CHEROKEE CITIZENSHIP COMMISSION DOCKETS 1880-1884 AND 1887-1889 VOLUME II

Jan. 29, 1881
Case #85   Subina Beason
              (Vs)   Petit...
           Cherokee Nation   Citiz...

Tahlequah, C.N. July 14th, 1887

The above case submitted by both parties after hearing the testimony, Jan. 31, 1881.
The testimony of William Harnage shows that the claimant is his niece and a Cherokee by blood.
The Commission therefore hereby issued this then decree admitting the said Subina Beason to all the rights, privileges, and franchises of Cherokee citizenship by blood. Jan 31, 1881.

                        Roach Young, President
                        William Harnage
                        G.W. Mayes
J.B. Mayes   Asst. Comm
    Clerk Commission

TRANSCRIBED BY
JEFF BOWEN

NATIVE STUDY
Gallipolis, Ohio
USA

Copyright © 2010
by Jeff Bowen

ALL RIGHTS RESERVED
No part of this publication may be reproduced
or used in any form or manner whatsoever
without previous written permission from the
copyright holder or publisher.

Originally published:
Baltimore, Maryland
2010

Reprinted by:

Native Study LLC
Gallipolis, OH
www.nativestudy.com
2020

Library of Congress Control Number: 2020916859

ISBN: 978-1-64968-059-4

Made in the United States of America.

Other Books and Series by Jeff Bowen

1901-1907 Native American Census Seneca, Eastern Shawnee, Miami, Modoc, Ottawa, Peoria, Quapaw, and Wyandotte Indians (Under Seneca School, Indian Territory)

1932 Census of The Standing Rock Sioux Reservation with Births And Deaths 1924-1932

Census of The Blackfeet, Montana, 1897- 1901 Expanded Edition

Eastern Cherokee by Blood, 1906-1910, Volumes I thru XIII

Choctaw of Mississippi Indian Census 1929-1932 with Births and Deaths 1924-1931   Volume I
Choctaw of Mississippi Indian Census 1933, 1934 & 1937, Supplemental Rolls to 1934 & 1935 with Births and Deaths 1932-1938, and Marriages 1936-1938 Volume II

Eastern Cherokee Census Cherokee, North Carolina 1930-1939 Census 1930-1931 with Births And Deaths 1924-1931 Taken By Agent L. W. Page Volume I
Eastern Cherokee Census Cherokee, North Carolina 1930-1939 Census 1932-1933 with Births And Deaths 1930-1932 Taken By Agent R. L. Spalsbury   Volume II
Eastern Cherokee Census Cherokee, North Carolina 1930-1939 Census 1934-1937 with Births and Deaths 1925-1938 and Marriages 1936 & 1938 Taken by Agents R. L. Spalsbury And Harold W. Foght Volume III

Seminole of Florida Indian Census, 1930-1940 with Birth and Death Records, 1930-1938

Texas Cherokees 1820-1839 A Document For Litigation 1921

Choctaw By Blood Enrollment Cards 1898-1914 Volumes I thru XVII

Starr Roll 1894 (Cherokee Payment Rolls) Districts: Canadian, Cooweescoowee, and Delaware Volume One
Starr Roll 1894 (Cherokee Payment Rolls) Districts: Flint, Going Snake, and Illinois   Volume Two
Starr Roll 1894 (Cherokee Payment Rolls) Districts: Saline, Sequoyah, and Tahlequah; Including Orphan Roll   Volume Three

Cherokee Intruder Cases Dockets of Hearings 1901-1909 Volumes I & II

Indian Wills, 1911-1921 Records of the Bureau of Indian Affairs Books One thru Seven;
Native American Wills & Probate Records 1911-1921

Other Books and Series by Jeff Bowen

Turtle Mountain Reservation Chippewa Indians 1932 Census with Births & Deaths, 1924-1932

Chickasaw By Blood Enrollment Cards 1898-1914 Volume I thru V

Cherokee Descendants East An Index to the Guion Miller Applications Volume I
Cherokee Descendants West An Index to the Guion Miller Applications Volume II (A-M)
Cherokee Descendants West An Index to the Guion Miller Applications Volume III (N-Z)

Applications for Enrollment of Seminole Newborn Freedmen, Act of 1905

Eastern Cherokee Census, Cherokee, North Carolina, 1915-1922, Taken by Agent James E. Henderson   Volume I (1915-1916)
Volume II (1917-1918)
Volume III (1919-1920)
Volume IV (1921-1922)

Complete Delaware Roll of 1898

Eastern Cherokee Census, Cherokee, North Carolina, 1923-1929, Taken by Agent James E. Henderson   Volume I (1923-1924)
Volume II (1925-1926)
Volume III (1927-1929)

Applications for Enrollment of Seminole Newborn Act of 1905 Volumes I & II

North Carolina Eastern Cherokee Indian Census 1898-1899, 1904, 1906, 1909-1912, 1914 Revised and Expanded Edition

1932 Hopi and Navajo Native American Census with Birth & Death Rolls (1925-1931) Volume 1 - Hopi
1932 Hopi and Navajo Native American Census with Birth & Death Rolls (1930-1932) Volume 2 - Navajo

Western Navajo Reservation Navajo, Hopi and Paiute 1933 Census with Birth & Death Rolls 1925-1933

Cherokee Citizenship Commission Dockets 1880-1884 and 1887-1889 Volume I

Visit our website at **www.nativestudy.com** to learn more about these and other books and series by Jeff Bowen

This series is dedicated to Joyce Tranter,
for giving me the inspiration of a lifetime.
And also to Dominick Lane Dugan.
Remember Isaiah 40:31
God bless!

INTRODUCTION

This publication was previously published by another publisher in 2009 and has now been reproduced by Native Study LLC. There are five volumes in this series concerning the Cherokee Citizenship Commission Dockets 1880 to 1889. This is material that was never before transcribed containing 2,288 Cherokee docket decisions.

This is somewhat of an explanation concerning the reasoning behind the proceedings that led the Cherokee tribal courts to take charge of these docket hearings.

The Cherokee relied upon their leaders to guide them but they ended up hanging in the balance after the Civil War, with their loyalties split worse than ever and their country ravished. Fathers and brothers were off fighting a war that didn't even concern them. By the time the war was over the Cherokee people had lost any form of stability. The men fighting the war came back to the same old political hatreds and in-fighting. The Nation was being over run with many that claimed they were Cherokee, hoping to benefit from false claims of citizenship. These people, known as intruders, did nothing but make it more difficult for the Cherokees because of the pressures from the Government to control their boundaries. The blood Cherokees that were seeking their homeland were again in question as to who they were. They found nothing but scrutiny and distrust, the war had made them choose a side, and the U.S. Government didn't care for the choice of the majority.

Intruder after intruder was encroaching on Cherokee land and what was to seem like a never ending battle. Many Cherokee citizens had lost their rights while intruders that didn't belong stayed using up what little resources there were. The government was telling the Cherokee leaders to settle their own intruder problems or else they would have to intercede. In an effort to clarify who were true Cherokee citizens and who were not, or who had been wrongfully taken off of the rolls, was a problem.

There were part-bloods, full-bloods, and no bloods along with mass confusion, prejudice, vendettas, and deceptions. The intruders wanted a free ride and were willing to use the confusion as a camouflage to achieve their purpose and greed.

This was a situation where the government was threatening to come in and turn the Cherokee Nation into a Federal Territory because it appeared to them that the Tribal Council would not be able to organize an effort to control the problem. But this wasn't the issue at hand as far as the Cherokee were concerned. They felt as if, according to their treaty stipulations, the United States was responsible for intruder removal. They felt as if the United States had let things get out of hand and that the government had not lived up to its contractual agreement. According to treaty stipulations this was true, but, they were told to either come up with a solution or lose their rights as a sovereign nation.

From William G. McLoughlin's book , *After the Trail of Tears, The Cherokees Struggle for Sovereignty 1839-1880*, it references on page 354, "Still, the Nation remained very uneasy about the fundamental question of its right to define who were its own citizens and its right to expect the United States to remove those who the Nation judged were not. Ever since 1872, federal agents had refused to expel from the Nation those former slaves whom the Nation considered 'aliens' and since 1874, federal agents had been under instructions from the Bureau of Indian Affairs to compile their own list of black or white persons who, in their opinion, had some claim to citizenship despite previous rulings of the Cherokee Courts on their claims."

On page 355-356, "On the basis of the affidavits and reports submitted, the Secretary of Interior, Zachariah Chandler, sent E.C. Watkins to the Nation in 1875, to investigate the citizenship problem and gather information that Chandler could use to ask Congress to take action on behalf of these 'men without a country'. Watkins reported in February, 1876, that many of those on Ingall's list were 'clearly entitled' to Cherokee citizenship. Oochalata denied it. He counter charged that Ingalls was meddling in Cherokee affairs and wrote to the Bureau of Indian Affairs to complain. Receiving no satisfactory response, he wrote directly to President Grant on November 13, 1876, enclosing a petition from the Cherokees Cooweescoowee District, complaining that the agent had not removed thousands of intruders in their area though ordered to do so by the Council. Some of these intruders were former slaves from the Deep South, but most were white U.S. citizens from Kansas, Missouri, and Arkansas.

Grant referred this letter to Commissioner J.Q. Smith. Annoyed that Oochalata had gone over the head of the Interior Department to the President, on December 8, Smith wrote Oochalata a long, assertive, and highly provocative letter outlining for the first time the department's position on this question. Smith said that from the evidence he had received, both from various federal agents and from the investigations of E.C. Watkins, the Cherokee Nation had failed to deal consistently and impartially with the problems of former slaves and others who claimed Cherokee citizenship. Therefore, the Bureau of Indian Affairs would continue to compile its own list of those who had 'prima facie' evidence for citizenship [whether the Cherokee courts had acted negatively on their claims or not], and it would take no action to remove them until the Cherokees carried four stipulations to resolve the issue. First, the Council must establish a clear, legal procedure providing due process for adjudicating all prima facie claims. Second, the rules by which such cases were decided must be approved by the Secretary of the Interior to ensure their impartiality. Third, he suggested that the Cherokee Circuit Courts be designated as the appropriate bodies for such hearings. Finally, claimants' appeals of the decisions of the Cherokee Circuit Courts must be forwarded to the Secretary of the Interior, and no claimant for citizenship should be removed from the Nation until the Secretary had made his own ruling. In effect, Smith asserted the right of the Bureau of Indian Affairs to decide who was and was not a Cherokee citizen. A crucial decision concerning the issue of the sovereignty of Indian nations was about to be reached.

Oochalata was stunned and wrote a 139-page letter to Smith explaining why this procedure was totally unacceptable and contrary to law, treaties, precedent, and the U.S. Constitution."

On page 357, "Acting on instructions from Oochalata, the Cherokee Delegation sent another letter to President Grant on Jan. 9, 1877, insisting that treaty rights, the Trade and Intercourse Act, and precedent gave the Nation the right 'to determine the question as to who are and who are not intruders.' The president referred their letter to Secretary of the Interior, Carl Schurz, who, on April 21, 1877, told the delegation that he supported Smith's four stipulations for settling the matter. Oochalata ignored this response and in August, 1877, sent to the new Commissioner of Indian Affairs, Ezra A. Hayt, a list of all the intruders whom the Cherokees wished to be immediately removed. On Nov. 7, Hayt replied flatly that the Bureau of Indian Affairs would not do so: 'while the department reserves to itself the right to finally determine who are and are not intruders under the law, **it expects the Cherokee Nation Council to enact some general and uniform law by which the Cherokee courts shall hear and determine the rights of claimants to citizenship,** subject only to the review of the Secretary of Interior after a final adjudication has been reached.'"

On page 358-9, "The department's claim that it had the right to judge intruders was, in Oochalata's opinion, 'a new doctrine for construing treaty or contracts in writing, to add to it verbally, a new clause, after the expiration of 92 years from date of that compact or treaty and without the consent of [one] party. . . . It is a dangerous doctrine to which I can never agree.'

While he urged the Council to send a protest through its delegation, Oochalata also asked it to enact a law that would establish a court to decide citizenship claims in a legal and uniform manner. The Council complied on Dec. 5, 1877, but the compromise was fatally weakened by the Council's failure to address two aspects of the law governing the Citizenship Court's actions.

First, the law provided no guidelines for deciding cases that would meet the demands of the Bureau of Indian Affairs, and consequently, in cases involving former slaves, the Citizenship Court relied, as the Cherokee Supreme Court had in 1870-71, simply on the wording in the Treaty of 1866. Second, the Council explicitly refused to allow the right of the Secretary of the Interior to review the decisions of the Court, stating that the Cherokee Citizenship Court was 'a tribunal of last resort'. The three persons appointed to the court, were John Chambers, O.P. Brewer, and George Downing. Also referred to as the Chamber's Commission, the Court began to hold hearings early in 1878. All persons claiming to have grounds for citizenship were required to present them or be declared intruders."

On pages 359-360, McLoughlin continues, "By the end of 1878, Oochalata struggling to find some new approach to the problem. On Dec. 3, he went over the head of the Bureau of Indian Affairs again, and wrote to Pres. Rutherford B. Hayes, forwarding a complete account of all of the cases adjudicated by the Citizenship Court and asking him to order the expulsion of those rejected and all other intruders. He told Hayes that the Cherokee Nation had an 'inherent national right' to define its own citizens, while the United States had a well-established obligation to expel non-citizens. Suspecting that Hayes would reject this request, Oochalata approached Commissioner Ezra A. Hayt and tried to work out a compromise. He said that the Cherokees would stop confiscating the property of those former slaves judged to be intruders pending the appointment of a joint commission of Cherokees and members of the Bureau to review the rejected claims. Hayt agreed only on the condition that decisions of this commission must be unanimous or the Bureau would retain the right to make its own decision in each case. Oochalata and the delegation could not accept such a condition, and the negotiations broke down. Finally, as a last resort, the council decided to submit a series of questions to the Secretary of Interior, Carl Schurz, about their right to determine citizenship and the obligation of the United States to accept their determinations. They asked Schurz to present their questions to Attorney General Charles Devens for his opinion. They sent the letter on March 3, 1879, and after Hayt informed Devens of his views on the matter, Devens held hearings at which both sides presented their views. Realizing the importance of the decision, the Cherokees spent the money necessary to hire the best lawyers they could find to assist them. Hayt said that the status of at least one-thousand persons was at issue, the Council argued that there were over twice that many intruders whom the Department was refusing to move.

Throughout the dispute, the Bureau of Indian Affairs declined to act against intruding squatters from Kansas who made no pretense to citizenship.

"The three questions that the Council asked Devens to answer were: Did the Cherokee Nation have the right to determine its own citizenship? Did the former slaves who were citizens have any share in the use of Cherokee land or in the money derived from the sale of the Cherokee land? Was it, or was it not, the duty of the Federal government to remove intruders under treaty stipulations and Trade and Intercourse Act? By the time Devens sent his reply, the Citizenship Court had heard 416 claims for citizenship and rejected 338."

Devens' opinion was clearly in the negative as far as the Cherokee Nation's sovereignty and decision processes were concerned. On page 364, McLoughlin observes, "Clearly, as since the days of Andrew Jackson, Federal refusal to honor the requirement of removing intruders was to be the means of forcing the Indian nations to do what they did not want to do." Ochalata would not run again as the election of August 1879 neared and Dennis W. Bushyhead became the new chief on August 4, 1879 but in the end it didn't matter who was chief the fight to keep Cherokee sovereignty along with self government was all but lost by 1880. On pages 365-366, McLoughlin wrote, "The turning point was reached in 1887 when Congress passed the Dawes Severalty Act. The act expressed what was now the national consensus among white voters (including Indian reformers, railroad magnates, and entrepreneurs) -that the solution to '"the Indian question'" was to denationalize the tribes in the Indian Territory, survey and allot their land in severalty, and establish a white-dominated territorial government over '"Oklahoma'" the Choctaw word for '"red man.'"

The sovereignty of the Western Cherokee tribe was taken, and to this day they still don't have a true land base as a nation. Even though others were able to take away the land that was promised to remain theirs forever; nobody was able to take away their right and ability to choose who was a true citizen and who was not. The dockets transcribed within this series are exactly as they appeared on the microfilm copies from the original court records involving citizenship during the time periods of 1880-1889.

These dockets were referenced and transcribed from microfilm series; 7RA25-0001 (American Genealogical Lending Library), Cherokee Citizenship Commission Docket Books, 1880-1884 and 1887-1889.

Jeff Bowen
Gallipolis, Ohio
NativeStudy.com

Cherokee Citizenship Commission Docket Books
(1880-84, 1887-89) Volume II
Tahlequah, Cherokee Nation

WALDON

Docket #287
Rolls 1835
filed July 14th /87 — Application for Cherokee Citizenship

Post Office: Tulsa, IT   **Attorney:** A.E. Ivey

N°	NAMES	AGE	SEX
1	Berry Waldon	48	Male
2	Robbie Waldon	18	"
3	Nona Waldon	14	Female

Ancestor: Nannie Waldon

The application in the above named case was filed the 18th day of June 1887. It is not supported by any evidence and an hour having been set by request of Attorneys for hearing the same and which was continued more than twenty four hours and no answer being made on the calling of the case again this day three several times at intervals of not less than one hour apart the Commission decide adversely to applicant Berry Walden aged 48 years and his son Robbie Walden aged 18 years and daughter Nona Walden aged 14 years. Post Office Tulsa, Ind. Ter.

                        Will P. Ross Chairman
Attest   John E Gunter   Com
    E.G. Ross
        Clk. of Commission Citizenship
May 1st 1889

Docket #288   Missing from archival records

DUNCAN

Docket #289
Rolls 1835 to 52
filed July 15th /87 — Applicant for Cherokee Citizenship

Post Office: Tulsa, I.T.   **Attorney:** A.E. Ivey

N°	NAMES	AGE	SEX
1	Sarah C. Duncan	32	Female
2	Hiram Duncan	15	Male
3	George W. Duncan	13	"
4	Charles M. Duncan	11	"

Cherokee Citizenship Commission Docket Books
(1880-84, 1887-89) Volume II
Tahlequah, Cherokee Nation

5	Allen T. Duncan	8	"
6	Georgia Ann Duncan	5	Female
7	Mary Ellen Duncan	11 mo	Female

Ancestor: Stephen & Annie Bolin

Now on this the 25th day of June 1888, come the above entitled case up for final hearing. The case having been submitted by Messrs Hutchins & Ivey. The testimony in this case was all taken in the state of Kentucky and is wholly ex parte in favor of applicants. In this case herewith, the testimony was admitted without cross examination, and considered admissible. The applicants claim as this ancestor, from whom they profess to form a lineal descent, that they are Cherokee Indians, are Stephen Bowlin and Annie Bowlin. Hon. R.F. Wyley, Nations Attorney, submitted on part of the Nation the authenticated census & pay rolls of Cherokees taken in the years 1835, 1848, 1851 and 1852, by the United States. Under the provisions of Sec. 7 of the Act creating and empowering this Commission, approved Dec. 8th 1886, which says: "The Commission when organized shall give a hearing to any person applying for citizenship in the Cherokee Nation upon the grounds of Cherokee blood or descent, but such applicant must be a person, or the lineal descendant of a person, whose name appears upon the census rolls of Cherokees taken by the United States after the treaty of 1835, and known as the "rolls of 1835", and the rolls of 1848 known as the "Mullay Roll", and the census rolls of Cherokees taken in the year 1851, and known as the "Silar Roll", and the pay roll of Cherokees made by the United States in 1852, and known as the "Chapman Rolls". The testimony of Plaintiff, together with the rolls, above mentioned, on part of the Nation, have been duly and considerably considered. In summing up this case it is not necessary to enter into it further than to mention that the applicants claim to be descended from one Stephen & Annie Bowlin do not appear upon any of the before mentioned rolls of Cherokees. Therefore, we the Commission on Citizenship after a careful and thorough investigation of this case, fail to find for Plaintiff, and declare that Sarah C. Duncan, Hiram Duncan, George W. Duncan, Charles M. Duncan, Allen T. Duncan, Georgia Ann Duncan, and Mary Ellen Duncan are not Cherokees by blood, and are not entitled to any of the rights and privileges of Cherokee citizens by virtue of such blood, and are intruders upon the public domain of the Cherokee Nation.

J.T. Adair   Chairman Commission
D.W. Lipe   Commissioner

Cherokee Citizenship Commission Docket Books
(1880-84, 1887-89) Volume II
Tahlequah, Cherokee Nation

MILLER

Docket #290
Rolls 1835
filed July 16th/87

Applicant for Cherokee Citizenship

Post Office: Sanders P O I.T.   **Attorney:** J.A. Scales

N°	NAMES	AGE	SEX
1	James J. Miller		Male
2	Henry Miller		"
3	G.W. Miller		"
4	Louisa Miller		Female
5	Lucy Miller		"
6	Wm F. Miller		Male
7	Thomas Miller		"
8	John Miller		"
9	Francis Miller		Female
10	Caladonia Miller		"
11	Mary Catharine Waters Grand Daughter	29	"

Ancestor: Jack Miller

Commission on Citizenship, Cherokee Nation Ind. Ter.
Tahlequah June 6th 1889.

The evidence in the above named case shows that applicant alleges that he is the grand son of one John Miller whose name will be found on the census roll of Cherokees by blood taken and made in the year 1852. It also shows that John Miller a well known citizen of the Cherokee Nation by blood and nativity and a resident of Illinois District at the time of his death did recognize James J. Miller the father of applicant as his son under oath before R.C. Blackstone, Clerk of Canadian District on the 20th day of November 1875, and that he was recognized as such by the relatives of the said John Miller whose name is found on the Census roll aforesaid of 1852. The Commission therefore decide that the applicant James Jackson Miller, and his brother Pleasant Henry Miller, George Washington Miller, William Franklin Miller, Thomas Miller, John Miller, and Sisters Lucy Jane Miller, Louisa Jane Miller, Caldonia Miller, Lenora Miller, Francis Miller, and Mary Catherine Waters nee Miller, wife of George Waters of Illinois District are of Cherokee blood & are hereby readmitted to citizenship in the Cherokee Nation, under the provisions of the Act of Dec. 5th 1888, creating this Commission on Citizenship.

Cherokee Citizenship Commission Docket Books
(1880-84, 1887-89) Volume II
Tahlequah, Cherokee Nation

Will P. Ross Chairman
J.E. Gunter Com.

Attest
    D.S. Williams
        Asst. Clk. Com.

HUNNICUT

Docket #291
Rolls 1835
filed July 16th/87   Applicant for Cherokee Citizenship
Post Office: Webbers Falls, CN   **Attorney**: S.A. Scales

N°	NAMES	AGE	SEX
1	Mary Ann Hunnicut		Female

Ancestor: Jack Miller

Now on this the first day of May 1889, comes the case of Mary Ann Hunnicut for the final hearing. The application was filed the 9th day of July 1887, and alleges that Mary Ann is the daughter of one John Miller whose name would be found on the census rolls of Cherokees by blood taken and made in the year 1835 by the United States. The evidence fails to sustain this allegation John or Jack Miller as he was commonly called, was a well known citizen of the Cherokee Nation by virtue of his blood, who resided in Illinois District and died within a few years from his sworn statement it appears that he lived with Sally White about two years in Tennessee, and that James J. Miller was born during that time and that he recognized him as his son. From other testimony it appears that Sally White refused to accompany the father of James J. Miller on the removal of the Cherokees to this country and a separation then took place. If the applicant had been recognized by John Miller as a child of his he would doubtless have so stated. The only witness who makes any reference to the applicant as being the daughter of John Miller is the said James J. Miller who was a tender infant at the time his father left Tennessee and could have no knowledge in reference to the to the relationship which he testifies other than hearsay and which in the opinion of the Commission is not sufficient to to[sic] show she was of Cherokee blood as the child of said John Miller. The Commission therefore decide that the applicant is not of Cherokee blood and is not entitled to Citizenship in the Cherokee Nation. This opinion includes the two children of Mrs. Hunnicut as identified by James J. Miller to wit; John Thomas Hunnicut and Robert Lee Hunnicut.

Cherokee Citizenship Commission Docket Books
(1880-84, 1887-89) Volume II
Tahlequah, Cherokee Nation

Will P. Ross Chairman
John E. Gunter   Com.

Attest
E.G. Lipe Clerk Commission

ADDINGTON

Docket #292
Rolls 1835
Filed July 20th 1887   Applicant for Cherokee Citizenship
Post Office: Stebo Ark   **Attorney:** A.E. Ivey

N°	NAMES	AGE	SEX
1	Lucinda Adington[sic]	58	Female
2	Cynthia Addington	40	"
3	Adaline Addington	38	"
4	Texas Addington	34	"
5	Altha Addington	32	"
6	R.N. Addington	30	Male
7	China J. Addington	28	Female
8	Mollie Addington	25	"

Ancestor: Robert & Cynthia Smith

Now on this the 27 day of August 1887. Comes the above case for a final hearing. And submitted by agreement between the attorney for Plaintiff and the atty on part of the Nation, on the evidence taken and submitted in the case of Lucinda Addington, Cynthia Addington, Adaline Addington, Texas Addington, Altha Addington, R.N. Addington, China J. Addington, Mollie Addington, we the Commission on Citizenship after a careful & impartial investigation of the testimony & having also examined the Census Rolls of 1835 and failed to find the [sic] of Ancestor Robt & Cynthia Smith and the evidence in behalf of applicant not being sufficient. The Commission therefore declare that the above named parties are not Cherokees by blood and not entitled to any of the rights or privileges of Cherokee Citizens.

J.T. Adair   Chairman Com.
Attest   D.W. Lipe
    C.C. Lipe
        Clerk Com.

Cherokee Citizenship Commission Docket Books
(1880-84, 1887-89) Volume II
Tahlequah, Cherokee Nation

SMITH

Docket #293
Rolls 1835
filed July 20th/87   Applicant for Cherokee Citizenship
  Post Office: Springtown. Ark   **Attorney:** A.E. Ivey

N°	NAMES	AGE	SEX
1	Andrew J. Smith	53	Male
2	Lula A. Smith	20	Female
3	J.R. Smith	18	Male
4	Emma V. Smith	16	Female
5	H.L. Smith	11	Male
6	Alice M. Smith	8	Female
7	Mary Smith	2	Female

Ancestor: Robt & Cynthia Smith

Office Commission on Citizenship
Cherokee Nation Ind Ter
Tahlequah June 6th 1889.

The Commission this day decide against Andrew J. Smith the applicant aged 53 years and his daughters Lula A. Smith aged 20 yrs, Emma V. Smith aged 17 yrs, Alice M. Smith aged 8 yrs, Mary Smith aged 2 yrs, and his sons J.R. Smith aged 18 yrs and H.L. Smith aged 11 yrs, and adjudge that they are not of Cherokee blood. See decision in case of Lucinda Addington Dock 190 Book A, Page 191 and in Case of Rena Johnson Docket 292 Book B, Page 5. P.O. Spring Town Arkansas.

	Will P. Ross	Chairman
Attest	R. Bunch Com.	
D.S. Williams	J.E. GunterCom	
Asst. Clk. Com.		

LEWIS

Docket #293[sic]
Rolls 1835
filed August 9th 1887   Applicant for Cherokee Citizenship
  Post Office: Red Oak, Mo.   **Attorney:** E.C. Boudinot

N°	NAMES	AGE	SEX
1	Martha Lewis	55	Female
2	E.B. Lewis	20	Male

Cherokee Citizenship Commission Docket Books
(1880-84, 1887-89) Volume II
Tahlequah, Cherokee Nation

3	Annie Lewis	16	Female

Ancestor: Eddie Grant

Office Commission on Citizenship Tahlequah I.T. Aug 9th 88
The above case being submitted, the evidence was fully considered, also the rolls of Cherokees laid down in the 7th Sec. of the Act of Dec. 8th 1886, as well as those mentioned in the amendment of Feb'y. 7th 1888, but fail to find the name of Edith Grant or that of the applicant, Martha Lewis enrolled thereon in the absence of which this Commission cannot admit them to citizenship in the Cherokee Nation; therefore declare, Martha Lewis and her two children, viz; E.B. and Annie Lewis <u>not</u> to be entitled to the rights and privileges of Cherokee citizens by blood.

      J.T. Adair   Chairman Commission
      H.C. Barnes Commissioner

HUGHES

Docket #294
Rolls 1835
filed Aug 9th, 87   Applicant for Cherokee Citizenship
  Post Office: Oakes, I.T. **Attorney:** Boudinot & Rasmus

N°	NAMES	AGE	SEX
1	Charles B. Hughes		Male

Ancestor: Burton ~~Skylock~~ Syleox

The above case was filed the 9th day of August 1887 and was submitted April 30th by Attorneys without evidence. The Commission therefore decide that Charles B. Hughes is not a Cherokee by blood and is not entitled to admission to Citizenship in the Cherokee Nation. Post Office Oaks, Indian Territory.

      Will P. Ross   Chairman
Attest   John E. Gunter Com
  E.G. Lipe
    Clerk Commission

Cherokee Citizenship Commission Docket Books
(1880-84, 1887-89) Volume II
Tahlequah, Cherokee Nation

WELDON

Docket #295
O.S. Rolls 1851
filed Aug 9th 1887   Applicant for Cherokee Citizenship
Post Office: Gibson Station I.T.   **Attorney:** Boudinot & Rasmus

N°	NAMES	AGE	SEX
1	Rebecca D. Weldon	39	Female
2	Bell West	19	"
3	Nettie West	14	"
4	Viola Weldon	6	"
5	Robt. Lee Weldon	14 mos	Male

Ancestor: Susanah McIntosh

We the Commission on Citizenship after examining the evidence in the above case and also the "Old Settler" pay rolls of 1851, find that the above applicant, and her four children, viz; Bell West and Nettie West and Viola & Robt. Lee Weldon, are Cherokees by blood, and are hereby re-admitted to all the rights and privileges of Cherokee citizens by blood. Which is in compliance with an Act of the National Council creating this Commission dated December 8th 1886 and the amendment thereto dated Feb'y. 7th 1888.

D.W. Lipe   Actg. Chairman Commission
John E. Gunter   Commissioner

Office Commission on Citizenship
Tahlequah Ind. Ter. July 12th 1888.

HAILEY

Docket #296
O.S. Rolls 1851
filed Aug 9th 1887   Applicant for Cherokee Citizenship
Post Office: Gibson Station I.T.   **Attorney:** Boudinot & Rasmus

N°	NAMES	AGE	SEX
1	Sallie M. Hailey	42	Female

Ancestor: Susannah McIntosh

In compliance with the Act of the National Council dated Dec. 8th 1886 and amendment thereto of Feb'y 7th 1888, creating this Commission and

Cherokee Citizenship Commission Docket Books
(1880-84, 1887-89) Volume II
Tahlequah, Cherokee Nation

defining its authority – the Commission has this day given final hearing in the above entitled cause and after carefully considering all the testimony presented and after having examined the Census Rolls of 1851, known as the "Old Settler Rolls" find the applicant Sallie M. Hailey – to be Cherokee by blood, descended from Susannah M. McIntosh, a Cherokee by blood, whose name appears upon the Rolls above described and the Commission do therefore by virtue of authority in them vested by law, do hereby re-admit the said Sallie M. Hailey to all the rights and privileges to Cherokee Citizenship by blood.

                        D.W. Lipe   Actg. Chairman Commission
                        John E. Gunter   Commissioner

Office Commission on Citizenship
Tahlequah, Ind. Ter. July 12th 88

SCOTT

Docket #297
O.S. Rolls 1851
filed Aug. 9th 1887   Applicant for Cherokee Citizenship
    Post Office: Creek Nation I.T.   **Attorney:** Boudinot & Rasmus

N°	NAMES	AGE	SEX
1	Daniel Scott	28	Male
2	Kiah Scott	1	Female

Ancestor: Susannah McIntosh

In compliance with an Act of the National Council dated Dec. 8th 1886, and amendment thereto of Feb'y 7th 1888 – creating this Commission and enforcing its authority – the Commission has this day given final hearing in the above cause and after carefully examining all the testimony presented and after having examined the Census Rolls of 1851 known as the "Old Settler Rolls" find the applicant Daniel Scott and his child Kiah, to be Cherokees by blood, descended from Susannah McIntosh a Cherokee by blood, whose name appears upon the rolls above described and the Commission do therefore by virtue of authority in them vested by law, do hereby re-admit the said Daniel Scott, aged 28 years and his child aged 1 year, to all the rights and privileges of Cherokee citizenship by blood.

                D.W. Lipe   Actg. Chairman Commission
                John E. Gunter Commissioner

Cherokee Citizenship Commission Docket Books
(1880-84, 1887-89) Volume II
Tahlequah, Cherokee Nation

Office Commission on Citizenship
Tahlequah, Ind. Ter. July 12th 1888.

FISHER

Docket #298
O.S. Rolls 1851
filed Aug. 9th 1887   Applicant for Cherokee Citizenship
Post Office: Creek Nation   **Attorney**: Boudinot & Rasmus

N°	NAMES	AGE	SEX
1	Lucy B. Fisher	27	Female
2	Carrie Fisher	4	"
3	Ollie Fisher	2	"
4	(Dead) Oslah Hailey Fisher Died *(illegible)* filing of application	5 mo	Male

Ancestor: Susannah McIntosh

    In compliance with an Act of the National Council dated December 8th 1886, creating this Commission, and the amendment thereto approved Feb'y. 7th 1888 and the above case having come up for final hearing, We the Commission on Citizenship after carefully examining all the evidence in the case, and also the "Old Settler" pay rolls of the year 1887, find that Lucy B. Fisher and her two children Carrie and Olley Fisher are Cherokees by blood, and are hereby re-admitted to all the rights & privileges of Cherokee Citizens by blood.

                   D.W. Lipe   Actg. Chairman Commission
                   John E. Gunter   Commissioner

Office Commission on Citizenship
Tahlequah, I.T. July 12th 1888.

COLLINS

Docket #299
O.S. Rolls 1851
filed Aug. 9th 1887   Applicant for Cherokee Citizenship
Post Office: Creek Nation I.T.   **Attorney**: Boudinot & Rasmus

N°	NAMES	AGE	SEX
1	Aurora Collins	30	Female

Cherokee Citizenship Commission Docket Books
(1880-84, 1887-89) Volume II
Tahlequah, Cherokee Nation

2	Bessie Collins	7	"
3	Roscoe S. Collins	6 mo	Male

Ancestor: Susannah McIntosh

In compliance with an Act of the National Council creating this Commission dated 8th December 1886, and the amendment thereto dated Feb'y 7th 1888, and the above case having come up for final hearing, We the Commission on Citizenship after carefully examining all the evidence in the case, and also the "Old Settler" pay rolls, taken in the year 1851, find that Aurora Collins and her two children, Bessie and Roscoe S. Collins are Cherokees by blood, and are hereby re-admitted to all the rights and privileges of Cherokee citizens by blood.

                D.W. Lipe   Actg. Chairman Commission
                John E. Gunter   Commissioner

Office Commission on Citizenship
Tahlequah, Ind. Ter. July 12th 1888.

WILLISON

Docket #300
O.S. Rolls 1851
filed Aug. 9th 1887   Applicant for Cherokee Citizenship
Post Office: Gibson Station   **Attorney:** Boudinot & Rasmus

N°	NAMES	AGE	SEX
1	James D. Willison	34	Male
2	Howard D. Willison	8	"
3	Irene B. Willison	6	Female
4	May C. Willison	2	"
5	Jim M. Willison	4	Male

Ancestor: Susannah McIntosh

We the Commission on Citizenship after examining the evidence in the above case and also the "Old Settler" pay rolls of 1851, find that the above applicant and his four children, viz: Howard D, Irene B, Jim M, and May C. Willison are Cherokees by blood and are hereby re-admitted to all the rights & privileges of Cherokee citizens by blood, which is in compliance with an Act of

Cherokee Citizenship Commission Docket Books
(1880-84, 1887-89) Volume II
Tahlequah, Cherokee Nation

the National Council dated Dec. 8th 1886, and amendment thereto dated Feb'y. 7th 1888.

                    D.W. Lipe   Actg. Chairman Commission
                    John E. Gunter   Commissioner

Office Commission on Citizenship
Tahlequah, Ind. Ter. July 12th 1888.

SHANNON

Docket #301
O.S. Rolls 1851
filed Aug. 9th 1887   Applicant for Cherokee Citizenship
   Post Office: Gibson Station   **Attorney:** Boudinot & Rasmus

Nº	NAMES	AGE	SEX
1	Mary B. Shannon	43	Female
2	Pauline Shannon	13	"
3	Daisy Shannon	12	"
4	Lucy Shannon	10	"
5	Floyd D. Shannon	8	Male
6	Sallie H. Shannon	4	Female

          Ancestor: Susannah McIntosh

    We the Commission on Citizenship after examining the evidence in the above named case and also the "Old Settler" pay rolls of 1851, find that Mary B. Shannon and her five children, viz: Pauline, Daisey, Lucy, Floyd & Sallie Shannon are Cherokees by blood and are re-admitted to all the rights and privileges of Cherokee citizens by blood, which is in compliance with an Act of the National Council dated Dec. 8th 1886 and amendment thereto of Feb'y 7th 1888. creating this Commission.

                    D.W. Lipe   Actg. Chairman Commission
                    John E. Gunter   Commissioner

Office Commission on Citizenship
Tahlequah, Ind. Ter. July 12th '88.

Cherokee Citizenship Commission Docket Books
(1880-84, 1887-89) Volume II
Tahlequah, Cherokee Nation

BRUNER

Docket #302
Rolls 1851 & 52
filed Aug. 9th 1887   Applicant for Cherokee Citizenship
    Post Office: **Attorney**: Boudinot Rasmus

N°	NAMES	AGE	SEX
1	Mary Bruner	62	Female
2	Lethia Bruner	29	Male
3	John R. Bruner	26	"
4	Isaac A. Bruner	24	"
5	Geo S. Bruner	20	"
6	Theodore S. Bruner	18	"

Ancestor: Self

    Now on this the 9th day of August 1887, comes the above case for final hearing and having made application pursuant to the provisions of an Act of the National Council approved December 8th 1886 and all the evidence having been duly considered and found to be sufficient and satisfactory to the Commission it is adjudged and determined by the Commission that Mary Bruner, Lethia Bruner, John R. Bruner, Isaac N. Bruner, George S. Bruner and Theadore S. Bruner are Cherokees by blood; and are hereby re-admitted to all the rights privileges and immunities of Cherokees by blood.
    And a certificate of said decision of the Commission and re-admission was made and furnished to said parties accordingly.

                     J.T. Adair   Chairman Commission
Attest   John E. Gunter   Commissioner
    Henry Eiffert
    Asst Clerk Com.

ROBERTS

Docket #303
Rolls 1835
filed 10 August 1887   Applicant for Cherokee Citizenship
    Post Office: Duluth, Ga   **Attorney**: C.J. Harris

N°	NAMES	AGE	SEX
1	Alexander C. Roberts	10	Male
2	Henry G. Roberts	6	"

Cherokee Citizenship Commission Docket Books
(1880-84, 1887-89) Volume II
Tahlequah, Cherokee Nation

| 3 | Rozella Roberts | 4 | Female |

Ancestor: Annie C. Lewis

The above case was decided by the former Commission on Citizenship on this 26th day of October 1887. Admitted to Citizenship in the Cherokee Nation. See decision in the envelope with application.

D.S. Williams
Clk. Com of 1889

Docket #304   Missing from archival records

JOURDAN

Docket #305
Rolls 1835
filed Aug 10th 87   Applicant for Cherokee Citizenship
   Post Office: *(Illegible)* Ark.   **Attorney:** C.H. Taylor

N°	NAMES	AGE	SEX
1	Jessie Jourdan	70	Female
2	Mary S. Jourdan	34	Female
3	Chisterfer[sic] Jourdan	29	Male
4	Jefferson D. Jourdan	25	Male

Ancestor: River Jourdan

Rejected May 3rd 1889

Office Commission on Citizenship
Cherokee Nation Ind. Ter.
Tahlequah May 3rd 1889

The application in the above case was filed this 11th day of August 1887. This applicant alleging as the ground of his claim to Citizenship that he is the son of one River Jourdan whose name can be found on the Census roll of Cherokee by blood taken and made by the United States in the year 1835. This case was decided adversely to the applicant Jesse Jourdan et. al. by the Commission on Citizenship commonly known as the Spears Commission on this 28th day of September, 1884, and again comes up for rehearing under the 9th Section of the Act of December 8th 1886 under which this Commission is sitting. The evidence introduced shows that Jesse Jourdan the applicant resided until quite recently for

Cherokee Citizenship Commission Docket Books
(1880-84, 1887-89) Volume II
Tahlequah, Cherokee Nation

more than forty years in Washington County Arkansas, on the immediate border of the Cherokee Nation and during that time made no effort to become a Citizen of the Nation. This fact taken in Consideration with the failure to show that his father was of Cherokee blood and that the name of River Jourdan is not found on the Census roll of 1835 together with the circumstances surrounding the claim which shows it to be of a questionable character in itself fully justify the Commission in deciding and declaring as they hereby do, that Jesse Jourdan and his children Mary S. Jourdan aged 34 years, Christopher Jourdan aged 29 years, Jefferson Jourdan aged 25 years, are not of Cherokee blood and not entitled to Cherokee Citizenship.

Attest
D.S. Williams
Clk. Com.

Will P. Ross
John E. Gunter

Chairman
Comm.

BOYD

Docket #306
Rolls 1835 to 1852
filed August 11th 87   Applicant for Cherokee Citizenship
Post Office: Fort Smith, Ark.   **Attorney:** Boudinot & Rasmus

N°	NAMES	AGE	SEX
1	Luther Boyd	51	Male
2	Albert Boyd	10	"
3	Janna Boyd	5	Female
4	John Boyd	3	Male
5	Luther Boyd	10 mo	"

Ancestor: Susan Taylor

Office Commission on Citizenship
Tahlequah May 27th 1889

This application was filed the 13th day of August 1887 and submitted by both parties May 22nd 1889 without evidence. The Commission therefore decide that Luther Boyd aged 51 years and his daughter Janna Boyd aged five years and his son Albert Boyd aged ten years, John Boyd aged three years and Luther Boyd aged ten months are not of Cherokee blood and not entitled to Citizenship in the Cherokee Nation.

Cherokee Citizenship Commission Docket Books
(1880-84, 1887-89) Volume II
Tahlequah, Cherokee Nation

E.G. Ross	Will P. Ross	Chairman
Clerk Commission	R. Bunch	Com
	J.E. Gunter	Com

DAWSON

Docket #307
R[sic]
filed August 11th 1887   Applicant for Cherokee Citizenship
    Post Office: Catoosa I.T.   **Attorney:** Bell & Bryant

N°	NAMES	AGE	SEX
1	S.R. Dawson	66	
2	Parlee Dawson	44	Female
3	America J. Dawson	35	"
4	Katharine J. Dawson	33	"
5	J.G. Dawson	31	Male
6	Elias F. Dawson	29	"
7	Toliver Dawson	27	"
8	Emma Dawson	20	Female
9	Fanny Dawson	18	"
10	John Riley Dawson	11	Male
11	Robt E. Dawson	9	"
12	Claud Dawson	7	
13	Cleveland Dawson	3	

Ancestor: John Rogers

Rejected April 26th 1889

Now this day comes the above case for final hearing. Samuel R. Dawson bases his application for readmission to Citizenship in the Cherokee Nation upon the ground that he is the son of Samuel Dawson, a white man, Polly Rogers the alleged daughter of Captain John Rogers and Epilsy Pruitt said to be a half sister of Joseph Vann *(illegible)* known as rich and who were of Cherokee blood. It is admitted that John Rogers and Epilsy Pruitt died before the rolls upon which their names would appear if living at the time, and specified in the 7th Section of the Act of December 8th 1886, creating this Commission on Citizenship were made but in support of the application it is urged that certain members of the Dawson family and full brothers of the applicant were readmitted to Citizenship by the Commission on Citizenship commonly known as the "Tehee Court" and "The Spears Court" and are now residing as citizens in

Cherokee Citizenship Commission Docket Books
(1880-84, 1887-89) Volume II
Tahlequah, Cherokee Nation

the Cherokee Nation. In the opinion of this of this Commission, the sufficiency of the consideration which determined the decision of those Commissioners or of the testimony now introduced to authorize the admission of this present applicant – is not relevant to the issue now pending. The 7th Section of the Act of December 8th 1886 before named provides that "the Commission shall give a hearing to any person applying for citizenship in the Cherokee Nation upon the grounds of Cherokee blood or descent but such applicant must be a person, or the lineal descendant of a person whose name appears on the census roll of Cherokees taken by the United States" as are thereafter enumerated. Neither the names of the applicant nor that of the person he claims to be a lineal descendant appearing on either of said rolls the Commission adjudge and decree that Samuel R. Dawson and family are not entitled to readmission to Citizenship in the Cherokee Nation as Cherokees by blood. This opinion includes the cases of Andrew J. Dawson, James K.P. Dawson, Jounnah Barber n<u>ee</u> Jaunnah Dawson, and Jane Queen n<u>ee</u> Jane Dawson, and their families as enumerated in their respective applications.

This April 26th 1889.
D.S. Williams
Clk. Com.

Will P. Ross   Chairman
R. Bunch   Commissioner
John E. Gunter   Commissioner

MILLER

Docket #308
Rolls 1835 to 52
filed August 11th 1887

Applicant for Cherokee Citizenship

Post Office: Van Buren Ark   **Attorney:** Ivey & Sanders

N°	NAMES	AGE	SEX
1	Richard J. Miller	34	Male
2	Mabel Miller	9	Female
3	Othelia Miller	8	"
4	Jessie Bell Miller	5	"
5	James Dick Miller	3	Male
6	Clara Miller	1	Female

Ancestor: William Miller

Rejected June 3rd 1889

Office of Commission on Citizenship
Cherokee Nation Ind. Ter'y.
Tahlequah June 3rd 1889

Cherokee Citizenship Commission Docket Books
(1880-84, 1887-89) Volume II
Tahlequah, Cherokee Nation

The only evidence in support of the above application is the statement before the Commission on Citizenship Oct. 3rd 1888 by Walt Christian a Cherokee Citizen of Goingsnake District Ch. Nat. who swears that he knew a man by the name of George Miller twenty five or thirty years ago who kept a grocery store Log Town near Van Buren Ark and who spoke Cherokee and had the appearance of a Cherokee. Such a statement amounts to nothing in a case like this one under consideration and the Commission decides that Richard Miller has failed to show that he is of Cherokee blood and that he and his children Mabel Miller aged 9 yrs, Clara Miller aged one year daughter and Othelan Miller aged 8 yrs, James Dick Miller aged 3 yrs son and Jessie Bell Miller aged 4 yrs daughter are not entitled to readmission to Citizenship in the Cherokee Nation.

Attest
   D.S. Williams
   Asst. Clk. Com.

Will P. Ross
R. Bunch
J.E. Gunter

Chairman
Commissioner
Com.

MILLER

Docket #309
Rolls 1835 to 52
filed August 11th 1887   Applicant for Cherokee Citizenship
   Post Office: Van Buren Ark   **Attorney:** Ivey & Sanders

N°	NAMES	AGE	SEX
1	Samuel A. Miller	29	Male

Ancestor: William Miller

Rejected June 3rd 1889

Office Commission on Citizenship
Cherokee Nation Ind. Ter'y.
Tahlequah June 3rd 1889

The Commission the above case against the Claimant for reasons set forth in case of Richard Miller, See Docket 308 Book B page 21.

Attest
   D.S. Williams
   Asst. Clk Com

Will P. Ross
R, Bunch

Chairman
Commissioner

Cherokee Citizenship Commission Docket Books
(1880-84, 1887-89) Volume II
Tahlequah, Cherokee Nation

COX

Docket #310
Rolls 1835 to 1852
filed August 11th 1887   Applicant for Cherokee Citizenship
Post Office: Webbers Falls CN   **Attorney:** L.B. Bell

N°	NAMES	AGE	SEX
1	Frances Cox	24	Female

Ancestor: Lear Daugherty

Rejected May 2nd 1889

This case was filed the 11th day of August 1887. The applicant alleging that she is the grand daughter of one Lear Daugherty whose name would be found on the census rolls of Cherokees by blood taken and made in the year 1835, 1851-1852. The application is supported by no evidence nor does the name Lear Daugherty appear on either of the rolls named. The Commission therefore decide that Francis Cox is not of Cherokee blood and is not entitled to Citizenship in the Cherokee Nation.

                Will P. Ross   Chairman
This May 2nd 1889   John E. Gunter   Comm
D.S. Williams
Clk. Com. Tah. I.T.

COX

Docket #311
Rolls 1835 to 1852
filed August 11th 1887   Applicant for Cherokee Citizenship
Post Office: Webbers Falls CN   **Attorney:** L.B. Bell

N°	NAMES	AGE	SEX
1	Serena Cox	33	Female

Ancestor: Lear Daugherty

Rejected May 2nd 1889

This case was filed the 11th day of August 1887. The applicant alleging that she is the grand daughter of one Lear Daugherty whose name would be found on the rolls 1835-1851-1852. The application is supported by no evidence nor is the name of Lear Daugherty on either of the rolls named of Cherokees by blood taken and made by the United States. The Commission

Cherokee Citizenship Commission Docket Books
(1880-84, 1887-89) Volume II
Tahlequah, Cherokee Nation

therefore decide that Serena Cox is not of Cherokee blood and not entitled to readmission to Citizenship in the Cherokee Nation.

This May 2nd 1889
D.S. Williams
Clk. Com. Tah. I.T.

Will P. Ross
John E. Gunter

Chairman
Com.

HUDSON

Docket #312
Rolls 1835 to 1852
filed August 11th 1887

Applicant for Cherokee Citizenship

Post Office: **Attorney:** Wm. A. Thompson

N°	NAMES	AGE	SEX
1	L.B. Hudson	46	Male
2	Harrison Hudson	18	"
3	Sarah Francis Hudson	16	Female
4	Edney E. Hudson	14	"
5	Samuel Hudson	12	Male
6	Leuan Hudson	10	Female
7	Barnet Hudson	8	Male
8	Mandy Hudson	4	Female

Ancestor: Polly Blackburn

Now on this the 11th day of August 1887 comes the above case for final hearing and having made application pursuant to the provisions of an Act of the National Council approved December 8th 1886 and all the evidence having been duly considered and found to be sufficient and satisfactory and upon an examination the name of Ancestor Polly Blackburn appears upon the Rolls of 1851 & 2, it is therefore adjudged and determined by the Commission that L.B. Hudson, Harrison Hudson, Sarah Francis Hudson, Edney E. Hudson, Samuel Hudson, Leuan Hudson, Barnet Hudson and Mandy Hudson are Cherokees by blood and are thereby re-admitted to all the rights. privileges and immunities of Cherokees by blood.

And a certificate of said decision of the Commission and of re-admission was made and furnished said parties accordingly.

Cherokee Citizenship Commission Docket Books
(1880-84, 1887-89) Volume II
Tahlequah, Cherokee Nation

J.T. Adair   Chairman Commission
                Commissioner
D.W. Lipe   Commissioner

Henry Eiffert
   Clk. Com.

QUEEN

Docket #313
Rolls 1835
filed August 12   Applicant for Cherokee Citizenship
    Post Office: Vinita I.T.   **Attorney:** L.B. Bell

N°	NAMES	AGE	SEX
1	Jane Queen	67	Female
2	E.G. Queen	47	"
3	E.O. Queen	43	Male
4	E.M. Queen	37	"
5	H.A. Queen	32	"
6	O.J. Queen	29	"
7	S.D. Queen	27	"
8	S.P. Queen	25	"

      Ancestor: John Rogers & Alcey or Anna Prewitt
Rejected April 26th 1889

Adverse to Claimant

See Decision in this case in that of G.R. Dawson in this book page 20.
Entered April 26th 1889

                             Will P. Ross
D.S. Williams   Chairman
     Clk. Com.   J.E. Gunter   Com.

Cherokee Citizenship Commission Docket Books
(1880-84, 1887-89) Volume II
Tahlequah, Cherokee Nation

NEAL

Docket #314
Rolls 1835 to 1852
filed August 12th 87   Applicant for Cherokee Citizenship
    Post Office: Muscogee[sic] I.T.   **Attorney:** Boudinot & Rasmus

N°	NAMES	AGE	SEX
1	Mary Rebecca Neal	48	Female

Ancestor: Billy Taylor

   The above case having come up for final hearing and all the points having been duly considered find that there is not sufficient evidence to justify the Court to admit said applicant to Citizenship. It is plainly shown by the evidence in the testimony of John Ross, that Billy Taylor was a resident of Georgia up to the year 1852 & that he was a full blood Cherokee. If such had been the case his name should appear on some one of the Rolls either 1835, 51 & 52, but after carefully examining the several Rolls, we find one William Taylor, who was enrolled in Cherokee County, North Carolina, and he if living, would be only eight years older than the applicant, which is impossible for him to be the father and it shows plainly that he was altogether of a different family. His father being David Taylor, and the said Billy Taylor's father was Davenport or Port Taylor, and the law governing this case plainly says that any person claiming Cherokee blood or descent must be a person or lineal descendant of a person whose name appears on some one of the Census Rolls of the Cherokee taken by the United States after the Treaty of 1835. Now after carefully and impartially considering the above case, the Commission decide that Mary R. Neal is not a Cherokee by blood and not entitled to any of the rights and privileges of Cherokee Citizenship.

             J.T. Adair   Chairman Commission
Attest   D.W. Lipe   Commissioner
    C.C. Lipe   H.C. Barnes
        Clerk

Cherokee Citizenship Commission Docket Books
(1880-84, 1887-89) Volume II
Tahlequah, Cherokee Nation

BARBER

Docket #315
Rolls 1835
filed August 12th 1887   Applicant for Cherokee Citizenship
   Post Office: Vinita I.T.   **Attorney:** L.B. Bell

N°	NAMES	AGE	SEX
1	Jounnah Barber	51	Female
2	Ailcy J. Barber	34	"
3	Irena Barber	24	"
4	Emma Barber	22	"
5	Atta Barber	20	"
6	Mary Barber	13	"
7	Ouice Barber	17	"
8	Joel Barber	31	Male
9	Caliway Barber	27	"
10	Toliven Barber1	26	"
11	Riley Barber	15	"
12	Edgar Barber	9	"

   Ancestor: John Rogers & Alcy Prewitt
Rejected April 26th 1889

See Decision in this case in that of L.R. Dawson <u>adverse</u> to claimant in this Book Page 20

This April 26th 1889   Will P. Ross
   D.S. Williams   Chairman
         Clk Comm.   J.E. Gunter, Com.

HENDRIX

Docket #316
Rolls 1835
filed August 15 1887   Application for Cherokee Citizenship
   Post Office: Oklahoma I.T.   **Attorney:**

N°	NAMES	AGE	SEX
1	Daisy C.N. Hendrix	15	Female
2	Henrietta Hendrix	13	"
3	Milo Hendrix	11	Male

Cherokee Citizenship Commission Docket Books
(1880-84, 1887-89) Volume II
Tahlequah, Cherokee Nation

| 4 | Theodosha Hendrix | 9 | Female |

Ancestor: Geo. Lowery

Now on this the 1st day of September 1887 comes the above case for final hearing and the above named parties having made application pursuant to the provisions of an Act of the National Council appeared December 8th 1886, and as the evidence having been duly considered and found to be sufficient and satisfactory to the Commission, it is adjudged and determined by the Commission that Daisy C.N. Hendrix, Henrietta Hendrix, Milo Hendrix and Theodosha Hendrix are Cherokees by blood and are hereby re-admitted to all the rights, privileges and immunities of Cherokee Citizens by blood.

And a certificate of said decision of the Commission and of re-admission was made and furnished said parties accordingly.

Henry Eiffert
Clk Comm

J.T. Adair
John E. Gunter

Chairman Commission
Commissioner
Commissioner

HAIL

Docket #317
Rolls 1851
filed August 15th 87

Application for Cherokee Citizenship

Post Office: Van Buren Ark   **Attorney:** B.H. Stone

N°	NAMES	AGE	SEX
1	Joseph L. Hail	34	Male

Ancestor: Michael Hail

The above named applicant's claim for citizenship this day came up for final hearing and the testimony taken in the case was carefully examined together with the Rolls of 1851 & '52 taken by the U.S. Government East of the Mississippi River. The three affidavits taken in the case plainly shows that the applicant is a son of the alleged ancestor Michael Hail who was enrolled in the year 1851 by Mr. Siler, and also drew his per capita money in the year 1852, as the rolls will show it appears that the applicant was born out of wedlock but all the testimony in the case points out plainly that Joseph Hail is undoubtedly the son of Micheal[sic] Hail. Therefore we the Commission on Citizenship acting under the law passed by the National Council and approved Dec. 8th 1886 and

Cherokee Citizenship Commission Docket Books
(1880-84, 1887-89) Volume II
Tahlequah, Cherokee Nation

the amendments thereto unanimously agree and so decide that Joseph L. Hail is a Cherokee by blood and is hereby re-admitted to all the rights and privileges of a Cherokee Citizen by blood in the Cherokee Nation.

Oct. 31st 1888

J.T. Adair   Chairman Commission
D.W. Lipe   Commissioner
H.C. Barnes   Commissioner

MONTGOMERY

Docket #308
Rolls 1835 to 1852
Filed August 15th 1887   Applicant for Cherokee Citizenship
Post Office: Tahlequah C.N.   **Attorney:** H.B. Stone

N°	NAMES	AGE	SEX
1	Thomas Montgomery	59	Male
2	William A. Montgomery	38	"
3	James N. Montgomery	36	"
4	Nora B. Montgomery	16	Female

Ancestor: Thomas Gobbest

Office Commission on Citizenship

Tahlequah, Ind. Ter. Sept. 25th 1888

Thomas Montgomery, et.al.
   (vs)   Applicants for Cherokee Citizenship
Cherokee Nation

    In the matter of the above applicants whose case was set for final hearing, and their names was[sic] called by the Sheriff on three several days, at the Court house door in the town of Tahlequah I.T. as required by law, and the parties not answering to these names personally, or by attorney. The Court then ordered, that the applicants, Thomas Montgomery and his three children, viz: William H, James H and N.B. Montgomery, be entered upon the docket by default, and declared not to be Cherokees by blood, and not entitled to any rights and privileges of this Nation. and stand as intruders upon the public domain of the Cherokee Nation.

J.T. Adair   Chairman of Commission
D.W. Lipe   Commissioner
H.C. Barnes   Commissioner

Cherokee Citizenship Commission Docket Books
(1880-84, 1887-89) Volume II
Tahlequah, Cherokee Nation

CHISHOLM

Docket #319
Rolls 1851 & 2
filed August 16th 1887   Applicant for Cherokee Citizenship
Post Office: Shawnee town I.T.   **Attorney:**

N°	NAMES	AGE	SEX
1	Frank Chisholm	26	Male

Ancestor: Jessie Chisholm

We the Commission on Citizenship after examining the evidence in the above case, and also the Old Settler pay rolls of 1851, find that the above applicant, Frank Chisholm is a Cherokee by blood, and is hereby re-admitted to all the rights and privileges of a Cherokee citizen by blood which is in compliance with an Act of the National Council dated December 8th 1886 and also the amendments to said Act dated Feb'y 7th 1888, creating this Commission.

      J.T. Adair   Chairman Commission
      D.W. Lipe   Commissioner
Office Com. on Citizenship
Tahlequah, I.T. July 2nd 1888

CHISHOLM

Docket #320
Rolls 1851 & 2
Filed August 16th 1887   Applicant for Cherokee Citizenship
Post Office: Shawneetown I.T.   **Attorney:**

N°	NAMES	AGE	SEX
1	Mary Chisholm	20	Female

Ancestor: Jessie Chisholm

We the Commission on Citizenship after carefully examining the evidence and also the Old Settler pay rolls of 1851 find that the applicant, Mary Chisholm, is a Cherokee by blood, and is hereby re-admitted to all the rights and privileges of a Cherokee citizen by blood, which is in compliance with an Act of the National Council dated December 8th 1886, creating this Commission, and also amendments to said Act approved Feb'y 7th 1888.

Cherokee Citizenship Commission Docket Books
(1880-84, 1887-89) Volume II
Tahlequah, Cherokee Nation

J.T. Adair Chairman Commission
D.W. Lipe Commissioner

Tahlequah I.T. July 2-1888
Office Com on Citizenship

CHISHOLM

Docket #321
Rolls 1851 & 52
Filed August 16th 1887   Applicant for Cherokee Citizenship
Post Office: Shawneetown I.T.   **Attorney:**

N°	NAMES	AGE	SEX
1	William Chisholm	10	Male

Ancestor: Jessie Chisholm

We the Commission on Citizenship after examining the evidence in the above case, and also the Old Settler pay rolls of 1851, find that the above applicant, William Chisholm, is a Cherokee by blood, and is hereby re-admitted to all the rights and privileges of a Cherokee citizen by blood, which is in compliance with an Act of the National Council dated Dec. 8-86, creating this Commission, and also amendments thereto approved Feb'y. 7th 1888.

J.T. Adair Chairman Commission
D.W. Lipe Commissioner

Office Com on Citizenship
Tahlequah I.T. July 2-1888

BEAVER

Docket #322
Rolls 1851 & 52
filed August 16th 1887   Applicant for Cherokee Citizenship
Post Office: Shawneetown I.T.   **Attorney:**

N°	NAMES	AGE	SEX
1	Jane Beaver	29	Female
2	Cora Beaver	8	"
3	Lucinda Beaver	6	"
4	Lucy Beaver	4	"

Cherokee Citizenship Commission Docket Books
(1880-84, 1887-89) Volume II
Tahlequah, Cherokee Nation

5	Frank Beaver	2	Male

Ancestor: Jessie Chisholm

We the Commission on Citizenship after examining the evidence, and also the Old Settler pay rolls of 1851, find that the above applicant, Jane Beaver and her four children – Cora – Lucinda – Lucy and Frank Beaver to be Cherokees by blood, and are hereby re-admitted to all the rights and privileges of Cherokee citizens by blood, which is in compliance with an Act of the National Council dated Dec. 8th 1886, creating this Commission, and also the amendments thereto approved Feb'y. 7th 1888.

                              J.T. Adair   Chairman Commission
                              D.W. Lipe   Commissioner

Office Com on Citizenship
Tahlequah I.T. July 2-1888

HILL

Docket #323
Rolls 1851 & 52
filed August 16th 1887   Applicant for Cherokee Citizenship
    Post Office: Shawneetown I.T.   **Attorney:**

N°	NAMES	AGE	SEX
1	Caroline Hill	27	Female
2	Mary Hill	4	"

Ancestor: Jessie Chisholm

We the Commission on Citizenship after examining the evidence in the above case and also the Old Settler pay rolls of 1851, find that the applicant, Caroline Hill and her daughter Mary are Cherokees by blood, and are hereby re-admitted to all the rights and privileges of Cherokee citizens by blood, which is in compliance with an Act of the National Council dated December 8th 1886, and also the amendment thereto approved Feb'y. 7th 1888.

                              J.T. Adair   Chairman Commission
                              D.W. Lipe   Commissioner

Office Com on Citizenship
Tahlequah I.T. July 2-'88

Cherokee Citizenship Commission Docket Books
(1880-84, 1887-89) Volume II
Tahlequah, Cherokee Nation

NICHOLS

Docket #324
Rolls 1835, 1852
filed August 17th 1887
Post Office: Dalton Ga

Applicant for Cherokee Citizenship
Attorney: Boudinot & Rasmus

N°	NAMES	AGE	SEX
1	Oceola Taylor Nichols	15	Male

Ancestor: Polly Blackburn

We the Commission on Citizenship after examining the evidence in the above case, and also the rolls of 1851 & 1852, find that Oceola T. Nichols is a Cherokee by blood, and a descendant of Polly Blackburn who was an acknowledged Cherokee. The Commission therefore decide that the applicant is a Cherokee by blood, and is hereby re-admitted to all the rights and privileges of Cherokee citizen by blood.

       J.T. Adair Chairman Commission
       D.W. Lipe Commissioner
               Commissioner

Office Com on Citizenship
Tahlequah I.T. Sept. 24th 1888

WARREN

Docket #325
Rolls 1835 to 1852
Filed August 17th 1887
Post Office: Kingston Texas

Applicants for Cherokee Citizenship
Attorney: C.H. Taylor

N°	NAMES	AGE	SEX
1	Mary E. Warren	25	Female
2	James L. Warren	7	Male
3	Jacob E. Warren	4	"

Ancestor: Elis B. Shoemake
Rejected April 26th 1889
Adverse to Claimant
See Decision in this case in that of L.R. Dawson in this Book Page 20.

This April 26th 1889.   Will P. Ross
  D.S. Williams   Chairman
     Clk Com   J.E. Gunter Com

Cherokee Citizenship Commission Docket Books
(1880-84, 1887-89) Volume II
Tahlequah, Cherokee Nation

COVINGTON

Docket #326
Rolls 1835 to 1852
filed August 18th 1887 Applicant for Cherokee Citizenship
Post Office: Kingston Texas **Attorney:** C.H. Taylor

N°	NAMES	AGE	SEX
1	George A. Covington	20	Male
2	Mordicia J. Covington	3	Male

Ancestor: Eli B. Shoemake
Rejected May 2nd 1889

The application in the above case was filed August 18th 1887 and submitted by Attorneys for applicant and for the Cherokee Nation this day for decision. There being no evidence presented in the case the Commission decide against the applicant George A. Covington as a Cherokee by blood. (Post Office Kingston Texas.)

This May 2nd 1887
D.S. Williams
Clk Com Tah I.T.

Will P. Ross
Chairman
John E. Gunter Com.

SHOEMAKE

Docket #327
Rolls 1835 to 1852
filed August 19th 1887 Applicant for Cherokee Citizenship
Post Office: Kingston Texas **Attorney:** C.H. Taylor

N°	NAMES	AGE	SEX
1	Altha J. Shoemake	11	Female
2	Bulah Shoemake	8	"

Ancestor: Eli Shoemake
Rejected May 2nd 1889

Application for Cherokee Citizenship Now comes on this day for the final hearing of the above entitled case. The Commission after investigating the papers in said case find that the applicant produces no evidence whatever to sustain the allegation set forth in his application relying entirely on his

Cherokee Citizenship Commission Docket Books
(1880-84, 1887-89) Volume II
Tahlequah, Cherokee Nation

application. Therefore the Commission render a decision adversely to claimant Wm L. Shoemake & the following named minor children, Altha J. Shoemake female aged 11 years, Bulah B. Shoemake aged 8 years. (Post Office Kingston Texas.)

This May 2nd 1887　　　　　　Will P. Ross
D.S. Williams　　　　　　　　　　Chairman
Clk Com Tah I.T.　　　　John E. Gunter　Com.

SHOEMAKE

Docket #328
Rolls 1835 to 1852
filed August 19th 1887　　　　Applicant for Cherokee Citizenship
Post Office: Kingston Texas　　**Attorney:**　C.H. Taylor

N°	NAMES	AGE	SEX
1	William L. Shoemake	31	Male
2	Jessie B. Shoemake	6	"
3	Frances J. Shoemake	4	Female
4	Tammie Shoemake	2	"
5	Lena Shoemake	1	"

Ancestor:　Eli B. Shoemake

Rejected May 16th 1889

Office Commission on Citizenship
Cherokee Nation Ind. Ter'y.
Tahlequah　May 16th-1889

Now on this day comes the above named case for final hearing. The applicant alleges that he is descended from Eli B. Shoemake whose name may be found on the Census rolls of Cherokee taken and made of Cherokees by blood in the years 1835/52 – Old Settler. The evidence fails to show that Eli B. Shoemake was of Cherokee blood while his name is not found on the rolls named. The Commission therefore decide that William L. Shoemake is not of Cherokee blood and not entitled to readmission to Citizenship in the Cherokee Nation. This decision included the family of applicant to wit:　Jesse B. Shoemake aged 6 years, Francis J. Shoemake (daughter) aged 4 years, Tammie J. Shoemake (daughter) aged two years, and Lena Shoemake (daughter) aged one year.

Cherokee Citizenship Commission Docket Books
(1880-84, 1887-89) Volume II
Tahlequah, Cherokee Nation

Attest   Will P. Ross
   D.S. Williams   Chairman
   Asst Clk Com.   R. Bunch   Commissioner
                       John E. Gunter   Com

JOURDAN

Docket #329
Rolls 1835
filed August 20th 1887   Applicant for Cherokee Citizenship
   Post Office: Rays Mill Ark   **Attorney:** C.H. Taylor

N°	NAMES	AGE	SEX
1	Jessie P. Jourdan	39	Male
2	William A. Jourdan	17	"
3	Sarah Jourdan	15	Female
4	Laura Jourdan	10	"
5	Taylor Jourdan	7	"
6	Emma Jourdan	3	Female
7	Sam Jourdan	1	Male
8	Mary Jourdan	5	Female

                Ancestor: River Jourdan
Rejected May 4th 1889
                       Office Commission on Citizenship
                            Cherokee Nation Ind. Ter'y.
                            Tahlequah May 4th 1889.

The application of Jesse P. Jourdan was filed Aug. 20th 1887 and submitted this day by Attorneys. The evidence refered[sic] to in support of the case will be found in the case of Jesse Jourdan which fails to show that River Jourdan was of Cherokee blood from whom applicant alleges his descent whose name is not found on the census roll of Cherokees [sic] blood taken in the year 1835. The Commission decide that Jesse P. Jourdan aged 39 years is not of Cherokee blood and is not entitled to Citizenship in the Cherokee Nation. This decision includes his children, William A. Jourdan aged 17 years, Sarah Jourdan 15 years, Laura Jourdain[sic] 10 years, Taylor Jourdan 7 years, Mary Jourdan 5 years, Emma Jourdan 3 years and Sam or Samuel Jourdan aged one year.
Attest   Will P. Ross
   D.S. Williams   Chairman
         Clk Com.   John E. Gunter   Com

Cherokee Citizenship Commission Docket Books
(1880-84, 1887-89) Volume II
Tahlequah, Cherokee Nation

SHOEMAKE

Docket #330
Rolls 1835 1851 & 2 Old Settler Rolls
filed Aug. 21st 1887 Applicant for Cherokee Citizenship
Post Office: Kingston Texas **Attorney:** C.H. Taylor

N°	NAMES	AGE	SEX
1	Wm L. Shoemake	39	Male
2	Rosetta Shoemake	17	Female
3	Ida B. Shoemake	13	"
4	Zidda W. Shoemake	10	

Ancestor: Eli B. Shoemake

May 2nd 1889

Now comes on this day for the final hearing of the above case. The Commission after investigating the papers in said case find that the applicant provides no evidence whatever to sustain the allegation set forth in his application relying entirely on his application. Therefore the Commission render a decision adverse to claimant Wm L. Shoemake and the following named minor children whose names appear in the application of Wm L. Shoemake and recorded as Guardian; Rosetta Shoemake Female aged 17 years, Ida B. Shoemake Female aged 13 years. Zidda W. Shoemake aged 10 years. Post Office address is Kingston Texas.

Will P. Ross
E.G. Ross   Chairman
   Clerk Commission   John E. Gunter   Com.

FISHER

Docket #331
Rolls 1835
filed Aug 26th 1887 Applicant
Post Office: Sheep Ranch **Attorney:** Wm A. Thompson

N°	NAMES	AGE	SEX
1	Leoda T. Fisher	24	Female
2	Geo G. Fisher	3	Male

Cherokee Citizenship Commission Docket Books
(1880-84, 1887-89) Volume II
Tahlequah, Cherokee Nation

3	Viva C. Fisher	1	Female

Ancestor: Clem V. McNair

Now on this the 26th day of August 1887, comes the above case for final hearing and having made application pursuant to the provisions of an Act of the National Council approved December 8th 1887 and all the evidence having been duly considered and found to be sufficient and satisfactory to the Commission and the name of C.V. McNair, ancestor found to *(illegible)* on the rolls 1835; it is adjudged and determined by the Commission that Leoda T. Fisher, Geo. G. Fisher and Viva C. Fisher are Cherokees by blood and are hereby re-admitted to all the rights, privileges and immunities of Cherokees by blood.

And a certificate of said decision of the Commission and readmission was made and furnished to said parties accordingly.

	J.T. Adair	Chairman Com
Henry Eiffert	D.W. Lipe	Commissioner
Clk Comm.		Commissioner

JOURDAN

Docket #332
Rolls 1835
Filed August 20th 1887   Applicant for Cherokee Citizenship
Post Office: Cincinnati Ark   **Attorney:** C.H. Taylor

N°	NAMES	AGE	SEX
1	John A. Jourdan	44	Male

Ancestor: River Jourdan

Rejected May 4th 1889

Office Commission on Citizenship
Cherokee Nation Ind. Ter'y.
Tahlequah May 4th 1889

The applicant aged 44 years, filed his application August 20th 1887 and it was submitted this day by Attorneys for decision. The evidence is the same as that in the case of Jesse Jourdan and is decided adversely to Claimant because the evidence does not show that River Jourdan was of Cherokee blood and because his name is not found on the Census roll of 1835.

Cherokee Citizenship Commission Docket Books
(1880-84, 1887-89) Volume II
Tahlequah, Cherokee Nation

                    Will P. Ross.
Attest   Chairman
    D.S. Williams   John E. Gunter Com
    Clk Com.

JORDAN

Docket #333
Rolls 1835
Filed August 20th 1887   Applicant for Cherokee Citizenship
Post Office: Rays Mill Ark   **Attorney:** C.H. Taylor

N°	NAMES	AGE	SEX
1	Alva D. Jordan	28	Female
2	William Jordan	4	Male
3	Ettie Jordan	2	Female

             Ancestor: River Jordan

Rejected May 4th 1889

                Office Commission on Citizenship
                  Cherokee Nation Ind. Ter'y.
                  Tahlequah May 4th 1889

The application in the above case was filed the 20th August 1887 and submitted by Attorneys this day for decision. The evidence in this case is the same as in the case of Jesse Jourdan and is decided adversely to Claimant and includes his[sic] son Willie Jourdan aged 4 years and daughter Ettie Jourdan aged 2 years.

                Will P. Ross
Attest   Chairman
    D.S. Williams   John E. Gunter Com.
    Clk. Com.

WEST

Docket #334
Rolls 1835
Filed August 20th 1887   Applicant for Cherokee Citizenship
Post Office: Viney Grove Ark   **Attorney:** C.H. Taylor

N°	NAMES	AGE	SEX
1	Elizabeth West	47	Female

Cherokee Citizenship Commission Docket Books
(1880-84, 1887-89) Volume II
Tahlequah, Cherokee Nation

2	William A. West	16	Male

Ancestor: River Jourdan

Rejected May 4th 1889

                      Office Commission on Citizenship
                          Cherokee Nation Ind. Ter'y.
                          Tahlequah May 3rd 1889.

Applicant for Cherokee Citizenship

Now on this day comes the above entitled for a final hearing there being no evidence submitted to establish the fact that the said Elizabeth West was a grand daughter of one River Jourdan whom she alleges to be her ancestor & admitting that she was either or not related to said River Jourdan there is no evidence to justify the readmission of River Jourdan to Citizenship therefore the Commission decide that the above applicant whose age is 47 years old. Post Office Vina Grove Ark. are not Cherokees and are not entitled to readmission to Cherokee Citizenship in the Cherokee Nation.

Attest
    D.S. Williams
    Clk. Com.

                Will P. Ross
                  Chairman
            John E. Gunter Com.

JOURDAN

Docket #335
Rolls 1835
filed August 20th 1887   Applicant for Cherokee Citizenship
    Post Office: Siloam Arks   **Attorney:** C.H. Taylor

N°	NAMES	AGE	SEX
1	William S. Jourdan	50	Male
2	Charles Jourdan	21	"
3	Mary Jourdan	17	Female
4	Jessie Jourdan	11	Male
5	Frank Jourdan	7	"
6	Fred Jourdan	5	"
7	Nora Jourdan	1	Female

Ancestor: River Jourdan

Cherokee Citizenship Commission Docket Books
(1880-84, 1887-89) Volume II
Tahlequah, Cherokee Nation

Office Commission on Citizenship
May 3rd 1889.

The application in this case was filed the 20th day of August 1887 and submitted by Attorney this day with the case of Jessie Jourdan as deriving his Cherokee blood from River Jourdan. And is decided adversely on the ground that the name of River Jourdan is not found on the roll of 1835 and his Cherokee descent is not established. This decision includes the family of William S. Jourdan, viz. Charles Jourdan aged twenty one years, Mary Jourdan aged seventeen years, Jessie Jourdan aged eleven years, Frank Jourdan aged seven years, Fred Jourdan aged five years and Nora Jourdan Female aged one year.

Attest
    E.G. Ross
    Clerk Commission

Will P. Ross
    Chairman
John E. Gunter   Com.

JOURDAN

Docket #336
Rolls 1825
filed August 20th 1887   Applicant for Cherokee Citizenship
Post Office: Sanders Station IT   **Attorney:** C.H. Taylor

N°	NAMES	AGE	SEX
1	Jackson Jourdan	65	Male
2	James Jourdan	14	"
3	Martin Jourdan	8	"
4	Susan Jourdan	6	Female
5	Josie Jourdan	1	"

Ancestor: Annis Jourdan

Commission on Citizenship
Tahlequah I.T. July 20th 1888

Jackson Jourdan, et.al.
    (vs)   Applicant for Citizenship
Cherokee Nation

The above case having come up for final hearing which was filed in compliance with the Act of the National Council creating this Commission dated Dec. 8th 1886. And the amendment thereto approved Feb'y 7th 1888.

Cherokee Citizenship Commission Docket Books
(1880-84, 1887-89) Volume II
Tahlequah, Cherokee Nation

Now the Commission after carefully examining all the evidence submitted in the case and also the Census rolls taken by Mr. Siler in the year 1851, find that the proff[sic] is not sufficient to establish this claim to Cherokee Citizenship. The testimony of Mary Martin shows that she was acquainted with Jackson Jourdan & his family in Lumpkin County, Ga. in the year 1860, and was some what acquainted with his mother Annice Jourdan, and that they were recognized as Cherokees, but she knows nothing of how she (Annice Jourdan) derived her Cherokee blood. mother maiden name before she was married. John M. McAllister the *(illegible)* witness for the defendant, states he saw Jackson Jourdan a few times in Georgia and heard his father and Charles Duncan speak of them as being Cherokee, which is about all he knows of this family. The Census rolls taken by Mr. Siler in the year 1851, east of the Missippi[sic] river shows that he did enroll one Annice Jourdan, which no doubt was the ancestor of Jackson Jourdan the applicant, but after enrolling, it appears from the remarks made by Mr. Siler on the said rolls, that he made a mistake, and from his remarks he was satisfied they were not Cherokees by blood "and could not produce the slightest degree of proff[sic] and according to her (Annice Jourdan) own statement they lived more than three hundred [miles] from the nearest point of the Cherokee Country, and that she did not know of any one who could state she was of Cherokee descent."

Now after summing up the whole of the evidence, the Commission decide that the foregoing applicant Jackson Jourdan & his four children viz. James – Martin – Susan and Jessie Jourdan are **not** Cherokees by blood and not entitled to any of the rights & privileges of Cherokee Citizens by blood.

                           D.W. Lipe   Act'g Chairman of Com
                           John E. Gunter   Commissioner

SLATON

Docket #337
Rolls 1835
filed Aug 20th 1887   Applicants for Cherokee Citizenship
     Post Office: Fort Gibson I.T.   **Attorney:**   C.H. Taylor

N°	NAMES	AGE	SEX
1	Martha E. Slaton	32	Female
2	Jas. V. Slaton	7	Male
3	Chas. Slaton	5	"

Cherokee Citizenship Commission Docket Books
(1880-84, 1887-89) Volume II
Tahlequah, Cherokee Nation

| 4 | | Jessie Slaton | 3 | " |
| 5 | | Elner Slaton | 6 mo | Female |

Ancestor: Drewsiller Green

May 3rd 1889

The application in the above case was filed the 20th day of August 1887 and is this day submitted without evidence by Attorney for claimant. The Commission therefore decide that Martha E. Slatton is not of Cherokee blood and is not entitled to Citizenship in the Cherokee Nation. This includes the family of said Martha E. Slatton, to wit; James V. Slatton aged seven years, Charles Slatton aged five years, Jesse Slaton aged three years and Elner Slaton (Female) aged six months.

                Will P. Ross

E.G. Ross   Chairman
   Clerk of Commission   John E. Gunter   Com.

SHOEMAKE

Docket #338
Rolls 1835 – 42 – 51 – 52
filed Aug 20th 1887   Applicants for Cherokee Citizenship
Post Office: Webbers Falls I.T.   **Attorney:** Boudinot & Rasmus

N°		NAMES	AGE	SEX
1		Jas D. Shoemake	36	Male
2		John H. Shoemake	15	"
3		Annie E. Shoemake	13	Female
4		Cyrus D. Shoemake	8	Male
5		Ric'd. E. Shoemake	5	"
6		Marion F. Shoemake	2	"

Ancestor: Annie Shoemake

Commission on Citizenship.

CHEROKEE NATION, IND. TER.

James D. Shoemake, Et al.   *Tahlequah,*   Oct. 25th 1888
   (vs)
Cherokee Nation

Cherokee Citizenship Commission Docket Books
(1880-84, 1887-89) Volume II
Tahlequah, Cherokee Nation

Now on this the 25th day of Oct. 1888, comes the above case up for final disposition, if having been submitted by plaintiff's attorney, E.C. Boudinot, Jr.

The application, as well as the testimony in this case, alleges one Annie Shoemake as the Cherokee ancestor of the applicants, and that she was of Cherokee blood, and that her name will appear on some of the rolls of Cherokees, East.

We, the Commission on Citizenship, have carefully examined the rolls laid down in the 7th Sec. of the law of Dec. 8th 1886 in relation to citizenship for the name of Annie Shoemake, but fail to find the name enrolled thereon in any shape though it is in proof that these parties were in Jackson County in the state of Alabama, up as late as the year 1854.

The testimony of W.H. Shoemake, who is Judge of the Southern Judicial district of the Cherokee Nation, and Uncle to the applicant, James D. Shoemake who is the son of Bettie Ann Shoemake, who was the full sister of W.H. Shoemake, goes to show that he was re-admitted to citizenship in the Cherokee Nation on the 5th day of January 1883, by the Tehee Commission on Citizenship, and that he now holds the office as Circuit Judge, as stated, of Canadian Dist.

In the absence of the rolls of 1848, 1851-1835 and 1852 of Cherokees taken in the Old Cherokee Nation in the state of North Carolina, Tennessee, Georgia and Alabama, containing the name of the ancestor Annie Shoemake, or that of the applicants themselves, we cannot grant citizenship to these applicants, for the law says "such applicant must be a person, or the lineal descendent of a person, whose name appears on the census rolls of Cherokees taken by the United States after the treaty of 1835" and before mentioned, which in this case is clearly shown that they do not.

We are of the opinion therefore, that this case is enshrouded in some way, that we cannot find out just how it is, and if Cherokees, as some would naturally suppose from the fact that some of this family had proven to the satisfaction of the Tehee Commission in 1883 that they were, that their names should appear on some of the rolls of Cherokees already mentioned, and as other Cherokee names do, who were living in Alabama at the same time these parties were. James D. Shoemake and his five children, namely: John H. – Amy E. – Cyrus D. – Richard E. and Marion F. Shoemake are not Cherokees under the law of Dec. 8th

Cherokee Citizenship Commission Docket Books
(1880-84, 1887-89) Volume II
Tahlequah, Cherokee Nation

1886 in relation to citizenship, consequently not citizens of the Cherokee Nation.

        J.T. Adair   Chairman Commission
        D.W. Lipe   Commissioner
        H.C. Barnes Commissioner

STORY

Docket #339
Rolls 1835
filed Aug. 20th 1887   Applicants for Cherokee Citizenship
   Post Office: Blue Tent, Cala.   **Attorney**: A.J. Ridge

N°	NAMES	AGE	SEX
1	Sarah Nevada Story	27	Female
2	Geo. Henry Story	8	Male

        Ancestor: Franklyn

Rejected June 28th 1889

        Office Commission Citizenship
        Cher. Nat. June 28th 1889

There being no evidence in support of the above named case, the Commission decide that Sarah Nevada Story age 27 yrs and her son, George Henry Story age 8, male. Are not Cherokees by blood. Post Office Blue Tent, Cal.

        Will P. Ross
D.S. Williams   Chairman
Clerk Commission   John E. Gunter Com.

CAMPBELL

Docket #340
Rolls 1835
Filed Aug. 20th 1887   Applicants for Cherokee Citizenship
   Post Office: Blue Tent, Cala   **Attorney**: A.J. Ridge

N°	NAMES	AGE	SEX
1	Annie Duncan Campbell	29	Female
2	Oscar Dunreath Campbell	9	Male
3	Dan'l. Alford Campbell	7	"

Cherokee Citizenship Commission Docket Books
(1880-84, 1887-89) Volume II
Tahlequah, Cherokee Nation

4	Jesse Kenneth Campbell	4	"

Ancestor: Franklyn

Rejected June 28th 89

Office Commission Citizenship
Cher. Nat. June 28th 1889

There being no evidence in support of the above named case the Commission decides that Annie D. Campbell aged 27 yrs and the following children; Oscar D. Campbell male age 9 yrs, Daniel A. Campbell age 7 yrs, Jesse K. Campbell male age 4 yrs are not Cherokees by blood. P.O. Blue Tent California.

                Will P. Ross
D.S. Williams   Chairman
Clerk Commission   John E. Gunter   Com.

BAKER

Docket #341
Rolls 1835
filed Aug. 20th 1887   Applicant for Cherokee Citizenship
Post Office: Blue Tent, Cala.   **Attorney:** A.J. Ridge

N°	NAMES	AGE	SEX
1	Melissa Jane Baker	11	Female

Ancestor: Franklyn

Rejected June 28th 1889

Office Commission Citizenship
Cher. Nat. June 28th 1889

There being no evidence in support of the above named case, the Commission decides that Melissa Jane Baker age 11 yrs, is not a Cherokee by blood. P.O. Blue Tent California.

                Will P. Ross
D.S. Williams   Chairman
Clerk Commission   John E. Gunter   Com.

Cherokee Citizenship Commission Docket Books
(1880-84, 1887-89) Volume II
Tahlequah, Cherokee Nation

HAGER

Docket #342
Rolls 1835
filed Aug. 20th 1887   Applicants for Cherokee Citizenship
Post Office: Blue Tent, Cala.   **Attorney:** A.J. Ridge

N°	NAMES	AGE	SEX
1	Mary Adeline Hager	24	Female
2	Nevada Lillian Hager	4	"
3	Horato Leroy Hager	1	Male

Ancestor: Franklyn

Rejected June 28th 1889

Office Commission Citizenship
Cher. Nat. June 28th 1889

There being no evidence in support of the above named case the Commission decides that Mary Adaline Hager age 24 yrs, and her following children; Nevada L. Hager 4 yrs Female, Horato Leroy Hager age 1 male, are not Cherokees by blood. P.O. Blue Tent California.

Will P. Ross
D.S. Williams   Chairman
Clerk Commission   John E. Gunter   Com.

DAVIS

Docket #343
Rolls 1835 to 52
filed Aug. 20th 1887   Applicants for Cherokee Citizenship
Post Office: Childers Station   **Attorney:** B.H. Stone

N°	NAMES	AGE	SEX
1	James Davis	44	Male
2	Charles Davis	21	"
3	Johny Davis	19	"
4	Nancy Davis	17	Female
5	Eva Davis	15	"
6	James Davis	13	Male
7	Andy Davis	11	"
8	Georgia Davis	9	Female
9	Alfred Davis	7	Male

Cherokee Citizenship Commission Docket Books
(1880-84, 1887-89) Volume II
Tahlequah, Cherokee Nation

10	Elizabeth Davis	2	Female

Ancestor:

Now on this the 29th day of August 1887 comes the above case for final hearing and the above named parties having made application pursuant to the provisions of an Act of the National Council approved December 8th 1886 and all the evidence having been duly considered and found to be sufficient and satisfactory to the Commission, it is adjudged and determined by the Commission that James Davis, Charles Davis, Johny Davis, Nancy Davis, Eva Davis, James Davis, Andy Davis, Georgia Davis, Alfred Davis, Elizabeth Davis are Cherokees by blood and are hereby re-admitted to all the rights, privileges and immunities of Cherokees by blood.

And a certificate of said decision of the Commission and readmission was made and furnished said parties accordingly.

Henry Eiffert
Clerk Comm.

J.T. Adair   Chairman Commission
John E. Gunter   Commissioner
                  Commissioner

IRVING

Docket #344
Rolls 1835
filed Aug. 20th 1887

Applicants for Cherokee Citizenship

Post Office: **Attorney:**   A.J. Ridge

N°	NAMES	AGE	SEX
1	Hester L. Irving	20	Female
2	Lowell Irving	1	Male

Ancestor: Franklyn

Rejected June 28th 1889

Office Commission Citizenship
Cher. Nat.   June 28th 1889

There being no evidence in support of the above named case, the Commission decides that Hester Luvina Irving age 20 is not a Cherokee by blood. P.O. Grass Valley, Cal.

Cherokee Citizenship Commission Docket Books
(1880-84, 1887-89) Volume II
Tahlequah, Cherokee Nation

D.S. Williams
Clerk Commission

Will P. Ross
Chairman
John E. Gunter Com.

LANDRETH

Docket #345
Rolls 1835
filed Aug. 20th 1887   Applicant for Cherokee Citizenship
Post Office: Van Buren Ark   **Attorney:** C.H. Taylor

N°	NAMES	AGE	SEX
1	Geo. R. Landreth	32	Male

Ancestor: C.H. Taylor

Rejected June 3rd 1889

Office Commission on Citizenship
Cherokee Nation Ind. Ter'y.
Tahlequah June 3rd 1889

The application in the above case is supported by no evidence and the Commission decide that George R. Landreth is not of Cherokee blood.

Attest
D.S. Williams
Asst Clk Com

Will P. Ross
Chairman
R. Bunch   Commissioner
J.E. Gunter Com

MONTGOMERY

Docket #346
Rolls 1835 to 52
Filed Aug 20th 1887   Applicants for Cherokee Citizenship
Post Office: Webbers Falls I.T. **Attorney:** B.H. Stone

N°	NAMES	AGE	SEX
1	Jos. W. Montgomery	61	Male
2	Jno S. Montgomery	36	"
3	Alverd Montgomery	40	Female
4	Thos. W. Montgomery	30	Male

Ancestor: Thos. Gabbor

Cherokee Citizenship Commission Docket Books
(1880-84, 1887-89) Volume II
Tahlequah, Cherokee Nation

Office Commission on Citizenship

Tahlequah, Ind. Ter. Sept. 25th 1888

James W. Montgomery, Et al.
    (vs)   Applicants for Cherokee Citizenship
Cherokee Nation

    In the matter of the above claimants for Cherokee Citizenship, the case was set for final hearing, and was called by the sheriff on three several days, at the Court House door in the town of Tahlequah, I.T. the parties did not answer personally, or by attorney. The Court then ordered that the applicants, James W. Montgomery, and his three children, viz; John S, Alfred and Thomas Montgomery, be entered up on the docket by default, and declaired[sic] not to be Cherokees by blood, and not entitled to any rights and privileges of this nation, and are intruders upon the public domain of the Cherokee Nation.

                         J.T. Adair   Chairman of Commission
                         D.W. Lipe   Commissioner
                         H.C. Barnes   Commissioner

COATS

Docket #347
Rolls 1835
filed Aug 20th 1887   Applicants for Cherokee Citizenship
     Post Office: Maysville Ark   **Attorney:** C.H. Taylor

N°	NAMES	AGE	SEX
1	Bell Coats	32	Female
2	Stella Coats	15	"
3	Cora Coats	9	"
4	Lola Coats	6	"

                 Ancestor: Samuel Parks
Rejected

Commission on Citizenship
                 Cherokee Nation IT
                 Tahlequah May 29th 1889

Cherokee Citizenship Commission Docket Books
(1880-84, 1887-89) Volume II
Tahlequah, Cherokee Nation

The application in the above case was filed on the 20th day of Aug. 1887 and was submitted for a final hearing without evidence. The Commission therefore decide that Bell Coats and three children whose names are as follows: Stealla[sic] Female age 15 yrs, Cora Female age 9 and Lula Coats Female 6 yrs, are not Cherokees by blood and are not entitled to Citizenship in the Cherokee Nation. Post Office Ardmore.

Maysville Arks.

George E. Miller
Clerk Commission

Will P. Ross
    Chairman
R. Bunch Com
J.E. Gunter Com

CAMPE

Docket #348
Rolls 1851 & 2
filed August 21st 1887

Applicants for Cherokee Citizenship

Post Office: Pond Sprgs Ga   **Attorney**: Bell & Akin

N°	NAMES	AGE	SEX
1	Missouri Campe	29	Female
2	Ora M. Campe	7	"
3	James M. Campe	5	Male

Ancestor: Nancy Compton

Now on this the 10th day of December 1887 comes the above case for final hearing and having made application pursuant to the provisions of an Act of the National Council approved December 8th 1886 and all the evidence being duly considered and found to be sufficient and satisfactory to the Commission it is adjudged and determined by the Commission that Missouri Campe and children, Ora M. Campe and James M. Campe are Cherokees by blood and they are hereby readmitted to all the rights, privileges and immunities of Cherokee Citizens by blood.

And a certificate of said decision of the Commission and of readmission was made and furnished said parties accordingly.

R.T. Hauks
Asst Clerk
Commission

J.T. Adair   Chairman Commission
John E Gunter   Commissioner
                     Commissioner

Cherokee Citizenship Commission Docket Books
(1880-84, 1887-89) Volume II
Tahlequah, Cherokee Nation

SCUDDER

Docket #349
Rolls 1835 to 52
filed August 21st 1887   Applicant for Cherokee Citizenship
Post Office: Pond Springs Ga   **Attorney**: Bell & Akin

N°	NAMES	AGE	SEX
1	Wm H.H. Scudder	45	Male
2	Ida J. Scudder	17	Female
3	Addie E. Scudder	15	"
4	Laura *(Illegible)* Scudder	13	"
5	Mary E. Scudder	11	"
6	Gordon H. Scudder	9	Male
7	Newton G. Scudder	5	Female
8	Maggie L. Scudder	3	"
9	Nellie V. Scudder	1	"

Ancestor: Polly Blackburn

Now on this the 9 day of Mar. 1887 comes the above case for a final hearing and all the parties having made application pursuant to the provisions of the National Council approved Dec. 8th 1886. And all the evidence being duly examined and found to be sufficient and satisfactory to the Commission and the name of the ancestor Polly Blackburn appearing on the rolls of 1835 to 52. It is adjudged and determined by the Commission that Wm H.H. Scudder, Ida J. Scudder, Addie E. Scudder, Laura *(Illegible)* Scudder, Mary E. Scudder, Gordon H. Scudder, Newton G. Scudder, Maggie Scudder, Nellie V. Scudder, are Cherokees by blood and are hereby readmitted to all the rights, privileges and immunities of Cherokees by blood. And a certificate of said decision of the Commission and re-admission now made are furnished to said parties accordingly.

J.T. Adair   Chairman Commission
C.C. Lipe   John E. Gunter   Commissioner
Clerk Commission

Cherokee Citizenship Commission Docket Books
(1880-84, 1887-89) Volume II
Tahlequah, Cherokee Nation

BREMER

Docket #350
Rolls 1835 & 52
filed 17TH August 1887   Applicant for Cherokee Citizenship
Post Office: Springfield I.T.   **Attorney:** L.B. Bell

N°	NAMES	AGE	SEX
1	George Bremer	47	Male
2	Eliza Bremer	22	female
3	Wm Bremer	20	Male

Ancestor: Walter Sanders

Commission on Citizenship.

CHEROKEE NATION, IND. TER.

George Bremer   *Tahlequah,* October 4th 1889
vs   Application for Cherokee Citizenship
The Cherokee Nation

  The applicant in the above case claims to be the grandson of one Water Walter Sanders, whose name he believes was enrolled on the census rolls of Cherokees by blood taken and made by the United States in the years 1835 51 2. The evidence in this case consists of the statement of William Robison of the *(Illegible)* Nation before the Commission on Citizenship on the 17th day of August 1887. Mr. Robison is 54 yrs of age a citizen of the said Nation by birth and of highly respectable standing. He testifies that he understands the claimant to be of Creek and Cherokee descent but that he knows nothing of his Cherokee blood. The hearing of this case was set for June 5th 1889 and continues to June 29 1889 and the parties in *(illegible)* not *(illegible)* but they have failed to respond and the Commission therefore in the absence of sufficient evidence to establish their Cherokee descent decide that George Bremer aged 47 years and his children, Eliza Bremer 22 yrs & William Bremer 20 yrs are not entitled to Citizenship in the Cherokee Nation.

         Will P. Ross Chairman
         J.E. Gunter Com.

Cherokee Citizenship Commission Docket Books
(1880-84, 1887-89) Volume II
Tahlequah, Cherokee Nation

ROBISON

Docket #351
Rolls 1835 – 51 & 52
filed 17th day of August 1887   Applicant for Cherokee Citizenship
Post Office: Springfield I.T.   **Attorney:** L.B. Bell

N°	NAMES	AGE	SEX
1	Jane Robison	26	female
2	Elizabeth J. Robison	5	"

Ancestor: Reuben Vann

Re-admitted Oct. 11th 1889

Office Commission on Citizenship
Cherokee Nation Ind. Ter.
Tahlequah Oct. 11th 1889.

The applicant in the above case is of Creek and Cherokee descent. The evidence shows that she is the daughter of Reuben Vann a person of Cherokee Indian blood, whose name will be found on the Old Settler Cherokee pay roll of 1851. The Commission therefore decide that the claimant Jane Robison 26 years of age and her daughter Elizabeth J. Robison, are of Cherokee Indian blood (George G. Robison, son of Wm Robison of the Creek Nation is the husband of Jane Robison nee Vann of Father of her child.)   P.O. Springfield Indian Territory.

                Will P. Ross   Chairman
Attest
    D.S. Williams   J.E. Gunter   Com.
    Asst. Clk. Com.

GEORGE

Docket #352
Rolls 1835, 48, 51 and 52
filed August 18th 1887   Applicant for Cherokee Citizenship
Post Office: Chocoville Ark   **Attorney:** Boudinot and Rasmus

N°	NAMES	AGE	SEX
1	John W. George	29	Male
2	Willie George	10 mo	female

Ancestor: Andrew Miller

Cherokee Citizenship Commission Docket Books
(1880-84, 1887-89) Volume II
Tahlequah, Cherokee Nation

Office Commission on Citizenship
Tahlequah May 14th 1889

Now on this day was submitted the case of John W. George applicant for Cherokee Citizenship for a final hearing this case having been filed the 18th day of August 1887. Now the Commission after an examination of the papers in the above case fail to find any evidence in support of application whom it alleges that John W. George is the Grand son of one Andrew Miller. Now the Commission in support of the above facts are of the opinion that John W. George aged 29 years with his family as follows, Willie George, Female, aged ten months, are not Cherokees by blood and are not entitled to Cherokee Citizenship. Post Office address: Chocoville Ark.

Attest	Will P. Ross	Chairman
E.G. Ross	R. Bunch	Com.
Clerk Commission	J.E. Gunter	Com.

PAULEY

Docket #353
Rolls 1835, 48, 51 and 52
filed August 18th 1887   Applicant for Cherokee Citizenship
Post Office: Chocoville Ark   **Attorney:** Boudinot & Rasmus

N°	NAMES	AGE	SEX
1	Sarah A. Pauley	64	Female

Ancestor: Andrew Miller

Office Commission on Citizenship
Tahlequah C.N. May 14, 1889

Now on this day the above case coming on for final hearing the application was filed on the 18th day of August 1887. After examining the papers we fail to find any evidence in support of the application. The applicant alleges that one Andrew Miller was his ancestor. After examining the census rolls, we fail to find the name of applicant's ancestor Andrew Miller. In view of these facts the Commission is of the opinion and so declare the applicant Sarah A. Pauley age 64 years is not a Cherokee by blood and are not entitled to Cherokee Citizenship in the Cherokee Nation.

Cherokee Citizenship Commission Docket Books
(1880-84, 1887-89) Volume II
Tahlequah, Cherokee Nation

	Will P. Ross	Chairman
E.G. Ross	R. Bunch	Com
Clk Commission	J.E. Gunter	Com

GEORGE

Docket #354
Rolls 1835, 48, 51 and 52
filed August 18th 1887   Applicant for Cherokee Citizenship
Post Office: Chocoville, Ark.   **Attorney:** Boudinot & Rasmus

N°	NAMES	AGE	SEX
1	Isaac C. George	32	Male

Ancestor: Andrew Miller

Rejected May 14th 89

Office Commission on Citizenship Cher, Nat. I.T.
Tahlequah May 14 1889

The above case which was set for the 14th day of May 1889, by the Attorneys for both parties for the final hearing, the same having been filed on the 18th day of Aug. 1887. The applicant claims his Cherokee descent through one Andrew Miller whose name would be found on the census roll of Cherokees taken and made in the years 1835-48-51 & 2. The Commission fail to find the name of the said Andrew Miller on either of the above mentioned rolls of Cherokees by blood. There being no evidence in support of the above named case of Isaac C. George, The Commission therefore adjudge that Isaac C. George aged 32 yrs. is not of Cherokee blood and are not entitled to Cherokee Citizenship within the Cherokee Nation and is hereby declared to be an intruder in the Cherokee Nation. Post Office address, Chocoville Ark.

Attest		
	Will P. Ross	Chairman
D.S. Williams	R. Bunch	Com
Asst Clk Com	J.E. Gunter	Com.

Cherokee Citizenship Commission Docket Books
(1880-84, 1887-89) Volume II
Tahlequah, Cherokee Nation

REED

Docket #355
Rolls 1835, 48, 51 and 52
filed August 28th 1887   Applicant for Cherokee Citizenship
Post Office: Chocoville Ark   **Attorney:** Boudinot and Rasmus

N°	NAMES	AGE	SEX
1	Julia A. Reed	27	Female
2	Nannie A. Reed	6	"
3	Lula Reed	4	"
4	Infant		

Ancestor: Andrew Miller

Office Commission on Citizenship
Tahlequah May 14th 1889

The above application was filed on the 18th day of August 1887, and having been called up for the final hearing and submitted without evidence to sustain the application. Therefore the Commission decree that Julia A. Reed aged 27 years and her children Nannie A. Reed Female aged six years, Lula Reed Female age 4 years and an Infant who is not named are not of Cherokee blood and not entitled to Citizenship in the Cherokee Nation. Post Office Van Buren Ark.

               Will P. Ross
Attest   Chairman
   E.G. Ross   R. Bunch   Chairman
   Clerk Commission   Commission
               J.E. Gunter   Com.

WARD

Docket #356
Rolls 1835, 48, 51 & 52
filed August 23rd 1887   Applicant for Cherokee Citizenship
Post Office: Blackfoot Grove, Tex. **Attorney:** Boudinot and Rasmus

N°	NAMES	AGE	SEX
1	Samuel C. Ward	40	Male

Ancestor: Bergess Ward

Rejected

Cherokee Citizenship Commission Docket Books
(1880-84, 1887-89) Volume II
Tahlequah, Cherokee Nation

Tahlequah May 21st 1889

Now comes this application for final hearing. It was filed the 22nd day of Aug 1887 and this day submitted after argument by Attorneys. The evidence in support of the application is exclusively in the form of <u>Exparte</u> affidavits of aged persons residing in Blount and Roane Counties in the State of Tennessee, now, the country around and occupied by the Cherokee prior to the Treaty of 1835, between the United States and the Cherokee Nation. David and Rhoda Ward the parents of Bergess Ward the father of applicant is claimed to have derived his Cherokee blood from Rhoda Ward whose maiden name is not given. Bergess Ward is shown to have been the Father of applicant & also of Nathan Ward, John Ward, Richard Ward, George W. Ward and Bergess C. Ward. The evidence does not show that Rhoda Ward and her husband Daniel Ward, or Bergess Ward lived within the limits of the Cherokee Country nor that they were covered by any of the operations of the Treaty of 1835 nor yet are their names found on the rolls of Cherokees by blood refered[sic] to in the 1st section of the Act of Dec. 8th 1886 or the amendments thereto which govern the Commission in *(illegible)* their decision in application for Citizenship. The Commission therefore decide that Samuel C. Ward & his children *(Illegible)* C. Ward aged 8 yrs, *(Illegible)* K. Ward 6 yrs, Samuel F. Ward 9 months and *(Illegible)* V. Ward 4 yrs are not Cherokees by blood.

	Will P. Ross	Chairman
George O. *(Illegible)*	R. Bunch	Com
Clerk Commission	John E. Gunter	Com

CODY

Docket #357
Rolls 1835 to 52
filed August 18th 1887   Applicant for Cherokee Citizenship
    Post Office: Chocoville Ark   **Attorney:** Boudinot & Rasmus

N°	NAMES	AGE	SEX
1	Sarah A. Cody	24	Female
2	Cloris C. Cody	3	Male
3	Elmer B. Cody	10 mo	"

Ancestor: Andrew Miller

Cherokee Citizenship Commission Docket Books
(1880-84, 1887-89) Volume II
Tahlequah, Cherokee Nation

Office Commission on Citizenship
Tahlequah C.N. May 14 1889

Now on this day comes the above named applicant for the final hearing the same having been submitted the application which was filed the 18th day of August 1887. The applicant Sarah A. Cody claims as her ancester[sic] one Andrew Miller whose name alleged to be found on the census rolls of 1835 & 1852. The Commission after a careful examination of the above mentioned rolls fail to find the name of Andrew Miller and there being no evidence introduced to sustain the fact that Sarah A. Cody is or was any ways related to Andrew Miller if his name had appeared upon any one of above mentioned census rolls made in the year 1835 or 1852, therefore the Commission decide that Sarah A. Cody age 24 years and her children Cloris C. Cody, male age 3 years, Elmer B. Cody, male age 10 months, are not Cherokees by blood and are not entitled to Citizenship in the Cherokee Nation. Post Office address Chocoville Ark.

Attest		Will P. Ross	Chairman
	E.G. Ross	R. Bunch	Com
	Clerk Com	J.E. Gunter	Com

CHASTIAN

Docket #358
Rolls 1835 to 1852
filed August 20th 1887 Applicant for Cherokee Citizenship
Post Office: Mulberry Ark. **Attorney:** A.E. Ivey

N°	NAMES	AGE	SEX
1	William M. Chastine	52	Male
2	William A.J. Chastine	23	"
3	Joseph E. Chastine	15	"
4	Lucinda E. Chastine	13	Female
5	John E.B. Chastine	3	Male

Ancestor: John Rogers

Now on this the 17th day of March, 1888, comes the above case for a final hearing, and the parties having made application pursuant to the provisions of an Act of the National Council approved December 8th 1886, and all the evidence being duly considered, and found to be insufficient and unsatisfactory, it is adjudged and declared by the Commission that William M. Chastian, William

Cherokee Citizenship Commission Docket Books
(1880-84, 1887-89) Volume II
Tahlequah, Cherokee Nation

A.J. Chastian, Joseph E. Chastian, Lucinda E. Chastian and John E.B. Chastian, are not Cherokees, and they are not entitled to the rights, privileges and immunities of Cherokee Citizens by blood.

                                        J.T. Adair   Chairman Commission
                                        John E. Gunter Commissioner
                                        D.W. Lipe   Commissioner

Attest
    C.C. Lipe
    Clerk Com.

The decision in the James C.C. Rogers case, found on Book C, page 637 and testimony on Journal page 325 to 333 – Governs this case.

HENRY

Docket #359
Rolls 1835
filed August 23rd 1887   Applicant for Cherokee Citizenship
    Post Office: Sheep Ranch Cal   **Attorney:** W A Thompson

N°	NAMES	AGE	SEX
1	Amelia D. Henry	27	Female
2	Archie B. Henry		Male
3	Eva M. Henry		Female
4	Ada A. Henry		"
5	Elsie A. Henry		"
6	Mary B. Henry		"

                  Ancestor: Clem V. McNair

Now on this the 23 day of August 1887 comes the above case for final hearing and having made application pursuant to the provision of an Act of the National Council approved December 8th 1866[sic] and all the evidence having been duly considered and found to be sufficient and satisfactory to the Commission, and upon examination the Ancestor Clement V. McNair's name appears on the Rolls of 1835 – it is adjudged and determined by the Commission that Amelia D. Henry, Archie B. Henry, Eva M. Henry, Ada A. Henry, Elsie A. Henry, and Mary B. Henry, are Cherokees by blood and are hereby readmitted to all the rights and privileges and immunities of a Cherokee Citizen by blood.

Cherokee Citizenship Commission Docket Books
(1880-84, 1887-89) Volume II
Tahlequah, Cherokee Nation

And a certificate of said decision of the Commission and of readmission was made and furnished to said parties accordingly.

Henry Eiffert	J.T. Adair	Chairman Com
Clk Commission	D.W. Lipe	Commissioner

TUCKER

Docket #360
Rolls 1851 & 52
filed August 22nd 1887   Applicant for Cherokee Citizenship
Post Office: Fleat P.O. I.T.   **Attorney:**

N°	NAMES	AGE	SEX
1	J.W.E. Tucker	25	Male
2	Mary M. Tucker	4	Female
3	Lennie Tucker	2	"

Ancestor: James Tucker

Now on this the 22nd day of August 1887 comes the above case for final hearing and having made application pursuant to the provisions of an Act of the National Council approved December 8th 1886 and all the evidence having been duly considered and found to be sufficient and satisfactory to the Commission, and upon an examination the name of Ancestor James Tucker appears upon the Rolls 1851 & 2, it is adjudged and determined by the Commission that J.W.E. Tucker, Mary M. Tucker and Lennie Tucker are Cherokees by blood and are hereby re-admitted to all the rights and privileges and immunities of Cherokee Citizens by blood.

And a certificate of said decision of the Commission and of re-admission was made and furnished to said parties accordingly.

Henry Eiffert	J.T. Adair	Chairman Commission
Clk Com	D.W. Lipe	Commissioner
		Commissioner

Cherokee Citizenship Commission Docket Books
(1880-84, 1887-89) Volume II
Tahlequah, Cherokee Nation

CRUTCHFIELD

Docket #361
Rolls 1835
filed August 22nd 1887   Applicant for Cherokee Citizenship
   Post Office: Jacksboro Tex   **Attorney:**

N°	NAMES	AGE	SEX
1	Leroy L. Crutchfield	43	Male
2	Annie Crutchfield	18	Female
3	Josephine Crutchfield	12	"
4	John H. Crutchfield	3	Male

Ancestor: James Crutchfield

Now on this 27th day of January 1888, comes the above case for a final hearing and the parties having made application pursuant to the provisions of an Act of the National Council approved December 8th 1886. and all the evidence having been duly examined and found to be sufficient and satisfactory to the Commission, and the name of the ancestor appearing on the Rolls, it is adjudged and determined by the Commission, that Leroy L. Crutchfield, Annie Crutchfield, Josephine Crutchfield and John H. Crutchfield are Cherokees by blood, and are hereby readmitted to all the rights, privileges of Cherokees by blood.

And a certificate of said decision of the Commission and of readmission was made and furnished said parties accordingly.

                        J.T. Adair   Chairman Commission
                        John E. Gunter   Commissioner
                                        Commissioner

Attest
    C.C. Lipe
    Clk Commission

Cherokee Citizenship Commission Docket Books
(1880-84, 1887-89) Volume II
Tahlequah, Cherokee Nation

WING

Docket #362
Rolls 1835
filed August 23 1887   Applicant for Cherokee Citizenship
<u>Post Office</u>: Childers Station I.T.   <u>Attorney</u>: H.B. Stone

N°	NAMES	AGE	SEX
1	Malissa Wing	47	Female
2	John H. Furguson	28	Male
3	Ophelia Furguson	25	Female
4	Oceola Furguson	20	Male
5	Joseph Furguson	16	"
6	Pearl Furguson	12	Female

<u>Ancestor</u>: Rebeccah Schell

Tahlequah
May ?[th] 1888

The application of Mallissa Wing was presented to the Commission the 23rd day of August 1887. It is supported by no evidence. The Commission therefore decide that Mallissa Wing is not of Cherokee blood and is not entitled to Citizenship in the Cherokee Nation. In the application are presented the names of John H. Ferguson, aged 28 years, Ophelia Ferguson aged 25 years, Oceola Ferguson aged 20 years, Joseph Ferguson aged 16 years, and Pearl Ferguson (daughter) aged twelve years, who appear from the face of the application to be the children of the applicant but whether named Wing or Ferguson, is not shown but the Commission include them in the decision as not Cherokees.

Attest   Will P. Ross
   E.G. Ross   Chairman
   Clerk Commission   John E. Gunter   Com.

Cherokee Citizenship Commission Docket Books
(1880-84, 1887-89) Volume II
Tahlequah, Cherokee Nation

SOMMERS

Docket #363
Rolls 1835
filed August 20th 1887   Applicant for Cherokee Citizenship
    Post Office: We wo ka I.T.   **Attorney:**

N°	NAMES	AGE	SEX
1	Martha Sommers	25	Female
2	Louisa Berryhill	5	"
3	*(Blank on original)*		

Ancestor: Wat Sanders

Office Commission on Citizenship
Oct. 4th 1889

The Commission decide adversely to Claimant, Martha Sommers 25 yrs of age and her daughter Louisa Berryhill aged 5 yrs for reasons given in this decision in the case of George Bremer. See docket 350, Book B, Page 60. Post Office of Claimant, We woka, Ind. Ty.

Attest   Will P. Ross
    E.G. Ross   Chairman
        Clerk Commission   R. Bunch   Com.
                              J.E. Gunter Com

HULSEY

Docket #364
Rolls 1835
filed August 24 1887   Applicant for Cherokee Citizenship
    Post Office: We wo ka I.T.   **Attorney:**

N°	NAMES	AGE	SEX
1	Eliza Hulsey	29	Female
2	Emma Hulsey	14	"
3	Catherine Hulsey	12	"
4	Louisa Hulsey	9	"
5	Ida Hulsey	7	"
6	Ross Hulsey	6	Male
7	Geo W. Hulsey	4	"

Cherokee Citizenship Commission Docket Books
(1880-84, 1887-89) Volume II
Tahlequah, Cherokee Nation

8	McAfee Hulsey	3	"

Ancestor: Wat Sanders

Office Commission on Citizenship
Cherokee Nation Ind. Ter.
Tahlequah Oct. 4th 1889

The Commission decide adversely to claimant Eliza Hulsey 29 years of age and her daughters Emma age 14 years, Katharine age 12 years, Louisa 9 years, Ada 7 years, and sons Ross 6 years, George W. 4 years, and McAfee Hulsey 3 years for reasons set forth in their decision in the case of George Bremer. See Docket 350, Book B, Page 63. P.O. We wo ka Indian Territory.

Attest
E.G. Ross
Clerk Commission

Will P. Ross
Chairman Com
R. Bunch   "
J.E. Gunter   "

LARKIN

Docket #365
Rolls 1835
filed August 24th 1887`   Applicant for Cherokee Citizenship
Post Office: Mayesville Ark   **Attorney:** C.H. Taylor

N°	NAMES	AGE	SEX
1	Columbia Larkin	29	Female
2	Nora Larkin	14	"
3	Olla Larkin	8	"
4	Henry A. Larkin	2	Male

Ancestor: *(Illegible)* Parks

Commission on Citizenship Cherokee Nation I.T.
Tahlequah May 20th 1998

The application in the above case was filed on the 20th day of Aug and was submitted May 23rd 1889 for a final hearing without any evidence. The Commission therefore decide that Columbus[sic] Larkin and his children whose names are as follows; Nora, Female age 14 yrs, Olla, Female age 8, Henry A.

Cherokee Citizenship Commission Docket Books
(1880-84, 1887-89) Volume II
Tahlequah, Cherokee Nation

Larkin male age 2 yrs, are not of Cherokee blood and are not entitled to Citizenship in the Cherokee Nation. Post office address Maysville Ark.

George O. *(Illegible)*
Clerk Commission

Will P. Ross
Chairman
R. Bunch   Com
J E Gunter   Com

STEWART

Docket #366
Rolls 1835
filed Aug 24th 1887   Applicant for Cherokee Citizenship
Post Office: Sanders Station I.T.   **Attorney:** C.H. Taylor

N°	NAMES	AGE	SEX
1	Dr. Thomas Steward[sic]	45	Male
2	Florence Stewart	7	Female
3	John Stewart	6	Male
4	Earnest Stewart	3	"

Ancestor: Mariah Stewart

Rejected May 9th 1889

Office Commission on Citizenship
Cherokee Nation Ind. Ter.
Tahlequah May 9th 1889

The application in this case was filed the 24th day of August 1887.

It is sustained by no evidence and having been called here several times at intervals of not less than one hour apart, the Commission therefore decide that said Dr. Thomas Stewart aged 45 years and his children, Florence Stewart female age 7 years, John Stewart male age 6 years, Ernest Stewart male age 3 years old, are not Cherokees by blood and not entitled to Citizenship in the Cherokee Nation. Post office address: Sanders Station I.T.

Attest
    D.S. Williams
    Clk Com

Will P. Ross
Chairman
John E. Gunter   Com

Cherokee Citizenship Commission Docket Books
(1880-84, 1887-89) Volume II
Tahlequah, Cherokee Nation

STEWART

Docket #367
Rolls 1835
filed August 24 1887

Applicant for Cherokee Citizenship

Post Office: Sanders I.T.   Attorney: C.H. Taylor

N°	NAMES	AGE	SEX
1	William Stewart	56	Male
2	Windfield Stewart	23	"
3	Leandrew Stewart	19	"
4	Agnes Stewart	15	Female
5	Dennis Stewart	13	Male
6	Earnest Stewart	9	"
7	Claud Stewart	7	Female
8	Della M. Stewart	4	Female
9	Ralf Stewart	1	Male

Ancestor: Mariah Stewart

Rejected May 9th 1889

Office Commission on Citizenship
Cherokee Nation Ind. Ter.
Tahlequah May 9th 1889.

The application in this case was filed this 16th day of August 1887. It is supported by no evidence and the parties having been called three several times at intervals of not less than one hour apart without answer. The Commission decides that William E. Stewart aged fifty years and his family, Windfield Stewart aged twenty three years, Leander F. Stewart aged nineteen years, Agnes Stewart aged fifteen years, Dennis Steward aged thirteen years, Ernest Stewart ages nine years, Claud Stewart aged seven years, Della M. Stewart (female) aged four years and Ralph Stewart aged one year, are not of Cherokee blood and not entitled to Citizenship in the Cherokee Nation.

Attest
    D.S. Williams
    Clk Com

Will P. Ross
    Chairman
John E. Gunter   Com

Cherokee Citizenship Commission Docket Books
(1880-84, 1887-89) Volume II
Tahlequah, Cherokee Nation

STEWART

Docket #368
Rolls 1835
Filed August 25th 1887   Applicant for Cherokee Citizenship
   Post Office: Lancaster Ark   **Attorney:** A.E. Ivey

N°	NAMES	AGE	SEX
1	T.C. Stewart	39	Male
2	Daisy Bell Stewart	5	Female
3	Delilah May Stewart	3	"

Ancestor: Mima Edwards

Now on this the 9th day of January 1888, comes the above case for a final hearing, and the parties having made application pursuant to the provisions of an Act of the National Council, approved December 8th 1886, and all the evidence being duly examined and found <u>not</u> to be sufficient and satisfactory to the Commission and the name of the Ancestor not appearing on the Rolls as claimed in the application.

It is adjudged and determined by the Commission, that T.C. Stewart, Daisy Bell Stewart and Delilah May Stewart are <u>not</u> Cherokees by blood, and are hereby rejected and declared intruders.

J.T. Adair   Chairman Commission
John E. Gunter   Commissioner
                 Commissioner

Attest
   C.C. Lipe
      Clerk Commission

BISWELL

Docket #369
Rolls 1835
filed August 25th 1887   Applicant for Cherokee Citizenship
   Post Office: Union Town Ark   **Attorney:** AE Ivey

N°	NAMES	AGE	SEX
1	Elizabeth A. Biswell	50	Female
2	Artimiss Biswell	21	"
3	Martha D. Biswell	16	"

Cherokee Citizenship Commission Docket Books
(1880-84, 1887-89) Volume II
Tahlequah, Cherokee Nation

4	Dillie M. Biswell	14	"
5	Emily T.B. Biswell	8	"

Ancestor: Elizabeth Ross

Office Commission on Citizenship
Cherokee Nation, Ind. Ter.
Tahlequah, August 16th 1889

The applicant in the above case alleges that she is the daughter of one N.J. Azbill and great grand daughter of Elizabeth Ross whose name she believes was duly enrolled in the census rolls of Cherokees by blood. Citizens of the Cherokee Nation taken and made in the years 1835 & 52. The evidence shows that the declarant is the daughter of Neomas Azbill the son of John Azbill, the son of Cherokee "Indian Bill Azbill" who went from North Carolina or Virginia and settled in Estill County, Kentucky in the year 1804 and so far west as it tends to show the Cherokee Indian descent of applicant is of a hearsay character. The claimant and her father and Grand Father have resided for many years (30 or 40) in Crawford County, State of Arkansas, on the immediate boundary line between that state and the Cherokee Nation and so far as shown has made no effort to obtain the admission to Cherokee rights of Citizenship if entitled to them. Besides these facts, neither the name of Elizabeth Ross nor Azbill is found on the census rolls referred to. The Commission therefore decide that Elizabeth A. Biswell age 50 years and her daughters Artimiss 21 years, Martha D. 16 years, Dillie M. 14 years and Emily T. Biswell 8 years are not of Cherokee blood and not entitled to the rights and privileges of Citizenship in the Cherokee Nation as Cherokee Indians. Post Office Uniontown, Crawford County, Arkansas.

	Will P. Ross	Chairman
Attest		
E.G. Ross	R. Bunch	Com
Clerk Commission	J.E. Gunter	"

Cherokee Citizenship Commission Docket Books
(1880-84, 1887-89) Volume II
Tahlequah, Cherokee Nation

GERMANY

Docket #370
Rolls 1835
filed August 25th 1887   Applicant for Cherokee Citizenship
Post Office: Whitesboro Texas   **Attorney:** AE Ivey

N°	NAMES	AGE	SEX
1	Mary C. Germany	40	Female
2	Wm E. Germany	14	Male
3	Florida Germany	4	Female

Ancestor: Mrs. Dawson

Office Commission on Citizenship
Tahlequah May 15th 1889

Now on this day comes the applicant for a final hearing to Citizenship in the Cherokee Nation, the case having been called three several times not less than one hour apart and no response from applicant of by Attorney and there being no evidence in support of application, the Commission are of the opinion that Mary C. Germany with her children Wm E. Germany male 14 years of age and Florida Germany Female, 4 years of age are not Cherokees by blood and are not entitled to any of the rights as citizens of the Cherokee Nation. Post Office address Whitesboro, Texas.

	Will P. Ross	Chairman
Attest	R. Bunch	Com
E.G. Ross	J.E. Gunter	Com
Clerk Commission		

MILLER

Docket #371
Rolls 1835
filed August 25 1887   Applicant for Cherokee Citizenship
Post Office: Wah-hil-law IT   **Attorney:** J.L. McCoy

N°	NAMES	AGE	SEX
1	Clelan J. Miller	34	
2	Ada M. Miller	8	
3	Pearlie J. Miller	6	
4	Esbella J. Miller } twins	4	
5	Ola D. Miller	4	

Cherokee Citizenship Commission Docket Books
(1880-84, 1887-89) Volume II
Tahlequah, Cherokee Nation

6	Walter D. Miller	1	

Rejected May 9th 1889

Ancestor: Elizabeth Merril

Office Commission on Citizenship
Cherokee Nation Ind. Ter'y.
Tahlequah May 9th 1889

The application in the above named case was filed the 20th day of August 1887. It is supported by no evidence and having been called three several times at an interval of at least one hour without answers, the Commission decide that Celand J. Miller and children, to wit; Addie M. Miller aged eight years, Pearlie J. Miller aged six years, Ethel (2) Miller aged five years and twin sister, Ola D. Miller and Walter D. Miller aged one year are not of Cherokee blood and not entitled to Citizenship in the Cherokee Nation. Post Office Wau-hillaw Ind. Ter'y.

         Will P. Ross
Attest   Chairman
D.S. Williams   John E. Gunter Com
 Clk Com

CROW

Docket #372
Rolls
filed Aug 25th 1887   Applicant for Cherokee Citizenship
 Post Office: St. Joe Texas   **Attorney:** AE Ivey

N°	NAMES	AGE	SEX
1	William M. Crow	32	Male

      Ancestor: Mrs. Dunston
"Copy"
      Commission on Citizenship Cherokee Nation Ind Ter'y
         Tahlequah May 15th 1889
Before the Commission on Citizenship
       Hon Jno E. Gunter Chairman
       " R. Bunch   Commissioner

Cases of
William M. Crow   Applicants for Cherokee Citizenship
James P. Rich

Cherokee Citizenship Commission Docket Books
(1880-84, 1887-89) Volume II
Tahlequah, Cherokee Nation

Sophie Sewell
John R. Rich
Phillip Sweeton
v.s.
Cherokee Nation

Now comes George O. Butler, Act. Atty for Cherokee Nation, and moves that judgment be entered against the above entitled cases together with their children for the following reasons. 1st.. the cases were filed in 1887 by the applicants as appears from their papers, respectfully, therefore they knew that their personal attention was necessary.
2nd.. The applicants have failed to produce any evidence in support of this claimant.
3rd.. They have had ample notice. The Commission has given thirty days notice of the time fixed for its setting in all of the news papers in the country and the further notice of nearly one month of this time when the call of this docket would begin also given in the news papers of this country not withstanding this due notice given they have failed to answer either in person or by Attorney, at the call of this *(illegible)* cases and thereby disregarding the Commission on Citizenship.

                            Respectfully submitted

Attest   George O. Butler Act Atty for C.N.
       D.S. Williams Asst Clk Com.

This motion sustained by the Commission on Citizenship <u>Adversely</u> to claimants. John E. Gunter Chairman & R. Bunch Commission
                D.S. Williams Asst. Clk Com

BURK

Docket #373
Rolls 1835
filed August 25   Applicant for Cherokee Citizenship
    Post Office: McAlester I.T.   **Attorney:** A.E. Ivey & Harris

N°	NAMES	AGE	SEX
1	Mary S. Burk	41	Female

              Ancestor: Wm Robnson[sic]

Cherokee Citizenship Commission Docket Books
(1880-84, 1887-89) Volume II
Tahlequah, Cherokee Nation

CROW

Docket #374
Rolls 1835
filed August 25 1887   Applicant for Cherokee Citizenship
Post Office: *(Illegible)* Town   **Attorney:** A.E. Ivey

N°	NAMES	AGE	SEX
1	L.H. Crow	26	Male
2	M E F Crow	3	"
3	Allie M. Crow	1	Female

Ancestor: Mrs Dunston

Now on this the 27 day of August, 1887, comes the above case for a final hearing. And submitted by agreement between the Attorney for plaintiff and the Atty on part of the Nation, on the evidence taken and submitted in the case of L.H. Crow, M.E.F. Crow, Allie M. Crow. We the Commission on Citizenship after a careful and impartial investigation of the testimony & having also examined the Census Rolls of 1835, & failed to find the name of the Ancestor Mrs. Dunston. And the evidence in behalf of applicant not being sufficient, The Commission therefore declare that the above names parties are not Cherokees by blood and not entitled to any of the rights or privileges of Cherokee Citizens.

J.T. Adair   Chairman Com
D.W. Lipe   Commissioner

Attest
    C.C. Lipe
    Clerk Com.

CROW

Docket #375
Rolls
filed August 25 1887   Applicant for Cherokee Citizenship
Post Office: Henderson Texas   **Attorney:** AE Ivey

N°	NAMES	AGE	SEX
1	John M. Crow	38	Male
2	Levi M. Crow	17	"
3	Alla A. Crow	15	Female
4	Margarett Crow	13	"
5	Florence Crow	11	"

Cherokee Citizenship Commission Docket Books
(1880-84, 1887-89) Volume II
Tahlequah, Cherokee Nation

6	Flora Crow	9	"
7	Annie Crow	8	"
8	Robt W. Crow	5	Male
9	Hellen Crow	2	Female

Ancestor: Mrs. Dunson

Office Commission on Citizenship
Tahlequah May 15th 1889

Now on this day the case of John M. Crow was taken up for final hearing. The applicant claims as his ancestor a Mrs. Dunson nee Vann, but fails to name either of the census rolls in order for the Commission to examine the census rolls to see whether or not his alledged[sic] ancestor's name appear upon the rolls. The applicant produces several affidavits in support of his claim, but all fails to sustain his claim in any particular. As the law governing this Commission expressly says "that all applicants for Cherokee Citizenship must be a person or the lawful descendant of a person whose name appears on the census rolls of the Cherokees taken by the United States after the Treaty of 1835 and known as the rolls of 1835 and the roll of 1848 known as the Mullay rolls and the Census roll of the Cherokees taken by the United States in 1851 and known as the Silar Rolls and the census rolls of the Cherokees taken by the United States in 1852 known as the Chapman rolls. After examining the applicants evidence we find that it does not support his claim of Cherokee blood and as he does not state what census rolls of either 1835, 48, 51-52 to find the name of his ancestor that by not complying with section seventh of the Act creating this Commission in view of these facts we are of the opinion that the applicant John M. Crow, 38 together with his children Levi M. Crow age 13[sic] years, Alla A. Crow, age 15 years, Margaret Crow age 13[sic] years, Florence Crow age 11 years, Flora Crow age 9 years, Annie Crow age 8 years, Robt. W. Crow age 5 years, Hellen Crow age 2 years, are not Cherokees by blood and not entitled to any rights and privileges of Cherokee Citizenship and we declare them intruders within the limits of the Cherokee Nation.

Attest	Will P. Ross -	Chairman
E.G. Ross	R. Bunch	Com
Clerk Commission	J.E. Gunter	Com

Cherokee Citizenship Commission Docket Books
(1880-84, 1887-89) Volume II
Tahlequah, Cherokee Nation

JONES

Docket #376
Rolls 1835
filed August 25th 1887   Applicant for Cherokee Citizenship

Post Office: Henderson Texas   **Attorney:** AE Ivey

N°	NAMES	AGE	SEX
1	Margaret L. Jones	27	
2	Mary O. Jones	10	
3	Jane L. Jones	6	
4	Emma E. Jones	4	
5	Wm J. Jones	2	
6	Homer C Jones	5 mo	

Ancestor: Mrs. Dunson

Rejected May 15th 1889

Office Commission Citizenship Cherokee Nation Ind. Ter'y.
Tahlequah May 15th 1889

Now comes the above applicant whose application was filed 24th day of August 1887 for a final hearing this applicant claims her Cherokee blood through one Mrs Dunson nee Vann. Now the case having been called three several times not less than one at[sic] intervals and the applicant fail to respond either in person or by Atty. The Commission after examining the papers fail to find any evidence in surport[sic] of said facts therefore the Commission are of the opinion that Margaret L. Jones and her family Mary O, Jane L, Emma E. William J. and Homer C. Jones are not Cherokees by blood and are not entitled to Citizenship in the Cherokee Nation.

	Will P. Ross	Chairman
Attest	R. Bunch	Com.
D.S. Williams	J.E. Gunter	Com.
Asst Clk Com		

Cherokee Citizenship Commission Docket Books
(1880-84, 1887-89) Volume II
Tahlequah, Cherokee Nation

GRAVITT

Docket #377
Rolls 1851 & 52
filed August 26 1887   Applicant for Cherokee Citizenship
Post Office: Talking Rock Ga   **Attorney:** AE Ivey

N°	NAMES	AGE	SEX
1	James M. Gravitt	48	Male
2	~~Frances M. Gravitt~~	~~57~~	~~Female~~
3	~~Columbus F. Gravitt~~	~~30~~	~~Male~~
4	Artemissa Gravitt	24	Female
5	Jefferson M Gravitt	22	Male
6	~~Minta A. Gravitt~~	~~20~~	~~Female~~

Ancestor: Alfred Gravitt

Now on this the 18th day of June 1888, comes the above case up for final hearing. We the Commission on Citizenship after a careful and impartial examination of the testimony and the census & pay rolls of 1851 and 1852, (also the Hester rolls of 1883 in the way of identifying children) find that James M. Gravitt, aged (1 year added) 49 years, Artemissa, female, aged 25 years and Jefferson M. Gravitt aged 23 years, are Cherokees by blood, and they are hereby re-admitted to all the rights and privileges of Cherokee citizens by blood. (See Sec. 7th of an Act, approved Dec. 8th 1886.)

          J.T. Adair   Chairman Commission
          John E. Gunter   Commissioner
          D.W. Lipe   Commissioner

GRAVITT

Docket #378
Rolls 1851 & 52
filed August 26th 1887   Applicant for Cherokee Citizenship
Post Office: Talking Rock Ga   **Attorney:** AE Ivey

N°	NAMES	AGE	SEX
1	Columbus F. Gravitt	30	Male
2	Ella Gravitt	28	Female
3	Luther O. Gravitt	4	Male
4	Ora B Gravitt	3	Female
5	Pearl Gravitt	2	"

Cherokee Citizenship Commission Docket Books
(1880-84, 1887-89) Volume II
Tahlequah, Cherokee Nation

6	Infant	3 mo	"

Ancestor: James M. Gravitt

Office Commission on Citizenship
Cherokee Nation Ind. Ter.
Tahlequah May 18th 1889

The applicant in the above named case having proved to the satisfaction of the Commission that he is the son of James M. Gravitt who was the son of Sally Parris a person of Cherokee descent and was admitted to citizenship in the Cherokee Nation by the Adair Commission on the 18th day of June 1888 and whose name is found on the Census roll of Cherokees taken in the year 1852 is hereby declared to be of Cherokee blood and is re-admitted to the rights of Citizenship in the Cherokee Nation together with his children to wit. Luther O Gravitt a son aged four years and Ora B Gravitt aged three years, Pearl Gravitt two years and an infant aged three months, daughters. Post Office, Talking Rock Georgia under the Act of December 5th 1889.

Attest	Will P. Ross	Chairman
E.G. Ross	R. Bunch	Com
Clerk Commission	J.E. Gunter	Com.

BULLOCK

Docket #379
Rolls 1835 & 1852
filed August 26th 1887   Applicant for Cherokee Citizenship
Post Office: Fort Gibson CN   **Attorney:**

N°	NAMES	AGE	SEX
1	Dennis Bullock	38	
2	Cynthia E Bullock	19	Female
3	Joseph W. Bullock	17	Male
4	William H Bullock	16	"
5	Henry Bullock	6	"
6	Alvo C Bullock	4	"
7	Walter Bullock	2	"

Ancestor: Ellis Hooker

Rejected May 9th 1889

Cherokee Citizenship Commission Docket Books
(1880-84, 1887-89) Volume II
Tahlequah, Cherokee Nation

Office Commission on Citizenship
Cherokee Nation Ind. Ter.
Tahlequah May 9th 1889.

The application in this case was filed the 23rd day of August 1887. It is accompanied by no evidence to sustain the allegations set forth. The Commission therefore decide that the applicant Dennis Bullock and his children Cynthia E Bullock age nineteen years, Joseph W Bullock aged seventeen years, William H Bullock aged sixteen years (16), Henry Bullock aged six years, Alvo C. Bullock aged four years and Walter Bullock aged two years, are not Cherokees by blood and not entitled to re-admission to Citizenship in the Cherokee Nation. Post Office Fort Gibson Ind. Ter.

Attest	Will P. Ross
D.S. Williams	Chairman
Clk Com	John E. Gunter Com.

SMITH

Docket #380
Rolls
filed August 26th 1887

Applicant for Cherokee Citizenship

Post Office: Attorney:

N°	NAMES	AGE	SEX
1	Louisa Smith		
2	Nancy J Smith		
3	Elizabeth Smith		
4	John B Smith		

Ancestor:

Rejected May 9th 1889

Office Commission on Citizenship
Cherokee Nation Ind. Ter'y.
Tahlequah May 9th 1889.

The application in this case was filed the 26th August 1887. It is supported by no evidence. The Commission therefore decide that the applicant Louisa Smith and her children, Nancy J Smith aged (29) twenty nine years, Elizabeth Smith twenty three years and John B Smith aged twenty one years are not of Cherokee

Cherokee Citizenship Commission Docket Books
(1880-84, 1887-89) Volume II
Tahlequah, Cherokee Nation

blood and not entitled to readmission to Citizenship in the Cherokee Nation.
Post Office Fort Gibson Ind. Ter'y.

Attest
   D.S. Williams
   Clk Com.

Will P. Ross
   Chairman
John E. Gunter   Com.

FOREMAN

Docket #381
Rolls
filed August 26th 1887   Applicant for Cherokee Citizenship
    Post Office: *(Illegible)*   **Attorney:** A. E. Ivey

N°	NAMES	AGE	SEX
1	Stephen Foreman	36	Male
2	Joe Foreman	20	"
3	Susie Foreman	16	female
4	Thomas Foreman	14	Male

Ancestor: *(Illegible)* Foreman

    Now on the 26th day of August 1887 comes the above case for final hearing, ant the above parties having made application pursuant to the provisions of an Act of the National Council approved December 8th 1886 and all the evidence having been duly examined and found to be sufficient and satisfactory to the Commission, it is adjudged and determined by the Commission that Stephen Foreman, Joe Foreman, Susie Foreman and Thomas Foreman are Cherokees by blood and are hereby readmitted to all the rights privileges and immunities of Cherokees by blood.

    And a certificate of said decision of the Commission and re-admission was made and furnished to said parties accordingly.

Henry Eiffert   J.T. Adair   Chairman Commission
Clk Comm.   John E. Gunter   Commissioner
                                                                           Commissioner

Cherokee Citizenship Commission Docket Books
(1880-84, 1887-89) Volume II
Tahlequah, Cherokee Nation

BRUNER

Docket #382
Rolls 1835 to 1852
filed August 26 1887   Applicant for Cherokee Citizenship
Post Office: **Attorney:**

N°	NAMES	AGE	SEX
1	Polly Bruner	34	female
2	Nancy Bruner	15	"
3	David Bruner	11	male
4	Katy Bruner	10	female
5	Thomas Bruner	6	male
6	Edward Bruner	5	"
7	Walter Bruner	3 mo	"

Ancestor: Walt Sanders

Rejected

Office Commission on Citizenship

The applicant in the above case having failed to establish her Cherokee blood the Commission decide that Polly Bruner 34 yrs of age and her daughters Nancy Bruner 15 yrs, Katy Bruner 10 yrs, and sons David Bruner 11 yrs, Thomas Bruner 6 yrs, Edward Bruner 2 yrs & Walter Bruner 3 months are not entitled to Citizenship in the Cherokee Nation. See decision of Commission in case of George Bremer, Docket 350 Book B, Page 63. PO Springfield Ind. Ter.

Attest	Will P. Ross	Chairman
	R. Bunch	Com
D.S. Williams	J.E. Gunter	Com
Asst. Clk Com.		

SEWELL

Docket #383
Rolls 1835 to 1852
filed August 27th 1887   Applicant for Cherokee Citizenship
Post Office: *(Illegible)* I.T.   **Attorney:**

N°	NAMES	AGE	SEX
1	Sophia Sewell	27	female
2	Benjamin Sewell	7	male

Cherokee Citizenship Commission Docket Books
(1880-84, 1887-89) Volume II
Tahlequah, Cherokee Nation

3	George Sewell	4	"

Ancestor: Walt Sanders

Adversely

See decision in this case in this Book Page 8.

D.S. Williams
Asst. Clk. Com.

HIBBS

Docket #384
Rolls 1835 to 1852
filed August 27th 1887   Applicant for Cherokee Citizenship
Post Office: Rudy, Ark.   **Attorney:** A.E. Ivey

N°	NAMES	AGE	SEX
1	Nancy Malissa Jane Hibbs	27	
2	John Alexander Hibbs	5	
3	Mary Elizabeth Hibbs	2	
4	David Andrew Hibbs	6 mo	

Ancestor: Thomas Tikonees Key

Now on this the 2nd day of October 1888 comes the above case for a final hearing and the parties having made application pursuant to the provisions of an Act of the National Council approved December 8th 1886 and all the evidence having been duly examined and found to be sufficient and satisfactory, it is adjudged and determined by the Commission that Nancy Malissa Jane Hibbs and her three children, John Alexander Hibbs, Mary Elizabeth Hibbs and David Andrew Hibbs are Cherokees by blood and are hereby readmitted to all the rights, privileges and immunities of other Cherokees by blood.

And a certificate of said decision of the Commission, and of readmission was made and furnished said parties accordingly.

Attest	J.T. Adair,	Chairman Commission
C.C. Lipe	H.C. Barnes	Commissioner
Clerk Commission		

Cherokee Citizenship Commission Docket Books
(1880-84, 1887-89) Volume II
Tahlequah, Cherokee Nation

WILLIS

Docket #385
Rolls 1851 and 1852
filed August 27th 1887   Applicant for Cherokee Citizenship
   Post Office: Dawsonville Ga   **Attorney:** A.E. Ivey

N°	NAMES	AGE	SEX
1	Priestly E. Willis	62	

Ancestor: Mary Barnhill

Now on this the 13th day of September 1887 comes the above case for final hearing and having made application pursuant to the provisions of an Act of the National Council approved December 8th 1886, and all the evidence being duly considered and found to be sufficient and satisfactory to the Commission, it is adjudged and determined by the Commission that Priestly E. Willis is a Cherokee by blood and is hereby readmited[sic] to all the rights, privileges and immunities of a Cherokee by blood, and a certificate of said decision of the Commission and readmission was made and furnished to said parties accordingly.

C.C. Lipe   J.T. Adair   Chairman Commission
Clerk Commission   John E. Gunter   Commissioner
                                                                  Commissioner

PETERS

Docket #386
Rolls 1835
filed August 27th 1887   Applicant for Cherokee Citizenship
   Post Office: Calisburg, Tex   **Attorney:** A.E. Ivey

N°	NAMES	AGE	SEX
1	Sarah W. Peters	35	female
2	John W. Peters	17	male
3	Eudora Peters	16	female
4	Dora S. Peters	14	"
5	Jennie E. Peters	12	"
6	Mattie L. Peters	10	"
7	Ivin L. Peters	7	male

Ancestor: Mrs. Dunson nee Vann

Cherokee Citizenship Commission Docket Books
(1880-84, 1887-89) Volume II
Tahlequah, Cherokee Nation

Office Commission on Citizenship
Tahlequah May 15th 1889

Now on this day comes the applicant Sarah M.[sic] Peters for a final hearing, the case having been called three several times not less than one hour at intervals, and no response from applicant or by Attorney, the Commission after examining the papers in said case find no evidence in support of application the Commission are of the opinion that Sarah W. Peters and her family John W. Peters male aged 17 years, Eudora Peters Female aged 16 years, Dora S. Peters, Female aged 14 years, Jinnie E. Peters, Female aged 12 years, Mattie L. Peters, female aged 10 years, Ivin L. Peters Male aged 7 years are not Cherokees by blood and are not entitled to Citizenship in the Cherokee Nation. Post Office address Calisburg, Texas.

Attest
E.G. Ross
Clerk Commission

Will P. Ross Chairman
R. Bunch   Com
J.E. Gunter Com

RICH

Docket #387
Rolls 1835 to 1852
filed August   Applicant for Cherokee Citizenship
   Post Office: Kidrow I.T.   **Attorney:** A.E. Ivey

N°	NAMES	AGE	SEX
1	Thomas T. Rich	27	male
2	Fred Rich	3	"

Ancestor: Jane Lowery

Adversely

See Decision in this case in this Book Page 85.

DS Williams
Asst Clk Comm.

Cherokee Citizenship Commission Docket Books
(1880-84, 1887-89) Volume II
Tahlequah, Cherokee Nation

RICH

Docket #388
Rolls 1835 to 1852
filed August 27th 1887   Applicant for Cherokee Citizenship
     Post Office: Kiddrow I.T.   **Attorney:** A.E. Ivey

N°	NAMES	AGE	SEX
1	John H. Rich	21	male

     Ancestor: Jane Rich formerly Lowery

Adversely

See Decision in this case in this Book Page 85.

DS Williams
Asst Clk Comm.

WATKINS

Docket #389
Rolls 1835
filed August 29th 1887   Applicant for Cherokee Citizenship
     Post Office: Tahlequah CN   **Attorney:** C.H. Taylor

N°	NAMES	AGE	SEX
1	Gordon Watkins	29	Male
2	Thomas Watkins	27	"
3	Mack Watkins	25	"
4	Mary Watkins	23	Female

     Ancestor: Jack Watkins

Rejected March 11th 1889

Now on this the 11th day of March 1889 comes the above case to wit, Gordon Watkins versus the Cherokee Nation for a final hearing, he having made application pursuant to the provisions of an Act of the National Council approved December 8th 1886 for readmission to Citizenship for himself and Thomas Watkins aged 27 years, Mack Watkins age 25 years, Mary Watkins aged 23 years, through Jack Watkins alleged to be of Cherokee blood. Now on examination of the rolls of 1835, and other rolls named seventh section of the before named Act, fails to show the names of Jack Watkins from whom applicant claims descent while the testimony which is of a hearsay character and

Cherokee Citizenship Commission Docket Books
(1880-84, 1887-89) Volume II
Tahlequah, Cherokee Nation

embodied in exparte affidavits does not show that the said Jack Watkins through whom descent is claimed was of Cherokee blood or at any time resided in the Cherokee Nation. The evidence does not establish the fact that Gordon Watkins has any Cherokee blood in his veins. It is therefore adjudged and declared by the Commission on Citizenship that said Gordon Watkins, Thomas Watkins, Mack Watkins, Mary Watkins above named are not Cherokee Indians and are not entitled to Citizenship in the Cherokee Nation.

	Will P. Ross	Chairman
Attest	John E. Gunter	Commissioner
E.G. Ross		
	Clerk of Commission	

WATKINS

Docket #390
Rolls 1835
filed August 29th 1887   Applicants for Cherokee Citizenship
Post Office: Carrolton Ark   **Attorney:** CH Taylor

N°	NAMES	AGE	SEX
1	Paschal Watkins	42	Male
2	Garland Watkins	12	"
3	Larkin Watkins	10	"
4	Charles Watkins	6	"
5	Dora Watkins	4	Female
6	Grover Watkins	1	Male

Ancestor: Jack Watkins

Rejected March 11th 1889

Now on this the 11th day of March 1889 comes the above case to wit, Paschal Watkins versus the Cherokee Nation, for a final hearing, he having made application pursuant to the provisions of an Act of the National Council approved December 8th 1886 for re-admission to Citizenship for himself and Garland Watkins aged 12 years, Larkin Watkins, aged 10 years, Charles Watkins aged 6 years, Dora Watkins, aged 4 years, Grover Watkins age 1 year, through Jack Watkins alleged to be of Cherokee blood. Now on examination of the rolls of 1835 and other rolls named in the seventh section of the before named Act, fails to show the name of Jack Watkins from whom applicant claims descent while the testimony which is of a hearsay character and embodied in

Cherokee Citizenship Commission Docket Books
(1880-84, 1887-89) Volume II
Tahlequah, Cherokee Nation

exparte affidavits does not show that the said Jack Watkins through whom descent is claimed, was of Cherokee blood or at any time resided in the Cherokee Nation. The evidence does not establish the fact that Paschal Watkins has any Cherokee blood in his veins. It is therefore adjudged and declared by the Commission on Citizenship that said Paschal Watkins and children above named are not Cherokee Indians and not entitled to Citizenship in the Cherokee Nation.

                          Will P. Ross   Chairman
Attest   John E. Gunter Commissioner
    E.G. Ross
        Clerk of Commission

WATKINS

Docket #391
Rolls 1835
filed   Applicant for Cherokee Citizenship
    Post Office: Berryville Ark   **Attorney**: C H Taylor

N°	NAMES	AGE	SEX
	Charles W Watkins	45	Male
	Joe Watkins	15	"
	Hellen Watkins	12	Female
	Ida Watkins	8	"
	G.D. Watkins	7	Male
	Johnie Watkins	5	"
	Nettie Watkins	4	Female
	Paschal Watkins	1	Male

                    Ancestor: Jack Watkins
Rejected March 11th 1889

    Now on this the 11th day of March 1889 comes the above case to wit; Charles W. Watkins versus the Cherokee Nation, for a final hearing, he having made application pursuant to the provisions of an Act of the National Council approved December 8th 1886, for readmission to Citizenship for himself and Joe Watkins female aged 15 years, Helen Watkins aged 12 years, Ida Watkins aged 8 years, John Watkins aged 5 years, Nellie Watkins aged 4 years, G.D. Watkins male age 7 years, Paschal Watkins aged one year, through Jack Watkins alleged to be of Cherokee blood. Now on an examination of the rolls of 1835 and other rolls named in the seventh section of the before named Act, fail to show the

Cherokee Citizenship Commission Docket Books
(1880-84, 1887-89) Volume II
Tahlequah, Cherokee Nation

name of Jack Watkins from whom applicant claims descent while the testimony which is of a hearsay character and embodied in expartie[sic] affidavits does not show that the said Jack Watkins through whom descent is claimed was of Cherokee blood or at any time resided in the Cherokee Nation the evidence does not establish the fact that Charles W. Watkins has any Cherokee blood in his veins. It is therefore adjudged and declared by the Commission on Citizenship that said Charles W. Watkins and children above named are not Cherokee Indians and are not entitled to Citizenship in the Cherokee Nation.

E.G. Ross
   Clerk of Com

Will P. Ross   Chairman
John E. Gunter   Comm.

MONTGOMERY

Docket #392
Rolls 1835 to 1852
filed August 29th 1887   Applicant for Cherokee Citizenship
Post Office: Tahlequah CN   **Attorney:** B.H. Stone

N°	NAMES	AGE	SEX
1	Thomas Montgomery	59	Male
2	William H. Montgomery	38	"
3	Janus H. Montgomery	36	Female
4	Nora B. Montgomery	16	"

Ancestor: Thomas Gobbert

See decision in this case on page 31, in this Book the same having been filed twice, and are the same case   adverse to claimant.

Attest
   D.S. Williams
Asst. Clk. Com

Will P. Ross
   Chairman
J.E. Gunter   Com

Cherokee Citizenship Commission Docket Books
(1880-84, 1887-89) Volume II
Tahlequah, Cherokee Nation

HAIL

Docket #393
Rolls 1851
filed August 29th 1887 Applicant for Cherokee Citizenship
Post Office: Van Buren Ark **Attorney:** B H Stone

N°	NAMES	AGE	SEX
1	Joseph L. Hail	34	Male

Ancestor: Micheal Hail

Joseph Hail Commission on Citizenship
vs Tahlequah I T
Cherokee Nation October 31st 1888.

The above named applicants claim for Citizenship this day came up for final hearing and the testimony taken in the case was carefully examined together with the rolls of 1851 & 52 taken by the U.S. Government east of the Mississippi River. The three affidavits taken in the case plainly shows that the applicant is a son of the aledged[sic] ancestor Micheal Hail, who was enrolled in the year 1851 by Mr. Siler, and also drew his per capita money in the year 1852, as the rolls will show, it appears that the applicant was born out of wedlock but all the testimony in the case points out plainly that Joseph Hail is undoubtedly the son of Micheal Hail.

Therefore we the Commission on Citizenship acting under the law passed by the National Council and approved December 8th 1886, and the amendments thereto, unanimously agree, and so decide, that Joseph L. Hail is a Cherokee by blood, and is hereby readmitted to all the rights and privileges of a Cherokee citizen by blood in the Cherokee Nation.

J.T. Adair Chairman of the Commission
D.W. Lipe Commissioner
H.C. Barnes Commissioner

Cherokee Citizenship Commission Docket Books
(1880-84, 1887-89) Volume II
Tahlequah, Cherokee Nation

GEORGE

Docket #394
Rolls 1835 to 1852
filed August 29 1887   Applicant for Cherokee Citizenship
  Post Office: Tokerville Ark   **Attorney:** Boudinot & Rasmus

N°	NAMES	AGE	SEX
1	Margaret I George	55	
2	James T. George	34	
3	Calvin M. George	21	
4	Ester J. George	18	
5	Ellennora George	15	
6	Robert George	12	

Ancestor: Andrew Miller

Office Commission on Citizenship
Tahlequah May 14th 1889

The above entitled case was submitted by both parties and on this day comes for a final hearing. The applicant claims as ancester[sic] one Andrew Miller and further submits as evidence the testimony of one John F. Hardcastle. After carefully examining the rolls the applicant set forth in his application, we fail to find the name of Andrew Miller the Ancestor of applicant. The evidence of John F. Hardcastle fails to sustain the applicants Cherokee blood. Therefore taking the above facts into consideration, the Commission is of the opinion and so declare that the applicant together with children are not Cherokees by blood and not entitled to the rights and privileges of Cherokee Citizenship, and declare applicant with family to be intruders within the Cherokee Nation. Names of the children of Maggie J. George are as follows: James T. George son aged 34 years, Calvin M. George son aged 21 years. Ester J. George Daughter aged 18 years, Ellenora George Daughter aged 15 years, Robert H. George son aged 12 years. Post Office address Chocoville Ark.

	Will P. Ross	Chairman
E.G. Ross	R. Bunch	Com
Clerk Commission	J.E. Gunter	Com

Cherokee Citizenship Commission Docket Books
(1880-84, 1887-89) Volume II
Tahlequah, Cherokee Nation

CLARK

Docket #395
Rolls 1835
filed Aug 29th 1887   Applicant for Cherokee Citizenship
    Post Office: Rule Ark   **Attorney:** C.H. Taylor

N°	NAMES	AGE	SEX
1	Bettie A. Clark	33	Male
2	Dalis Clark	6	Female
3	Nellie Clark	4	"
4	Mary Clark	2	"

Ancestor: Jack Watkins

Rejected May 14, 1889

                Office Commission on Citizenship
                Cherokee Nation Ind. Ter'y.
                Tahlequah May 14th 1889

Now on this day comes the above case for the final hearing. The case having been submitted by the Attys for both parties being unsustained by any evidence The Commission decide that the applicant Bettie A. Clark aged 33 yrs and her children, Dalis Clark male aged 6 yrs, Nellie Clark female aged 4 yrs and Mary Clark female aged 2 yrs, are not of Cherokee blood and not entitled to the privileges as such within the limits of the Cherokee Nation.
Post Office address, Rule Ark.

Attest	Will P. Ross	Chairman
D.S. Williams	R. Bunch	Com.
Asst Clk Com	J.E. Gunter	Com

BOBO

Docket #396
Rolls 1835
filed August 29th 1887   Applicant for Cherokee Citizenship
    Post Office: Harrison Ark   **Attorney:** C.H. Taylor

N°	NAMES	AGE	SEX
1	Alabama Bobo	30	Female
2	Charlie Bobo	11	Male
3	Nellie Bobo	9	Female

Cherokee Citizenship Commission Docket Books
(1880-84, 1887-89) Volume II
Tahlequah, Cherokee Nation

4	George Bobo	5	Male

Ancestor: Jack Watkins

Rejected March 11th 1889

Now on this the 11th day of March 1889, comes the above case to wit, Alabama Bobo versus the Cherokee Nation for a final hearing, she having made application pursuant to the provisions of an Act of the National Council approved December 8th 1886 for readmission to Citizenship for herself and Charles Bobo aged 11 years, Nellie Bobo aged 9 years, George Bobo aged 5 years, through Jack Watkins alleged to be of Cherokee blood. Now on examination of the rolls of 1835 and other rolls named on the seventh section of the before named Act, fails to show the name of Jack Watkins from whom applicant claims descent while the testimony which is of a hearsay character and embodied in expartie[sic] affidavits does not show that the said Jack Watkins through whom descent is claimed was of Cherokee blood or at any time resided in the Cherokee Nation. The evidence does not establish the fact that Alabama Bobo has any Cherokee blood in her veins. It is therefore adjudged and declared by the Commission on Citizenship that said Alabama Bobo, Charlie Bobo, Nellie Bobo, George Bobo above named are not Cherokee Indians and not entitled to Citizenship in the Cherokee Nation.

                        Will P. Ross   Chairman
                        John E. Gunter Commis.

Attest
    E.G. Ross
        Clerk Commission

ADAMS

Docket #397
Rolls 1835
filed August 29th 1887   Applicant for Cherokee Citizenship
   Post Office: Scullaville   **Attorney:** C.H. Taylor

N°	NAMES	AGE	SEX
1	Nancy Adams	51	Female
2	John C. Adams	17	Male
3	Powhattan Adams	10	Male

Ancestor: Delilah Taylor

Cherokee Citizenship Commission Docket Books
(1880-84, 1887-89) Volume II
Tahlequah, Cherokee Nation

Office Commission on Citizenship
Tahlequah May 14th 1889

Now on the day above named comes the above application for the final hearing. The same having been submitted by the Attorneys for both parties. The application which was filed the 29th day of August 1887, being unsustained by any evidence, the Commission decide that the applicant Nancy A. Adams aged fifty one years and her children, John C. Adams male aged seventeen years and Powhattan Adams female aged ten years is not entitled to readmission to Citizenship in the Cherokee Nation by virture[sic] of having Cherokee blood. Post Office Rule Ark.

	Will P. Ross	Chairman
Attest	R. Bunch	Com
E.G. Ross	J.E. Gunter	Com
	Clerk Commission	

PARKER

Docket #398
Rolls 1835
filed August 29th 1889 Applicant for Cherokee Citizenship
Post Office: Vinita Ind. Terry **Attorney:** H.T. Landrew

N°	NAMES	AGE	SEX
1	E.A. Parker	28	Male
2	Earnest Parker	4	"
3	Clauda Parker	1	"

Ancestor: Ches-quay-ah

See decision in this case in that of George W. Parker in Book "A" page 119 – Adverse to claimant.

Cornell Rogers
Clk Com on Citizenship

Office Com on Citizenship
Tahlequah, I.T. Sept 25th 1888

Cherokee Citizenship Commission Docket Books
(1880-84, 1887-89) Volume II
Tahlequah, Cherokee Nation

SWEETEN

Docket #399
Rolls 1852
filed August 29th 1887   Applicant for Cherokee Citizenship

Post Office: **Attorney:** Geo Bible

N°	NAMES	AGE	SEX
1	Phillip Sweeten	21	Male
2	Eng Sweeten	18	"
3	Emaline Sweeten	12	Female
4	Carrie Sweeten	10	"
5	Clem Sweeten	8	Male
6	Sam M. Sweeten	6	"

Ancestor: Rebecca Sweeten nee Bible
The above case reconsidered and Admitted Sept 5th 1889

Adversely

See decision in this case in this Book, Page 85.

D.S. Williams
Asst. Clk Com.

Office Commission on Citizenship
Tahlequah I T Sept 5th 1889

    The application of claimants in the above named case was rejected on the 15th day of May 1889 because of the absence of proof. But is having been proven to the satisfaction of the Commission that it was through no fault or neglect on the part of the applicants that their case had been allowed to go by default and that it was meritorious in character. It was reopened on the 31st day of August for final hearing. On that day it was proven by witnesses well known to the Commission to their satisfaction that the applicants were the children of the body of Rebecca Sweeten, nee Rebecca Bible who derived her Cherokee blood from her mother Eliza Bible nee Eliza Green, a woman of Cherokee blood and that the name of Rebecca Sweeten nee Rebecca Bible is entered as a Cherokee Indian on the pay roll of the Old Settlers taken and made in the year 1851. The Commission therefore decide that Phillip G. Sweeten age 21 years and his brothers Eng Sweeten 18 years, Clem Sweeten 8 years, and Sam M. Sweeten age 6 years, and his sisters Emeline Sweeten age 12 years, Carrie

Cherokee Citizenship Commission Docket Books
(1880-84, 1887-89) Volume II
Tahlequah, Cherokee Nation

Sweeten age 10 years, are of Cherokee blood and are hereby re-admitted to Citizenship in the Cherokee Nation in accordance with the Constitution and laws thereof.

Attest
    E.G. Ross
    Clerk Commission

Will P. Ross   Chairman
J.E. Gunter   Com

ZARTMAN

Docket #400
Rolls 1835 to 1851
filed August 29th 1887   Applicant for Cherokee Citizenship
Post Office: Chetopa Kansas   **Attorney:** Boudinot & Rasmus

N°	NAMES	AGE	SEX
1	Catharine B. Zartman	44	Female
2	Eliza R. Zartman	14	"
3	Erdie W. Zartman	12	"
4	Oscar B. Zartman	10	Male
5	Owen L. Zartman	8	"
6	Perlie P. Zartman	6	Female

Ancestor: Joseph B. Dorn

(This line illegible)

    The applicant in the above case alleges that she is the grand daughter of one Joseph B. Dorn or Dorns and Tammy *(Illegible)* whos[sic] names will be found on the Census rolls of Cherokees by blood taken in the year 1835. The exparte affidavits of one Phillip Smith or Chetopa Kansas before J.T. Caldwell, Notary Public, August 8th 1889, states that he is 80 yrs old and that he was acquainted with Bernard Dorn who lived on *(Illegible)* Creek on the line between Tennessee and Georgia from the years 1827 to 1847 and that the *(illegible)* also Tammy *(Illegible)* the mother of said Dorn who was a Cherokee. While this statement is not sufficient to establish the right of the applicant to Citizenship in the Cherokee Nation the fact that neither the names of Bernard Dorn or Dorns nor that of Tammy *(Illegible)* can be found on the rolls of Cherokees by blood taken in 1835 is regarded as conclusive against the applicant. The Commission therefore decide that Catherine B. Zartman and her daughters, Lizzie R. Zartman age 14 yrs, Erdie W. Zartman aged 12 yrs, Perlie

Cherokee Citizenship Commission Docket Books
(1880-84, 1887-89) Volume II
Tahlequah, Cherokee Nation

P. Zartman aged 6 yrs and sons Oscar B. Zartman aged 10 yrs and Owen L. Zartman aged 8 yrs are not of Cherokee blood and not entitled to readmission to Citizenship in the Cherokee Nation.

George O. Butler
Clerk Commission

Will P. Ross
R. Bunch
John E. Gunter

Chairman
Commissioner
Com

RICH

Docket #401
Rolls 1835 to 1852
filed August 29 1887   Applicant for Cherokee Citizenship
Post Office: Fort Gibson I.T.   **Attorney**: B.H. Stone

N°	NAMES	AGE	SEX
1	Reil Rich	52	Male
2	Lucetta Rich	28	Female
3	Nancy Rich	26	"
4	Bennett Rich	24	Male
5	F Rich	23	Female

Ancestor: Ellie Hooker

The above case was filed in pursuance with an Act of the National Council approved Dec 8th 1886, in the office of the Commission on Citizenship, and was this day duly considered. The parties claiming a descent from Ellie Hooker, whom they allege was of Cherokee Indian blood.

The rolls of Cherokees mentioned in the 7th Sec. of an Act of Dec 8th 1886 in relation to Citizenship fail to contain the names of Ellie Hooker, or those of the applicants themselves, therefore it is useless to make mention of the testimony, as we cannot grant citizenship other than is prescribed by the law under which we are working, and Reil Rich and his four children, viz: Lucetta, Nancy J., Bennett and Ferhia Rich are not Cherokee by blood and are not entitled to any of the rights and privileges of Cherokee citizens by blood, and are intruders upon the public domain of the Cherokee Nation.

J.T. Adair   Chairman Commission
H.C. Barnes   Commissioner

Office Com on Citizenship
Tahlequah, I.T. Oct. 13t '88

Cherokee Citizenship Commission Docket Books
(1880-84, 1887-89) Volume II
Tahlequah, Cherokee Nation

DESHAZO

Docket #402
Rolls 1835
filed August 30th 1887   Applicant for Cherokee Citizenship
Post Office: Harrison Ark   **Attorney:** C.H. Taylor

N°	NAMES	AGE	SEX
1	Tennessee Deshazo	27	Female
2	Willie Deshazo	9	Male
3	Eddie Deshazo	8	Male
4	Hellen Deshazo	3	Female
5	Tilda Deshazo	4 mo	"

Ancestor: Jack Watkins

Rejected March 11th 1889

Now on this the 11th day of March 1889, comes the above case, to wit; Tennessee Deshazo versus the Cherokee Nation for a final hearing, she having made application pursuant to the provisions of an Act of the National Council approved December 8th 1886 for re-admission to Citizenship for herself and Willie Deshazo aged 9 years, Eddie Deshazo aged 8 years, Hellen Deshazo aged 3 years, Tilda Deshazo aged 4 months through Jack Watkins alleged to be of Cherokee blood. Now on examination of the rolls of 1835 and other rolls named in the seventh section of the before named Act, fails to show the name of Jack Watkins from whom applicant claims descent while the testimony which is of a hearsay character and embodied in expartie[sic] affidavits does not show that the said Jack Watkins through whom descent is claimed was of Cherokee blood or at any time resided in the Cherokee Nation. The evidence does not establish the fact that Tennessee Deshazo has any Cherokee blood in her veins. It is therefore adjudged and declared by the Commission on Citizenship that said Tennessee Deshazo, Willie Deshazo, Eddie Deshazo, Hellen Deshazo, Tilda Deshazo, above named are not Cherokee Indians and not entitled to Citizenship in the Cherokee Nation.

                                  Will P. Ross   Chairman
Attest   John E. Gunter   Commissioner
    E.G. Ross
        Clerk of Com.

Cherokee Citizenship Commission Docket Books
(1880-84, 1887-89) Volume II
Tahlequah, Cherokee Nation

LAYTON

Docket #403
Rolls 1835 to 1852
filed August 30 1887   Applicant for Cherokee Citizenship
Post Office: Tahlequah CN   **Attorney:** WA Thompson

N°	NAMES	AGE	SEX
1	Martha C. Layton	39	Female
2	Ida J. Layton	13	"
3	Sarah F. Layton	11	"
4	Emma B. Layton	8	"

Ancestor: Joseph Walker

Rejected May 16 – 89

Office Commission on Citizenship
Cherokee Nation Ind. Ter'y.
Tahlequah May 16th 1889

Now comes the above case for the final hearing which was filed on the 20th day of August 1887. The applicant claims that she is the descendant of Joseph Walker and Sallie Nunoly Walker, whose names she firmly believes was enrolled on the census rolls of Cherokees by blood taken and made in the years of 1835-51 & 2. The Commission fail to find the names above named on either of the above mentioned rolls and the case having been called three several times at intervals of not less than one hour apart and no answer and there being no evidence in support of said claimants case. The Commission decide that Martha C. Layton aged 39 yrs and her children, to wit; Ida J. Layton aged 13 yrs (daughter), Sarah F. Layton (daughter) aged 11 yrs and Emma B. Layton (daughter) aged 8 yrs is not of Cherokee blood and not entitled to Citizenship in the Cherokee Nation.

	Will P. Ross	Chairman
Attest	R. Bunch	Com
D.S. Williams	J.E. Gunter	Com
Asst. Clk Com		

Cherokee Citizenship Commission Docket Books
(1880-84, 1887-89) Volume II
Tahlequah, Cherokee Nation

HAYES

Docket #404
Rolls 1835
filed August 30th 1887　　　　　　　Application for Cherokee Citizenship

Post Office: Fishertown Ind Terry　**Attorney:** Boudinot & Rasmus

N°	NAMES	AGE	SEX
1	Rachel M. Hayes	47	Female
2	John H. Hayes	8	Male

Ancestor: Malinda Simmons

– Rejected –

　　　　　　　　　　　　Office Commission on Citizenship
　　　　　　　　　　　　　　Tahlequah May 22nd 1889

The application in this case was filed the 30th August 1887 and submitted by Attorneys without evidence. The Commission therefore decide that Rachel M. Hayes and her son, John H. Hayes aged eight years of Fishertown, Indian Territory are not of Cherokee blood and not entitled to readmission to Citizenship in the Cherokee Nation.

	Will P. Ross	Chairman
Attest	R. Bunch	Com
EG Ross	JE Gunter	Com
Clerk Commission		

HAYES

Docket #405
Rolls 1835
filed August 30 1887　　　　　　　Applicant for Cherokee Citizenship

Post Office: Fishertown I.T.　**Attorney:** Boudinot & Rasmus

N°	NAMES	AGE	SEX
1	William M Hayes	29	Male
2	Walter Hayes	2	"

Ancestor: Malinda Simmons

　　　　　　　　　　　　Office Commission on Citizenship
　　　　　　　　　　　　　　Tahlequah May 22nd 1889

Cherokee Citizenship Commission Docket Books
(1880-84, 1887-89) Volume II
Tahlequah, Cherokee Nation

The application in the above case was filed the 30th day of August 1887 and this day submitted by Attorneys without evidence. The Commission therefore decide that William M Hayes and Walter Hayes aged two years of Fishertown, Ind. Ter. are not of Cherokee blood and <u>not</u> entitled to readmission to Citizenship in the Cherokee Nation.

Attest	Will P. Ross	Chairman
EG Ross	R. Bunch	Com
Clerk Commission	JE Gunter	Com

BAKER

Docket #406
Rolls 1835
filed August 30th 1887   Applicant for Cherokee Citizenship
Post Office: Alma Ark   **Attorney:** Boudinot & Rasmus

N°	NAMES	AGE	SEX
1	Eliza J Baker	68	Female
2	Samuel B. Baker	32	Male
3	William A Baker	27	"

Ancestor: Elizabeth Brooks

Office Commission on Citizenship
Tahlequah May 27th 1889

This application was filed on the 30th day of August 1887 and is supported by no evidence, and was submitted on the 22nd day of May 1889 for a final hearing. The Commission therefore decide against Eliza J Baker and the following named children, Samuel B. Baker male aged 32 years, William A Baker male age 27 years, are not Cherokees by blood, and are not entitled to Citizenship in the Cherokee Nation.

	Will P. Ross	Chairman
EG Ross	R. Bunch	Com
Clerk Commission	JE Gunter	Com

Cherokee Citizenship Commission Docket Books
(1880-84, 1887-89) Volume II
Tahlequah, Cherokee Nation

HAYES

Docket #407
Rolls 1835
filed August 30 1887   Application for Cherokee Citizenship
Post Office: Fishertown Ind Ter   **Attorney:** Boudinot & Rasmus

N°	NAMES	AGE	SEX
1	James L. Hayed	24	Male
2	Bertha Hayes	3	Female
3	Kia Hayes	4 mo	"

Ancestor: Malinda Simmons

Office Commission on Citizenship
Tahlequah May 22nd 1889

This application filed the 30th day of August 1887 was submitted by Attorneys this day without evidence. The Commission therefore decide that James L. Hayes and daughters Bertha Hayes aged three years and Kia Hayes aged four months of Fishertown Ind. Ter. are not of Cherokee blood and not entitled to Citizenship in the Cherokee Nation.

Attest	Will P. Ross	Chairman
EG Ross	R. Bunch	Com
Clerk Commission	J.E. Gunter	Com

FLOTHO

Docket #408
Rolls 1835
filed August 30 1887   Applicant for Cherokee Citizenship
Post Office: Fishertown I.T.   **Attorney:** Boudinot & Rasmus

N°	NAMES	AGE	SEX
1	Francis G. Flotho	21	Female
2	Oscar Flotho	4	Male
3	James Flotho	6 mo	"

Ancestor: Malinda Simmons

Cherokee Citizenship Commission Docket Books
(1880-84, 1887-89) Volume II
Tahlequah, Cherokee Nation

Office Commission on Citizenship
Tahlequah CN May 22nd 1889

    The above case was this day submitted by Attorneys without evidence. The Commission therefore decide that Francis G. Flotho and her sons Oscar Flotho aged four years and James Flotho aged six months are not of Cherokee blood.

	Will P. Ross	Chairman
Attest	R. Bunch	Com
EG Ross	JE Gunter	Com
Clerk Commission		

YOUNG

Docket #409
Rolls 1835
filed August 30 1887   Applicant for Cherokee Citizenship
Post Office: Oklahoma IT   **Attorney:** AE Ivey

N°	NAMES	AGE	SEX
1	J.D. Young	28	Male
2	Mollie Young	5	Female
3	Gus Young	3	Male
4	Oscar Young	2	"

Ancestor: John Thompson

Rejected May 16 '89

Office Commission on Citizenship Cherokee Nation
Tahlequah May 16th 1889

Application for Cherokee Citizenship.

    This day the above case coming on for final hearing, and examining the application of claimant we fail to find any evidence produced to sustain the claimant's claim of Cherokee blood and in view of this fact The commission decide that applicant J.D. Young aged 28 and his children, Mollie Young aged 5 yrs, Gus Young aged 3 yrs, Oscar Young aged 2 yrs. Post Office Oklahoma, I.T. are not entitled to any rights or privileges of Citizenship in the Cherokee Nation.

Attest	Will P. Ross	Chairman
D.S. Williams	R. Bunch	Commissioner
Asst Clk Com	John E. Gunter	Com

Cherokee Citizenship Commission Docket Books
(1880-84, 1887-89) Volume II
Tahlequah, Cherokee Nation

WATSON

Docket #410
Rolls 1825
filed August 30 1887 Application for Cherokee Citizenship
  Post Office: Oklahoma IT **Attorney**: AE Ivey

N°	NAMES	AGE	SEX
1	Josephine Watson	35	Female
2	Geo S. Baker	15	Male

Ancestor: John Thompson

Rejected 16 – 89

Office Commission on Citizenship Cherokee Nation I.T.
Tahlequah May 16th 1889

This day comes the above named application for final hearing. This application was filed the 30th day of August 1887. The evidence in support of it will be found in the affidavit made before the Commission on Citizenship August 3rd 1888, by the applicant who was born in Polk, now Howard County, Arkansas near the Cherokee line and in which ~~Nation~~ state she resided three years and came into the Cherokee Country the February presiding the filing of her application. There are also filed the affidavits taken <u>Exparte</u> before the Clerk of the Circuit Court of Howard County, Arkansas, of John Waldon and James Young who swear that Josephine Watson is the daughter of George Young and Martha Young. George Young was the son of John Young and Millie Young. Also was a daughter of John Thompson who they say, was a half blood Cherokee Indian. These affiants are uncles of Josephine Watson. The grounds upon which they swear that John Thompson was a half blood Cherokee are not given and the facts that there us no evidence that Mrs. Watson or any members of her family resided at anytime within the limits of the Nation or ever made applications to become citizens although born and living for so many years within a short distance of the Cherokee Country previous to the date of the application. Now presented and that the name of John Thompson is not found on the rolls of Cherokees by blood taken and made in the year 1835 as alleged lend this Commission to decide as they now do that Josephine Watson is not of Cherokee blood and entitled to Cherokee Citizenship. The foregoing decision includes the names of Josephine Watson, George S. Baker aged fifteen years at the filing of this application.

Cherokee Citizenship Commission Docket Books
(1880-84, 1887-89) Volume II
Tahlequah, Cherokee Nation

Attest	Will P. Ross	Chairman
D.S. Williams	R. Bunch	Com
Asst Clk Com	J.E. Gunter	Com

CHAMBERS

Docket #411
Rolls 1835

Applicant for Cherokee Citizenship

Post Office: Center Point Ark   **Attorney:** AE Ivey

N°	NAMES	AGE	SEX
1	Milly A Chambers	37	Female
2	Emily J Chambers	10	"
3	Sarah C Chambers	6	"
4	Thomas S Chambers	4	Male
5	Josephine Bell Chambers	2	"

Ancestor: John Thompson

Rejected May 16 – 89

Office Commission on Citizenship Cher Nat I.T.
Tahlequah May 16th 1889

Application for Cherokee Citizenship

This day the above case was taken up for a final hearing. The application being filed on the 30th day of August after examining the application we fail to find any evidence filed in support of applicant claim and in view of this fact the Commission decide that claimant Milly A Chambers aged 37 yrs and her children, Emily J Chambers aged 10 yrs, Sarah C. Chambers aged 6 yrs, Thomas S. Chambers aged 4 yrs, Josephine Bell Chambers age 2 yrs. Post Office Center Point Ark are not entitled to Cherokee Citizenship in the Cherokee Nation.

Attest	Will P. Ross	Chairman
D.S. Williams	R. Bunch	Commissioner
Asst Clk Com	John E. Gunter	Com

Cherokee Citizenship Commission Docket Books
(1880-84, 1887-89) Volume II
Tahlequah, Cherokee Nation

ROGERS

Docket #412
Rolls 1835

Applicant for Cherokee Citizenship

Post Office: Belemont Ark   **Attorney:** AE Ivey

N°	NAMES	AGE	SEX
1	James CC Rogers	32	Male
2	H.L. Rogers	19	"
3	Rose Rogers	17	Female
4	Lillie May Rogers	15	"
5	John C. Rogers	13	Male
6	William C Rogers	11	"
7	Chas W Rogers	9	"
8	Daisie B Rogers	6	Female
9	Mary M Rogers	5	"
10	Pink Rogers	2	"

Ancestor: John Rogers

See Decision in this case on Book C. Page 627. Adversely to Claimant.

Attest   Will P. Ross
  D.S. Williams   Chairman
  Asst Clk Com   J.E. Gunter   Com

HALL

Docket #413
Rolls 1835 to 1852

Applicant for Cherokee Citizenship

Post Office: Springtown Ark   **Attorney:** A.E. Ivey

N°	NAMES	AGE	SEX
1	Thursetta Hall	56	female
2	D.M. Hall	35	male
3	David A. Hall	33	
4	Lee Ann Hall		
5	John Hall		
6	Annie L Hall		
7	Amanda Hall		

Cherokee Citizenship Commission Docket Books
(1880-84, 1887-89) Volume II
Tahlequah, Cherokee Nation

8		Robert Hall		

Ancestor: Raleigh Hood

Rejected May 16 – 89

Office Commission on Citizenship Cher Nat I.T.
Tahlequah May 16th 1889

Now on this day comes the application of one Thursetta Hall for Cherokee Citizenship for a final hearing. This application was filed 1st day of September 1887 and alleging that Thursetta Hall nee Hood was the daughter of one Raleigh Hood whose name would be found on the census roll of Cherokees taken and made in the year 1835 to 52. Now the Commission after an examination of papers in the above case fail to find any evidence in support of said application, therefore the Commission are of the opinion that Thursetta Hall & her family D.M. Hall 35 yrs, David A. Hall, Lee Ann, Annie L, John, Amanda and Robert Hall are not Cherokees by blood and are not entitled to Cherokee Citizenship in the Cherokee Nation. Post Office Spring Town Arkansas.

Attest	Will P. Ross	Chairman
D.S. Williams	R. Bunch	Commissioner
Asst Clk Com	John E. Gunter	Com

EDWARDS

Docket #414
Rolls 1835 to 1852

Applicant for Cherokee Citizenship

Post Office: Rudy Ark   **Attorney:** A.E. Ivey

N°	NAMES	AGE	SEX
1	Silas P. Edwards		

Ancestor: Mima Edwards

Now on this the 9th day of January 1888, comes the above case for a final hearing, and the parties having made application pursuant to the provisions of an Act of the National Council approved December 8th 1886, and all the evidence being duly examined and found <u>not</u> to be sufficient and satisfactory to the Commission and the name of the Ancestor not appearing on the Rolls as claimed in the application.

Cherokee Citizenship Commission Docket Books
(1880-84, 1887-89) Volume II
Tahlequah, Cherokee Nation

It is adjudged and determined by the Commission that Silas P. Edwards is not a Cherokee by blood and is hereby rejected and declared an intruder.

        J.T. Adair   Chairman Commission
        John E. Gunter Commissioner
        D.W. Lipe   Commissioner

Attest
    C.C. Lipe
        Clerk Commission

BROOKS

Docket #415
Rolls 1835 to 1852

Applicant for Cherokee Citizenship

Post Office: Alma Ark   **Attorney:** A.E. Ivey

N°	NAMES	AGE	SEX
1	Mary Manervia Brooks	25	female
2	Rosa Maybell Brooks	7	"
3	Adell Brooks	5	"

Ancestor: Mima Edwards

Now on this the 9th day of January 1888 comes the above case for a final hearing and the parties having made application pursuant to the provisions of an Act of the National Council approved December 8th 1886 and all the evidence being duly examined and found not to be sufficient and satisfactory to the Commission and the name of the ancestor not appearing on the Rolls as claimed in the application.

It is adjudged and determined by the Commission that Mary Manervia Brooks, Rosa Maybell Brooks and Adell Brooks are not Cherokees by blood and are hereby rejected and declared intruders.

        J.T. Adair   Chairman Commission
        John E. Gunter Commissioner
        D.W. Lipe   Commissioner

Attest
    C.C. Lipe
        Clerk Commission

Cherokee Citizenship Commission Docket Books
(1880-84, 1887-89) Volume II
Tahlequah, Cherokee Nation

EDWARDS

Docket #416
Rolls

Applicant for Cherokee Citizenship

Post Office: Rudy Ark   **Attorney:** A.E. Ivey

N°	NAMES	AGE	SEX
1	William C.P. Edwards	27	Male
2	George W. Edwards	8	"
3	Anna Lee Edwards	6	female
4	Elizabeth Edwards	4	"
5	Silas Edwards	2	male
6	James Daniel Edwards	6 mo	"

Ancestor: Mima Edwards

Now on this the 9th day of January 1888 comes the above case for a final hearing, and the parties having made application pursuant to the provisions of an Act of the National Council approved December 8th 1886. and all the evidence being duly examined and found <u>not</u> to be sufficient and satisfactory to the Commission and the name of the ancestor not appearing on the Rolls as claimed in the application.

It is adjudged and determined by the Commission, that Wm C.P. Edwards, George W. Edwards, Anna Lee Edwards, Elizabeth Edwards, Silas Edwards and James Daniel Edwards, are <u>not</u> Cherokees by blood, and are hereby rejected and declared intruders.

J.T. Adair   Chairman Commission
John E. Gunter   Commissioner
D.W. Lipe   Commissioner

Attest
　　C.C. Lipe
　　　Clerk Commission

Cherokee Citizenship Commission Docket Books
(1880-84, 1887-89) Volume II
Tahlequah, Cherokee Nation

BELLU

Docket #417
Rolls 1835 to 1852

Applicant for Cherokee Citizenship

Post Office: Mountainburg Ark **Attorney:** A.E. Ivey

N°	NAMES	AGE	SEX
1	W.H. Bellu	56	Male
2	John A. Bellu	19	"
3	Adah H. Bellu	12	female
4	William C Bellu	10	male
5	Peter A. Bellu	8	"
6	George G. Bellu	5	"
7	Job C. Bellu		

Ancestor: Mima Edwards

Now on this the 9th day of January 1888 comes the above case for a final hearing, and the parties having made application pursuant to the provisions of an Act of the National Council approved December 8th 1886. and all the evidence being duly examined and found not to be sufficient & satisfactory to the Commission and the name of the ancestor not appearing on the Rolls as claimed in the application.

It is adjudged and determined by the Commission, that W.H. Bellu, John A. Bellu, Adah H. Bellu, Wm C. Bellu, Peter A. Bellu, George G. Bellu and Job C. Bellu are not Cherokees by blood, and are hereby rejected and declared to be intruders.

        J.T. Adair Chairman Commission
        John E. Gunter Commissioner
        D.W. Lipe Commissioner

Attest
  C.C. Lipe
    Clerk Commission

Cherokee Citizenship Commission Docket Books
(1880-84, 1887-89) Volume II
Tahlequah, Cherokee Nation

WAGONER

Docket #418
Rolls 1835 to 1852

Applicant for Cherokee Citizenship

Post Office: Mountainburg Ark   **Attorney**: A.E. Ivey

N°	NAMES	AGE	SEX
1	Lavina N Wagoner	46	female
2	Mary E. Wagoner	16	"
3	Peter G. Wagoner	14	male
4	Soloman E. Wagoner	12	"
5	Julia A. Wagoner	11	female
6	James W. Wagoner	8	male
7	Disia L. Wagoner	5	female

Ancestor: Mima Edwards

Now on this the 9th day of January 1888 comes the above case for a final hearing, and the parties having made application pursuant to the provisions of an Act of the National Council approved December 8th 1886. and all the evidence being duly examined and found <u>not</u> to be sufficient and satisfactory to the Commission and the name of the ancestor not appearing on the Rolls as claimed in the application.

It is adjudged and determined by the Commission, that Lavina N. Wagoner, Mary E. Wagoner, Peter G. Wagoner, Soloman E. Wagoner, Julia A. Wagoner, James W. Wagoner and Disia L. Wagoner are not Cherokees by blood, and are hereby rejected and declared intruders.

　　　　　　　　J.T. Adair　　Chairman Commission
　　　　　　　　John E. Gunter　Commissioner
　　　　　　　　D.W. Lipe　　Commissioner

Attest
　　C.C. Lipe
　　　Clerk Commission

Cherokee Citizenship Commission Docket Books
(1880-84, 1887-89) Volume II
Tahlequah, Cherokee Nation

WHITSON

Docket #419
Rolls 1835

Applicant for Cherokee Citizenship

Post Office: Lancaster Ark   **Attorney:** A.E. Ivey

N°	NAMES	AGE	SEX
1	Tempie Whitson	39	female
2	John Whitson	17	male
3	James Whitson	15	"
4	William Whitson	14	"
5	Ollie Whitson	12	female
6	Etta Whitson	10	"
7	Collumbus Whitson	8	male
8	Tempie Whitson	4	female
9	Emma Whitson	2	"

Ancestor: Mima Edwards

Now on this the 9th day of January 1888 comes the above case for a final hearing, and the parties having made application pursuant to the provisions of an Act of the National Council approved December 8th 1886. and all the evidence being duly examined and found not to be sufficient & satisfactory to the Commission and the name of the ancestor not appearing on the Rolls as claimed in the application.

It is adjudged and determined by the Commission, that Tempie Whitson, John Whitson, James Whitson, William Whitson, Ollie Whitson, Etta Whitson, Collumbus Whitson, Tempie Whitson and Emma Whitson, are not Cherokees by blood, and are hereby rejected and declared intruders.

J.T. Adair   Chairman Commission
John E. Gunter   Commissioner
D.W. Lipe   Commissioner

Attest
    C.C. Lipe
        Clerk Commission

Cherokee Citizenship Commission Docket Books
(1880-84, 1887-89) Volume II
Tahlequah, Cherokee Nation

DRAKE

Docket #420
Rolls 1835 to 1852

Applicant for Cherokee Citizenship

Post Office: Tahlequah CN   **Attorney:**

N°	NAMES	AGE	SEX
1	C.W. Drake	29	male
2	Charles S. Drake	1	"

Ancestor: William S. Taylor

See decision in Book "D" – page 455 in the case of Sidney R. Jamison – Adverse to claimant –

Cornell Burgess
Clk Com on Citizenship

Office Com on Citizenship
Tahlequah I.T. July 28th 1888

JAMISON

Docket #421
Rolls 1835 to 1852

Applicants for Cherokee Citizenship

Post Office: Locus Grove I.T.   **Attorney:** B.H. Stone

N°	NAMES	AGE	SEX
1	James W. Jamison	44	male
2	Herschal Jamison	16	"
3	William Jamison	15	"
4	Elija Jamison	13	"
5	Nancy Jamison	11	female
6	Maggie E. Jamison	8	"
7	Henry Jamison	6	male
8	James Jamison	4	"
9	Harriet Jamison	2	female

Ancestor: James and Mary Bell

Cherokee Citizenship Commission Docket Books
(1880-84, 1887-89) Volume II
Tahlequah, Cherokee Nation

Office Commission on Citizenship
Tahlequah C.N. May 17, 1889

Now comes the above case for final hearing. The applicant bases his claim upon descent from Mary Bell nee Lewis, who was the daughter of Dilsy Lewis. The witness on the part of the applicant are[sic] W.M. Bell and John R. Gourd and for the Nation John M. Taylor. The witness Bell, who is himself an applicant for Citizenship shows that Jamison has resided all his life on the immediate border of the Cherokee Country and he's not heretofore sought any rights on the Cherokee Nation. He also shows that the family in 1835 resided in Tennessee and settled in McDonald County Mo. as early as 1862 or 1863. The evidence of Mr. Gourd is conclusive of nothing on the subject further than that he claims to have known one Dilsy Lewis, but who she was and where she came from or went to he is ignorant. The evidence of Mr. Taylor tends to discredit the latter named witness and shows that claimant Jamison while running a saloon in Siloam Arkansas did not claim to be an Indian and that it was only after his failure in business that he moved into the Nation and claimed to be of Cherokee blood. In addition to the facts the names of neither Mary Bell nor Dilsy Lewis are found on the rolls of Cherokees by blood referred to in the Act of Dec 8th 1886. The Commission therefore decide that James W. Jamison and family are not of Cherokee blood and not entitled to Cherokee Citizenship.

Attest	Will P. Ross	Chairman
E.G. Ross	R. Bunch	Com
Clk Com	John E. Gunter	Com

LEE

Docket #422
Rolls 1835

Applicant for Cherokee Citizenship
Post Office: Walnut Ark   **Attorney:** B.H. Stone

N°	NAMES	AGE	SEX
1	Richard Lee	73	male
2	Mary B. Lee	37	female
3	Oliver Lee	35	male
4	Ellen Lee	30	female
5	Z.B. Lee	27	male
6	Susan A. Lee	25	female

Cherokee Citizenship Commission Docket Books
(1880-84, 1887-89) Volume II
Tahlequah, Cherokee Nation

7	William Lee	21	male
8	Margaret Lee	19	female
9	James Lee	17	male
10	Frank Lee	13	"

Ancestor: Dick and S. Lee

Rejected May 16 – 89

Office Commission on Citizenship Cher Nat I.T.
Tahlequah May 16th 1889

This case was filed the 1st day of September 1887.

There being no evidence to support the application and the names of the alleged ancestors not being found on the rolls of 1835, The Commission decide that the applicant Richard Lee aged 73 yrs, to wit; Mary B. Lee aged 37 yrs, Oliver Lee aged 38[sic] yrs, Ellen Lee aged 30 yrs, Z.B. Lee male aged 27 yrs, Susan A. Lee aged 25 yrs, William Lee 21 yrs, Margaret Lee 19 yrs, James Lee 17 yrs and Frank Lee aged 13 yrs. Post Office Tahlequah Ind. Ter'y.

Attest	Will P. Ross	Chairman
D.S. Williams	R. Bunch	Com
Asst Clk Com	J. E. Gunter	Com

SMITH

Docket #423
Rolls 1835 to 1852

Applicant for Cherokee Citizenship

Post Office: Van Buren Ark   **Attorney:** A.E. Ivey

Nº	NAMES	AGE	SEX
1	Mary Ann Smith	46	female
2	Samuel Smith	19	male
3	Mary M Smith	12	female

Ancestor: Mima Edwards

Now on this the 9th day of January 1888 comes the above case for a final hearing, and the parties having made application pursuant to the provisions of an Act of the National Council approved December 8th 1886. and all the evidence being duly examined and found not to be sufficient and satisfactory to the

Cherokee Citizenship Commission Docket Books
(1880-84, 1887-89) Volume II
Tahlequah, Cherokee Nation

Commission and the name of the ancestor not appearing on the Rolls as claimed in the application.

It is adjudged by the Commission, that Mary Ann Smith, Samuel Smith and Mary M. Smith, are <u>not</u> Cherokees by blood, and are hereby rejected and declared intruders.

                        J.T. Adair   Chairman Commission
                        John E. Gunter Commissioner
                        D.W. Lipe   Commissioner

Attest
    C.C. Lipe
        Clerk Commission

LANGLEY

Docket #424
Rolls 1835 to 1852

                        Applicant for Cherokee Citizenship
Post Office: Ellijay Ga.   **Attorney**: A.E. Ivey

Nº	NAMES	AGE	SEX
1	Zachary T. Langley	36	male
2	John W.D. Langley	19	"
3	Robert R. Langley	16	"
4	Louisa H.M.C. Langley	14	female
5	Lock Langley	11	male
6	Marion J. Langley	7	"
7	Martha E. Langley	5	female
8	Charles O. Langley	4 mo	male

Ancestor: Susan Langley

                    Tahlequah C.N.
                    Sept. 26th 1887

We the Commission on Citizenship after a careful examination of all the testimony in the case of Zachary T. Langley – John W.D. Langley – Robert R. Langley – Louisa H.M.C. Langley – Lock Langley – Marion J. Langley – Martha E. Langley and Charles O. Langley (VS) Cherokee Nation – find they are Cherokees by blood, and are hereby readmitted to all the rights privileges and immunities of Cherokees by blood.

Cherokee Citizenship Commission Docket Books
(1880-84, 1887-89) Volume II
Tahlequah, Cherokee Nation

J.T. Adair   Chairman Commission
John E. Gunter   Commissioner

SPRAGGINS

Docket #425
Rolls 1835 to 1852

Applicant for Cherokee Citizenship

Post Office: Alvarado Tex.   **Attorney:** A.E. Ivey

N°	NAMES	AGE	SEX
1	C.C. Spraggins	20	male

Ancestor: John Spraggins

Office Commission on Citizenship Cher. Nat. I.T.
Tahlequah May 16th 1889.

The application in the above case was filed 1st day of September 1998. It is supported by no evidence and the names of the ancestor John Spraggins not being found on census rolls of 1835 – 52. The Commission decide that C.C. Spraggins is not of Cherokee blood and not entitled to Citizenship in the Cherokee Nation. Post Office Alvarado, Texas.

Attest		
	Will P. Ross	Chairman
D.S. Williams	R. Bunch	Com
Asst Clk Com	J. E. Gunter	Com

CHOATE

Docket #426
Rolls 1835

Applicant for Cherokee Citizenship

Post Office: Fair Play, Cal.   **Attorney:** A.E. Ivey

N°	NAMES	AGE	SEX
1	John B. Choate, Sr.	63	Male
2	William S. Choate	31	"
3	Rufus M. Choate	28	"
4	John B. Choate, Jr.	24	"
5	Laura E. Choate	21	female

Cherokee Citizenship Commission Docket Books
(1880-84, 1887-89) Volume II
Tahlequah, Cherokee Nation

6	Mary C. Choate	19	"

Ancestor: Silas Choate

We the Commission on Citizenship after carefully examining the evidence in the above case, and also examining the Old Settler pay rolls of 1851, and the emigrant pay rolls of 1852, find that the above applicant John B. Choate, Sen. and his five children, viz: William Silas – Rufus Marc – John Brown – Laura Etta and Mary Carolina Chote[sic] are Cherokees by blood, and are hereby readmitted to all the rights and privileges of Cherokee citizens by blood, which is in compliance with an Act of the National Council creating this Commission, dated Dec 8th 1886, and amendment thereto approved Feb'y 7th 1888.

J.T. Adair   Chairman Commission
D.W. Lipe   Commissioner

Office Commission on Citizenship
Tahlequah, Ind. Ter. July 4th 1888

TIMMS

Docket #427
Rolls 1835

Applicant for Cherokee Citizenship

Post Office: Cheyenne Ga.   **Attorney:** AE Ivey

N°	NAMES	AGE	SEX
1	Mary Jane Timms	40	Female
2	Osceola Timms	14	"
3	Mathias Timms	12	Male
4	Ethan Comonodon Timms	10	"
5	V.G. Timms	9	"

Ancestor: Richard Redmon

Rejected May 16 – 89

Office Commission on Citizenship C.N.I.T.
Tahlequah May 16th 1889

The above application was filed the 2nd of September 1889, and is supported by no evidence. The Commission therefore decide that Mary Jane Timms and her daughter Osceola Timms aged fourteen yrs and Mathias Timms aged twelve years, Ethan Comonodon Timms aged ten years and V.G. Timms aged nine

Cherokee Citizenship Commission Docket Books
(1880-84, 1887-89) Volume II
Tahlequah, Cherokee Nation

years are not Cherokees by blood and not entitled to Citizenship in the Cherokee Nation.

	Will P. Ross	Chairman
Attest	R. Bunch	Com
D.S. Williams	J.E. Gunter	Com
Asst. Clk Com		

REASONER

Docket #428
Rolls 1835

Applicant for Cherokee Citizenship

Post Office: Blossom Prairie, Texas   **Attorney:** A.E. Ivey

N°	NAMES	AGE	SEX
1	J.W. Reasoner	42	Male

Ancestor: Elizabeth Reasoner

Rejected May 16 – 89

Office Commission on Citizenship C.N.I.T.
Tahlequah May 16th 1889

This application was presented the 2nd day of September, 1887, and this day submitted by Attorneys. It is supported by no evidence and the Commission decide that the applicant is not a Cherokee by blood.
P.O. Blossom Prairie, Texas.

	Will P. Ross	
Attest	Chairman	
D.S. Williams	R. Bunch	Commissioner
Asst. Clk Com	J.E. Gunter	Com

OUMILLER

Docket #429
Rolls1835

Applicants for Cherokee Citizenship

Post Office: Moorehead I.T.   **Attorney:**

N°	NAMES	AGE	SEX
1	Mary E Oumiller	28	Female
2	John H. Johnson	25	Male
3	Nancy Water	20	Female

Cherokee Citizenship Commission Docket Books
(1880-84, 1887-89) Volume II
Tahlequah, Cherokee Nation

4	Lizzie Oumiller	2½	Female

Ancestor: Anna Rogers

Rejected May 16 – 89

Office Commission on Citizenship C.N.I.T.
Tahlequah May 16th 1889

This application was filed the 15th day of August 1887, and was this day called three several times without answer. It is supported by no evidence and the Commission decide that Mary E. Oumiller and his[sic] Brother John H. Johnson aged 25 yrs and Sister Nancy Water aged 20 yrs and Daughter Lizzie Oumiller are not Cherokees by blood and not entitled to Citizenship in the Cherokee Nation.

P.O. Address Morehead In. Ter.

	Will P. Ross	Chairman
Attest	R. Bunch	Com
D.S. Williams	J.E. Gunter	Com
Asst. Clk Com		

COOPER

Docket #430
Rolls 1835

Applicants for Cherokee Citizenship

Post Office: Lewisville Texas **Attorney:** AE Ivey

N°	NAMES	AGE	SEX
1	T C Cooper	32	Male
2	Willie May Cooper	5	Female
3	Lou Eve Cooper	3	"

Ancestor: Lucrecy Wheeler

Now on this the 19th day of July 1888, the above case coming up for final action, it being submitted by Plaintiff's Atty Mr. Hitchcock.

The evidence on part of Plaintiff is of an exparte nature and while it was pronounced or admitted admissible, it fails to convince us that the applicant is of Cherokee descent. Now in summing up these cases, under the law, we are bound to take the rolls of Cherokees mentioned in the 7th Sec. of the Act creating and defining the authority of this Commission, which says: that the applicant must prove a lineal descent from some ancestor, or themselves, whose

Cherokee Citizenship Commission Docket Books
(1880-84, 1887-89) Volume II
Tahlequah, Cherokee Nation

name is on these rolls, before this Commission can readmit the applicants to Cherokee Citizenship.

Now therefore, be it remembered that the name of T.C. Cooper, or that of his alleged Cherokee ancestor, Lucrecy Wheeler, do not appear upon any of the rolls mentioned, as we have examined the same and found them to be wanting, and Thomas C. Cooper and his two children, Willie May and Lou Eva Cooper are not Cherokees by blood, and are not entitled to any of the rights and privileges of such by virtue of such blood.

D.W. Lipe   Acting Chairman Commission
John E. Gunter   Commissioner

SMITH

Docket #431
Rolls 1835

Applicant for Cherokee Citizenship

Post Office: Fort Gibson CN   **Attorney:** A.E. Ivey

N°	NAMES	AGE	SEX
1	James M Smith	32	Female[sic]
2	Eli T. Smith	7	Male
3	Fred Smith	4	"
4	John C Smith	2	"

Ancestor: Ellis Hooker

Rejected May 16 – 89

Office Commission on Citizenship
Cherokee Nation Ind. Ter'y.
Tahlequah   May 16th 1889

Application for Cherokee Citizenship

Now on this day the above case coming on for final hearing and after examining the application we fail to find any evidence filed in support of applicant's claim. The application was filed 2nd of September 1887. In the view of the fact that no evidence being filed in support of his claim the Commission decide that claimant James M. Smith aged 32 yrs, Eli T. Smith aged 7 yrs, Fred Smith aged 4 yrs, John C. Smith aged 2 yrs, Post Office Fort Gibson I.T. are not entitled to any rights or privileges in the Cherokee Nation.

Cherokee Citizenship Commission Docket Books
(1880-84, 1887-89) Volume II
Tahlequah, Cherokee Nation

Attest   Will P. Ross   Chairman
    D.S. Williams   R. Bunch   Com
    Asst Clk Com   J.E. Gunter   Com

CHASTIAN

Docket #432
Rolls 1835

Application for Cherokee Citizenship

Post Office: Dyer Ark   **Attorney:** A.E. Ivey

N°	NAMES	AGE	SEX
1	John S. Chastian	54	Male
2	John B. Chastian	17	"
3	Edward D. Chastian	17	"
4	James R. Chastian	15	"
5	Leona C. Chastian	12	Female
6	Milton B. Chastian	3	Male

Ancestor: John Rogers

Now on this the 17th day of March 1888, comes the above case for a final hearing, and the parties having made application pursuant to the provisions of an Act of the National Council approved December 8th 1886, and all the evidence being duly considered and found to be insufficient and unsatisfactory, it is adjudged and declared by the Commission that,

John S. Chastian, John B. Chastian, Edward D. Chastian, James R. Chastian, Leona C. Chastian and Milton B. Chastian, are not Cherokees, and they are not entitled to the rights, privileges and immunities of Cherokee Citizens by blood.

           J.T. Adair,   Chairman Commission
           John E. Gunter   Commissioner
           D.W. Lipe   Commissioner

Attest
    C.C. Lipe
    Clk Com.

The decision in the James C.C. Rogers case found on Book C, page 637 and testimony found in Journal page 325 to 333 – proves this case –

Cherokee Citizenship Commission Docket Books
(1880-84, 1887-89) Volume II
Tahlequah, Cherokee Nation

LYON

Docket #433
Rolls 1835

Applicant for Cherokee Citizenship

Post Office: Bentonville Ark **Attorney:** Boudinot & Rasmus

N°	NAMES	AGE	SEX
1	Lenora Lyon	20	Female

Ancestor: Asbell

Office Commission on Citizenship
Cherokee Nation July 3rd 1889

There being no evidence in support of the above named case the Commission decide that Lenora Lyon aged 20 years is not a Cherokee by blood. Post Office Bentonville Ark.

Attest
E.G. Ross
Clerk Commission

Will P. Ross
Chairman
John E. Gunter
Com

JACKSON

Docket #434
Rolls 1835

Application for Cherokee Citizenship

Post Office: Bentonville Ark **Attorney:** Boudinot & Rasmus

N°	NAMES	AGE	SEX
1	Martha Jackson	40	Female
2	Hugh J Jackson	19	Male
3	Arthur E Jackson	16	"
4	Arka J Jackson	14	Female
5	Maud E Jackson	10	"
6	Chester E. Jackson	6	Male
7	George P Jackson	3	"
8	Frank A Jackson	1	"

Ancestor: M Asbell

Cherokee Citizenship Commission Docket Books
(1880-84, 1887-89) Volume II
Tahlequah, Cherokee Nation

Office Commission on Citizenship
Cherokee Nation Ind. Ter.
Tahlequah July 2nd 1889

There being no evidence in support of the above named case the Commission decide that Martha S Jackson age 40 years, and the following children, Hugh male age 19 yrs, Arthur E. male age 16 yrs, Arka J. Female age 14 yrs, Maud E. Female age 10 yrs, Chester E, male age 6 yrs, George P, male age 3 yrs and Frank A. Jackson male age 1 yr are not Cherokees by blood. Post Office Bentonville Ark.

                              Will P. Ross
Attest   Chairman
    D.S. Williams   John E. Gunter   Com
Asst. Clerk Commission

TURNHAM

Docket #435
Rolls 1835

Applicant for Cherokee Citizenship
Post Office: Chocoville Ark   **Attorney:** Boudinot & Rasmus

N°	NAMES	AGE	SEX
1	Sarah A. Turnham	36	
2	Joseph M Turnham	17	
3	Sarah J Turnham		
4	Pinkney B Turnham		
5	Ellen M Turnham		
6	Miney L Turnham		
7	William A Turnham		
8	Edgar M Turnham		
9	Irvin W. Turnham		

Ancestor: Andrew Miller

Office Commission on Citizenship
Tahlequah May 14th 1889

Now on this day was submitted the case of Sarah A. Turnham, applicant for Cherokee Citizenship for a final hearing the case having been filed the 2nd day of September 1887. Now the Commission after an examination of the

Cherokee Citizenship Commission Docket Books
(1880-84, 1887-89) Volume II
Tahlequah, Cherokee Nation

papers in said case fail to find any evidence in support of application whom it alleges that Sarah A. Turnham was a Grand Daughter of one Andrew Miller now in support of the above facts the Commission are of the opinion that Sarah A. Turnham aged 36 years and her children named as follows: Joseph M. Turnham Male 17 years, Sarah J Turnham Female aged 14 years, Pinkney B. Turnham Male aged 12 years, Ellen M. Turnham Female aged 10 years, Miney L. Turnham Female aged 8 years, William A. Turnham Male aged 6 years, Edgar M. Turnham Male aged 4 years, and Irvan[sic] W. Turnham Male aged 1 year are not Cherokees by blood and are not entitled to Citizenship in the Cherokee Nation. Post Office Chocoville Ark.

                                        Will P. Ross   Chairman
                                        R. Bunch   Com
Attest   E.G. Ross   J.E. Gunter   Com
        Clk Com

COLEMAN

Docket #436
Rolls 1835

                              Applicant for Cherokee Citizenship

Post Office: Muskogee Ind Terry   **Attorney:** Boudinot & Rasmus

N°	NAMES	AGE	SEX
1	Nancy A Coleman	23	Female
2	James F Coleman	5	Male
3	Margaret G Coleman	2	Female

                 Ancestor: James U Richardson

                          Office Commission on Citizenship
                                Tahlequah CN June 15th 1889

There being no evidence in support of the above named case the Commission decide that Nancy A. Coleman age 23 years and the following named children James F. Coleman and Margaret G. Coleman aged 5 and 2 years respectfully are not of Cherokee blood. Post Office Muskogee IT

Attest   Will P. Ross
   E.G. Ross   Chairman
   Clerk Commission   R. Bunch   Com
                              JE. Gunter   Com

Cherokee Citizenship Commission Docket Books (1880-84, 1887-89) Volume II
Tahlequah, Cherokee Nation

GRAYSON

Docket #437
Rolls 1835

Applicant for Cherokee Citizenship
Post Office: Muskogee Nation   **Attorney:** W.P. Ross

N°	NAMES	AGE	SEX
1	Kate Grayson	28	Female
2	Della Grayson	6	"
3	Claud Grayson	3	Male

Ancestor: Richard Ross

Now on this 14th day of September 1887, comes the above case for final hearing and having made application pursuant to the provisions of an Act of the National Council approved December 8th 1886, and all of the evidence being duly examined and found to be sufficient and satisfactory to the Commission it is adjudged and determined by the Commission therefore, Kate R. Grayson, Della E. Grayson & Claud R. Grayson are Cherokee by blood, and they are hereby readmitted to all the rights, privileges and immunities of Cherokee Citizens by blood.

And a certificate of said decision of the Commission and of readmission was made and furnished said parties accordingly.

C.C. Lipe   J.T. Adair   Chairman Commission
Clk Commission   John E. Gunter   Commissioner
                                             Commissioner

DINSMORE

Docket #438
Rolls 1835

Applicant for Cherokee Citizenship
Post Office: Tahlequah C.N.   **Attorney:** C.H. Taylor

N°	NAMES	AGE	SEX
1	Lizzie Dinsmore	46	Female
2	William L. Dinsmore	19	Male

Ancestor: Polly Smith

Cherokee Citizenship Commission Docket Books
(1880-84, 1887-89) Volume II
Tahlequah, Cherokee Nation

The Application of Lizzie Dinsmore for admission to Citizenship in the Cherokee Nation of herself and son William L. Dinsmore aged nineteen years, filed Aug. 31st 1887. Also submitted by Attorney the 11th day of April 1889. The applicant alleges that she is the Grand Daughter of Polly Smith nee Polly Miller whose name would be found on the census roll of Cherokee by blood made in 1835. The census roll does not show the fact alleged while the age of applicant in 1887, is placed at fifty six years in her application and at thirty-seven in her sworn statement in support of her own claim before the Commission in 1888. The testimony of J.M. Taylor shows that he was well acquainted with her and her Family in Tennessee where they made no claim to Cherokee blood and that it was after her arrival in this country that she wished him to aid her in procuring evidence in support of her alleged Cherokee descent. For these reasons the Commission adjudge and decree that Lizzie Dinsmore the applicant and her son Wm L. Dinsmore are not of Cherokee blood and are not entitled to admission into the Cherokee Nation as Citizens.

                         Will P. Ross   Chairman
                         John E. Gunter   Commissioner

Attest
     D.S. Williams Clk Com

TAYLOR

Docket #439
Rolls 1887

                         Applicant for Cherokee Citizenship
Post Office: Tahlequah CN   **Attorney:** C.H. Taylor

N°	NAMES	AGE	SEX
1	Louisa J Taylor	24	Female

                Ancestor: Polly Smith

                    Office Commission on Citizenship
                         Tahlequah May 17th 1889

Now on this day the above case coming on for final hearing. The claimant filed on her application on the 2nd day of August 1887. She claims her Cherokee blood through one Polly Smith. After examining the papers submitted by applicant we find no evidence accompaning[sic] the application in support of her claim. In view of these facts the Commission decide that Louiza[sic] Taylor

Cherokee Citizenship Commission Docket Books
(1880-84, 1887-89) Volume II
Tahlequah, Cherokee Nation

age 24 years Post Office Tahlequah I.T. is not a Cherokee by blood and not entitled to any rights and privileges of Cherokee Citizenship.

Attest   Will P. Ross   Chairman
     E.G. Ross   R. Bunch   Com
          Clerk Commission   J.E. Gunter   Com.

MILLS

Docket #440
Rolls 1835

Applicant for Cherokee Citizenship

Post Office: Tahlequah CN   **Attorney:** C.H. Taylor

N°	NAMES	AGE	SEX
1	Malisa Mills	22	Female
2	James E Mills	4	Male

Ancestor: Polly Smith

Rejected May 16 – 89

         Office Commission on Citizenship Cher Nat Ind Ter'y
                 Tahlequah May 16 1889

The application in this case was filed 2nd day of September 1887 and this day submitted by Attorneys. It is accompanied by no evidence to sustain the alleged descent of the applicants from a Cherokee Indian named Polly Smith. The Commission therefore decide that Wm L Dinsmore age 19 yrs and Louisa J. Taylor nee Louisa J. Dinsmore the wife of James E. Taylor a citizen of the Cherokee Nation and Malisa Mills nee Malisa Dinsmore the wife of Otto Mills a white man are not of Cherokee blood. P.O. address Tahlequah Ind. Ter'y.

Attest   Will P. Ross
     D.S. Williams   Chairman
     Asst Clk Com   R. Bunch   Commissioner
                   J.E. Gunter   Com

Cherokee Citizenship Commission Docket Books
(1880-84, 1887-89) Volume II
Tahlequah, Cherokee Nation

PARKS

Docket #441
Rolls 1835

Applicant for Cherokee Citizenship

Post Office: Joplin Mo **Attorney:** C.H. Taylor

N°	NAMES	AGE	SEX
1	George W. Parks	56	Male
2	Samuel R. Parks	25	"
3	George E. Parks	23	"

Ancestor: Samuel Parks

Office Commission on Citizenship
Cherokee Nation I.T.
Tahlequah May 29, 1889

The application in the above case was filed on the 2nd day of September 1887 and was submitted May 23rd 1889 for a final hearing without evidence. The Commission therefore decide that George W. Parks whose age of fifty six years, and his children named as follows Samuel male, aged twenty five years and George E. Parks male aged twenty three years are not of Cherokee blood and are not entitled to Citizenship in the Cherokee Nation.

Attest
E.G. Ross
Clk Com

Will P. Ross   Chairman
R. Bunch   Com
J.E. Gunter   Com

BROWN

Docket #442
Rolls 1835 & 52

Applicant for Cherokee Citizenship

Post Office: Uniontown Ark **Attorney:** AE Ivey

N°	NAMES	AGE	SEX
1	John Thomas Brown	48	Male
2	Charles F. Brown	15	"
3	John Brown	13	"
4	Susan Lona Brown	8	Female

Ancestor: Alex Brown

Cherokee Citizenship Commission Docket Books
(1880-84, 1887-89) Volume II
Tahlequah, Cherokee Nation

Office Commission on Citizenship C.N.I.T.
Tahlequah May 17th 1889

The application in the above case was filed the 2nd day of September 1887. It is supported by no evidence nor is the name of the alleged ancestor Alex Brown found on the rolls of Cherokees as claimed – The Commission therefore decide that John Thomas Brown age 48 yrs and Charles F. Brown aged 15 yrs, John Brown 13 yrs and Susan Lona Brown aged 8 yrs are not Cherokees by blood and not entitled to Citizenship in the Cherokee Nation. P.O. Union Town, Ark.

Attest
   D.S. Williams
   Asst. Clk Com

Will P. Ross
   Chairman
R. Bunch   Com
J.E Gunter   Com

TAYLOR

Docket #443
Rolls 1835

Applicant for Cherokee Citizenship

Post Office: South West City Mo   **Attorney:** CH Taylor

N°	NAMES	AGE	SEX
1	William Taylor	28	Male
2	John H. Taylor	10	"
3	Tennessee C. Taylor	8	Female
4	Sarah Taylor	6	"
5	William E. Taylor	4	Male
6	Emily A. Taylor	2	Female
7	Emmerson Taylor	4 mo	Male

Ancestor: George Taylor

See decision in the John A. Taylor case in Book B. Page 158

Attest
   D.S. Williams
   Asst Clk Com

Will P. Ross
   Chairman
J E Gunter   Com

Cherokee Citizenship Commission Docket Books
(1880-84, 1887-89) Volume II
Tahlequah, Cherokee Nation

DAVIS

Docket #444
Rolls 1835

Applicant for Cherokee Citizenship

Post Office: Tiff City Mo   **Attorney:** CH Taylor

N°	NAMES	AGE	SEX
1	Emma J Davis	17	Female
2	Manda Davis	6 mo	"

Ancestor: George Taylor

See decision in the John A. Taylor case in Book B. Page 158.

Office Commission on Citizenship
Tahlequah CN May 17th 1889

Now on this day the above case comes up on for final hearing and after examining the application which was filed September 2nd we fail to find any evidence accompaning[sic] the application in support of applicant's claim of Cherokee by blood and in view of this fact we decide that claimant Emma J. David age 17 years and her daughter Manda Davis age 6 months are not Cherokees by blood and are not entitled to Cherokee Citizenship. Post Office Tiff City Mo.

Attest
E.G. Ross

Will P. Ross
Chairman
JE Gunter   Com

TAYLOR

Docket #445
Rolls 1835

Applicant for Cherokee Citizenship

Post Office: Tiff City Mo   **Attorney:** CH Taylor

N°	NAMES	AGE	SEX
1	John A Taylor	46	Male
2	Levada Taylor	14	Female
3	Arazona Taylor	7	"
	Idia Taylor	5	"

Ancestor: Geo Taylor

Cherokee Citizenship Commission Docket Books
(1880-84, 1887-89) Volume II
Tahlequah, Cherokee Nation

Commission on Citizenship.

CHEROKEE NATION, IND. TER.

John A. Taylor, et al   Tahlequah, Sept. 29th 1889
(vs)
Cherokee Nation

    In the matter of the claim of John A Taylor & family and William T. Taylor & family for Cherokee citizenship filed in this office on the 30th day of August 1887 and alleging George Taylor from whom they have attempted to prove a Cherokee descent. We the Commission on Citizenship have taken up these cases, and at once agree that the applicants are not Cherokees by blood as they have failed to prove from an ancestor whose name appears on some one of the rolls mentioned in the 7th Section of the Act of Dec 8th 1886, in relation to citizenship, therefore; John A. Taylor and his three children, viz: Levada, Arazona and Idia Taylor and William Taylor and his six children, viz: John H, Tennessee C, Sarah, William E, Emily A and Emerson Taylor, are not entitled to any of the rights, privileges and immunities of Cherokee Citizenship and the Commission do hereby so declare.

                        J.T. Adair   Chairman Commission
                        H.C. Barnes   Commissioner

WATTS

Docket #446
Rolls 1835

Applicant for Cherokee Citizenship
Post Office: Enan[sic] Ark   **Attorney:** CH Taylor

N°	NAMES	AGE	SEX
1	Sarah L Watts	27	Female
2	Minnie Watts	6	"
3	Fits Watts	4	Male
4	Francis M Watts	2	Male

Ancestor: Geo Taylor

Rejected

Cherokee Citizenship Commission Docket Books
(1880-84, 1887-89) Volume II
Tahlequah, Cherokee Nation

Office Commission on Citizenship
Tahlequah C N May 18th 1889

The application in the above case was filed the 2nd day of September 1887, and submitted by Attorney this day without evidence. The Commission therefore decide that Sarah L Watts aged 27 years and Minnie Watts aged six years and Fitts Watts aged four years and Francis M Watts, aged two years are not of Cherokee blood. Post Office Enan[sic], Ark.

Attest
    E.G. Ross
       Clerk Commission

Will P. Ross
    Chairman
J.E. Gunter   Com

CAPP

Docket #447
Rolls 1835

Applicant for Cherokee Citizenship

Post Office: Babtist[sic] Mission IT   **Attorney:** C.H. Taylor

N°	NAMES	AGE	SEX
1	Pricey Capp	84	female
2	Richard Capp	15	male
3	Samuel Capp	13	"

Ancestor: Charles and Katy *(Illegible)*

Office Commission Citizenship
Tahlequah C.N. May 18th 1889

This application was filed 2nd day of September 1887 and submitted this day without evidence further than her own statement. The Commission therefore decide that the applicant Pricy Capps, aged 84 years and Richard Capp Grand son aged fifteen years, and Samuel Capps Grand son aged thirteen years are not of Cherokee blood and not entitled to Cherokee Citizenship. P.O. Baptist Mission I.T.

                Will P. Ross   Chairman
Attest   J.E. Gunter   Com
    E.G. Ross
    Clk Com.

Cherokee Citizenship Commission Docket Books
(1880-84, 1887-89) Volume II
Tahlequah, Cherokee Nation

JONES

Docket #448
Rolls 1835

Applicant for Cherokee Citizenship
Post Office: Colfax, Placer Co, Cal   **Attorney:** A.J. Ridge

N°	NAMES	AGE	SEX
1	James Jones	54	Male

Ancestor: Jesse Jones

Rejected July 5th 1889

Office Commission Citizenship
Cher Nat.
July 5th 1889

There being no evidence in the above named case for its support, the Commission decides that James Jones, age 54 yrs, is not a Cherokee by blood. Post office, Colfax Placer Co Cal.

D.S. Williams	Will P. Ross
Clerk – Commission	Chairman
	John E. Gunter
	Com

CRAIG

Docket #449
Rolls 1835

Applicant for Cherokee Citizenship
Post Office: Howe Ark   **Attorney:** A.E. Ivey

N°	NAMES	AGE	SEX
1	John W. Craig	31	Male
2	Mary E Craig	16	female
3	Caleb Craig	14	male
4	Dartha J. Craig	12	female
5	William A. Craig	10	male
6	Lee N. Craig	8	"
7	L.M. Craig	5	female
8	Samuel Craig	2	male

Ancestor: John Craig

Cherokee Citizenship Commission Docket Books
(1880-84, 1887-89) Volume II
Tahlequah, Cherokee Nation

On the 23rd day of March A.D. 1888, comes the above case up for final hearing. the applicants having made application pursuant to the provisions of an Act of the National Council approved Dec 8th 1886, and all the evidence being duly examined and found to be insufficient and unsatisfactory to the Commission, it is adjudged and determined by the Commission that John W. Craig, Mary E – Caleb – Dartha J – William A – Lee N – L.M. – and Samuel Craig, are <u>not</u> Cherokees by blood and are hereby declared to be intruders.

                J.T. Adair   Chairman Commission
                John E. Gunter Commissioner
                D.W. Lipe   Commissioner

Cornell Rogers
Clk Commission

CRAIG

Docket #450
Rolls 1835

Applicant for Cherokee Citizenship
Post Office: Howe, Ark.   **Attorney:** A.E. Ivey

N°	NAMES	AGE	SEX
1	J.E. Craig	33	Male
2	Brassiter Craig	7	"
3	David M. Craig	5	"
4	Maggie J. Craig	1 mo	female

Ancestor: John Craig

On the 23rd day of March A.D. 1888, comes the above case up for final hearing. they having made application pursuant to the provisions of an Act of the National Council approved Dec 8th 1886, and all the evidence being duly examined and found to be insufficient and unsatisfactory to the Commission, it is adjudged and determined by the Commission that they J.E. – Brassiter – David M and Maggie J. Craig, are <u>not</u> Cherokees by blood and are not entitled to the immunities and rights of such, and are hereby declared to be intruders.

                J.T. Adair   Chairman Commission
                John E. Gunter Commissioner
                D.W. Lipe   Commissioner

Cherokee Citizenship Commission Docket Books
(1880-84, 1887-89) Volume II
Tahlequah, Cherokee Nation

Cornell Rogers
Clk Commission

The evidence in this case will be found on Journal pages 336 to 341 in the case of G.W. Craig.

CRAIG

Docket #451
Rolls 1835

Applicant for Cherokee Citizenship

Post Office: Tahlequah C.N.   **Attorney:** A.E. Ivey

N°	NAMES	AGE	SEX
1	G.W. Craig	44	Male
2	James G. Craig	19	"
3	Martha C. Craig	15	female
4	Josiah Craig	13	male
5	George W. Craig	11	"
6	Sarah A. Craig	9	female

Ancestor: John Craig

G.W. Craig & others   Office Commission on Citizenship
    (vs)   Tahlequah I.T. Mch 23rd 1888
Cherokee Nation

The above case was this day submitted to the Commission for final hearing, and by an agreement entered into by the Attorney for the defendant and plaintiff this case was made a *(illegible)* one, and the findings of this Commission shall govern all other cases who claim their Cherokee blood from John Craig or his descendants.

The first witness examined was George Wilkerson who states he is a resident of Tahlequah Dist and is Sixty Six years old and knew one John Craig in the Old Nation near Red Clay and started in the same detachment with him to this Nation, but took sick and stoped[sic] in Missouri. he had ~~childr~~ three or four children but didn't five their names, and did not know who this John Craig was a white man or not, but sayes[sic] his wife was a Cherokee, but don't know what family she was of, or what part of the Old Nation she was from, said it was in

Cherokee Citizenship Commission Docket Books
(1880-84, 1887-89) Volume II
Tahlequah, Cherokee Nation

the year 1836 he left John Craig in Mo, said he thought the applicant's father's name was Jim Craig.

David Bales states that Jim Craig was father of applicant, and John Craig was his grand father, and he (John) had two brothers Tom and Sam Craig, and states that Sam Craig's wife was a Haslaw and a Cherokee by blood.

Bates' statement as to Sam Craig is correct as the census rolls of 1835, show that he was enrolled as a white man and that his wife was a Cherokee by blood.

The statement of F.M. Bates and America Rose, is of a hear say nature and therefore cannot attach much importance to it.

The testimony of Judge Adair, a man ~~of~~ 75 years old and who was well acquainted in Georgia & Tenn, states that he never knew any Cherokees by the name of Craig, but his understanding was that one Sam Craig a white man married a Cherokee by the name of Haslaw.

The statement of Nancy Haslaw a resident of the Nation and a lady ~~of~~ 88 years old states she was acquainted with Sam Craig, he lived in Bradley Co Tenn, old Nation, and that he married her husbands cousin, who was Eliza Haslaw and a Cherokee by blood, and further states he came west in the year 1838 with the emigration, and stoped[sic] in the state of Missouri on account of sickness, and never came to this Nation.

It will be seen that Geo Wilkerson states that John Craig came to Missouri and stoped[sic] on account of sickness, but Mrs. Nancy Haslaw sayes[sic] that Sam Craig came with the emigration and stoped[sic] in Missouri on account of sickness, but makes no mention about John. it is evident to this Commission that Mrs Haslaw was in a better position to know the Craig family than Mr. Wilkerson, for the reason that she was connected by marriage and the census rolls of 1835 bear her out in her statements. the rolls show that Sam Craig appears and not John Craig.

Therefore we the Commission after examining all the evidence in the case, and the census rolls of 1835, find that, G.W. – James W – Martha C – Josiah – George W & Sarah A. Craig in Application No. 1 – Nancy J Null & Rosetta Drinen, in Application No. 2 – John W. – Mary E – Caleb – Dartha J –

Cherokee Citizenship Commission Docket Books
(1880-84, 1887-89) Volume II
Tahlequah, Cherokee Nation

Wm A – Lee N – L.M. and Samuel Craig in Application No. 3 J.E. – Braister M – David B and Maggie J Craig, in Application No. 4, are <u>not</u> Cherokees by blood and not entitled to any rights & privileges of this Nation.

                                      J.T. Adair   Chairman Commission
                                      John E. Gunter Commissioner
                                      D.W. Lipe   Commissioner

Evidence on Journal pages 336 to 341 in *(illegible)*.

NULL

Docket #452
Rolls 1835

                                                Applicant for Cherokee Citizenship
Post Office: Rago Mill Ark   **Attorney:** A.E. Ivey

N°	NAMES	AGE	SEX
1	Nancy J Null	28	female
2	Rosetta Drinen	9	"

Ancestor: John Craig

On on[sic] this the 23rd day of March A.D. 1888, comes the above case up for final action and hearing, the applicants having made application pursuant to the provisions of an Act of the National Council approved Dec 8th 1886, and all the evidence being duly examined and found not to be sufficient and not satisfactory to the Commission and the name of the ancestor John Craig, not appearing on the rolls as claimed in the application, it is adjudged and determined by the Commission that Nancy J. Null and Rosetta Drinen, are <u>not</u> Cherokees by blood and are hereby <u>rejected</u> and declared intruders.

                                      J.T. Adair   Chairman Commission
                                      John E. Gunter Commissioner
                                      D.W. Lipe   Commissioner

Cornell Rogers
    Clk Commission

    The evidence in this case will be found on Journal pages 336 to 341 in the case of G.W. Craig.

Cherokee Citizenship Commission Docket Books
(1880-84, 1887-89) Volume II
Tahlequah, Cherokee Nation

CRUTCHFIELD

Docket #453
Rolls 1852

Applicant for Cherokee Citizenship
Post Office: **Attorney:** A.E. Ivey

N°	NAMES	AGE	SEX
1	W.W. Cruchfield[sic]	22	Male
2	Claud Cruchfield[sic]	4	"
3	Mary Cruchfield[sic]	3	female

Ancestor: John Cruchfield[sic]

Now on this the 2nd day of October 1888 comes the above case for a final hearing, and the parties having made application pursuant to an Act of the National Council approved December 8th 1886, and all the evidence having been duly examined and found to be sufficient and satisfactory. It is adjudged and determined by the Commission that S.W. Cruchfield[sic] and his two children, Claude Cruchfield[sic] and Mary Cruchfield[sic] are Cherokees by blood and are hereby re-admitted to all the rights, privileges and immunities of other Cherokees by blood.

And a certificate of said decision of the Commission and re-admission are made and furnished said parties accordingly.

J.T. Adair   Chairman Commission
C.C. Barnes   Commissioner

Attest
   C.C. Lipe
   Clerk, Com.

SIZEMORE

Docket #454
Rolls 1835 to 1852

Applicant for Cherokee Citizenship
Post Office: Grant, Madison Co, Ark. **Attorney:** Boudinot & Rasmus

N°	NAMES	AGE	SEX
1	Willis D. Sizemore	57	Male

Cherokee Citizenship Commission Docket Books
(1880-84, 1887-89) Volume II
Tahlequah, Cherokee Nation

| 2 | Leander Sizemore | 16 | " |
| 3 | Tennessee Sizemore | 13 | female |

Ancestor: Henry Sizemore

See decision in this case in the Sarah A. Bond case on Book "A" page 235 – Adverse to applicant

                Cornell Rogers
                Clk Com on Citizenship

Office Com on Citizenship
Tahlequah I.T. Sept. 19th 1888

CLEMMONS

Docket #455
Rolls 1835

                                        Applicant for Cherokee Citizenship

Post Office: Whiteright[sic], Tex   **Attorney:** C.H. Taylor

N°	NAMES	AGE	SEX
1	M.P. Clemmons	56	Male
2	Jodie Clemmons	18	female
3	Ottis D. Clemmons	15	male

Ancestor: Agnes Childress

Rejected May 18 – 1889

                          Office Commission on Citizenship
                          Cherokee Nation Ind. Ter.
                          Tahlequah May 18 – 1889

The application in the above case was filed the 5th day of September 1887 and submitted by Attorneys May 18th 1889 without evidence. The Commission therefore decide that Mrs. M.P. Clemmons aged 56 yrs and Jodie R. Clemmons (daughter) aged 18 yrs, and Ottis D. Clemmons (son) aged fifteen yrs are not Cherokees by blood and not entitled to Citizenship in the Cherokee Nation.

Attest   Will P. Ross   Chairman
    D.S. Williams   J.E. Gunter   Com
    Asst Clk Com.

Cherokee Citizenship Commission Docket Books
(1880-84, 1887-89) Volume II
Tahlequah, Cherokee Nation

RAPER, Jr.

Docket #456
Rolls 1835 to 1852

Applicant for Cherokee Citizenship
Post Office: **Attorney:** Boudinot & Rasmus

N°	NAMES	AGE	SEX
1	Charles Raper, Jr.	32	Male
2	Cora Raper	6	female
3	Young Raper	2	male
4	Infant, unnamed	2 mo	"

Ancestor: Charles Raper, Sr.

Now on this the 23rd day of April 1888, comes the above case up for final hearing, and having made application pursuant to the provisions of an Act of the National Council approved Dec 8th 1886, and all the evidence being duly considered and found to be sufficient and satisfactory to the Commission, it is adjudged and determined by the Commission, that Charles Raper, Jr, Cora Raper, Young Raper and Infant, unnamed, are Cherokees by blood, and they are hereby re admitted to all the rights, privileges and immunities of Cherokee citizens by blood.   A certificate of re-admission was made and furnished said parties accordingly.

J.T. Adair,   Chairman Commission
John E. Gunter   Commissioner

PERIMAN

Docket #457
Rolls 1835 to 1852

Applicants for Cherokee Citizenship
Post Office: Dudenville, Mo.   **Attorney:** Boudinot and Rasmus

N°	NAMES	AGE	SEX
1	Mary E Periman	33	female
2	Minnie Periman	17	"
3	William Periman	15	male
4	Ada Periman	13	female
5	Oscar Periman	22	male
6	Agnes Periman	7	female
7	Glenard Periman	5	male

Cherokee Citizenship Commission Docket Books
(1880-84, 1887-89) Volume II
Tahlequah, Cherokee Nation

8	Mattie Periman	3	female

Ancestor: Edith Grant

Office Commission on Citizenship Tahlequah I.T. Aug. 9 – '88

The above case being submitted it was duly considered, together with the rolls mentioned in the 7th Sec. of the Act of Dec 8th 1886, as well as those laid down in the amendment of Feb'y 7th 1888, in connection thereto, but fail to find the name of Edith Grant, or Martha Alsup, or that of the applicant, Mary E. Periman enrolled thereon. In the absence of which not withstanding the testimony this Commission cannot admit them to citizenship & therefore declared Mary E Periman and her seven children, viz: Minnie, William, Ada, Oscar, Agnes, Glenard, and Mattie Periman, not to be Cherokees by blood and not entitled to the rights and privileges of such.

        J.T. Adair   Chairman Commission
        H.C. Barnes Commissioner

MURRELL

Docket #458
Rolls 1835

Applicants for Cherokee Citizenship

Post Office: Lynchburg, Va. **Attorney:** Wm P. Ross

N°	NAMES	AGE	SEX
1	Amanda R. Murrell	58	female
2	George Ross Murrell	25	male
3	Fanney E. Murrell	23	female
4	Rosanna E Murrell	20	"
5	Lewis Edward Murrell	13	male

Ancestor: Lewis Ross

Now on this the 26th day of August 1887 comes the above case for final hearing and the above named parties having made application pursuant to the provisions of the National Council approved December 8th 1887 and all the evidence having been duly considered and found to be sufficient and satisfactory to the Commission, it is adjudged and determined to the by the Commission that Amanda R. Murrell, Geo Ross Murrell, Fannie E. Murrell, Rosanna E. Murrell and Lewis Edward Murrell are Cherokees by blood and are hereby readmitted to all rights, privileges and immunities of Cherokees by blood.

Cherokee Citizenship Commission Docket Books
(1880-84, 1887-89) Volume II
Tahlequah, Cherokee Nation

And a certificate of said decision of the Commission and of re-admission was made and furnished said parties accordingly.

Henry Eiffert
    Clk Com.

J.T. Adair   Chairman Commission
John E Gunter   Commissioner
D.W. Lipe   Commissioner

TAYLOR

Docket #459
Rolls 1835 to 1852

Applicant for Cherokee Citizenship

Post Office: Hanford, Tulare Co, Cal.   **Attorney:**

N°	NAMES	AGE	SEX
1	Susan C. Taylor	33	female
2	Alma R. Taylor	3	"

Ancestor: John B. Choate

We the Commission on Citizenship after carefully examining the evidence in the above case, and also the Old Settler pay rolls of 1851, and the Emigrant pay rolls of 1852, find the applicants Susie C. Taylor and her child Alma R. Taylor, to be Cherokees by blood, and they are hereby re-admitted to all the rights and privileges of Cherokee citizens by blood, which is in compliance with an Act of the National Council dated Dec. 8th 1886, and amendment thereto dated Febr'y. 7th 1888.

J.T. Adair   Chairman Commission
D.W. Lipe   Commissioner

Office Commission on Citizenship
Tahlequah Ind. Ter. July 4th 1888.

Cherokee Citizenship Commission Docket Books
(1880-84, 1887-89) Volume II
Tahlequah, Cherokee Nation

COTNER

Docket #460
Rolls 1835

Application for Cherokee Citizenship

Post Office: Sanders, I.T.   **Attorney:** A.E. Ivey

N°	NAMES	AGE	SEX
1	Pauline Cotner	33	Female
2	William Cotner	10	Male
3	Allie Cotner	8	Female
4	Babe Cotner	6	"
5	Robert J.H. Cotner	4	Male
6	Melt in "	2	"

Ancestor: Shade and Eleza Gentry

Office Commission on Citizenship
Tahlequah C.N. May 18th 1889

This application was filed on the 9th day of September 1887. There being no evidence in support of the application and the names of alleged ancestors not being found on the census roll of Cherokees made in the[sic] 1835, the Commission decide that Pauline Cortner[sic] the applicant is not of Cherokee blood and not entitled to Citizenship in the Cherokee Nation.

Attest   Will P. Ross
  E.G. Ross   Chairman
      Clerk Commission   R. Bunch   Com

BLANCETT

Docket #461
Rolls 1835

Applicant for Cherokee Citizenship

Post Office: Sanders, I.T.   **Attorney:** A.E. Ivey

N°	NAMES	AGE	SEX
1	Hardin Blancett	37	Male
2	Sarah E. Blancett	10	female
3	Laura A Blancett	8	"
4	Myrtie F. Blancett	6	"
5	Desdemonia Blancett	2	"

Cherokee Citizenship Commission Docket Books
(1880-84, 1887-89) Volume II
Tahlequah, Cherokee Nation

6	Akie Blancett	6 mo	"

Ancestor: Shade and Eleza Gentry

Office Commission on Citizenship C.N. I.T.
Tahlequah May 18th 1889

Now on this day comes the application of Harden Blancett for a final hearing to Cherokee Citizenship. This case was filed on the 8th day of September 1887 alleging that Harden Blancett to be a grand son of one Shade & Eliza Gentry nee Ballard and whose name would be found on census rolls of Cherokees taken and made in the year 1835; the above case was called 3 several times at not less than one hour at intervals and then comes the Attorney & submitted the case without any evidence in support of application. Now, we the Commission are of the opinion the Harden Blancett with his Family, Sarah E. 10 yrs, Laura A. 8 yrs, Myrtie F. 6 yrs. Desdemonia 2 yrs & Akie Blancett age 6 months are not Cherokees by blood & are not entitled to Cherokee Citizenship. P.O. Sanders I.T.

	Will P. Ross	Chairman
Attest	R. Bunch	Com
D.S. Williams	J.E. Gunter	Com
Asst Clk Com		

LAWRENCE

Docket #462
Rolls 1835 to 1852

Applicant for Cherokee Citizenship

Post Office: Carr, Mo.   **Attorney:** A.E. Ivey

N°	NAMES	AGE	SEX
1	James F. Lawrence	24	Male

Ancestor: Lucy Bryant

Rejected May 18 – 89

Office Commission on Citizenship Cher Nat I.T.
Tahlequah May 18th 1889

This Application filed the 9th day of September 1887, was this day submitted by Attorney without evidence. The Commission therefore decide that the applicant is not of Cherokee blood.
P.O. Carr Mo.

Cherokee Citizenship Commission Docket Books
(1880-84, 1887-89) Volume II
Tahlequah, Cherokee Nation

Attest		Will P. Ross	Chairman
	D.S. Williams	R. Bunch	Com
	Att. Clk Com	J.E. Gunter	Com

TERRY

Docket #463
Rolls 1835 to 1852

Applicant for Cherokee Citizenship

Post Office: Carr, Mo.   **Attorney:** A.E. Ivey

N°	NAMES	AGE	SEX
1	Isaac Terry	40	Male
2	Joseph R. Terry	19	"
3	William Terry	17	"
4	Elizabeth Terry	15	female
5	John Terry	13	male
6	Dora Bell Terry	11	female
7	Wiley C. Terry	9	male
8	Robert Terry	7	"
9	A.M. Terry	5	"
10	Manda Terry	3	female

Ancestor: Hiram Bryant

Now on this the 26th day of June 1888, comes the above case up for final hearing, it being one of eleven case claiming a descent from one Hiram Bryant. Testimony will be found on Court pages 74 to 81. Decision will be found in this book page 211 in the Rachel Wilder case – Adverse to claimant.

	J.T. Adair	Chairman Commission
	D.W. Lipe	Commissioner

LAWRENCE

Docket #464
Rolls 1835

Applicant for Cherokee Citizenship

Post Office: Carr, Mo.   **Attorney:** A.E. Ivey

N°	NAMES	AGE	SEX
1	T.R. Lawrence	42	male

Cherokee Citizenship Commission Docket Books
(1880-84, 1887-89) Volume II
Tahlequah, Cherokee Nation

| 2 | Daniel B. Lawrence | 14 | " |

Ancestor: Hiram Bryant

Rejected May 18 – 89

Office Commission on Citizenship Cher. Nation I.T.
Tahlequah May 18th 1889

This application filed the 9th day of September 1887 and submitted by Attorney this day without evidence is decided adversely by the Commission. This decision includes the applicant – T. R. Lawrence aged forth two years, and Daniel B. Lawrence aged fourteen years. P.O. Carr, Mo.

Attest	Will P. Ross	Chairman
D.S. Williams	R. Bunch	Com
Asst. Clk Com	J.E. Gunter	Com

WOMAK

Docket #465
Rolls 1835 to 1852

Applicant for Cherokee Citizenship

Post Office: Chatfield, Texas.   **Attorney:** Boudinot & Rasmus

N°	NAMES	AGE	SEX
1	John W. Womack	43	male
2	Daisey Dell Womack	7	female
3	John Everts Womack	2	male

Ancestor: Elizabeth Womack

Rejected May 18 – 1889

Office Commission on Citizenship
Cherokee Nation Ind. Ter'y.
Tahlequah May 18th 1889.

The application in the above case was filed the 11th day of September 1887 And submitted by Attorneys May 18 1887. It is supported by no evidence and the Commission decide that John W. Womack is not of Cherokee blood and that he and Daisy Dell Womack aged 7 years and John Everts Womack aged two years, are not entitled to Citizenship in the Cherokee Nation.

Attest	Will P. Ross	Chairman
D.S. Williams	JE Gunter	Com
Asst Clk Com		

Cherokee Citizenship Commission Docket Books (1880-84, 1887-89) Volume II
Tahlequah, Cherokee Nation

RICHERSON

Docket #466
Rolls 1835 to 1852

Applicant for Cherokee Citizenship

Post Office: Detroit, Texas   **Attorney:** Boudinot and Rasmus

N°	NAMES	AGE	SEX
1	James W. Richerson	67	Male
2	John Richerson	19	female[sic]
3	Wm Brice Richerson	17	male
4	Mattie Ann Richerson	15	female

Ancestor: John Richerson

Office Commission on Citizenship
Tahlequah C.M. May 18th 1889

The application in this case was filed the 10th day of September 1887 and submitted this day by the Attorneys. As there is no evidence in support of it the Commission decide that James W. Richerson aged 67 years and his sons John Richerson aged nineteen years, and Wm Rice[sic] Richerson aged seventeen years and daughter Mattie Ann Richerson aged fifteen years, are not of Cherokee blood and not entitled to Cherokee Citizenship. Post Office Detroit, Texas.

	Will P. Ross	Chairman
Attest	J.E. Gunter	Com
E.G. Ross	R. Bunch	Commissioner
Clerk Commission		

SHAW

Docket #467
Rolls 1835 to 1852

Applicant for Cherokee Citizenship

Post Office: Childers Station, C.N.   **Attorney:** C.H. Taylor

N°	NAMES	AGE	SEX
1	George W.C. Shaw	48	Male
2	Samuel B. Shaw	24	"
3	James G.W. Shaw	13	"

Cherokee Citizenship Commission Docket Books
(1880-84, 1887-89) Volume II
Tahlequah, Cherokee Nation

4	Mathew Benj. F. Shaw	13	"
5	Hardy Rodman Shaw	8 mo	"

Ancestor: Betsey Waldroop

Rejected May 27 – 89

Office Commission on Citizenship Cherokee Nation I.T.
Tahlequah May 20th 1889

This day comes the above case for final hearing. The applicant *(illegible)* had his case before the Commission on Citizenship commonly known as the Tehee Court. That Court on January 23rd 1883 decide adversely to claimant. The evidence presented to this Commission is the same as that presented to the Tehee Court with the addition of a statement made before the Commission on Citizenship July 21st 1888 by Malinda *(Illegible)* who recoginzed[sic] G.W.C. Shaw as a relation but could not state whether from the white or Indian side and whose acquaintance with him did not excel a period of about six years. She had no personal knowledge of applicant and no information from other sources pertinent to this case. Aside from the insufficiency of the evidence to establish the Indian descent of this applicant the name of the ancestor claimed as of Cherokee blood, Betsey Waldroop is not found on the rolls of Cherokees taken and made in the years 1835-1852. The Commission therefore decide that G.W.C. Shaw and his children Samuel B. Shaw aged 24 yrs, Jas. G.W. Shaw and his twin brother Mathew Benj. F. Shaw aged 13 yrs and Hardy Rodman Shaw aged 8 months are not of Cherokee blood and not entitled to Cherokee Citizenship.

         Will P. Ross Chairman
Attest   R. Bunch and J.E. Gunter Commissioners
  D.S. Williams Asst Clk Com

HESLERODE

Docket #468
Rolls 1835 to 1852

Applicant for Cherokee Citizenship
Post Office: Fort Smith Ark **Attorney:** Wm A. Thompson

N°	NAMES	AGE	SEX
1	George Alice Heselrode[sic]	29	female
2	Bertha A. Heslerode	14	"
3	Katie E. Heslerode	12	"
4	Elie[sic] W. Heslerode	8	male

Cherokee Citizenship Commission Docket Books
(1880-84, 1887-89) Volume II
Tahlequah, Cherokee Nation

5	Charles O. Heslerode	6	"
6	Robert E. Heslerode	3	"

Ancestor: Jessie Rich

Office Commission on Citizenship
Tahlequah May 23rd 1889

The application in the above case was filed on the 12th day of September 1887 and is supported by no evidence; the Commission therefore decide that George Alice Heslerode and children Bertha Ann aged fourteen years, Katie Elmyra aged twelve years, Eli Walter aged eight years, Charles Otto, aged six years, Robert Edward Heslerode aged three years, whose Post Office was Fort Smith, Ark at the time of filing, are not Cherokees by blood and are not entitled to Citizenship in the Cherokee Nation.

Attest   Will P. Ross   Chairman
E.G. Ross   JE Gunter   Com
    Clerk Commission

MIDLETON

Docket #469
Rolls 1835 to 1852

Applicant for Cherokee Citizenship
Post Office: Carlington C.N.   **Attorney:** Wm A. Thompson

N°	NAMES	AGE	SEX
1	Mary Jane Midleton[sic]	39	female
2	Charles Haggins	19	male
3	James A. Haggins	13	"
4	Lulu May Haggins	11	female
5	Berdie K.E. Haggins	5	"

Ancestor: Martha J. Waldroop

Office Commission on Citizenship
Tahlequah C.N. May 20th 1889

The application in the above case was filed on the 12th day of September 1887 and is supported by no evidence. Therefore the Commission decide that Mary Jane Middleton and her children, Charles Haggins male nineteen years,

Cherokee Citizenship Commission Docket Books
(1880-84, 1887-89) Volume II
Tahlequah, Cherokee Nation

James A. Haggins, male thirteen years, Lulu May Haggins female aged eleven years, Berdie K.E. Haggins female aged five years at the time of filing whose Post Office was Carlington I.T. are not Cherokees by blood and are not entitled to Citizenship in the Cherokee Nation.

    E.G. Ross   Will P. Ross
    Clerk Commission   Chairman
                          R. Bunch   Commissioner
                          JE Gunter   "

HAMMACK

Docket #470
Rolls 1835 to 1852

Applicant for Cherokee Citizenship

Post Office: Chester, Crawford Co, Ark   **Attorney:** Wm A. Thompson

N°	NAMES	AGE	SEX
1	Samuel M. Hammack	27	Male

Ancestor: Rhoda Gideon

Office Commission on Citizenship
Tahlequah May 15th 1889

Now comes the above application which was filed the 12th day of September 1887 for the final hearing. The applicant claims his Cherokee blood through one Rhoda Gideons[sic] whose name he claims will be found on the census rolls of Cherokees by blood taken and made in the years of 1835 and 1852. The Commission fail to find the name of Rhoda Gideons[sic] on either of the above named rolls, and the case having been called three several times at intervals of not less than one hour apart and no answer. There being no evidence in support of the said claimant application, the Commission decide that Samuel M. Hammack aged 27 years is not of Cherokee blood and not entitled to Citizenship in the Cherokee Nation. Post Office address, Chester, Crawford Co, Ark.

                         Will P. Ross   Chairman
E.G. Ross   R. Bunch   Com
Clerk Commission   JE Gunter   Com

Cherokee Citizenship Commission Docket Books (1880-84, 1887-89) Volume II
Tahlequah, Cherokee Nation

SWEET

Docket #471
Rolls 1835 to 1852

Applicant for Cherokee Citizenship

Post Office: Chester, Crawford Co, Ark **Attorney:** Wm A. Thompson

N°	NAMES	AGE	SEX
1	John M. Sweet	34	Male

Ancestor: Rhoda Gideon

Office Commission on Citizenship
Tahlequah CM May 15th 1889

Now comes this case for the final hearing having been filed on the 12th day of September 1887. The applicant alleges that he is the Great Grand son of Rhoda Gideons whose name he claims will be found on the census rolls of Cherokees by blood taken and made in the years of 1835 and 1852. The Commission fail to find the name of Rhoda Gideons on either of the above named rolls and there being no evidence in support of the above claimant allegations set forth in his application and after the third calling of the above named case and no answer, the Commission allege that John F.[sic] Sweet whose name is not signed to his application aged 34 years, is not of Cherokee blood and not entitled to Citizenship in the Cherokee Nation. Post Office address Chester, Crawford Co, Ark.

E.G. Ross　　　　　　　　Will P. Ross　　　Chairman
　　Clerk Commission　　　JE Gunter　　　　Com

ASWEET

Docket #472
Rolls 1835

Applicant for Cherokee Citizenship

Post Office: Chester, Crawford Co, Ark **Attorney:** Wm A. Thompson

N°	NAMES	AGE	SEX
1	Wm E. Sweet	47	male
2	Walter R. Sweet	17	"
3	Carrie J. Sweet	14	female
4	R.A. Sweet	12	"
5	Guardie Sweet	8	"

Cherokee Citizenship Commission Docket Books
(1880-84, 1887-89) Volume II
Tahlequah, Cherokee Nation

6	Manda B Sweet	6	"
7	Emma C. Sweet	4	"
8	Cleveland Sweet	2	male
9	J.Y. Sweet	3 mo	"

Ancestor: Rhoda Gideon

Office Commission on Citizenship
Tahlequah C.N. May 15th 1889

Now comes the above application for a final hearing which was filed 12th Sept. 1887. The applicant claims his Cherokee blood through one Rhoda Gideon whose name the applicant claims will be found on the census rolls of 1851 & 1852. The Commission fails to find the name of Rhoda Gideons on either of the census rolls of 1851 & 1852 and the case having been called three several times at intervals of an hour apart and no answer and there being no evidence produced in support of applicant's case. The Commission decide that William E. Sweet age 47 years, Walter R. Sweet age 17 years, Carrie J Sweet age 14 years. R.A. Sweet age 12 years. Guardie Sweet age 8 years, Manda B. Sweet age 6 years, Emma C. Sweet age 4 year, Cleveland Sweet age 2 years, J.Y. Sweet age 3 months are not Cherokees by blood and not entitled to Citizenship in the Cherokee Nation.

	Will P. Ross	Chairman
E.G. Ross	R. Bunch	Com
Clk Commission	JE Gunter	Com

ROGERS

Docket #473
Rolls 1835 to 1852

Applicant for Cherokee Citizenship
Post Office: Chester, Crawford Co, Ark. **Attorney:** Wm A. Thompson

N^o	NAMES	AGE	SEX
1	James M Rogers	47	Male
2	R.B. Rogers	15	"
3	S.C. Rogers	12	"
4	J.C. Rogers	9	"
5	F.C. Rogers	6	"
6	James O Rogers	3	"

Ancestor: John Rogers

Cherokee Citizenship Commission Docket Books
(1880-84, 1887-89) Volume II
Tahlequah, Cherokee Nation

Now on this the 17th day of March 1888, comes the above case for a final hearing, and the parties having made application pursuant to the provisions of an Act of the National Council approved December 8th 1886, and all the evidence being duly considered and found to be insufficient and unsatisfactory, it is adjudged and declared by the Commission that

James M. Rogers, R.B. Rogers, S.C. Rogers, J.C. Rogers, P.C. Rogers and James O. Rogers are not Cherokees, and they are not entitled to the rights. privileges and immunities of Cherokee Citizens by blood.

        J.T. Adair Chairman Commission
        John E. Gunter Commissioner
        D.W. Lipe Commissioner

Attest
  C.C. Lipe
  Clk Com.

The decision in the James C.C. Rogers case found on Book C, page 622 and testimony on Journal page 325 to 333, governs this case.

SWEET

Docket #474
Rolls 1835 to 1852

            Applicant for Cherokee Citizenship
Post Office: Chester, Crawford Co, Ark. **Attorney:** Wm A. Thompson

N°	NAMES	AGE	SEX
1	C.S. Sweet	41	Male
2	John P. Sweet	13	"
3	Isam T. Sweet	10	"
4	Hester L. Sweet	1	female

       Ancestor: Rhoda Gideon

       Office Commission on Citizenship
       Tahlequah C.N. May 15 1889

Now comes the above application for a final hearing which was filed 12th day of September 1887. The applicant claims his Cherokee blood through one Rhoda Gideon whose name the applicant claims would be found on the census

Cherokee Citizenship Commission Docket Books
(1880-84, 1887-89) Volume II
Tahlequah, Cherokee Nation

rolls of 1851 and 1852. The Commission after examining the papers in the above case fail to find any evidence in support of the above fact, and the case having been called three times not less than one hour apart and no response from applicant in person or by Attorney, therefore the Commission are of the opinion that C.S. Sweet, John P. Sweet, Isam T Sweet and Hester L. Sweet are not Cherokees by blood and are not entitled to Cherokee Citizenship.

	Will P. Ross	Chairman
E.G. Ross	R. Bunch	Com
Clerk Commission	J E Gunter	Com

TUCKER

Docket #475
Rolls 1835

Applicant for Cherokee Citizenship

Post Office: Oonala I.T.   **Attorney:** ~~Wm A Thompson~~
A.E. Ivey

N°	NAMES	AGE	SEX
1	E.J. Tucker	32	Male
2	Sally M Tucker	8	female
3	Calvin Tucker	6	male
4	Thomas T Tucker	3	"
5	Wesley Tucker	1	"

Ancestor: Polly Tucker

Tahlequah, C.N.
Sept. 24th 1887

We the Commission on Citizenship after a careful examination of all the testimony in the case of E.A.J. Tucker and Sally May Tucker – Calvin Tucker – Thomas Taylor Tucker & Wesley Tucker (VS) Cherokee Nation, find that they are Cherokees by blood, and is hereby re-admitted to all the rights, privileges and immunities of Cherokees by blood.

J.T. Adair	Chairman Commission
John E. Gunter	Commissioner

Cherokee Citizenship Commission Docket Books
(1880-84, 1887-89) Volume II
Tahlequah, Cherokee Nation

LONG

Docket #476
Rolls 1835 to 1852

Applicant for Cherokee Citizenship

Post Office: Webbers Falls, I.T.   **Attorney:** Wm A. Thompson

N°	NAMES		AGE	SEX
1	Fernecy Jane Long		56	female
2	Serena C Long		19	"
3	George F. Long		18	male
4	Daniel E. Long		16	"
5	Rebecca E. Long		13	female
6	John Barnett	grand	16	male
7	Thomas J. Hutchison	children	13	"
8	Gustina Shipman		4	female

Ancestor: Robert Rogers

In the matter of the above applicant and her children, we the Commission after carefully looking into the case, find that they have no shadow of rights in the Cherokee Nation. The said Fernecy Long claims to be the granddaughter of Robert Rogers. The Siler rolls of 1851 shows that the only daughter Robt. Rogers had at that time was named Sarah and was only 11 years old in the year 1851, and was then living in the state of Georgia. The testimony of Iks Glass shows that the applicant's mother was named Lizzie and moved to this country before the emigration and was termed an "Old Settler" and remained here about a year and moved to the "Neutral land" – there was no Neutral Land prior to the treaty of 1835. The application of Fernecy J. Long shows that she was 56 years old when this application was made out. The only daughter that Robert Rogers had in 1851, if now living, would only be 48 years old, which is nine years younger than the applicant herself.

We the Commission do not hesitate in declaring that Fernecy Jane Long, and her seven children, viz: George T, Serena C, Daniel E, Rebecca E. Long, John Barnett, Thomas J. Hutchinson and Gustina Shipman are not Cherokees by blood, and are not entitled to any of the rights, privileges of the C.N. and are hereby declared to be intruders upon the public domain of the Cherokee Nation.

J.T. Adair   Chairman Commission
D.W. Lipe   Commissioner
H.C. Barnes   Commissioner

Cherokee Citizenship Commission Docket Books
(1880-84, 1887-89) Volume II
Tahlequah, Cherokee Nation

Office Com on Citizenship
Tahlequah I.T. Sept 24th 1888.

McCLURE

Docket #477
Rolls 1851 & 1852

Applicant for Cherokee Citizenship

Post Office: Evansville Ark   **Attorney:** A.E. Ivey

N°	NAMES	AGE	SEX
1	Alice L. McClure	21	female

Ancestor: Martin & Sallie Ward

We the Commission on Citizenship after fully examining the testimony in the above case and the Old Settler pay rolls of 1851, find that Alice L. McClure is a Cherokee by blood and entitled to all the rights and privileges of a citizen of the Cherokee Nation on account of such blood – Law of December 8th 1886 in relation to citizenship approved on the before mentioned date and the amendment thereto, approved Feb'y, 7th 1888.

                         J.T. Adair   Chairman Commission
                         John E. Gunter   Commissioner
                                                Commissioner

Office Commission on Citizenship
Tahlequah Ind. Ter. July 7th 1888

HOWELL

Docket #478
Rolls 1852

Applicant for Cherokee Citizenship

Post Office: Marietta, Ga.   **Attorney:** Henry C. Rogers

N°	NAMES	AGE	SEX
1	Emily C. Howell	50	female
2	Robert Edie Howell	20	male
3	Charles C. Howell	18	"
4	Mary D. Howell	17	Female
5	Eaton E. Howell	14	male
6	Thomas C. Howell	12	"

Cherokee Citizenship Commission Docket Books
(1880-84, 1887-89) Volume II
Tahlequah, Cherokee Nation

| 7 | Frank R. Howell | 11 | " |
| 8 | Evan C. Howell | 9 | " |

Ancestor: Elmina Waters

Now on this the 12th day of October, 1887, comes the above case for a final hearing, and the parties having made application pursuant to the provisions of an Act of the National Council approved December 8th 1886, - And all the evidence being duly examined and found to be sufficient and satisfactory to the Commission, and the name of the ancestor Elmina Waters, appearing on the roll of 1852. It is adjudged and determined by the Commission that Emily C. Howell, Robert E. Lee Howell, Charles C. Howell, Mary D. Howell, Eaton E. Howell, Thomas C. Howell, Frank R. Howell, Evan C. Howell – are Cherokees by blood and are hereby re-admitted to all the rights, privileges and immunities of Cherokees by blood. And a certificate of said decission[sic] of the Commission and readmission was made and furnished to said parties accordingly.

                                J.T. Adair   Chairman Com.
Henry Eiffert   D.W. Lipe   Commissioner
Clk Com.   Commissioner

MATES

Docket #479
Rolls 1835

                                      Applicant for Cherokee Citizenship
      Post Office: Colfax, Cal.   **Attorney:** A.J. Ridge

N^0	NAMES	AGE	SEX
1	Phillip Matea	52	male

Ancestor: James Matea

                                Office Commission on Citizenship
                                    Cherokee Nation, Ind. Ter.
                                    Tahlequah, August 19, 1889

There being no evidence in support of this case the Commission decide that Phillip Matea aged fifty two years is not a Cherokee by blood. Post Office Colfax California.

Cherokee Citizenship Commission Docket Books
(1880-84, 1887-89) Volume II
Tahlequah, Cherokee Nation

Attest
  E.G. Ross
  Clerk Commission

Will P. Ross
      Chairman
  J.E. Gunter   Com.

BROWNING

Docket #480
Rolls 1835

Applicant for Cherokee Citizenship

Post Office: Exiter[sic], Mo   **Attorney:** C.H. Taylor

N°	NAMES	AGE	SEX
1	Jessie Browning	21	male

Ancestor: Elizabeth House

Office Commission on Citizenship
Tahlequah C.N. May 20th 1889

The application in this case was filed the 13th day of September 1887 and is decided against by the Commission on the grounds stated in the case of George House Docket 485, Book B, page 198.

E.G. Ross
  Clerk Commission

Will P. Ross
      Chairman
  R. Bunch Commissioner

HARRELL

Docket #481
Rolls 1835

Applicant for Cherokee Citizenship

Post Office: Cassville, Mo   **Attorney:** C.H. Taylor

N°	NAMES	AGE	SEX
1	Bettie Harrell	24	female
2	Rosie Harrell	3	"

Ancestor: Elizabeth House

The above application was filed on the 13th day of Sept. 1887 and is supported by no evidence. The Commission therefore decide that Bettie Harrell age 24 and her daughter one Rosie Harrell female age 3 years at the time of filing and

Cherokee Citizenship Commission Docket Books
(1880-84, 1887-89) Volume II
Tahlequah, Cherokee Nation

whose Post Office was Cassville Mo are not Cherokees by blood and are not entitled to Citizenship in the Cherokee Nation.

George O. Butler
Asst Clerk Commission

Will P. Ross
    Chairman
R. Bunch Commissioner

EARLE

Docket #482
Rolls 1835

Applicant for Cherokee Citizenship
Post Office: Cassville, Mo.   **Attorney:** C.H. Taylor

N°	NAMES	AGE	SEX
1	Sarah Earle	36	female
2	Grantburn Earle	16	male
3	Albert Earle	14	"
4	Benjamin Earle	12	"
5	Cora Earle	10	female
6	William Earle	8	male
7	John Earle	6	"
8	George Earle	3	"

Ancestor: Elizabeth House

Office Commission on Citizenship
Tahlequah C.N. May 20th 1889

The application in the above case was filed on the 13th day of September 1998 and is supported by no evidence. Therefore the Commission decide that Sarah Earle and her children, Grantburn Earle, aged sixteen years, Albert Earle aged fourteen years, Benjamin Earle, aged twelve years, Cora Earle, William Earle aged eight years, John Earle aged six years, George Earle aged three years, whose Post Office was Cassville Mo. at the time of filing are not Cherokees by blood and are not entitled to Citizenship in the Cherokee Nation.

Attest
  E.G. Ross
  Clerk Commission

Will P. Ross

R. Bunch

Chairman
Commissioner

Cherokee Citizenship Commission Docket Books
(1880-84, 1887-89) Volume II
Tahlequah, Cherokee Nation

WOODARD

Docket #483
Rolls 1835

Applicant for Cherokee Citizenship

Post Office: Exeter, Mo.   **Attorney:** C.H. Taylor

N°	NAMES	AGE	SEX
1	Mollie Woodard	26	female
2	James Woodard	3	male
3	Guie Woodard	1	"

Ancestor: Elizabeth House

Office Commission on Citizenship
Tahlequah C.N. May 20, 1889

The above case was this[sic] considered and the Commission decide that Mollie Woodard who claims to be the Grand daughter of Elizabeth House nee Elizabeth McLemore and her sons James Woodward age three years and Guy or Guie Woodward aged one year are not of Cherokee blood and not entitled to readmission to Citizenship in the Cherokee Nation. See the evidence and the opinion of the Commission in the case of George House Docket 485, Book B, Page 198.

Will P. Ross
Attest   Chairman
E.G. Ross   R. Bunch   Commissioner
Clerk commission

ELROD

Docket #484
Rolls 1835

Applicant for Cherokee Citizenship

Post Office: Carthage, Mo.   **Attorney:** C.H. Taylor

N°	NAMES	AGE	SEX
1	Columbia Elrod	30	female
2	Mertle[sic] Elrod	10	"

Ancestor: Elizabeth House

Cherokee Citizenship Commission Docket Books
(1880-84, 1887-89) Volume II
Tahlequah, Cherokee Nation

Office Commission on Citizenship
Tahlequah C.N. May 20, 1889

The Commission decide against the applicant in the above case upon the grounds set forth in the George House case, the alleged ancestor being the same. See docket 485, Book B, Page 198. This decision includes the applicant Columbia Elrode[sic] age 30 years, and Myrtle Elrode[sic] age 10 years.

E.G. Ross
    Clerk Commission

Will P. Ross
    Chairman
R. Bunch   Commissioner

HOUSE

Docket #485
Rolls 1835

Applicant for Cherokee Citizenship

Post Office: Cassville, Mo.   **Attorney:** C.H. Taylor

N°	NAMES	AGE	SEX
1	George House	66	Male
2	James House	28	"
3	Charlie House	11	"
4	Ida House	21	female
5	Virginia House	14	"

Ancestor: Elizabeth House

Commission on Citizenship
Tahlequah May 20th 1889

Now comes the above case for final hearing, George House the applicant at the date of filing his application the 13th day of September 1887 alleges that he is the son of one Mansfield House and a Cherokee woman named Elizabeth McLemore or House, whose name he believes will be found on the census rolls of Cherokees by blood taken in the year 1835. The only evidence in the case is based upon the statement of the House brothers, George and Thomas and shows that they were born out of marriage and alleges that they were left at the house of their Father by their mother and that they are by him apprenticed to trades in the state of Tennessee when their father resided. The affiants Thomas Ragsdale and Obediah Ragsdale whose sister Thomas House married were not personally

Cherokee Citizenship Commission Docket Books
(1880-84, 1887-89) Volume II
Tahlequah, Cherokee Nation

acquainted with the mother Elizabeth McLemore. They left Tennessee in 1848 several years after the census roll of 1835 was taken and neither the names of Elizabeth McLemore nor those of George and Thomas House appear upon it. The Commission therefore decide that George House is not of Cherokee blood, and that he and his children James House aged 29 years, Charles House aged 11 years, Ida House, aged 21 years and Virginia House aged 14 years are not of Cherokee blood and not entitled to readmission to Citizenship in the Cherokee Nation.

        Will P. Ross   Chairman
        R. Bunch and J.E. Gunter Com.

HAWKINS

Docket #486
Rolls 1835

Applicants for Cherokee Citizenship
Post Office: Exeter, Mo.   **Attorney:** C.H. Taylor

N°	NAMES	AGE	SEX
1	Samuel Hawkins	22	male
2	Dora Hawkins	17	female
3	Golden Hawkins	15	male
4	Nancy Hawkins	13	female
5	Celia Hawkins	11	"
6	Rebecca Hawkins	9	"

Ancestor: George House

        Office Commission on Citizenship
        Tahlequah C.N. May 20th 1889

The applicant in this case claims to be the Grand son of George House. The Commission decide that Samuel Hawkins is not of Cherokee blood and in support of this decission[sic] refer to their decision in the case of George House. See Docket 485, Book B, page 198. This decision in the case of Samuel Hawkins includes Dora Hawkins female aged 17 years, Golden Hawkins male aged 15 years, Money[sic] Hawkins male aged 13 years, Celia Hawkins female aged 11 years, and Rebecca Hawkins female aged 9 years, children of said Samuel Hawkins.

Cherokee Citizenship Commission Docket Books
(1880-84, 1887-89) Volume II
Tahlequah, Cherokee Nation

Attest   Will P. Ross
   E.G. Ross   Chairman
   Clerk Commission   R. Bunch   Commissioner

BROWNING

Docket #487
Rolls 1835

Applicant for Cherokee Citizenship

Post Office: Exeter, Mo.   **Attorney:** C.H. Taylor

N°	NAMES	AGE	SEX
1	Lillie Browning	18	female
2	Jennie Browning	1	"

Ancestor: Elizabeth House

Office Commission on Citizenship
Tahlequah C.N. May 20th 1889

The Commission decide against the applicant in the above case upon the grounds set fourth[sic] in the decision in the case of George House. See Docket 485, Book B, page 198. This decision includes the applicant Lillie Browning aged 18 years and her daughter Jennie Browning age one year.

               Will P. Ross
E.G. Ross   Chairman
   Clerk Commission   R. Bunch   Commissioner

STONE

Docket #488
Rolls 1835

Applicant for Cherokee Citizenship

Post Office: Alma, Ark.   **Attorney:** A.E. Ivey

N°	NAMES	AGE	SEX
1	W.R. Stone (husband)	32	male
2	J.A. Stone (wife)	30	female
3	Robert A. Stone (son)	5	male
4	Lelia M. Stone	3	female

Cherokee Citizenship Commission Docket Books
(1880-84, 1887-89) Volume II
Tahlequah, Cherokee Nation

5	Bean Stone	5 mo	male

Ancestor: Mima Edwards

Now on this the 9th day of January 1888, comes the above case up for final hearing, the applicants having made application pursuant to the provisions of an Act of the National Council approved December 8th 1886, and all the evidence in the Mary A. Couch case, which was made by agreement of attys a test, one to govern all cases claiming a direct lineage from this same ancestor Mima Edwards. It is adjudged and determined by the Commission that W.R. Stone – J.A. – Robert A. – Lelia M. – and Bean Stone are not Cherokees by blood and in consequence not entitled to the rights of such.

The decision of Mary A. Couch, found on Docket "A" page 100 governs this case.

J.T. Adair   Chairman Commission
D.W. Lipe   Commissioner

Attest
C.C. Lipe
Clerk Com.

STONE

Docket #489
Rolls 1835

Applicant for Cherokee Citizenship

Post Office: Alma, Ark   **Attorney:** A.E. Ivey

N°	NAMES	AGE	SEX
1	James C. Stone	25	male

Ancestor: Mima Edwards

Now on this the 9th day of January 1888, comes the above case up for final hearing, the applicant having made application pursuant to the provisions of an Act of the National Council approved Dec. 8th 1886, and all the evidence in the Mary A. Couch case being fully considered, which was by agreement made a test case governing all cases claiming a direct ancestry from the same ancestor, Mima Edwards, it is adjudged and determined by the Commission that James C. Stone is not a Cherokee by blood and in consequence not entitled to the rights of such.

Cherokee Citizenship Commission Docket Books
(1880-84, 1887-89) Volume II
Tahlequah, Cherokee Nation

The decision in the Mary A Couch case, found on page 100 Docket "A", governs this case.

                        J.T. Adair   Chairman Commission
                        D.W. Lipe   Commissioner

Attest
    C.C. Lipe
    Clerk Com.

STONE

Docket #490
Rolls 1835

Applicant for Cherokee Citizenship

Post Office: Alma, Ark   **Attorney:** A.E. Ivey

N°	NAMES	AGE	SEX
1	Samuel H. Stone	27	male

Ancestor: Mima Edwards

Now on this the 9th day of January 1888, comes the above case up for final hearing, the applicant having made application pursuant to the provisions of an Act of the National Council approved Dec. 8th 1886, and all the evidence being duly considered in the Mary A. Couch case, which was by an agreement of attys. made a test case to govern all cases claiming a direct ancestry from the same ancestor, Mima Edwards; it adjudged and determined by the Commission that Samuel H. Stone is <u>not</u> a Cherokee by blood and not entitled to the rights of such.

The decision in the Mary A Couch case, found on page 100 Docket "A", governs this case.

                        J.T. Adair   Chairman Commission
                        D.W. Lipe   Commissioner

Attest
    C.C. Lipe
    Clerk Com.

Cherokee Citizenship Commission Docket Books
(1880-84, 1887-89) Volume II
Tahlequah, Cherokee Nation

DENHAM

Docket #491
Rolls 1835 to 1852

Applicant for Cherokee Citizenship

Post Office: Bridgeport, Ill   **Attorney:** A.E. Ivey

N°	NAMES	AGE	SEX
1	William Denham	56	Male

Ancestor: John S. Dunham[sic]

Now on this the 31st day of May 1888, comes the above case up for final disposition. The application of Wm Denham for Cherokee Citizenship, filed on the 18th day of July 1887 alleges one John S. Denham as his ancestor, and that he was of Cherokee Indian blood.

Under the 7th Section of the Act empowering and creating this Commission, approved Dec. 8th 1886, the law sayes[sic] "that the applicant must prove a lineal descent from some person whose name appears on the census rolls of Cherokees taken by the United States after the treaty of 1835 and known as the "rolls of 1835", the rolls of 1848 known as the "Mullay Rolls" and the census rolls of Cherokees taken by the United States and known as the "Siler roll", and the pay roll of 1852 known as the "Chapman rolls". The evidence in this case is not altogether admissible as most of it is more heresay[sic] testimony and does not plainly state of its self that Mr. Denham is a Cherokee Indian only from the general "make up" and looks of him that they (the parties testifying) believed him to be a Cherokee.

The rolls where referred to do not show the name of John S. Denham or the name of the applicant, William Denham. – Taking this fact into consideration, no matter how good and conclusive the evidence might seem, it is beyond the province of this Commission to re-admit any applicant for Cherokee citizenship whose ancestor (their names) do not appear upon some of these records of Cherokees.

The Commission are of the opinion that William Denham is not a Cherokee Indian and so declare.

J.T. Adair   Chairman Commission
John E Gunter   Commissioner
D.W. Lipe   Commissioner

Attest
  Cornell Rogers, Clk.

Cherokee Citizenship Commission Docket Books
(1880-84, 1887-89) Volume II
Tahlequah, Cherokee Nation

EDWARDS

Docket #492
Rolls 1835

Applicant for Cherokee Citizenship
Post Office: Oak Lodge, I.T. **Attorney**: A.E. Ivey

N°	NAMES	AGE	SEX
1	G.W. Edwards	36	male
2	Anna L. Edwards	15	female
3	James W. Edwards	13	male
4	Mary M. Edwards	12	female
5	Lucy A. Edwards	9	"
6	Perry W. Edwards	6	male

Ancestor: ~~Henry Edwards~~
Mima Edwards

Now on this the 9th day of January 1888, comes the above case for a final hearing, and the parties having made application pursuant to the provisions of an Act of the National Council approved December 8th 1886, and all the evidence being duly examined and found not to be sufficient and satisfactory to the Commission, and the name of ancestor not appearing on the Rolls as claimed in the application.

It is adjudged and determined by the Commission that, G.W. Edwards, Anna L. Edwards, James W. Edwards, Mary M. Edwards, Lucy A. Edwards and Perry W. Edwards, are Not Cherokees by blood, and are hereby rejected and declared to be intruders.

                        J.T. Adair   Chairman Commission
                        John E Gunter Commissioner
Attest   D.W. Lipe   Commissioner
    C.C. Lipe
    Clerk Commission

Cherokee Citizenship Commission Docket Books
(1880-84, 1887-89) Volume II
Tahlequah, Cherokee Nation

WILLIAMS

Docket #493
Rolls 1852

Applicant for Cherokee Citizenship

Post Office: Waldron, Ark   **Attorney:** A.E. Ivey

N°	NAMES	AGE	SEX
1	Lucinda Jane Williams		

Ancestor: Jack & Ruth *(Illegible)*

Rejected May 21 – 89

Office Commission on Citizenship Cher. Nat. I.T.
Tahlequah May 21st 1889

The above application was filed the 14th day of September 1887, and is supported by no evidence.

The Commission therefore decide that Lucinda Jane Williams, age nine years, whose Post Office address at the time of the filing was Waldron Ark. is not of Cherokee by blood and is not entitled to Citizenship in the Cherokee Nation.

Attest
D.S. Williams
Asst Clk Com

Will P. Ross
JE Gunter
R Bunch   Com

Chairman
Com

MARSHAL

Docket #494
Rolls 1835 to 1852

Applicant for Cherokee Citizenship

Post Office: Lancaster, Ark   **Attorney:** A.E. Ivey

N°	NAMES	AGE	SEX
1	E.F. Marshal	64	male

Ancestor: Lawrence S. Slaughter

Rejected May 21 – 89

Office Commission on Citizenship Cher. Nat. Ind. Ter'y.
Tahlequah May 21st 1889

This application filed 14th day of September 1887. Supported by no evidence. The Commission therefore decide adversely to claimant. P.O. Lancaster Arkansas.

Cherokee Citizenship Commission Docket Books
(1880-84, 1887-89) Volume II
Tahlequah, Cherokee Nation

Attest	Will P. Ross	Chairman
D.S. Williams	R. Bunch	Com
Asst Clk. Com	J.E. Gunter	Com.

JOHNSON

Docket #495
Rolls 1835

Applicant for Cherokee Citizenship

Post Office: Alma, Ark.   **Attorney:** A.E. Ivey

N°	NAMES	AGE	SEX
1	Sarah E. Johnson	29	female

Ancestor: Mima Edwards

Now on this the 9th day of January 1888, comes the above case up for final hearing, the applicant having made application pursuant to the provisions of an Act of the National Council approved December 8th 1886, and all the evidence being duly considered, in the M.A. Couch case which was by an agreement of the Attys made a list and to govern all cases claiming a lineal ancestry from the same ancestor, Mima Edwards, it is adjudged and determined by the Commission that Sarah E. Johnson is not a Cherokee by blood, and in consequence and *(illegible)* to the rights of each.

The decision in the Mary A. Couch case, found on page 100 Docket "A" governs this case.

J.T. Adair   Chairman Commission
D.W. Lipe   Commissioner

COZBY

Docket #496
Rolls 1835

Applicant for Cherokee Citizenship

Post Office: Lewisville, Tex   **Attorney:** A.E. Ivey

N°	NAMES	AGE	SEX
1	Virginia J Cozby	36	female
2	John H Cozby	17	male
3	James R. Cozby	14	"
4	Andrew L Cozby	12	"

Cherokee Citizenship Commission Docket Books
(1880-84, 1887-89) Volume II
Tahlequah, Cherokee Nation

5	Eva J Cozby	10	female
6	Wm A. Cozby	6	male
7	Frank Cozby	1	"

Ancestor: Ivin & Sarah Austill

Rejected May 21 – 89

Office Commission on Citizenship Cherokee Nation Ind Tery.
Tahlequah May 21st 1889

The above application was filed the 14th day of September 1887. and Supported by no evidence.

The Commission therefore decide that Virginia J. Cozby and her children, John H. male age 17 years, James R. male age 14 years, Andrew L. male age 12 yrs, Eva J. female age 10 yrs, Wm A. male age 6 yrs, and Frank Cozby male age 2 yrs, whose Post office at the time of filing was Lewisville Tex. are not Cherokees by blood and are not entitled to Citizenship in the Cherokee Nation.

Attest	Will P. Ross	Chairman
D.S. Williams	R. Bunch	Com
Asst Clk Com.	J.E. Gunter Com.	

EWART

Docket #497
Rolls 1835

Applicant for Cherokee Citizenship

Post Office: Lewisville Tex   **Attorney:** A.E. Ivey

N°	NAMES	AGE	SEX
1	Lethea A. Ewart	34	female
2	Amrilla N Ewart	10	"
3	Alford P. Ewart	9	male
4	Dora Ewart	6	female
5	Myrtle Ewart	2	"

Ancestor: Iven & Sarah Austill

Rejected

The above application was filed on the 14th day of September 1887, and is supported by no evidence.

Cherokee Citizenship Commission Docket Books
(1880-84, 1887-89) Volume II
Tahlequah, Cherokee Nation

The Commission therefore decide that Lethea A. Ewart and her children, Amrilla N. Ewart 10, Alford P. Ewart, aged 9, Dora Ewart aged 6, Myrtle Ewart aged 2 yrs whose Post Office at the time of filing Lewisville Tex, are not Cherokees by blood and are not entitled to Citizenship in the Cherokee Nation.

(Name Illegible) Will P. Ross   Chairman
Asst. Clerk Commission   J.E. Gunter   Com

GAY

Docket #498
Rolls 1835

Applicant for Cherokee Citizenship

Post Office: Waketon Tex.   **Attorney:** A.E. Ivey

N°	NAMES	AGE	SEX
1	R.B. Gay	31	male
2	Amand[sic] Gay	4	fem

Ancestor: Iven & Sarah Austill

Rejected May 21 – 89

Office Commission on Citizenship Cherokee Nation I.T.
Tahlequah May 21st 1889

This application filed 14th day of September 1887 is supported by no evidence. The Commission therefore decide adversely to applicant, R.B. Gay and Amanda Gay. The former aged thirty one years and latter aged four years. P.O. Waketon Texas.

Attest   Will P. Ross   Chairman
   D.S. Williams   R. Bunch   Com
   Asst Clk Com   JE Gunter   Com

Cherokee Citizenship Commission Docket Books
(1880-84, 1887-89) Volume II
Tahlequah, Cherokee Nation

CLINE

Docket #499
Rolls 1835 to 1852

Applicant for Cherokee Citizenship

Post Office: Fort Graham, Tex   **Attorney:** A.E. Ivey

N°	NAMES	AGE	SEX
1	G.W. Cline	61	male
2	R.D. Cline	18	"
3	G.W. Cline	16	"
	D.F. Cline	14	"

Ancestor: David Cline

Rejected May 21 – 89

Office Commission on Citizenship
Cherokee Nation I.T.
Tahlequah May 21st 1889

The above application was filed on the 14th day of September 1887, and is supported by no evidence.

The Commission therefore decide that G.W. Cline age 61 yrs and his children, R.D. Cline male eighteen years, G.W. Cline male aged 16 years and D.F. Cline male age 14 years of age, whose Post office address at the time of filing was Fort Graham Tex. are not Cherokees by blood and are no entitled to Citizenship in the Cherokee Nation.

Attest   Will P. Ross   Chairman
  D.S. Williams   R. Bunch   Com
  Asst Clk Com   JE Gunter Com

EDWARDS

Docket #500
Rolls 1835 to 1852

Applicant for Cherokee Citizenship

Post Office: Oak Lodge, I.T.   **Attorney:** A.E. Ivey

N°	NAMES	AGE	SEX
1	W.H. Edwards	31	male
2	Sarah E Edwards	1	female

Ancestor: Henry Baker

Cherokee Citizenship Commission Docket Books
(1880-84, 1887-89) Volume II
Tahlequah, Cherokee Nation

Rejected May 21 – 89

Office Commission on Citizenship Cherokee Nation I.T.
Tahlequah May 21st 1889

The above application was filed on the 14th day of September 1887 and is supported by no evidence.

The Commission therefore decide that W.H. Edwards and his daughter Sarah E. Edwards 1 year old at the time of filing and whose Post Office was Oak Lodge I.T. are not Cherokees by blood and are not entitled to Citizenship in the Cherokee Nation.

Attest	Will P. Ross	Chairman
D.S. Williams	R Bunch	Com
Asst Clk Com	JE Gunter	Com

HERNDON

Docket #501
Rolls 1835

Applicant for Cherokee Citizenship
Post Office: McKinney Tex   **Attorney:** William A. Thompson

N°	NAMES	AGE	SEX
1	J.M. Herndon	46	male
2	Elwood Herndon	19	"
3	Wallace Herndon	2	"
4	Grover C. Herndon	6 mo	"

Ancestor: Peter *(Illegible)*
Jack Mc*(Illegible)*

Office Commission on Citizenship
Cherokee Nation Tahlequah
June 26 1889

The above named case having been submitted by Attorney for applicant without evidence the Commission decide that the applicant J.M. Herndon aged 46 years and his sons, Elwood Herndon aged 19 years, Wallace Herndon two

Cherokee Citizenship Commission Docket Books
(1880-84, 1887-89) Volume II
Tahlequah, Cherokee Nation

years, and Grover C. Herndon six months of McKinney Texas are not of Cherokee blood.

Attest	Will P. Ross Chairman
E.G. Ross	R. Bunch Com
Clerk Commission	John E. Gunter Com

CLARK

Docket #502
Rolls 1835

Applicant for Cherokee Citizenship

Post Office: Childers Station I.T.   **Attorney:** C.H. Taylor

N°	NAMES	AGE	SEX
1	Elizabeth Clark	43	female
2	Austin Clark	17	male
3	Ennia Clark	14	female
4	Ora Clark	12	"
5	Ollie L. Clark	11	"
6	Donie Clark	6	"

Ancestor: Rebecca Fields

Rejected May 21st 1889

Office Commission on Citizenship Cher. Nat. I.T.
Tahlequah May 21st 1889

The above application was filed the 13th day of September 1887 and is supported by no evidence.

The Commission therefore decide that Elizabeth Clark and her children Austin age 17 years male, Ennia female age 14 years, Ora, female age 12 years, Ollie L. female age 10 years, Donie Clark female age 6 years are not Cherokees by blood and are not entitled to Citizenship in the Cherokee Nation. Post Office Childers Station, I.T.

Attest	Will P. Ross	Chairman
D.S. Williams	R. Bunch	Com
Asst Clk Com	J.E. Gunter	Com

Cherokee Citizenship Commission Docket Books
(1880-84, 1887-89) Volume II
Tahlequah, Cherokee Nation

HUBBARD

Docket #503
Rolls 1835

                                      Applicant for Cherokee Citizenship
Post Office: Fort Smith, Ark.   **Attorney:** C.H. Taylor

N°	NAMES	AGE	SEX
1	Alvilda Hubbard	24	female
2	Oda Wilson		daughter

Ancestor: Rebecca Fields

Rejected May 31st 1889

                      Office Commission on Citizenship
                          Cherokee Nation Ind. Ter'y.
                            Tahlequah May 21st 1889

This application was filed 15th September 1887 and submitted this day by Atty for claimant without evidence. The Commission therefore decide Alvilda Hubbard and Oda Wilson her daughter are not of Cherokee blood and not entitled to Citizenship in the Cherokee Nation.

Attest   Will P. Ross   Chairman
    D.S. Williams   R. Bunch   Com
    Asst Clk Com   J.E. Gunter   Com

GRIST

Docket #504
Rolls 1835

                                    Applicant for Cherokee Citizenship
Post Office: Childers Station I.T.   **Attorney:** C.H. Taylor

N°	NAMES	AGE	SEX
1	Emma Grist	17	female
2	Sadie Grist	1	"

Ancestor: Rebecca Fields

                      Office Commission on Citizenship
                      Cherokee Nation May 27th 1889

This application was filed the 13th day of September 1998 and is submitted by both parties May 22nd 1889, without evidence. The Commission

Cherokee Citizenship Commission Docket Books
(1880-84, 1887-89) Volume II
Tahlequah, Cherokee Nation

therefore decide that Emma Grist and her daughter Sadie Grist aged one year are not of Cherokee blood and not entitled to Citizenship in the Cherokee Nation.

E.G. Ross
Clerk Commission

Will P. Ross   Chairman
R. Bunch   Com
J.E. Gunter   Com.

GRAY

Docket #505
Rolls 1835

Applicant for Cherokee Citizenship
Post Office: Lewisville, Tex.   **Attorney:** A.E. Ivey

N°	NAMES	AGE	SEX
1	Aurilla P. Gray	59	female

Ancestor: Sarah Austill

Office Commission on Citizenship
Tahlequah May 27th 1889

There being no evidence presented in support of the application in the above named case the Commission decide that the applicant is not of Cherokee blood.

E.G. Ross
Clerk Commission

Will P. Ross   Chairman
R. Bunch   Com
J.E. Gunter   Com

GRAY

Docket #506
Rolls 1835

Applicant for Cherokee Citizenship
Post Office: Lewisville, Tex.   **Attorney:** A.E. Ivey

N°	NAMES	AGE	SEX
1	William N. Gray	26	Male
2	S.H. Gray	24	"

Ancestor: Iven & Sarah Austill

Cherokee Citizenship Commission Docket Books
(1880-84, 1887-89) Volume II
Tahlequah, Cherokee Nation

Office Commission on Citizenship
Tahlequah May 27th 1889

The above named case is decided against applicants William N. Gray an S.H. Gray, there being no evidence submitted in sup. or the allegations set forth in the application.

E.G. Ross
Clerk Commission

Will P. Ross   Chairman
R. Bunch   Com
J.E. Gunter   Com

CANNADA

Docket #507
Rolls 1835

Applicants for Cherokee Citizenship

Post Office: Cannadaville, I.T.   **Attorney**: A.E. Ivey

N°	NAMES	AGE	SEX
1	G.L. Cannada	63	Male
2	Mansfield Cannada	34	"
3	James Cannada	32	"
4	Alonzo Cannada	26	"
	and		
	James L. Canada, et al		
	See Docket "C" No. 921 page 46		

Ancestor: Absalom Cannada

Office Commission on Citizenship Tahlequah I.T. August 14th 1889

The above entitled case being submitted by plaintiffs attorney, M. Hitchcock, on the 13th *(illegible)* it is adjudged and determined by the Commission on Citizenship that the above parties are not Cherokees by blood, for these reasons; first, the ancestor from whom their people claim a Cherokee descent, Absalom Canada and Biddie Canada, or the names of the applicants themselves, fail to appear on any of the rolls of Cherokees mentioned in the law of Dec. 8th 1886, or those mentioned in the amendment of Feb'y 7th 1888 – More over the testimony in this case shows that G.L. Canada and James L. Canada are brothers claiming a descent from the same ancestor, and that their father lived in the state of Tennessee prior to the treaty, or year 1835 and removed to the state of Indiana

Cherokee Citizenship Commission Docket Books
(1880-84, 1887-89) Volume II
Tahlequah, Cherokee Nation

The evidence is of a hearsay character entirely in these cases, none of the witnesses knowing for themselves that which they testified about - In the absence of proof, and the fact that these people are not contained in some of the rolls of Cherokees, G.L. Canada, Mansfield Canada, James Canada and Alonzo Canada and James L. Canada and his daughter Viney J. Canada are declared to be <u>intruders</u> upon the public domain of the Cherokee Nation, without any rights or privileges of citizens whatever.

                           J.T. Adair   Chairman Commission
                           H.C. Barnes   Commissioner

LLEWELLYN

Docket #508
Rolls 1835

Applicant for Cherokee Citizenship

Post Office: Wedington[sic], Ark   **Attorney**: C.H. Taylor

N°	NAMES	AGE	SEX
1	Dica Lewellen[sic]	67	female

Ancestor: James Parris

Commission on Citizenship.

CHEROKEE NATION, IND. TER.

Dicey Llewellyn, et al.   *Tahlequah,* August 29th 1888
    (VS)
Cherokee Nation

The above entitled case is composed of eight applications, First Dicey Llewellyn and Henry J. Llewellyn, claiming a Cherokee descent from James Parris; Secondly, William C. Llewellyn, James L. Llewellyn and Rebecca Johnson, claiming a Cherokee descent from their mother, Dicey Llewellyn, who is the grand daughter of James Parris: Thereby, Steve Llewellyn and America E. Rusk, claiming a Cherokee descent from Nancy Benum nee Parris, the grand daughter of James Parris.

Cherokee Citizenship Commission Docket Books
(1880-84, 1887-89) Volume II
Tahlequah, Cherokee Nation

The testimony in these cases will be found in the application of Dicey Llewellyn and was duly and impartially examined.

From the evidence of George Parris, and of the witnesses the above case, it will at once be observed that all he knows is from what he had[sic] his parents say, and that his grand father, George Parris. Son was married three times and that he had these children by his first marriage, viz: *(Illegible)* T. Jim & John, and that Dicey Llewellyn claims to be the great grand child of George Parris, the grandfather of George Parris, the affiant. Mr. Parris further states from a conversation he had with the mother of Dicey Llewellyn, that he believes that they are related to him, but does not know of his own knowledge that such is the case.

The testimony of James Dale, of Monroe County, state of Missouri, goes to show that he is 84 years old, and that Dicey Llewellyn is the daughter of James Parris, but says nothing about his, James Parris', Cherokee blood. The affidavits of Isom Thompson and Hubbard Johnson taken in the state of Missouri, fail to show that James Parris, the grandfather of Dicey Llewellyn, was of Cherokee Indian blood. The testimony of Polly Parris is of a hearsay character, and not much importance can be attached to it.

This is about all the testimony that needs to be recounted to arrive at a conclusion in the premise. From the testimony of George Parris, now 66 years old, who is the son of Robert Parris who is or was, a half brother of Jim Parris, who were the sons of George Parris, son, taken in connection with the allegation contained in the application of Dicey Llewellyn, now 64 years old, when she alleges that she is descended from one James Parris, her grandfather, who is now living, would be in the very nature of things, allowing a person to be 20 years old before they had any offspring, about 107 or 108 years old, therefore the James Parris mentioned by Mr. George Parris, as "Jim" and being one of the children by George Parris' son first wife and the uncle of George Parris, the affiant, who is 66 years old, could not have been the same James Parris as alleged as the ancestor of the applicant in this case, for it is hardly probable that James Parris the uncle of George Parris, Jr. could be, if now living more that 85 or 90 years old, tho it is possible. In the absence of dates and ages which have been omitted in getting this evidence together, the Commission is at a loss to freely and lucidly understand it from this stand point, more over the rolls of Cherokees of the year 1835 taken in the states of Tennessee, Alabama, North Carolina and Georgia, fail to show the names of James Parris, Dicey Llewellyn

Cherokee Citizenship Commission Docket Books
(1880-84, 1887-89) Volume II
Tahlequah, Cherokee Nation

or that of Nancy Benum, or any of the applicants herein mentioned, and are therefore by the Commission on Citizenship, declared and adjudged to have no rights or privileges in common with the Cherokee tribe of Indians, and Dicey Llewellyn, Robert Llewellyn, Henry J. Llewellyn, Nettie M. Llewellyn, Vincent B. Llewellyn, Sarah F. Llewellyn, Dora Llewellyn, Laura Llewellyn, John Llewellyn, Steve Llewellyn, Alfred B. Llewellyn, Cordora Llewellyn, James L. Llewellyn, Alonzo Llewellyn, Hugh Llewellyn, Bertie A. Llewellyn, William C. Llewellyn, Lawson Llewellyn, Florence Llewellyn, Stephen Llewellyn, James Llewellyn, Oscar Llewellyn, Rebecca Johnson, Amanda Johnson, Robert Johnson, Mitchell Johnson, Dicey Johnson, Mary Johnson, America Ellen Rusk, William L. Smith, James S. Smith, John W. Smith, Ada E. Rusk, Lula Rusk, William D. Rusk, John M. Rusk, Eliza E. Rusk, and Mary Rusk, the applicants in the above and foregoing case are hereby as declared.

They being residents of the states of the United States and not being within the confines of the Cherokee Nation.

                         D.W. Lipe   Acting Chairman Commission
                         H.C. Barnes   Commissioner

DAVIS

Docket #509
Rolls 1835 to 1852

Applicant for Cherokee Citizenship

Post Office: Neutral. Kans.   **Attorney:** A.E. Ivey

N°	NAMES	AGE	SEX
1	Elizabeth Davis	22	Female
2	Maude Davis		"

Ancestor: Richard Sizemore

See decision in this case in the Sarah A. Bond case on page 235 Book "A" – Adverse to Claimant

                         Cornell Rogers
                         Clerk Com. on Citizenship

Office Com. on Citizenship
Tahlequah, I.T. Sept 19th '88

Cherokee Citizenship Commission Docket Books
(1880-84, 1887-89) Volume II
Tahlequah, Cherokee Nation

SIZEMORE

Docket #510
Rolls 1835

Applicant for Cherokee Citizenship
Post Office: Neutral, Kans.   **Attorney:** A.E. Ivey

N°	NAMES	AGE	SEX
1	James C. Sizemore	57	male
2	America A. Sizemore	20	female
3	Ida Sizemore	13	"
4	George C. Dobins (grand child)	2	male

Ancestor: Richard Sizemore

See decision in this case in that of Sarah A. Bond case on page 235 Book "A". Adverse to Claimant

Cornell Rogers
Clerk Com. on Citizenship

Office Com. on Citizenship
Tahlequah, I.T. Sept 19th '88

SIZEMORE

Docket #511
Rolls 1835 to 1852

Applicant for Cherokee Citizenship
Post Office: Columbus, Kans   **Attorney:** A.E. Ivey

N°	NAMES	AGE	SEX
1	Wm F. Sizemore		

Ancestor: Richard Sizemore

See decision in this case in the case of Sarah A. Bond case on Book "A" page 235 – Adverse to Claimant

Cornell Rogers
Clerk Com. on Citizenship

Office Com. on Citizenship
Tahlequah, I.T. Sept 19th '88

Cherokee Citizenship Commission Docket Books
(1880-84, 1887-89) Volume II
Tahlequah, Cherokee Nation

KEITH

Docket #512
Rolls 1835 to 1852

Applicant for Cherokee Citizenship
Post Office: Neutral, Kans   **Attorney**: A.E. Ivey

N°	NAMES	AGE	SEX
1	Sarah Keith	31	female
2	James M. Keith	12	male
3	Minnie Keith	9	female
4	Jefferson Keith	7	male
5	Stella Keith	5	female
6	Elmer Keith	1	male

Ancestor: Richard Sizemore

See decision in this case in the case of Sarah A. Bond case on Book "A" page 235 – Adverse to Claimant

Cornell Rogers
Clerk Com. on Citizenship

Office Com. on Citizenship
Tahlequah, I.T. Sept 19th '88

SIZEMORE

Docket #513
Rolls 1835 to 1852

Applicant for Cherokee Citizenship
Post Office: Columbus, Kans   **Attorney**: A.E. Ivey

N°	NAMES	AGE	SEX
1	Allen G. Sizemore	30	male
2	Gertrude Sizemore	3	female
3	Adolph A. Sizemore	1	male

Ancestor: Richard Sizemore

See decision in this case in that of Sarah A. Bond case on Book "A" page 235 – Adverse to Claimant

Cornell Rogers
Clerk Com. on Citizenship

Office Com. on Citizenship
Tahlequah, I.T. Sept 19th '88

Cherokee Citizenship Commission Docket Books
(1880-84, 1887-89) Volume II
Tahlequah, Cherokee Nation

SIZEMORE

Docket #514
Rolls 1835 to 1852

Applicant for Cherokee Citizenship

Post Office: Columbus, Kans. **Attorney:** A.E. Ivey

N°	NAMES	AGE	SEX
1	Andrew J. Sizemore		
2	Lissa A. Sizemore		

Ancestor: Richard Sizemore

See decision in this case in that of Sarah A. Bond case on Book "A" page 235 – Adverse to Claimant

Cornell Rogers
Clerk Com. on Citizenship

Office Com. on Citizenship
Tahlequah, I.T. Sept 19th '88

SIZEMORE

Docket #515
Rolls 1835 to 1852

Applicant for Cherokee Citizenship

Post Office: Neutral, Kans. **Attorney:** A.E. Ivey

N°	NAMES	AGE	SEX
1	Richard G. Sizemore	38	male
2	James A. Sizemore	16	female[sic]
3	Hattie G. Sizemore	10	"
4	Della V. Sizemore	8	"
5	Charles A. Sizemore	3	male
6	Jessie Sizemore		

Ancestor: Richard Sizemore

See decision in this case in that of Sarah A. Bond case on Book "A" page 235. Adverse to Claimant

Cornell Rogers
Clerk Com. on Citizenship

Cherokee Citizenship Commission Docket Books
(1880-84, 1887-89) Volume II
Tahlequah, Cherokee Nation

Office Com. on Citizenship
Tahlequah, I.T. Sept 19th '88

SIZEMORE

Docket #516
Rolls 1835 to 1852

Applicant for Cherokee Citizenship

Post Office: Neutral, Kans   **Attorney:** A.E. Ivey

N°	NAMES	AGE	SEX
1	Mary A. Gaylor	30	female
2	Bertha R. Gaylor	8	"
3	America O. Gaylor	6	"
4	Garland G. Gaylor	3	male

Ancestor: Richard Sizemore

See decision in this case in that of Sarah A. Bond case on Book "A" page 235. Adverse to Claimant

Cornell Rogers
Office Com. on Citizenship   Clerk Com. on Citizenship
Tahlequah, I.T. Sept 19th '88

BOND

Docket #517
Rolls 1835 to 1852

Applicant for Cherokee Citizenship

Post Office: Stafford, Kans   **Attorney:** A.E. Ivey

N°	NAMES	AGE	SEX
1	Abel J Bond	33	male
2	J.A. Bond	13	"
3	Christina Bond	10	female
4	Laura Bond	8	"
5	Wm Bond	6	male
6	Bertha Bond	4	female
7	Anna P. Bond	2	"

Ancestor: Isom Sizemore

See decision in this case in that of Sarah A. Bond case on Book "A" page 235 –

Cherokee Citizenship Commission Docket Books
(1880-84, 1887-89) Volume II
Tahlequah, Cherokee Nation

Adverse to Claimant.

Cornell Rogers
Clerk Com. on Citizenship

Office Com. on Citizenship
Tahlequah, I.T. Sept 19th '88

MOLDEN

Docket #518
Rolls 1835

Applicant for Cherokee Citizenship

Post Office: Harrison, Ark   **Attorney:** C.H. Taylor

N°	NAMES	AGE	SEX
1	Mattie Molden	24	female
2	Arthur Molden	7	male
3	Aleis[sic] Molden	5	"
4	Sissie Molden	3 mo	female

Ancestor: Rena Johnson

Office Commission on Citizenship
Cherokee Nation Ind Ter'y.
Tahlequah June 6th 1889

The Commission this day decide against Mattie Molden age 24 years and her children whose names are as follows Arthur Molden 7 years Alice Molden age 5 years and Sissie Molden Female age 3 months are not of Cherokee blood. See decision in the case of Rena Johnson Docket 292 Book B Page 5. Post office address Harrison Ark.

Will P. Ross
Attest   Chairman
   D.S. Williams   JE Gunter   Com
   Asst Clk Com

Cherokee Citizenship Commission Docket Books
(1880-84, 1887-89) Volume II
Tahlequah, Cherokee Nation

JOHNSON

Docket #519
Rolls 1835

Applicants for Cherokee Citizenship

Post Office: Harrison, Ark   **Attorney:** C.H. Taylor

N°	NAMES	AGE	SEX
1	George Johnson	35	male
2	Lillie Johnson	7	female
3	Rena Johnson	5	"

Ancestor: Rena Johnson

Office Commission on Citizenship
Cherokee Nation Ind Ter'y.
Tahlequah June 6th 1889

The Commission this day decide that George Johnson age 35 years and his children whose names are as follows Lillie Female 7 years and Rena Johnson Female age 5 years are not of Cherokee blood. See decision in case of Rena Johnson Docket 292 Book B Page 5. Post office address Harrison Ark.

Will P. Ross
Chairman

Attest
D.S. Williams   JE Gunter   Com
Asst Clk Com

MITCHEL

Docket #520
Rolls 1835

Applicant for Cherokee Citizenship

Post Office: Harrison, Ark   **Attorney:** C.H. Taylor

N°	NAMES	AGE	SEX
1	Alta Mitchel[sic]	28	female
2	Stella Mitchel	8	"

Ancestor: Rena Johnson

Office Commission on Citizenship
Cherokee Nation Ind Ter'y.
Tahlequah June 6th 1889

Cherokee Citizenship Commission Docket Books
(1880-84, 1887-89) Volume II
Tahlequah, Cherokee Nation

The Commission this day decide against Alta Mitchell the applicant age 28 years her daughter Stella Mitchell age 8 years, are not of Cherokee blood. See decision in case of Rena Johnson Docket 292 Book B Page 5. Post office address Harrison Ark.

                            Will P. Ross
Attest   Chairman
    D.S. Williams   JE Gunter   Com
    Asst Clk Com

SLOOP

Docket #521
Rolls 1835

                            Applicant for Cherokee Citizenship
     Post Office: Harrison, Ark   **Attorney:** C.H. Taylor

N°	NAMES	AGE	SEX
1	Jane Sloop	31	female
2	Harvey Sloop	9	male
3	Jane Sloop	7	female

                Ancestor: Rena Johnson
Rejected June 6th 1889

                    Office Commission on Citizenship
                      Cherokee Nation Ind Ter'y.
                      Tahlequah June 6th 1889

The Commission this day decide against Jane Sloop the applicant age 31 years and his children whose names are as follows Harvey Sloop male age 9 years and Josie[sic] Female age 7 years, we adjudge that they are not of Cherokee blood. See decision in case of Rena Johnson Docket 292 Book B Page 5. Post office address Harrison Ark.

                          Will P. Ross
Attest   Chairman
    D.S. Williams   J.E. Gunter   Com
    Asst Clk Com

Cherokee Citizenship Commission Docket Books
(1880-84, 1887-89) Volume II
Tahlequah, Cherokee Nation

MOSS

Docket #522
Rolls 1835

Applicant for Cherokee Citizenship
Post Office: Harrison, Ark   **Attorney:** C.H. Taylor

N°	NAMES	AGE	SEX
1	Roxey Moss	26	female
2	Hugh Moss	8	male
3	Elbert Moss	6	"
4	Della Moss	4	female
5	Sissie Moss	1	female

Ancestor: Rena Johnson

Office Commission on Citizenship
Cherokee Nation Ind. Tery.
Tahlequah June 6th 1889

The Commission this day decide that Roxey Moss age 26 years and her children whose names are as follows Hugh Moss male age 8 years, Elbert Moss male age 6 years, Della Female age 4 years and Sissie Moss Female age 1 year are not Cherokee blood. See decision in case of Rena Johnson Docket 292 Book B, Page 5 Post office address Harrison Ark.

Attest   Will P. Ross
   DS Williams   Chairman
   Asst. Clk Com   J.E. Gunter   Com

JONES

Docket #523
Rolls 1835

Applicant for Cherokee Citizenship
Post Office: Harrison Ark   **Attorney:** C.H. Taylor

N°	NAMES	AGE	SEX
1	Anna Jones	33	female
2	Mary Jones	13	"
3	Ester Jones	11	"
4	Samuel Jones	9	"[sic]

Ancestor: Rena Johnson

Cherokee Citizenship Commission Docket Books
(1880-84, 1887-89) Volume II
Tahlequah, Cherokee Nation

Rejected June 6th 1889

Office Commission on Citizenship
Cherokee Nation Ind. Tery
Tahlequah June 6th 1889

The Commission this day decide that Anna Jones age 33 years and her children whose names are as follows Mary Jane Female age 13 years Ester Female age 11 years and Samuel Jones male age 9 years are not of Cherokee blood and are not entitled to Citizenship in the Cherokee Nation. See decision in case of Rena Johnson Docket 292 Book B Page 5 Post office address Harrison Ark.

Attest
   D.S. Williams
   Asst Clk Com.

Will P. Ross
   Chairman
J.E. Gunter   Com.

DAVIS

Docket #524
Rolls 1851 & 1852

Applicant for Cherokee Citizenship

Post Office: Dahlonega, Ga.   **Attorney:**

N°	NAMES	AGE	SEX
1	Miller Davis	26	male
2	Susan Davis (Sister)	31	female
3	Earl Davis (Brother)	24	male

Ancestor: Lorenzo D. Davis

Now on this the 16th day of December 1887. comes the above case for final hearing and having made application pursuant to the provisions of the Act of the National Council approved December 8th 1886, and all the evidence being duly considered and found to be sufficient and satisfactory to the Commission it is adjudged and determined by the Commission that Miller Davis, Susan Davis and Earl Davis are Cherokees by blood and they are hereby readmitted too all the rights privileges and immunities of Cherokee Citizens by blood.

And a certificate of said decision of the Commission and of readmission was made and furnished said parties accordingly.

Cherokee Citizenship Commission Docket Books
(1880-84, 1887-89) Volume II
Tahlequah, Cherokee Nation

R.T. Hauks
Asst. Clerk of Comm.
on Citizenship

J.T. Adair, Chairman Commission
John E. Gunter Commissioner

McGUIRE

Docket #525
Rolls 1835 to 1852

Applicant for Cherokee Citizenship
Post Office: Mason Valley Ark   **Attorney:** L.S. Sanders

N°	NAMES	AGE	SEX
1	James T. McGuire	43	male
2	William A. McGuire	19	"
3	Hettie Bell McGuire	14	female
4	Rosey Lee McGuire	11	"

Ancestor: Elizabeth Choate

Office Commission on Citizenship
Cherokee Nation Ind. Ter,
Tahlequah Aug 20th 1889

The above application was filed on the 16th day of September, 1887. The applicant claims to derive his Cherokee blood through his Grand Mother, Elizabeth Choate.

The claimant fails to find any evidence in support of his claim of Cherokee blood and in view of this fact, we decide that applicant James Taylor McGuire, age 43 together with his children William A. McGuire age 19 years, Hettie Bell McGuire age 14 years, Rosa Lee McGuire age 11 years, are not Cherokees by blood and are not entitled to Cherokee Citizenship in the Cherokee Nation.

	Will P. Ross	Chairman
Attest	R. Bunch	Com
E.G. Ross	J.E. Gunter	Com
Clerk Commission		

Cherokee Citizenship Commission Docket Books
(1880-84, 1887-89) Volume II
Tahlequah, Cherokee Nation

CHRISTEY

Docket #526
Rolls 1835 to 1852

Applicant for Cherokee Citizenship

Post Office: Siloam Springs, Ark.   **Attorney:** L.S. Sanders

N°	NAMES	AGE	SEX
1	John H. Christey	57	
2	Ellen L. Christey (wife)	46	

Ancestor: *(Illegible)* & Comingdeer

Rejected Aug. 21st 1889

Office Commission on Citizenship
Cherokee Nation Ind. Ter.
Tahlequah Aug. 21st 1889

The application in this case was filed on the 16 day of Sept. 1887, and there being no evidence in support of this case the Commission decide that Applicants John L.[sic] Christey age 57 yrs and his wife Ellen L. Christey are not Cherokees by blood and not entitled to Citizenship in the Cherokee Nation. P.O. Siloam Springs Ark.

Attest
D.S. Williams
Asst. Clk Com.

Will P. Ross   Chairman
R. Bunch   Com
J.E. Gunter   Com

HALL

Docket #527
Rolls 1835 to 1852

Applicant for Cherokee Citizenship

Post Office: Blue Jacket I.T.   **Attorney:** A.E. Ivey

N°	NAMES	AGE	SEX
1	Mary K. Hall	30	female
2	Minnie J. Hall	11	"
3	Daisy M. Hall	9	"
4	Paty L. Hall	6	"
5	Effie M. Hall	4	"
6	Archie C. Hall	2	male
7	Wm A. Hall	4 mo	"

Ancestor: Isom Sizemore

Cherokee Citizenship Commission Docket Books
(1880-84, 1887-89) Volume II
Tahlequah, Cherokee Nation

See decision in this case in that of Sarah A. Bond on Book "A" page 235. Adverse to claimant.

Cornell Rogers
Clerk Com on Citizenship

Office Com on Citizenship
Tahlequah I.T. Sept. 19th 1888

SIZEMORE

Docket #528
Rolls 1835 to 1852

Applicant for Cherokee Citizenship

Post Office: Neutral, Kans.   **Attorney:** A.E. Ivey

N°	NAMES	AGE	SEX
1	James K. Sizemore		
2	Gracie M. Sizemore		

Ancestor: Richard Sizemore

See decision in this case in that of Sarah A. Bond on Book "A" page 235 – Adverse to claimant.

Cornell Rogers
Clerk Com on Citizenship

Office Com on Citizenship
Tahlequah I.T. Sept 19th 1888.

BOND

Docket #529
Rolls 1835 to 1852

Applicant for Cherokee Citizenship

Post Office: Little River, Kans   **Attorney:** A.E. Ivey

N°	NAMES	AGE	SEX
1	Isom R. Bond	42	male
2	Almeeda Bond	17	female
3	Isom H. Bond	15	male
4	Ida Bond	14	female
5	Earl Bond	7	male
6	Ethel Bond	3 mo	twins

Cherokee Citizenship Commission Docket Books
(1880-84, 1887-89) Volume II
Tahlequah, Cherokee Nation

7	Mable Bond	3 mo	"

Ancestor: Isom Sizemore

See decision in this case in that of Sarah A. Bond on Book "A" page 235. Adverse to claimant.

                                Cornell Rogers
                                        Clerk Com on Citizenship

Office Com on Citizenship
Tahlequah I.T. Sept 19th 1888.

COPE

Docket #530
Rolls 1835 to 1852

                                Applicant for Cherokee Citizenship
Post Office: Blue Jacket I.T.   **Attorney:** A.E. Ivey

N°	NAMES	AGE	SEX
1	Martha A. Cope	35	female
2	William Cope	12	male
3	David Cope	9	"

Ancestor: Isom Sizemore

                          Office Commission on Citizenship
                              Tahlequah C.M. May 27 1889

The application in the above case was foiled on the 15th day of September 1887 and was submitted for a final hearing with out evidence May 27th 1889. The Commission therefore decide that Martha Cope aged thirty five years and the following named children William Cope male aged twelve years, David Cope male aged nine years are not of Cherokee blood and are not entitled to Citizenship in the Cherokee Nation Post Office address Blue Jacket I.T.

                        Will P. Ross   Chairman
Attest   R. Bunch   Com
     E.G. Ross   J.E. Gunter   Com
        Clerk Commission

Cherokee Citizenship Commission Docket Books
(1880-84, 1887-89) Volume II
Tahlequah, Cherokee Nation

HAYES

Docket #531
Rolls 1835 to 1852

Applicant for Cherokee Citizenship

Post Office: Tahlequah, C.N.   **Attorney:** Gideon Morgan

N°	NAMES	AGE	SEX
1	Elizabeth Morgan Hayes	30	female

Ancestor: Elizabeth Eblen

Now on this the 17th day of September 1887 comes the above case for final hearing, and having made application pursuant to the provisions of an Act of the National Council approved December 8th 1886, and all the evidence being duly considered and found to be sufficient and satisfactory to the Commission. It is adjudged and determined by the Commission, that Elizabeth Morgan Eblen, is a Cherokee by blood, and are hereby readmitted to all the rights privileges and immunities of a Cherokee by blood.

And a certificate of said decision of the Commission and readmission was made and furnished to said persons accordingly.

C.C. Lipe   J.T. Adair   Chair Commission
Clerk Commission   John E. Gunter   Commissioner

BOND

Docket #532
Rolls 1835 to 1852

Applicant for Cherokee Citizenship

Post Office: Blue Jacket I.T.   **Attorney:** A.E. Ivey

N°	NAMES	AGE	SEX
1	J.S. Bond	26	male
2	Annie Bone	1	female

Ancestor: Isom Sizemore

See decision in this case in that of Sarah A. Bond on Book "A" page 235 – Adverse to claimant.

Cornell Rogers
Clerk Com. on Citizenship

Cherokee Citizenship Commission Docket Books
(1880-84, 1887-89) Volume II
Tahlequah, Cherokee Nation

Office Com on Citizenship
Tahlequah I.T. Sept 19th 1888

DAVIS

Docket #533
Rolls 1852 & 2

Applicant for Cherokee Citizenship

Post Office: Dahlonega Ga. **Attorney**:

N°	NAMES	AGE	SEX
1	Daniel Davis	40	male
2	William E. Davis	8	"
3	Newton L. Davis		

Ancestor: Lorenzo D. Davis

Now on this the 16th day of December 1887 comes the above case for final hearing and having made application pursuant to the provisions of the Act of the National Council approved December 8th 1886, and all the evidence being duly considered and found to be sufficient and satisfactory to the Commission it is adjudged and determined by the Commission that Daniel Davis, William E. Davis and Newton L. Davis are Cherokees by blood and they are hereby readmitted to all the rights privileges and immunities of Cherokee Citizens by blood.

And a certificate of said decision of the Commission and of readmission was made and furnished said parties accordingly.

R.T. Hauks   J.T. Adair   Chairman Commission
Asst Clerk of Com   John E. Gunter   Commissioner
on Citizenship

SEITZ

Docket #534
Rolls 1852 & 2

Applicant for Cherokee Citizenship

Post Office: Dahlonega Ga. **Attorney**:

N°	NAMES	AGE	SEX
1	Jennie L. Seitz	30	Female
2	Mary D. Seitz	10	"

Cherokee Citizenship Commission Docket Books
(1880-84, 1887-89) Volume II
Tahlequah, Cherokee Nation

3	Eliza M. Seitz	8	"
4	Jetta A. Seitz	6	"
5	Amanda E. Seitz	5	"
6	George A. Seitz	4	
7	John C. Seitz		

Ancestor: Danl. and Rachel Davis

Now on this the 28th day of January 1888, comes the above case for a final hearing, and the parties having made application pursuant to the provisions of the Act of the National Council approved December 8th 1886, and all the evidence being duly examined and found to be sufficient and satisfactory to the Commission and the names of the ancestor appearing on the Rolls of 1852. It is adjudged and determined by the Commission that Jennie L. Seitz, Mary D. Seitz, Eliza M. Seitz, Jetta A. Seitz, Amanda E. Seitz, George A. Seitz and John C. Seitz are Cherokees and are hereby re-admitted to all the rights privileges of Cherokee by blood.

And a certificate of said decision of the Commission and of readmission were made and furnished said parties accordingly.

J.T. Adair — Chairman Commission
John E. Gunter — Commissioner
D.W. Lipe — Commissioner

Attest
C.C. Lipe
Clerk Commission

LLEWELLYN

Docket #535
Rolls 1835

Applicant for Cherokee Citizenship

Post Office: Wedington[sic] Ark   **Attorney:** *(Illegible)* and Sanders

N°	NAMES	AGE	SEX
1	*(Illegible)* J. Llewellyn	38	male
2	*(Illegible)* M. Llewellyn		

Ancestor: James Parris

Cherokee Citizenship Commission Docket Books
(1880-84, 1887-89) Volume II
Tahlequah, Cherokee Nation

See decision in the above case in the Dicey Llewellyn case on page 221 of this Book – adverse –

Cornell Rogers

August 29th 88

CORN

Docket #536
Rolls 1851 & 2

Applicant for Cherokee Citizenship

Post Office: Dahlonega Ga.   **Attorney:**

N°	NAMES	AGE	SEX
1	Hannah Corn	33	Female
2	Ola S. Corn	14	"
3	Arden Corn	9	male
4	Earl Corn	6	"
5	Wm H Corn	4	"

Ancestor: Lorenzo D. Davis

Now on this the 16th day of December 1887 comes the above case for final hearing and having made application pursuant to the provisions of the Act of the National Council approved December 8th 1886, and all the evidence being duly considered and found to be sufficient and satisfactory to the Commission it is adjudged and determined by the Commission that Hannah Corn, Ola Corn, Archie Corn, Earl Corn and William H. Corn, are Cherokees by blood and they are hereby readmitted to all the rights privileges and immunities of Cherokee Citizens by blood.

And a certificate of said decision of the Commission and of readmission was made and furnished said parties accordingly.

R.T. Hauks   J.T. Adair   Chairman Commission
Asst Clerk of Com   John E. Gunter   Commissioner
on Citizenship

Cherokee Citizenship Commission Docket Books
(1880-84, 1887-89) Volume II
Tahlequah, Cherokee Nation

DAVIS

Docket #537
Rolls 1851 – 2

Applicant for Cherokee Citizenship

Post Office: Dahlonega Ga   **Attorney:**

N°	NAMES	AGE	SEX
1	J.W. Davis	37	male
2	Mary E. Davis	15	Fem.
3	Danl. B. Davis	13	male
4	Dock Davis	11	"
5	Susan M. Davis	8	Fem
6	Berrella E. Davis	6	"
7	Amanda Davis	4	"
8	Florence Davis	2	"
9	Joseph J. Davis	1	male

Ancestor: Lorenzo D. Davis

Now on this the 16th day of December 1887 comes the above case for final hearing and having made application pursuant to the provisions of the Act of the National Council approved December 8th 1886, and all the evidence being duly considered and found to be sufficient and satisfactory to the Commission it is adjudged and determined by the Commission that J.W. Davis, Mary E. Davis, Daniel B. Davis, Dock Davis, Susan M. Davis, Berrella E. Davis, Amanda Davis, Florence Davis and Joseph J. Davis are Cherokees by blood and they are hereby readmitted to all the rights privileges and immunities of Cherokee Citizenship by blood.

And a certificate of said decision of the Commission and of readmission was made and furnished said parties accordingly.

R.T. Hauks   J.T. Adair   Chairman Commission
Asst Clerk of Com   John E. Gunter   Commissioner
on Citizenship

Cherokee Citizenship Commission Docket Books
(1880-84, 1887-89) Volume II
Tahlequah, Cherokee Nation

BOATRIGHT

Docket #538
Rolls 1835 to 52

Application for Cherokee Citizenship

Post Office: Siloam Springs Ark   **Attorney:** L.S. Sanders

N°	NAMES	AGE	SEX
1	Eveline Boatright	50	Fem
2	Geo M. Boatright	20	Male
3	Julia M. Boatright	18	Fem
4	Eveline Boatright	15	"
5	Jesse Boatright	13	Male
6	Jas R Boatright	11	"
7	Catherine E. Boatright	9	Fem
8	Medora P. Boatright	7	"
9	Myrtle Boatright	4	"

Ancestor: Isaac Miller

Office Commission on Citizenship
Tahlequah May 16th 1889

Now on this day comes the above named case for the final hearing the same having been filed on the 15th day of September 1887. The above named applicant claims her Cherokee blood through one Andrew Miller who she claims is enrolled on the census rolls of Cherokees taken and made in the years of 1835 & 1852. The Commission fail to find the name of Andrew Miller on either of the above named rolls and there being no evidence in support of said above claimants case the Commission decide that Eveline Boatright aged 50 years and her children to wit: George M. Boatright male aged 20 years, Julia M. Boatright Female aged 18 years, Eveline Boatright Female aged 15 years, Jesse Boatright Male aged 13 years, James R. Boatright male aged 11 years, Catharine E. Boatright Female aged 9 years, Medora P. Boatright Female aged 7 years, Myrtle Boatright. Female aged 4 years, are not of Cherokee blood and not entitled to Citizenship in the Cherokee Nation. Post Office Siloam Springs, Ark.

Will P. Ross   Chairman
R. Bunch   Com
E.G. Ross   JE Gunter   Com
Clerk Commission

Cherokee Citizenship Commission Docket Books (1880-84, 1887-89) Volume II
Tahlequah, Cherokee Nation

LANGLEY

Docket #539
Rolls 1835 – 51 & 52

Applicant for Cherokee Citizenship
Post Office: Dresden, I.T.   **Attorney:** Wm A Thompson

N°	NAMES	AGE	SEX
1	Sarah J Langley	37	Fem
2	Loncella Langley	16	"
3	Joannie Langley	14	"
4	Nellie C. Langley	8	"
5	Joseph M. Langley	6	Male
6	John F. Langley	2	"

Ancestor: *(Illegible)* Clarkes

Office Commission on Citizenship
Cherokee Nation July 3rd 1889

There being no evidence in support of the above named case the Commission decide that Sarah J. Langley aged 37 years and the following children, Loncella Female aged 16 years, Joannie Female aged 14 years, Nellie C. Female aged 8 years, Joseph M. Male aged 6 years and John F. Langley male aged 2 years are not Cherokees by blood. Post Office Dresden, I.T.

Attest
   E.G. Ross
   Clerk Commission

Will P. Ross
   Chairman
   John E. Gunter   Com

DICKERSON

Docket #540
Rolls 1835 to 52

Applicant for Cherokee Citizenship
Post Office: Severy, Greenwood Co, Kans   **Attorney:** L.S. Sanders and Boudinot & Rasmus

N°	NAMES	AGE	SEX
1	Mary P. Dickerson	29	Fem
2	Harry Dickerson	11	Male
3	Clarence Dickerson	9	"
4	Ernest Dickerson	6	"

Cherokee Citizenship Commission Docket Books
(1880-84, 1887-89) Volume II
Tahlequah, Cherokee Nation

| 5 | John M. Dickerson | 3 | " |
| 6 | Everet Male[sic] Dickerson | 4 | months |

Ancestor: Oliver and Maria McCoy

Commission on Citizenship.

CHEROKEE NATION, IND. TER.

Tahlequah, August 3rd 1888

Mary P. Dickerson, et al.
   (VS)
Cherokee Nation

    The above case being submitted by Plaintiff's Atty, it was first taken into consideration in the matter of changing the name of the ancestor, Oliver McCoy as laid down in the original application of applicant of Sept. 15th 1887 to that of Richard McCoy. The Descendants in this case claiming that they had made a mistake in filing to Oliver instead of Richard McCoy.

    In the testimony of James L. Dickerson, taken before a Notary Public of Greenwood County, state of Kansas, under date of July 19th 1888 in the matter of changing the name of ancestor in this case, it will be noticed that he said it was a mistake of Mr. Boatright, the gentleman who made out the application. The statement of Mr. Boatright made before this Commission in the matter of the alleged mistake in making out this application, is to the affect that he made it out upon the information furnished him and that he thought he had done it right, and that the name of Richard McCoy was not at the making of said application mentioned, and that it was in April following the date of application that he first became apprised, through Mr. Oliver Mears, the brother of applicant, that he had made a mistake in putting the ancestor Oliver instead of Richard McCoy. It will be remembered that Mr. McCoy (J.L.) made statement on the 10th of April 1888, before this Commission in which he says that he had a talk with a man by the name of Mears, (Oliver Mears) and that this conversation took place about two weeks ago, in which the name of Richard McCoy was mentioned as being his uncle, and that he, Richard, was to live with a Uncle Jack Martin, in the Old Nation, in Georgia, and that he had no family when he knew him and that he left there in the year 1821 or 1822, but does not know where he went to and that his family and relatives never heard of him afterwards, and that he does not know

Cherokee Citizenship Commission Docket Books
(1880-84, 1887-89) Volume II
Tahlequah, Cherokee Nation

what became of him and that he never heard of an Oliver McCoy. It will be remembered that the papers were found out to be wrong immediately after Uncle Jack McCoy had this conversation, mentioned, with Oliver Mears, a brother of Mary P. Dickerson, and the grand child of the same grand parents – The affidavits of Isaac Dye made on the 23rd day of March, 1888, before a County Clerk of Chautauqua County, state of Kansas, and of John Watkins before a District Clerk of the County of Wilson, in same state even written by the same party, and with the exception of the names and counties different, they are each a facsimile of the other, each party knowing the precise same thing and stating it in the same words – It will be further noticed that these affidavits were made on the 23rd and 24th of March, preceding the date of the statement of Mr. McCoy, when he said that he had a talk with a Mr. Mears in which conversation the name of Richard McCoy was mentioned, and he sys this was about a week ago before date of making statement – It is a notorious fact that Alexander McCoy died between 45 and 50 years ago at Old Dwight Mission in the Cherokee Nation, how – Richard McCoy was lost sight of 7 or 8 years before the birth of Isaac Dye, the party making this statement according to his evidence, in which he says that he is 60 years old – The same be said of John Watkins, when he said is 50 years old – neither of these parties state where or when they knew any of the McCoys mentioned in their statements. All of the circumstances connected with the making of these two affidavits of Isaac Dye and John Watkins betray the fact that they are simply spurious and unworthy of consideration.

We the Commission on Citizenship fail to see the propriety of changing the name on the application of Mrs. Mary P. Dickerson for Cherokee Citizenship from that of Oliver McCoy to Richard McCoy for these reasons: that parties should and do know their grandparents, and we are of the opinion that Oliver McCoy is the grandparent of Mrs. Dickerson, the applicant in this case, as laid down in the application, and that they – the applicants – in this case, stated the truth when they said Oliver McCoy was the grandparent of the applicant for it is evident that "Oliver" is a family name, as Mrs. Dickerson has a brother by name, Oliver Mears, and in all probability was named after his grandfather, and it is passing strange that they never knew it was Richard or if so, said nothing about it until they had an interview with Mr. J.S. McCoy, who in all probability inadvertently led them on in this scheme, *(illegible)* and prove a descent from an acknowledged Cherokee Indian, thereby giving them citizenship - The cupidity of man now a days is inexplicable – It is adjudged and determined that Mary P. Dickerson and her five children, viz: Harry, Clarence, Ernest, John M, and Everet Dickerson are not Cherokees by blood, and are not entitled to the rights

Cherokee Citizenship Commission Docket Books
(1880-84, 1887-89) Volume II
Tahlequah, Cherokee Nation

and privileges of such, as they have not established this fact. The name of Oliver McCoy does not appear on the Rolls of Cherokees laid down in the law of Dec. 8th 1886.

J.T. Adair, Chairman Commission
H.C. Barnes   Commissioner

DAVIS

Docket #541
Rolls 1852 & 2

Applicant for Cherokee Citizenship
Post Office: Dahlonega, Ga.   **Attorney**:

N°	NAMES	AGE	SEX
1	Joseph C. Davis	63	Male

Ancestor: Dan'l Davis

Now on this the 16th day of December 1887, comes the above case for final hearing and having made application pursuant to the provisions of the Act of the National Council approved December 8th 1886, and all the evidence being duly considered and found to be sufficient and satisfactory to the Commission it is adjudged and determined by the Commission that Joseph C. Davis is a Cherokee by blood and he is hereby readmitted to all the rights privileges and immunities of a Cherokee Citizen by blood.

And a certificate of said decision of the Commission and of readmission was made and furnished said parties accordingly.

R.T. Hauks   J.T. Adair   Chairman Commission
Asst Clerk of Commission   John E. Gunter   Commissioner
on Citizenship

DAVIS

Docket #542
Rolls 1851 – 2

Applicant for Cherokee Citizenship
Post Office: Dahlonega, Ga.   **Attorney**:

N°	NAMES	AGE	SEX
1	Lorenzo D. Davis	30	Male

Cherokee Citizenship Commission Docket Books
(1880-84, 1887-89) Volume II
Tahlequah, Cherokee Nation

2	Addie Davis	9	Fem
3	Biddie Davis	6	"
4	Lorenzo D. Davis, Jr.	4	Male
5	Berrilla Davis	4 mo	"

Ancestor: Lorenzo D. Davis

Now on this the 16th day of December 1887, comes the above case for final hearing and having made application pursuant to the provisions of the Act of the National Council approved December 8th 1886, and all the evidence being duly considered and found to be sufficient and satisfactory to the Commission it is adjudged and determined by the Commission that Lorenzo D. Davis, Addie Davis, Biddie Davis, Lorenzo D. Davis, Jr. and Berrilla Davis are Cherokees by blood and they are hereby readmitted to all the rights privileges and immunities of Cherokee Citizens by blood.

And a certificate of said decision of the Commission and of readmission was made and furnished said parties accordingly.

R.T. Hauks
Asst Clerk of Com
on Citizenship

J.T. Adair   Chairman Commission
John E. Gunter   Commissioner

COMBS

Docket #543
Rolls 1835 & 52

Applicant for Cherokee Citizenship
Post Office: Union Town, Arks.   **Attorney:** A.E. Ivey

N°	NAMES	AGE	SEX
1	Cornelia Combs	28	Fem
2	Jennie J. Combs	9	Male[sic]
3	Wm A. Combs	7	"
4	Sallie A. Combs	5	Fem
5	Lillie Combs	3	"
6	Cora Combs	1	"

Ancestor: Martha Ross

Office Commission on Citizenship
Tahlequah C.N. May 27, 1889

Cherokee Citizenship Commission Docket Books
(1880-84, 1887-89) Volume II
Tahlequah, Cherokee Nation

The application in the above case was filed on the 17th day of September 1887 and was submitted for a final hearing May 27th 1889 without evidence. The Commission therefore decide that Cornelia Combs whose age is twenty eight years and the following named children, Jennie J. Combs, Female aged nine years, Wm A. Combs male aged seven years, Sallie A. Combs Female aged five years, Lillie Combs Female aged three years, Cora Combs, Female aged one year are not of Cherokee blood, and are not entitled to Citizenship in the Cherokee Nation.

	Will P. Ross	Chairman
E.G. Ross	R. Bunch	Com
Clerk Commission	J.E. Gunter	Com.

BROWN

Docket #544
Rolls 1835 to 52

Applicant for Cherokee Citizenship

Post Office: Union Town, Arks.　　**Attorney:** A.E. Ivey

N°	NAMES	AGE	SEX
1	Sarah A. Brown	43	Female
2	Isaac Cox	16	male
3	Edward Cox	14	"
4	Isabell	12	Fem

Ancestor: Pettit

Office Commission on Citizenship
Tahlequah CN May 27, 1889

The application in the above case was filed on the 17th day of September 1887, and was supported by no evidence. The Commission therefore decide that Sarah A. Brown and her children whose names are as follows, Isaac Cox male aged 16 years, Edward Cox male aged 14 years, and Isabell Cox are not Cherokees by blood and are not entitled to Citizenship in the Cherokee Nation.

E.G. Ross	Will P. Ross	Chairman
Clerk Commission	R. Bunch	Com
	JE Gunter	Com

Cherokee Citizenship Commission Docket Books
(1880-84, 1887-89) Volume II
Tahlequah, Cherokee Nation

MOSS

Docket #545
Rolls 1835 to 52

Post Office: Union Town, Ark **Applicant for Cherokee Citizenship**
Attorney: A.E. Ivey

N°	NAMES	AGE	SEX
1	Elizabeth Moss	18	Fem.

Ancestor: Pettitt

Office Commission on Citizenship
Tahlequah C.N. May 17th 1889

The application in the above case was filed on the 17th day of September 1887 and was submitted for a final hearing May 27th 1889 without evidence. The Commission therefore decide that Elizabeth Moss is not of Cherokee blood and not entitled to Citizenship in the Cherokee Nation.

E.G. Ross Will P. Ross Chairman
Clerk Commission R Bunch Com
  J.E. Gunter Com

CLUBB

Docket #546

Post Office: Granby, Mo. **Applicant for C. Citizenship**
Attorney: A.E. Ivey

N°	NAMES	AGE	SEX
1	Villetty Clubb	22	Fem
2	Isiah[sic] Clubb	6	male
3	Lovenia Clubb	4	Fem
4	James Clubb		

Ancestor: Alex Brown

Office Commission on Citizenship
Tahlequah C.N. May 27th 1889

The application in the above case was filed on the 17th day of September 1887 and was submitted without evidence. The Commission therefore decide

Cherokee Citizenship Commission Docket Books
(1880-84, 1887-89) Volume II
Tahlequah, Cherokee Nation

that Villetty Clubb and her children named as follows, Isiah[sic] male aged six years, Lovenia Female aged four years, James Clubb male, aged two years are not of Cherokee blood and are not entitled to Citizenship in the Cherokee Nation.

	Will P. Ross	Chairman
Attest	R Bunch	Com
E.G. Ross	J.E. Gunter	Com
Clerk Commission		

BROWN

Docket #547
Rolls 1835 to 52

Applicant for Cherokee Citizenship

Post Office: Brigeton[sic], Mo.   **Attorney:** A.E. Ivey

N°	NAMES	AGE	SEX
1	Sarah T. Brown	18	Female
2	Baby Brown		

Ancestor: Alex Brown

Office Commission on Citizenship
Cherokee Nation, Ind. Ter.
Tahlequah May 27 1889

This application in the above case was filed the 17th day of September 1887 & is supported by no evidence and the Commission therefore decide against the applicant.

	Will P. Ross	Chairman
E.G. Ross	R. Bunch	Com
Clerk Commission	J.E. Gunter	Com.

EAVES

Docket #548
Rolls 1835 to 52

Applicant for Cherokee Citizenship

Post Office: Morrisville, Mo.   **Attorney:** A.E. Ivey

N°	NAMES	AGE	SEX
1	Villetty Eaves	58	Fem

Cherokee Citizenship Commission Docket Books
(1880-84, 1887-89) Volume II
Tahlequah, Cherokee Nation

2	Etta Eaves	16	"
3	Pete Eaves	14	male

Ancestor: Alex Brown

Office Commission on Citizenship
Tahlequah CN May 27th 1889

The application in the above case was filed on the 17th day of September 1887 and was submitted after a final hearing without evidence. The Commission therefore decide that Viletta Eaves and her children named as follows, Etta Eaves female aged sixteen years, Pete Eaves male aged 14 years, are not of Cherokee blood and not entitled to Citizenship in the Cherokee Nation.

E.G. Ross   Will P. Ross   Chairman
  Clerk Commission   R Bunch   Com
                      J.E. Gunter   Com

SNYDER

Docket #549
Rolls 1835 to 52

Applicant for Cherokee Citizenship
Post Office: Blue Jacket, I.T.   **Attorney:** ~~A.E. Ivey~~

N°	NAMES	AGE	SEX
1	Martesen E Snyder	43	Fem
2	Oscar L. Snyder	9	male
3	Mary C Snyder	8	Fem
4	Aleson C Snyder		

Ancestor: *(Illegible)* Davidson

Tahlequah C.N. May 27th 1889

The application in the above case was filed on the 17th day of September 1887 and is supported by no evidence. The Commission therefore decide that Martesen E Snyder and her children whose names are as follows, Oscar S. Snyder son age 9 yrs, Mary C Snyder Daughter 8 yrs, Aleson C. Snyder son 8 yrs whose Post Office address time of filing was Blue Jacket I.T. are not of[sic] Cherokees by blood and are not entitled to Citizenship in the Cherokee Nation.

Cherokee Citizenship Commission Docket Books
(1880-84, 1887-89) Volume II
Tahlequah, Cherokee Nation

George O. Butler   Will P. Ross   Chairman
                        R Bunch   Com
                        J.E. Gunter   Com

MENDENHALL

Docket #550
Rolls

Applicant for Cherokee Citizenship
Post Office: Blue Jacket I.T.   **Attorney:**

N°	NAMES	AGE	SEX
1	Francis V. Mendenhall	33	male[sic]
2	Evan Mendenhall	6	"
3	Walter H. Mendenhall	4	"
4	Lawrence E. Mendenhall	3	"

Ancestor: *(Illegible)* B. Davidson

Office Commission on Citizenship
Tahlequah C.N. May 27th 1889

The application in the above case was filed on the 27th day of September and is supported by no evidence. The Commission therefore decide that Francis V. Mendenhall and her children named as follows, Evan Mendenhall male aged six years, Walter H. male aged four years Lawrence E. Mendenhall male aged three years whose Post Office address at the time of filing was Blue Jack[sic] are not of Cherokee blood and are not entitled to Citizenship in the Cherokee Nation.

	Will P. Ross	Chairman
E.G. Ross	R. Bunch	Com
Clk Commission	J.E. Gunter	Com

THRIFT

Docket #551
Rolls

Applicant for Cherokee Citizenship
Post Office: Fairmount, Ind.   **Attorney:**

N°	NAMES	AGE	SEX
1	Mary Thrift	60	female

Cherokee Citizenship Commission Docket Books
(1880-84, 1887-89) Volume II
Tahlequah, Cherokee Nation

2	Martha J. Ellis	43	daughter
3	Margaret Gordon	42	"
4	Wm T. Thrift	39	son
5	Rebecca M. Brewer	37	daughter
6	David A. Thrift	35	son
7	Thomas H. Thrift	32	"
8	Sarah H. Riggslee	30	daughter
9	Samuel ? Thrift	22	son
10	Charles F.B. Thrift	17	"
11	Author T. Gordon	12	grand son
12	Daniel E. Gordon	10	"
13	Isham F. Gordon	7	"
14	Rachel S. Gordon	4	"[sic]

Ancestor: Sarah Elmore

Office Commission on Citizenship
Cherokee Nation Ind. Ter.
Tahlequah Aug 19th 1889

    The Commission decide against the applicant as a person of Cherokee blood and thereby not entitled to readmission to Citizenship in the Cherokee Nation for reasons set fourth[sic] in their decision in the case of John R. Henly[sic]. See Docket 553 Book B Page 266. This decision includes the applicant Mary Thrift age 61 years Martha J. Ellis (daughter) age 43 years, Margaret L. Gordon (daughter) age 42 years, William L. Thrift (son) age 39 years, Rebecca M. Brewer (daughter) age 37 years, Davis M. Thrift (son) age 35 years, Thomas H. Thrift (son) age 32 years, Sarah H. Riggslee age 30 years, Samuel L. Thrift (son) age 22 years, Chas F.B. Thrift (son) age 17 years. Nathan F. Gordon (Grand son) age 12 years, David E. Gordon (Grand son) age 10 years, Isham F. Gordon (Grand son) age 7 years, Rachel L. Gordon (Grand Daughter) age 4 years. Post Office Fair Mount, Ind. Jane H. Winslow, sister of Mary Thrift is included in this decision.

                              Will P. Ross   Chairman
Attest E.G. Ross   J.E. Gunter   Com
    Clerk Commission

Cherokee Citizenship Commission Docket Books
(1880-84, 1887-89) Volume II
Tahlequah, Cherokee Nation

HENLEY

Docket #552
Rolls

Applicant for Cherokee Citizenship

Post Office: Fairmount, Ind.   **Attorney:**

N°	NAMES	AGE	SEX
1	Alphena Henley	51	Male
2	Louisa Henley	46	Female
3	Glenn Henley	16	Male
4	Richard Henley	14	"

Ancestor: Sarah Elmore

Adverse decision of Commission in case John R. Henly[sic] Docket 553 Book B Page 266.

                        Will P. Ross   Chairman
Attest D.S. Williams   R. Bunch   Com   J.E. Gunter Com
Asst. Clk Com

HENLEY

Docket #553
Rolls

Applicant for Cherokee Citizenship

Post Office: Tebo, Kans   **Attorney:**

N°	NAMES	AGE	SEX
1	John R. Henley		
2	Sarah Henley		
3	Amanda Durbin		
4	Willis Durbin		
5	Sarah Durbin		

Ancestor: Sarah Elmore

Cherokee Citizenship Commission Docket Books
(1880-84, 1887-89) Volume II
Tahlequah, Cherokee Nation

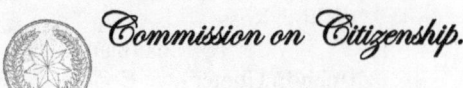

CHEROKEE NATION, IND. TER.

John R. Henly[sic]
vs
The Cherokee Nation

Tahlequah, August 19th 1889
The applicant in the above case alleges that he is the great grand son of one Sarah Elmore and from whom he claims to have derived his Cherokee blood.

In support of the above allegation two affidavits exparte taken by affirmation before Z.F. Rush, a Justice of the Peace in and for Randolph County State of North Carolina on the 28th day of October AD 1886 are presented. One of the affiants Kesiah Dillon 95 years of age claims to be one half Cherokee Indian testifies that she knows applicant from his birth and that he is of Cherokee descent being the child of Phineas Henly who was born in Randolph County, North Carolina in 1862 and died in Grant County, Indiana 1st March 1883. He was the son of John Henly who it is said was born in N.C. in 1767 and died there in 1842 and that he was the son of Sarah Henly nee Sarah Elmore a Cherokee woman who died in 1813. Nancy *(Illegible)* 98 yrs old, the other affiant *(illegible)* to testifies as to the same statement of alleged facts. The statements are not regarded by the Commission as being conclusive as to the Cherokee blood of the applicant because they are exparte and state detail which it is not probable that the witnesses of such extreme age would be likely to recall and because there is nothing to show that Sarah Elmore or any of her descendants at any time lived in the Cherokee Nation or *(several illegible words)* to avail themselves of any of the rights and benefits *(illegible)* or otherwise to which they were entitled if Cherokees by blood. But as conclusive of the question it is admittedly the Attorney for the applicant that neither his own name nor that of an ancestor is found enrolled on the census rolls of Cherokees by blood named in the 7th Sec. of the Act of Decr 8th 1886 and amendment there to taken by the United States and which governs the Commission in their action in the *(illegible).* The Commission therefore decide that applicant John R. Henly and his children wife Sarah Henly age 52 and Amanda Durbin aged 32 and grandchildren Willis Durbin age 12 and Sarah Durbin age 8(or 6) yrs are not of Cherokee blood. P.O. Tebo, Kansas. This decision also includes Alphena Henly and Kesiah Dillon whose names are included in the case of John R. Henly.

Cherokee Citizenship Commission Docket Books
(1880-84, 1887-89) Volume II
Tahlequah, Cherokee Nation

Will P. Ross Chairman
John E. Gunter Com

DILLON

Docket #554
Rolls

Applicant for Cherokee Citizenship

Post Office: Fairmount, Ind. **Attorney:**

N°	NAMES	AGE	SEX
1	Kusiah Dillon	53	female
2	Richard Dillon	27	male

Ancestor: Sarah Elmore

Adverse See decision of Commission in case John R. Henly[sic] Docket 553 Book B Page 266.

Will P. Ross Chairman
R. Bunch Com
J.E. Gunter Com

Attest D.S. Williams
Asst Clk Com

ROSS

Docket #555
Rolls 1835

Applicant for Cherokee Citizenship

Post Office: Muskogee, I.T. **Attorney:**

N°	NAMES	AGE	SEX
1	Joshua Ross	54	Male
2	Rosalee Ross Miles	19	Female
3	Susan Lowery Ross	16	"
4	Joshua Ewing Ross	10	male
5	John Yagu Ross	8	"
6	Richard Lewis Ross	4	"
7	Jennie P. Ross	1	female

Ancestor: Andrew Ross

Cherokee Citizenship Commission Docket Books
(1880-84, 1887-89) Volume II
Tahlequah, Cherokee Nation

Now on this the 28th day of January 1888 comes the above case for a final hearing and the parties having made application pursuant to the provisions of an Act of the National Council approved December 8th 1886, and all the evidence having been duly examined and found to be sufficient and satisfactory to the Commission and the names of the ancestor appearing on the Rolls as claimed in the application. It is adjudged and determined by the Commission, that Joshua Ross, Rosalee Ross Miles, Susan Lowery Ross, Joshua Ewing Ross, John Yargu Ross, Richard Lewis Ross and Jennie P. Ross are Cherokees and are hereby readmitted to all the rights privileges of Cherokees by blood.

And a certificate of said decision of the Commission and of readmission was made and furnished said parties accordingly.

          J.T. Adair   Chairman Commission
          John E. Gunter   Commission
          D.W. Lipe   Commission

Attest
    C.C. Lipe
        Clerk Commission

FORBES

Docket #556
Rolls

Applicant for Cherokee Citizenship

Post Office: *(Illegible)* Ga.   **Attorney:** A.E. Ivey

N°	NAMES	AGE	SEX
1	Francis E. Forbes	26	female
2	Cora Forbes	8	"

Ancestor: Nancy Forbes

Now on this the 16th day of may 1888, comes the above case up for final hearing and the Commission say: "We the Commission on Citizenship after examining the evidence and also the pay rolls find that the above applicants, Francis E. Forbes and Cora Forbes, her daughter to be Cherokees by blood, and are hereby re-admitted to all the rights and privileges of Cherokee citizens by blood.

                        Chairman of the Commission
          D.W. Lipe   Commissioner

Cherokee Citizenship Commission Docket Books
(1880-84, 1887-89) Volume II
Tahlequah, Cherokee Nation

MORTON

Docket #557
Rolls 1835 to 1852

Applicant for Cherokee Citizenship

Post Office: Union Town, Ark.   **Attorney:** A.E. Ivey

N°	NAMES	AGE	SEX
1	William Morton		male

Ancestor: J. ?. Morton

See decision on Page 278 this Book.

Attest
D.S. Williams
Asst Clk Com

Will P. Ross
Chairman
JE Gunter
Com

RUSSELL

Docket #558
Rolls 1835 to 1852

Applicant for Cherokee Citizenship

Post Office: Heidelheimer[sic], Tex   **Attorney:** A.E. Ivey

N°	NAMES	AGE	SEX
1	W.R. Russell	23	male
2	Robert L. Russell	19	"
3	Fannie L. Russell	21	female

Ancestor: Susan Russell

Now on this the 21st day of September 1887 comes the above case for final hearing and having made application pursuant to the provisions of an Act of the National Council approved December 8th 1886, and all the evidence having been duly examined and found to be sufficient and satisfactory to the Commission and the names of ancestor Susan Russell appearing upon the Rolls of 1835, it is adjudged and decided by the Commission that W.R. Russell, Robert L. Russell and Fannie L. Russell are Cherokees by blood and are hereby re-admitted to all the rights privileges and immunities of Cherokees by blood.

Cherokee Citizenship Commission Docket Books
(1880-84, 1887-89) Volume II
Tahlequah, Cherokee Nation

And a certificate of said decision and re-admission of the Commission was made and furnished to said parties accordingly.

	J.T. Adair	Chairman Com
Henry Eiffert	D.W. Lipe	Commissioner
Clk Com		Commissioner

MARSHALL

Docket #559
Rolls 1835 to 1852

Applicant for Cherokee Citizenship

Post Office: Heidelheimer[sic], Tex.   **Attorney:**

N°	NAMES	AGE	SEX
1	Mrs. M.J.R. Marshall	26	female
2	Wm B. Marshal[sic]	1	male

Ancestor: Susan Russell

Now on this the 21st day of September 1887 comes the above case for a final hearing and the applicants having made application pursuant to the provisions of an Act of the National Council approved December 8th 1886, and all the evidence having been duly considered and found to be sufficient and satisfactory to the Commission it is adjudged and determined by the Commission that M.J.R. Marshfield[sic] and Wm B. Marshfield are Cherokees by blood and are hereby readmitted to all the rights privileges and immunities of Cherokees by blood.

And a certificate of said decision of the Commission and re-admission was made and furnished to said parties accordingly.

	J.T. Adair	Chairman Com
Henry Eiffert	D.W. Lipe	Commissioner
		Commissioner

Cherokee Citizenship Commission Docket Books (1880-84, 1887-89) Volume II
Tahlequah, Cherokee Nation

RUSSELL

Docket #560
Rolls 1851 & 1852

Applicant for Cherokee Citizenship

Post Office: Briartown, I.T.   **Attorney:** A.E. Ivey

N°	NAMES	AGE	SEX
1	William H. Russell	39	male
2	Ed W. Russell	2	"

Ancestor: Susan Russell

Now on this the 21st day of September 1887 comes the above case for a final hearing and the applicants having made application pursuant to the provisions of an Act of the National Council approved December 8th 1886, and all the evidence having been duly considered and found to be sufficient and satisfactory to the Commission and the name of Ancestor Susan Russell appearing upon the Rolls of 1851 & 2 it is adjudged and determined by the Commission that William H. Russell and Edward W. Russell are Cherokees by blood; and are hereby readmitted to all the rights privileges and immunities of Cherokees by blood.

And a certificate of said decision of the Commission and re-admission was made and furnished said parties accordingly.

	J.T. Adair	Chairman Commission
Henry Eiffert	D.W. Lipe	Commissioner
Clk Com		Commissioner

HOWARD

Docket #561
Rolls 1835 to 1852

Applicant for Cherokee Citizenship

Post Office: Dougherty, Ga   **Attorney:** A.E. Ivey

N°	NAMES	AGE	SEX
1	Mary E. Howard	33	female
2	Ellen Howard	14	"
3	Russell Howard	12	male
4	Charles P. Howard	10	"
5	Hellen Howard	8	female

Ancestor: Susan Russell

Cherokee Citizenship Commission Docket Books
(1880-84, 1887-89) Volume II
Tahlequah, Cherokee Nation

Now on this the 21st day of September 1887 comes the above case for final hearing and having made application pursuant to the provisions of an Act of the National Council approved December 8th 1886, and all the evidence having been duly examined and found to be sufficient and satisfactory to the Commission, and the name of Ancestor Susan Russell appearing upon the Rolls of 1835, it is adjudged and decided by the Commission that Mary E Howard, Ellen Howard, Russell Howard, Charles P. Howard and Hellen Howard are Cherokees by blood and are hereby readmitted to all the rights privileges and immunities of Cherokees by blood.

And a certificate of said decision and re-admission of the Commission was made and furnished said parties accordingly.

Henry Eiffert	J.T. Adair	Chairman Commission
Clk Com	D.W. Lipe	Commissioner
		Commissioner

PALMOUR

Docket #562
Rolls 1851 to 1852

Applicant for Cherokee Citizenship

Post Office: Palmour, Ga. **Attorney:** A.E. Ivey

N°	NAMES	AGE	SEX
1	John D. Palmour	60	male
2	Mollie O. Palmour	20	female
3	Alaska Palmour	15	"
4	Keziah M. Palmour	13	"

Ancestor: Sarah Palmour

Now on this the 22nd day of September 1887 comes the above case for a final hearing, and the parties having made application pursuant to the provisions of an Act of the National Council approved December 8th 1886, and all the evidence being duly examined, and found to be sufficient and satisfactory to the Commission, and the names of the ancestor appearing on the Rolls of 1851 and 52, it is adjudged and determined by the Commission that John D. Palmour, Mollie O. Palmour, Alaska Palmour and Keziah Palmour, are Cherokees by blood, and are hereby readmitted to all the rights privileges and immunities of Cherokees by blood.

Cherokee Citizenship Commission Docket Books
(1880-84, 1887-89) Volume II
Tahlequah, Cherokee Nation

And a certificate of said decision of the Commission and re-admission was made and furnished to said parties accordingly.

J.T. Adair   Chairman Commission
John E. Gunter   Commissioner

Attest
   C.C. Lipe
      Clerk Commission

PALMOUR

Docket #563
Rolls 1851 & 1852

Applicant for Cherokee Citizenship

Post Office: Palmour, Ga   **Attorney:** A.E. Ivey

Nº	NAMES	AGE	SEX
1	Charles F. Palmour	27	male
2	Iva Palmour	3	female
3	Asa Palmour	6 mos	male

Ancestor: John D. Palmour

Now on this the 22 day of Sept. comes the above case for a final hearing, and the parties having made application pursuant to the provisions of an Act of the National Council approved Dec 8 1886. And all the evidence being duly examined, and found to be sufficient & satisfactory to the Commission. And the names of the ancestor John D. Palmour, appearing on the Rolls of 1851 and 1852. It is adjudged & determined by the Commission that Charles F. Palmour, Iva Palmour, Asa Palmour are Cherokees by blood. And are hereby readmitted to all the rights privileges & immunities of Cherokees by blood. And a certificate of said decision of the Commission & re-admission was made and furnished to said parties accordingly.

J.T. Adair   Chairman Commission
John E. Gunter   Commissioner

C.C. Lipe
Clek[sic] Commission

Cherokee Citizenship Commission Docket Books
(1880-84, 1887-89) Volume II
Tahlequah, Cherokee Nation

SMITH

Docket #564
Rolls 1851 & 1852

Applicant for Cherokee Citizenship

Post Office: Gainsville[sic], Ga   **Attorney:** A.E. Ivey

N°	NAMES	AGE	SEX
1	Sallie A. Smith	25	

Ancestor: John D. Palmour

Now on this the 22 day of Sept. 1887 comes the above case for a final hearing. And the parties having made application pursuant to the provisions of an Act of the National Council approved Dec 8, 1886. And all the evidence being duly examined, & found to be sufficient & satisfactory to the Commission and the name of the ancestor John D. Palmour, appearing on the Rolls of 1851 & 1852. It is adjudged & determined by the Commission that Sallie A. Smith is a Cherokee by blood. And are[sic] hereby re-admitted to all the rights privileges and immunities of Cherokees by blood. And a certificate of said decision of the Commission & re-admission was made & furnished to said parties accordingly.

                    J.T. Adair   Chairman Commission
                    John E. Gunter   Commissioner

C.C. Lipe
Clerk Commission

MORTON

Docket #565
Rolls 1835 to 1852

Applicant for Cherokee Citizenship

Post Office: Union Town, Ark.   **Attorney:** A.E. Ivey

N°	NAMES	AGE	SEX
1	William Morton		
2	James M. Morton		
3	Henry H. Morton		
4	Sherard Morton		
5	Annie R. Morton		
6	Quinn Morton		
7	Samantha Morton		

Ancestor: Alice Baily[sic]

Cherokee Citizenship Commission Docket Books
(1880-84, 1887-89) Volume II
Tahlequah, Cherokee Nation

Now on this the 1st day of October A.D. 1888, comes the above entitled case for final hearing. The applicants having made application in conformity with an Act of the National Council approved Dec 8, 1886, and all the evidence in said case having been duly examined is found not to be sufficient nor is it satisfactory to the Commission. Hence it is adjudged by the Commission on Citizenship that William Morton and children viz: James M, Henry H, Sherard, Annie R, Quinn and Samantha Morton are not Cherokees by blood and are not entitles to any of the rights and privileges of Cherokees by blood and are hereby declared intruders upon the Public Domain of the Cherokee Nation.

J.T. Adair   Chairman Commission
H.C. Barnes   Commissioner

DOUGHERTY

Docket #566
Rolls 1851

Applicant for Cherokee Citizenship
Post Office: Dawsonville, Ga.   **Attorney:** A.E. Ivey

N°	NAMES	AGE	SEX
1	Susan J. Dougherty	49	female

Ancestor: Benjamin Dougherty

Now on this the 16th day of May 1888, comes the above case up for final hearing, and the Commission say: "We the Commission on Citizenship after "examining the evidence in the above case of Susan J. Dougherty, and also the "census rolls of 1851 and 52, find the applicant to be a Cherokee by blood, and "is hereby re-admitted to all the rights and privileges of a Cherokee citizen by "blood.

J.T. Adair   Chairman of the Commission
D.W. Lipe   Commissioner

Cherokee Citizenship Commission Docket Books
(1880-84, 1887-89) Volume II
Tahlequah, Cherokee Nation

WILLIS

Docket #567
Rolls 1851

Applicant for Cherokee Citizenship
Post Office: Palmour, Ga.   **Attorney:** A.E. Ivey

N°	NAMES	AGE	SEX
1	Pickens E Willis		
2	John P. Willis		
3	Andrew E. Willis		
4	Nathaniel D. Willis		
5	Esther J. Willis		

Ancestor: Mary Barnhill

Now on this the 25th day of March A.D. 1888 comes the above case for final hearing, they having made application pursuant to the provisions of the National Council approved Dec 8, 1886, and the evidence being considered and found to be sufficient and satisfactory, the Commission say: "We the "Commission on Citizenship after carefully examining the evidence in the case "and also finding the ancestors on the rolls of 1851 and 52, find that Pickens E. "Willis, who proved to be the brother of Priestly Willis, is a Cherokee by blood, "also his four children, John P – Andrew E – Nathaniel D – Ester[sic] J. Willis, "and they are hereby re-admitted to all the rights & privileges of Cherokee "citizens by blood."

D.W. Lipe   Acting Chairman Commission
John E. Gunter   Commissioner

Cornell Rogers
Clk Commission

The evidence in this case will be found in Journal page 171 & 180, in the case of Priestly Willis & W.H. Russell, et al.

DOUGHERTY

Docket #568
Rolls 1851

Applicant for Cherokee Citizenship
Post Office: Dawsonville, Ga.   **Attorney:** A.E. Ivey

N°	NAMES	AGE	SEX
1	Charles E. Dougherty	28	male

Cherokee Citizenship Commission Docket Books
(1880-84, 1887-89) Volume II
Tahlequah, Cherokee Nation

2	Essie M. Dougherty	8	female
3	Maud Dougherty	6	"
4	Callie D. Dougherty	4	"
5	Homer Dougherty	2	male

Ancestor: Susan J. Dougherty

Now on this the 16th day of May 1888, comes the above case up for final hearing, and the Commission say: "We the Commission on Citizenship after "carefully examining the evidence and also the rolls of 1851 and 52, find that "Charles E. Dougherty and his four children, viz: Elsie M. Dougherty, Maud "Dougherty. Callie D. Dougherty, and Homer Dougherty are Cherokees by "blood, and are hereby re-admitted to all the rights and privileges of Cherokee "citizens by blood.

         J.T. Adair Chairman of the Commission
         D.W. Lipe Commissioner

MOSS

Docket #569
Rolls 1851

              Applicant for Cherokee Citizenship
Post Office: Palmour, Ga.   **Attorney:** A.E. Ivey

N°	NAMES	AGE	SEX
1	Mary M Moss	56	female

Ancestor: Lucy Satersfield

Now on this the 18th day of June 1888, comes the above case up for final hearing, and the Commission say: "We the Commission on Citizenship after examining the testimony in the above case and particularly the rolls of 1851 & 52, find that the applicant, Mary M. Moss is a Cherokee by blood, and is hereby re-admitted to all the rights and privileges of Cherokee citizens by blood. (See Sec. 7 Act approved Dec. 8th 1886.)

         J.T. Adair Chairman of the Commission
         John E. Gunter Commissioner
         D.W. Lipe Commissioner

Cherokee Citizenship Commission Docket Books
(1880-84, 1887-89) Volume II
Tahlequah, Cherokee Nation

DARNELL

Docket #570
Rolls 1851

Applicant for Cherokee Citizenship

Post Office: Dawsonville, Ga.   **Attorney:** A.E. Ivey

N°	NAMES	AGE	SEX
1	Eliza E. Darnell	31	female
2	Eva Darnell	11	"
3	Enla Darnell	5	"

Ancestor: Pickens E. Willis

Now on this the 16th day of May 1888, comes the above case up for final hearing, and the Commission say: "We the Commission on Citizenship after "examining the evidence and rolls of 1851 and '52, find the above named "applicant and her two daughters Eva – and Enla Darnell are Cherokees by "blood, and are hereby re-admitted to all the rights and privileges of Cherokee "citizens by blood.

J.T. Adair   Chairman of the Commission
D.W. Lipe   Commissioner

HULSEY

Docket #571
Rolls 1851

Applicant for Cherokee Citizenship

Post Office: Barrettsville, Ga.   **Attorney:** A.E. Ivey

N°	NAMES	AGE	SEX
1	Sarah M. Hulsey	39	female
2	Ella V. Hulsey	20	"
3	Alonzo Hulsey	16	male
4	Earl Hulsey	13	"
5	Rosalee Hulsey	11	female
6	Loucinda Hulsey	8	female
7	Charles Hulsey	4	male
8	Roscoe Hulsey	2	"

Ancestor: Priestly E. Willis

Now on this the 23rd day of March A.D. 1888, comes the above case up for final hearing. The applicant having made application pursuant to the

Cherokee Citizenship Commission Docket Books
(1880-84, 1887-89) Volume II
Tahlequah, Cherokee Nation

provisions of an Act of the National Council approved December 8th 1886, and all the evidence being duly considered and found to be sufficient and satisfactory, the Commission say:

"We the Commission on Citizenship after carefully examining the rolls "and evidence in the case of Sarah M. Hulsey, find that her and her (7) seven "children, viz: Ella V. – Alonzo – Earl – Rosalee – Loucinda – Charles and "Roscoe Hulsey are Cherokees by blood, and are hereby re-admitted to all the "rights & privileges of Cherokee citizens by blood.

         D.W. Lipe Acting Chairman Commission
         John E. Gunter   Commissioner

Cornell Rogers
Clk Commission

  The evidence in this case will be found on Journal page 171 & 180, in the case of Priestly Willis & W.H. Russell, et al.

BARNHILL

Docket #572
Rolls

               Applicant for Cherokee Citizenship
    Post Office: Dougherty. Ga.   **Attorney:** A.E. Ivey

N°	NAMES	AGE	SEX
1	Mary Barnhill	79	female

       Ancestor: James Dougherty

Now on this the 23rd day of March A.D. 1888, comes the above case up for final hearing; having made application pursuant to the provisions of an Act of the National Council approved Dec. 8th 1886, and all the evidence being duly considered and found to be sufficient and satisfactory, the Commission say:

"We the Commission on Citizenship after examining the evidence in the "case of Mary Barnhill, find that she is a Cherokee by blood, and is hereby re-"admitted to all the rights & privileges of Cherokee citizens by blood.

         D.W. Lipe Acting Chairman Commission
         John E. Gunter   Commissioner

Cherokee Citizenship Commission Docket Books
(1880-84, 1887-89) Volume II
Tahlequah, Cherokee Nation

Cornell Rogers
Clk Commission

The evidence in this case will be found on Journal page 171 & 180, in the case of Priestly Willis & W.H. Russell, et al.

HUGHES

Docket #573
Rolls 1851

Applicant for Cherokee Citizenship

Post Office: Dawsonville, Ga. **Attorney:** A.E. Ivey

N°	NAMES	AGE	SEX
1	Martha E. Hughes	30	female

Ancestor: Priestly E. Willis

Now on this 23rd day of March A.D. 1888, comes the above case up for final hearing, they having made application pursuant to the provisions of an Act of the National Council approved Dec. 8th 1886, and all the evidence being duly considered and found to be sufficient and satisfactory, the Commission say:

"We the Commission on Citizenship after carefully examining the "evidence and census and pay rolls of 1851 & 52, find that the above applicant, "Martha E. Hughes, is a Cherokee by blood, and is hereby re-admitted to all the "rights and privileges of Cherokee citizens by blood.

D.W. Lipe   Acting Chairman Commission
John E. Gunter   Commissioner

Cornell Rogers
Clk Commission

The evidence in this case will be found on Journal page 170 & 180, in the Priestly Willis case & W.H. Russell, et al.

Cherokee Citizenship Commission Docket Books
(1880-84, 1887-89) Volume II
Tahlequah, Cherokee Nation

WILLIS

Docket #574
Rolls

                                              Applicant for Cherokee Citizenship
Post Office: Palmour, Ga.   **Attorney:** A.E. Ivey

N°	NAMES	AGE	SEX
1	William B. Willis	27	male
2	Mary E. Willis	7	female
3	George E. Willis	2	male

Ancestor: Pickens E. Willis

Now on this the 16th day of May 1888, comes the above case up for final hearing, and the Commission say: "We the Commission on Citizenship after "examining the evidence and the rolls of 1851 & '52, find that William B. Willis "and his two children, Mary E. and George E. Willis are Cherokees by blood, "and they are hereby re-admitted to all the rights and privileges of Cherokee "citizens by blood.

                        J.T. Adair   Chairman of the Commission
                        D.W. Lipe   Commissioner

JULIAN

Docket #575
Rolls 1851

                                              Applicant for Cherokee Citizenship
Post Office: Big Creek, Ga.   **Attorney:** A.E. Ivey

N°	NAMES	AGE	SEX
1	Susan J. Julian	44	female
2	Edwin C. Julian	21	male
3	Robert W. Julian	16	"
4	Wm B. Julian	13	"
5	Eva M. Julian	7	female
6	Ella P. Julian	4	"

Ancestor: Priestly E. Willis

Now on this the 16th day of May 1888, comes the above case up for final hearing, and the Commission say: "We the Commission on Citizenship after "carefully examining the evidence and rolls of 1851 and '52, find that Susan J. "Julian and her five children, namely, Edwin C – Robert W. – William B. – Eva

Cherokee Citizenship Commission Docket Books
(1880-84, 1887-89) Volume II
Tahlequah, Cherokee Nation

"M. – and Ella P. Julian are Cherokees by blood, and are hereby re-admitted to "all the rights and privileges of Cherokee citizens by blood."

          J.T. Adair   Chairman of the Commission
          D.W. Lipe   Commissioner

FORBES

Docket #576
Rolls 1851

Applicant for Cherokee Citizenship
Post Office: Dougherty, Ga.   **Attorney:** A.E. Ivey

N°	NAMES	AGE	SEX
1	Nancy E. Forbes	49	female
2	Agnes E. Forbes	22	"
3	Robert F. Forbes	21	male
4	William M. Forbes	16	"
5	Nancy L. Forbes	13	female
6	Susan L. Forbes	8	"

Ancestor: Benjamin Dougherty

Now on this the 16th day of May 1888, comes the above case up for final hearing, and the Commission say: "We the Commission on Citizenship after "carefully examining the testimony and the rolls of 1851 & '52, find that Nancy "E. Forbes and her five children, viz: Agnes E. – Robert F. – William M. – "Nancy L. – and Susan L. Forbes are Cherokees by blood, and are hereby re-"admitted to all the rights and privileges of Cherokee citizens by blood.

          J.T. Adair   Chairman of the Commission
          D.W. Lipe   Commissioner

DOUGHERTY

Docket #577
Rolls

Applicant for Cherokee Citizenship
Post Office: Dougherty, Ga.   **Attorney:** A.E. Ivey

N°	NAMES	AGE	SEX
1	Sarah M. Dougherty	46	female

Cherokee Citizenship Commission Docket Books (1880-84, 1887-89) Volume II
Tahlequah, Cherokee Nation

2	John H. Dougherty	14	male

Ancestor: Benjamin Dougherty

Now on this the 16th day of May 1888, comes the above case up for final hearing, and the Commission say: "We the Commission on Citizenship after "carefully examining the evidence and the rolls of 1851 and '52, find that the "applicants, Sarah M. and her son John H. Dougherty are Cherokees by blood, "and are hereby re-admitted to all the rights and privileges of Cherokee citizens "by blood.

         J.T. Adair Chairman of the Commission
         D.W. Lipe Commissioner

DOUGHERTY

Docket #578
Rolls

              Applicant for Cherokee Citizenship
Post Office: Palmour, Ga.   **Attorney:** A.E. Ivey

N°	NAMES	AGE	SEX
1	Elizabeth Dougherty	73	female

Ancestor: James Dougherty

Now on this the 16th day of May 1888, comes the above case up for final hearing, the Commission say: "We the Commission on Citizenship after "carefully examining the evidence in the above case and also the census and pay "rolls of 1851 and '52, find that the above applicant, Elizabeth Dougherty, is a "Cherokee by blood, and is hereby re-admitted to all the rights and privileges of "a Cherokee citizen by blood."

         J.T. Adair Chairman of the Commission
         D.W. Lipe Commissioner

Cherokee Citizenship Commission Docket Books
(1880-84, 1887-89) Volume II
Tahlequah, Cherokee Nation

RUSSELL

Docket #579
Rolls

Applicant for Cherokee Citizenship

Post Office: Dougherty, Ga.   **Attorney:** A.E. Ivey

N°	NAMES	AGE	SEX
1	Susan Russell	60	female

Ancestor: Mary Barnhill

Now on this 23rd day of March A.D. 1888, comes the above case up for final hearing, and having made application pursuant to the provisions of an Act of the National Council approved December 8th 1886, and the evidence being duly considered and found to be sufficient and satisfactory, the Commission say: "We the Commission on Citizenship after carefully examining the evidence and the pay rolls of 1852, find that Susan Russell, is a Cherokee by blood, and is hereby re-admitted to all the rights and privileges of Cherokee citizens by blood.

D.W. Lipe   Act'g Chairman Commission
                    Commissioner
John E. Gunter   Commissioner

Cornell Rogers
Clk Commission

The evidence in this case will be found on Journal page 171 & 180, in the case of Priestly Willis & W.H. Russell, et al.

CAULK

Docket #580
Rolls 1835 to 1852

Applicant for Cherokee Citizenship

Post Office: Jeff City, Mo.   **Attorney:** L.B. Bell

N°	NAMES	AGE	SEX
1	Rhoda Caulk	61	female
2	Edward L. Caulk	26	male
3	Pleasant H Caulk	24	"
4	Laura E. Caulk	18	female

Ancestor: Catherine Childers & John Vann

Cherokee Citizenship Commission Docket Books
(1880-84, 1887-89) Volume II
Tahlequah, Cherokee Nation

Commission on Citizenship
Cherokee Nation, Ind. Ter.
Tahlequah Oct. 4, 1889

Rhoda Caulk
vs   Application for Cherokee Citizenship
The Cherokee Nation

  The applicant in the above case alleges that she is the grand daughter of one John Vann whose name she believes was duly enrolled on the census rolls of Cherokees by blood taken and made by the United States in the years 1835 and 1852. This case involves the re-opening of the question of right to citizenship in the Cherokee Nation of the claimant and a number of other persons which was decided adversely by the National Council in the year 1846. Among the persons whose right to citizenship then denied will be found the names of Laban Cork the husband of Mrs. Rhoda Caulk the claimant. John Schrimsher her father and Lemuel Childers her uncle by marriage and who were white persons claiming citizenship through their wives who were the daughters and grand daughters of said John Vann. In the absence of special authority to do so the Commission does not deem itself authorized to re-open the question settled by the law making power of the Nation more than forty years ago. Especially is this the case when a careful examination of the evidence introduced in behalf of the claimant and of the rolls of 1835, 1851 and 1852 fails to show that either the names of John Vann, Edith Vann, John Schrimser[sic] or Rhoda Caulk nee Rhoda Schrimsher was enrolled on neither of them. Such being the fact it is the duty of the Commission under the laws creating them to sustain the action of the National Council in 1846, in deciding that the applicant is not of Cherokee blood and therefore not entitled to re-admission to citizenship in the Cherokee Nation.

  In arriving at this conclusion, the Commission deems it proper to impart their decision with the accompanying evidence to the National Council for their information and further action if deemed necessary. The names of Lemuel Childers one of the persons denied the right of citizenship by the National Council in the year 1846 is entered on the census roll of 1835 as a white man with a Cherokee family in the care of Lemuel Parris a grandson of Lemuel Childers and his wife Nancy Childers whose maiden name was Nancy Vann the daughter of John Vann and sister of Edith Schrimsher nee Edith Vann the mother of Mrs. Rhoda Caulk the claimant and which was decided by the Adair Commission in favor of the claimant Lemuel Parris, a transcript was furnished

Cherokee Citizenship Commission Docket Books
(1880-84, 1887-89) Volume II
Tahlequah, Cherokee Nation

from the Department of the Interior of Washington, D.C. which shows that one John Vann was enrolled by the United States Agent in 1832 for Emigration from the limits of Georgia in the ~~nation~~ Cherokee Nation East to the Cherokee Nation West. This John Vann was the father of Mrs. Edith Schrimsher the mother of Mrs. Rhoda Caulk. The name of John Vann if alive at the date of the per capita payment to the "Old Settlers" in 1851 should appear on this pay roll or if dead and of recognized Cherokee blood the names of his descendants should be thereon enrolled. But such as before stated is not the fact. They were not then therefore regarded as of Cherokee descent. The testimony in the cases of Mrs. Caulk and Lemuel Parris was taken before the Adair Commission the two witnesses of most importance being in this Joseph L. Martin of *(Illegible)* District and Bluford W. Alberty of Tahlequah District. The wife of Mr. Martin was a daughter of Lem Childers and a grand daughter of John Vann and who he swears was always regarded and recognized as a Cherokee. He did not know John Vann but knew a brother of his by the name of Cah lah to li tu who was recognized as a Cherokee and that the family of Lemuel Childers was named as Cherokees and participated in the funds sat apart by the treaty of 1835 for the payment for improvements. Mr. Alberty testifies that he was a school mate of Mrs. Rhoda Caulk and knew her well as he did her ~~father~~ mother Mrs. Schrimsher and her grand father John Vann and regarded them as Cherokees and that they were so regarded in Flint District when they *(illegible)*. These two witnesses are both of well known character and high standing in the Cherokee Nation and entitled to full credit in relation to matters where they *(illegible)* testify as of their *(illegible)* knowledge.

The applicants, whose cases are determined by the adverse decision of the Commission on this claim of Mrs. Rhoda Caulk are the following names persons who are identified by herself as being her children and grand children claiming to have derived their Cherokee blood from John Vann through their mother, viz: Milton M. Caulk 39 years of age and his sons Edward H. Caulk 12 yrs, Arthur Caulk 6 years and daughters Nellie L. Caulk 15 yrs, Lena M. Caulk 10 yrs, Rosa M. Caulk 8 yrs, and Rhoda Caulk 6 years, Tiff City, Missouri; Mary A. Caulk 35 years of age and her son Jesse Caulk 4 years and daughters, Bessie Caulk 6 years and Laura Caulk 2 yrs, P.O. Joplin, Mo.

Fannie E. Gray nee Caulk 23 years of age & son Ora Gray 2 years, P.O. Tiff City, Mo.

Cherokee Citizenship Commission Docket Books
(1880-84, 1887-89) Volume II
Tahlequah, Cherokee Nation

Elmyra J. Crawford 20 yrs of age and daughter Ollie Crawford 2 yrs, P.O. Kent, Washington Territory.

Robert Hall 15 years, Newton Hall 12 yrs, Dora Hall 10 yrs and Henry Hall 7 yrs, children of a deceased daughter whose name is not given. P.O. Split Log, Mo. and Edward L. Caulk 26 yrs, Pleasant H. Caulk 24 yrs and Laura E. Caulk 18 years. P.O. Tiff City, Mo.

Will P. Ross
Chairman
J. E. Gunter Com.

CAULK

Docket #581
Rolls 1835 to 1852

Applicant for Cherokee Citizenship
Post Office: Tiff City, Mo.   **Attorney:** L.B. Bell

N°	NAMES	AGE	SEX
1	Milton M. Caulk	39	male
2	Nellie L. Caulk	15	female
3	Edward H. Caulk	12	male
4	Lena M. Caulk	10	female
5	Rosa M. Caulk	8	"
6	Arthur Caulk	6	male
7	Rhoda Caulk	4	female

Ancestor: Catherine Childers & John Vann
Office Commission Citizenship
Oct. 4th 1889

In the above case the Commission decide against claimant for reasons given in this decision in the case of Rhoda Caulk. See Docket 580 Book B, Page 293. P.O. Tiff City Missouri.

Will P. Ross   Chairman
R. Bunch   Com
J.E. Gunter   Com

Cherokee Citizenship Commission Docket Books
(1880-84, 1887-89) Volume II
Tahlequah, Cherokee Nation

CAULK

Docket #582
Rolls 1835 to 1852

Applicant for Cherokee Citizenship

Post Office: Joplin, Mo.   **Attorney:** L.B. Bell

N°	NAMES	AGE	SEX
1	Mary A. Caulk	35	female
2	Bessie Caulk	6	"
3	Jessie Caulk	4	"
4	Laura Caulk	2	"

Ancestor: Catherine Childers & John Vann

Office Commission on Citizenship
Oct. 4th 1889

In the above case the Commission decide against claimant for reasons embraced in this decision in the case of Rhoda Caulk. See Docket 580, Book B, Page 293. P.O. Joplin Missouri.

      Will P. Ross   Chairman
      R. Bunch   Com
      J.E. Gunter   Com

CRAWFORD

Docket #583
Rolls 1835 to 1852

Applicant for Cherokee Citizenship

Post Office: Kent, Washington Terr.   **Attorney:** L.B. Bell

N°	NAMES	AGE	SEX
1	Elmyra J. Crawford	20	female
2	Ollie Crawford	2	"

Ancestor: Catherine Childers & John Vann

Office Commission on Citizenship
Oct. 4th 1889

In the above case the Commission decide adversely to claimant. See case of Rhoda Caulk. See Docket 580, Book B, Page 293. P.O. Kent Wash Ter.

Cherokee Citizenship Commission Docket Books
(1880-84, 1887-89) Volume II
Tahlequah, Cherokee Nation

Will P. Ross	Chairman
R. Bunch	Com
J.E. Gunter	Com

GRAY

Docket #584
Rolls 1835 to 1852

Applicant for Cherokee Citizenship

Post Office: Tiff City, Mo.   **Attorney:** L.B. Bell

N°	NAMES	AGE	SEX
1	Fannie E. Gray	23	female
2	Ora Gray	2	male

Ancestor: Catherine Childers & John Vann

Office Commission Citizenship
Oct. 4th 1889

In the above case the Commission decide against claimant for reasons given in their opion[sic] in the case of Rhoda Caulk. See Docket 580 Book B, Page 293. P.O. Tiff City Missouri.

Will P. Ross	Chairman
R. Bunch	Com
J.E. Gunter	Com

HALL

Docket #585
Rolls 1835 to 1852

Applicant for Cherokee Citizenship

Post Office: Split Log, Mo.   **Attorney:** L.B. Bell

N°	NAMES	AGE	SEX
1	Robert Hall	15	male
2	Newton Hall	12	"
3	Dora Hall	10	female
4	Henry Hall	7	male

Ancestor: Catherine Childers & John Vann

Office Commission on Citizenship
Oct. 4th 1889

Cherokee Citizenship Commission Docket Books
(1880-84, 1887-89) Volume II
Tahlequah, Cherokee Nation

The Commission in the above case decide against claimants for reasons given their decision in the case of Rhoda Caulk. See Docket 580 Book B, Page 293. P.O. Split Log Mo.

                          Will P. Ross   Chairman
                          R. Bunch   Com
                          J.E. Gunter   Com

LLOYD

Docket #586
Rolls 1835

                          Applicant for Cherokee Citizenship
Post Office: Tulsa, I.T.   **Attorney:** A.E. Ivey

N°	NAMES	AGE	SEX
1	G.C. Lloyd	34	male

Ancestor: Water Hunter

Commission on Citizenship.

CHEROKEE NATION, IND. TER.

Tahlequah,   September 10th 1888

G.C. Lloyd. et al.
    (VS)
Cherokee Nation

The above case is one composing the applications of G.C. Lloyd, James P. Lloyd, Virgil M. Lloyd, et al, Ida Brady and Josephine Barthel and child, all claiming a Cherokee ancestry from one Water Hunter.

The testimony of Mary Lloyd shows that Dr. George Lloyd, the father of applicants lived in Floyd County in the state of Georgia from the time he was a young man until after the war of the late Rebellion. He must have moved into that state ~~and among the~~ about the year 1840 when he was about 18 or 20 years old and remained there until, or states, after the late War. The testimony of Mrs. Lloyd further shows that Mr. Lloyd's mother's maiden name was Susan Parsons, and that Dr. Lloyd came to this country from Georgia in the year 1872, leaving him with his family in Ga. during the years 1851, ~~1848~~ & 1852, and that Dr. Lloyd claimed his Cherokee blood from his mother – Parsons. The evidence of

Cherokee Citizenship Commission Docket Books
(1880-84, 1887-89) Volume II
Tahlequah, Cherokee Nation

Peter Parson or as he is more properly called Peter Kill-er-nee-ter, shows that his grand father was named Water Hunter (Parson). That his English name was Parson and his Cherokee name Water Hunter, and that the applicant's great grand mother was named Susan Parson, and that Susan's father was named Parson, and from his *(illegible)* information the applicants are Cherokee, and that he, Peter, was born in Oo-ka-la-ga Valley in the state of Georgia, and that the applicants came to this county since the war and that this is the third time that they have been before Court or Commission praying for citizenship in the Cherokee Nation. The balance of the testimony in this case is of about the same impact, though the most important to claimants have been recited herein.

Now in looking up the evidence together with the "Rolls" submitted by the Nation's Attorney. on part of plaintiffs in this cause, it will first be observed that Peter Parson, whose real name is no doubt Peter Kill-er-nee-ter, for the rolls of Cherokees made in the year 1835 goes to show this name, and it is his family, living in the *(illegible)* location in the state of Georgia that Peter says that he came from, and where he lived, identifying Peter's real name as Kill-er-nee-ter – and further the rolls do not contain the name of Parson at all – The evidence of Mr. Isaac Hitchcock in this matter is good, for he says that some of Peter's family attended school at Park Hill and that Mr. Worcester in all probability and it is very likely, given this name "Passon" to the Kill-er-nee-ter children – for what reason we cannot say unless it was that it sounded more euphonious than as a great many people are *(illegible)* to call this name as being first acquainted with it. "Kill-er-nigger". More over according to the testimony of Mr. Hitchcock who is considerable of a linguist, it will be remembered that the name Passon is not the English definition of Kill-er-ne-ter, and that the two names are not synonymous – It will further be noticed that Parson is not Passon – and that Parson is entirely an English name and a common one too.

We the Commission on Citizenship after carefully examining the testimony in this case together with the different census and pay rolls of Cherokees laid down in the 7th Section of the Act of Dec. 8th 1886, are of the opinion that the above applicants are not Cherokees by blood, and are not entitled to the rights and privileges of such, on account of their blood, and G.C. Lloyd, and the children of Virgil M. Lloyd, dec'd, viz: John G, William W, and Minnie M. Lloyd, and Josephine Barthel and her child Florence Barthel, are hereby declared to be Intruders upon the public domain of the Cherokee Nation with no interest in common with the Cherokee Indians. The testimony in this cause goes to show that James R. Lloyd married one Rachel Twist, a Cherokee

Cherokee Citizenship Commission Docket Books
(1880-84, 1887-89) Volume II
Tahlequah, Cherokee Nation

woman but that he did not comply with the Cherokee law of intermarriage with citizens of the United States and foreigners and Cherokee women; and further that Ida Brady – nee Lloyd, married a Cherokee man by the name of ~~Brady~~ – John G. Brady.

G.C. Lloyd is living on an improvement that he claims as his own in Cooweescoowee Dist. and John G. and William W. Lloyd have improvements on the public domain claiming them as their own.

J.T. Adair Chairman Commission
D.W. Lipe Commissioner
H.C. Barnes Commissioner

LLOYD

Docket #587
Rolls 1835

Applicant for Cherokee Citizenship

Post Office: Tulsa, I.T.   **Attorney:** A.E. Ivey

N°	NAMES	AGE	SEX
1	James P. Lloyd	29	male

Ancestor: Water Hunter

The decision in this case will be found on page 299 of this Book in the G.C. Lloyd case – Adverse to claimant.

Cornell Rogers
Clerk Com.

LLOYD

Docket #588
Rolls 1835

Applicant for Cherokee Citizenship

Post Office: Tulsa I.T.   **Attorney:** A.E. Ivey

N°	NAMES	AGE	SEX
1	Virgil M. Lloyd	32	male
2	John G. Lloyd	27	male ~~female~~

Cherokee Citizenship Commission Docket Books
(1880-84, 1887-89) Volume II
Tahlequah, Cherokee Nation

3	Wm W. Lloyd	20	male
4	Minnie M. Lloyd	7	female

Ancestor: Water Hunter

The decision in this case will be found on page 299 of this Book in the G.C. Lloyd case – Adverse to claimant.

      Cornell Rogers
       Clerk Commission

BARTHEL

Docket #589
Rolls 1835

      Applicant for Cherokee Citizenship
Post Office: Tulsa I.T. **Attorney:** A.E. Ivey

N°	NAMES	AGE	SEX
1	Josephine Barthel	31	female
2	Florence Barthel	1	"

Ancestor: Water Hunter

The decision in this case will be found on page 299 of this Book in the G.C. Lloyd case – Adverse to claimant.

      Cornell Rogers
       Clerk Commission

BRADY

Docket #590
Rolls 1835

      Applicant for Cherokee Citizenship
Post Office: Skiatook I.T. **Attorney:** A.E. Ivey

N°	NAMES	AGE	SEX
1	Ida Brady	23	female

Ancestor: Water Hunter

Cherokee Citizenship Commission Docket Books
(1880-84, 1887-89) Volume II
Tahlequah, Cherokee Nation

The decision in this case will be found on page 299 of this Book in the G.C. Lloyd case – Not a Cherokee by blood but has married a Cherokee by the name of John G. Brady.

Cornell Rogers
Clerk Commission

HALL

Docket #591
Rolls 1835

Applicant for Cherokee Citizenship

Post Office: South West City   **Attorney:** L.B. Bell

N°	NAMES	AGE	SEX
1	Martha Hall	45	female
2	Frank Hall	18	male
3	Rebecca Hall	16	female
4	Catherine Hall	11	"
5	Ibie Hall	8	"
6	Rhoda Hall	5	"
7	Fredrick Hall	3	male

Ancestor: Nancy Childers

Now on this the 28th day of September 1887 comes the above case for a final hearing and the parties having made application pursuant to the provisions of an Act of the National Council approved December 8th 1886. And all the evidence being duly examined and found to be sufficient and satisfactory to the Commission and the name of the ancestor Nancy Childers appearing upon the Rolls of 1835. It is adjudged and determined by the Commission that Martha Hall, Frank Hall, Rebecca Hall, Catharine Hall, Ibie Hall, Rhoda Hall and Fredrick Hall are Cherokees by blood and are hereby re-admitted to all the rights privileges and immunities of Cherokees by blood.

And a certificate of said decision of the Commission and of re-admission was made and furnished to said parties accordingly.

Henry Eiffert   J.T. Adair   Chairman Commission
Clk Com   D.W. Lipe   Commissioner
                                      Commissioner

Cherokee Citizenship Commission Docket Books
(1880-84, 1887-89) Volume II
Tahlequah, Cherokee Nation

PARRIS

Docket #592
Rolls 1835

Applicant for Cherokee Citizenship
Post Office: Chelsea I.T.   **Attorney:** L.B. Bell

N°	NAMES	AGE	SEX
1	Levi Parris	35	male
2	Frank Parris	1	"

Ancestor: Nancy Childers

Now on this the 28th day of September 1887 comes the above case for a final hearing. And the parties having made application pursuant to the provisions of an Act of the National Council approved December 8th 1886. And all the evidence having been duly examined and found to be sufficient and satisfactory to the Commission and the name of the ancestor Nancy Childers appearing on the Rolls of 1835. It is adjudged and determined by the Commission that Levi Parris and Frank Parris are Cherokees by blood and are hereby re-admitted to all the rights privileges and immunities of Cherokees by blood.

And a certificate of said decision of the Commission and re-admission was made and furnished to said parties accordingly.

Henry Eiffert
Clk Com

J.T. Adair   Chairman Commission
D.W. Lipe   Commissioner
              Commissioner

PARRIS

Docket #593
Rolls 1835

Applicant for Cherokee Citizenship
Post Office: Chelsea I.T.   **Attorney:** L.B. Bell

N°	NAMES	AGE	SEX
1	W.F. Parris	30	male

Ancestor: Nancy Childers

Cherokee Citizenship Commission Docket Books
(1880-84, 1887-89) Volume II
Tahlequah, Cherokee Nation

Now on this the 28th day of September 1887 comes the above case for a final hearing. And the parties having made application pursuant to the provisions of an Act of the National Council approved December 8th 1886. And all the evidence duly examined and found to be sufficient and satisfactory to the Commission and the name of the ancestor Nancy Childers appearing upon the Rolls of 1835. It is adjudged and determined by the Commission that W.F. Parris is a Cherokee by blood and he is hereby re-admitted to all rights privileges and immunities of a Cherokee by blood.

And a certificate of said decision of the Commission and re-admission was made and furnished to said parties accordingly.

Henry Eiffert
Clk Com

J.T. Adair   Chairman Commission
D.W. Lipe   Commissioner
             Commissioner

CARMICLE

Docket #594
Rolls 1835

Applicant for Cherokee Citizenship

Post Office: Chelsea I.T.   **Attorney:** L.B. Bell

N°	NAMES	AGE	SEX
1	Mary Carmicle	29	female
2	Allen F. Carmicle	10	male
3	Wm C. Carmicle	8	"
4	Ora Carmicle	6	female
5	Clarence Carmicle	4	male
6	Annie J. Carmicle	1	female

Ancestor: Nancy Childers

Now on this the 28 day of September 1887 comes the above case for a final hearing and the parties having made application pursuant to the provisions of the National Council approved December 8th 1886. And all the evidence being duly examined and found to be sufficient and satisfactory to the Commission and the name of the ancestor Nancy Childers appearing upon the Rolls of 1835. It is adjudged and determined by the Commission that Mary Carmicle, Allen F. Carmicle, Wm C. Carmicle, Ora Carmicle, Clarence

Cherokee Citizenship Commission Docket Books
(1880-84, 1887-89) Volume II
Tahlequah, Cherokee Nation

Carmicle, Annie J. Carmicle [sic] Cherokees by blood and re-admission was made and furnished to said parties accordingly.

Henry Eiffert	J.T. Adair	Chairman Commission
Clk Com	D.W. Lipe	Commissioner
		Commissioner

BRINK

Docket #595
Rolls 1835

Applicant for Cherokee Citizenship
Post Office: Chelsea I.T. **Attorney:** L.B. Bell

N°	NAMES	AGE	SEX
1	Lidia Brink	21	female
2	G.F. Brink	2	male
3	Mary A. Brink	5 mos	female

Ancestor: Nancy Childers

Now on this the 28th day of September comes the above case for a final hearing and the parties having made application pursuant to the provisions of an Act of the National Council approved Dec. 8th 1886. And all the evidence being duly examined and found to be sufficient and satisfactory, the Commission and the names[sic] of the ancestor Nancy Childers appearing on the Roll of 1835. It is adjudged and determined by the Commission that Martha Hall, Frank Hall, Rebecca Hall, Catharine Hall, Ibie Hall, Lydia Brink, G.F. Brink and Mary A. Brink are Cherokees by blood and are hereby re-admitted to all the rights privileges and immunities of Cherokees by blood. And a certificate of said decision of the Commission and re-admission was made and furnished to said parties accordingly.

Henry Eiffert	J.T. Adair	Chairman Commission
Clk Com	D.W. Lipe	Commissioner
		Commissioner

Cherokee Citizenship Commission Docket Books
(1880-84, 1887-89) Volume II
Tahlequah, Cherokee Nation

HALL

Docket #596
Rolls 1835

Applicant for Cherokee Citizenship

Post Office: Vinita I.T.   **Attorney:** L.B. Bell

N°	NAMES	AGE	SEX
1	William O. Hall	7	male
2	J.W. Hall	5	"
3	D.H. Hall	3	"

Ancestor: Nancy Childers

Now on this the 28th day of September 1887 comes the above case for a final hearing and the parties having made application pursuant to the provisions of an Act of the National Council approved Dec. 8th 1886. And all evidence being duly examined and found to be sufficient and satisfactory to the Commission and the name of the ancestor Nancy Childers appearing on the roll of 1835. It is adjudged and determined by the Commission that William Hall, J.W. Hall, D.H. Hall are Cherokees by blood and hereby re-admitted to all the rights privileges and immunities of Cherokees by blood. And a certificate of said decision of the Commission and re-admission was made and furnished to said parties accordingly.

Henry Eiffert   J.T. Adair   Chairman Commission
Clk Com   D.W. Lipe   Commissioner
                            Commissioner

WYLY

Docket #596[sic]
Rolls 1851 & 52

Applicant for Cherokee Citizenship

Post Office: Sunnydale, Ga.   **Attorney:** A.E. Ivey

N°	NAMES	AGE	SEX
1	Oliver L. Wyly	35	male
2	Robert N. Wyly	4	"

Ancestor: Amanda C. Wyly

Cherokee Citizenship Commission Docket Books
(1880-84, 1887-89) Volume II
Tahlequah, Cherokee Nation

Now on this the 20th day of September 1887 comes the above case for final hearing and having made application pursuant to the provisions of an Act of the National Council approved Dec. 8th 1886, and all evidence having been duly examined and found to be sufficient and satisfactory to the Commission and the name of the ancestor Amanda C. Wyly appearing on the Rolls of 1851 & 52 it is adjudged and determined by the Commission that Oliver L. Wyly and Robt M. Wyly are Cherokees by blood and are hereby re-admitted to all the rights privileges and immunities of Cherokees by blood.

And a certificate of said decision of the Commission and re-admission was made and furnished to said parties accordingly.

Henry Eiffert	J.T. Adair	Chairman Commission
Clk Commission	D.W. Lipe	Commissioner
		Commissioner

ROGERS

Docket #597
Rolls 1851 & 1852

Applicant for Cherokee Citizenship

Post Office: Sunnydale, Ga.   **Attorney:** A.E. Ivey

N°	NAMES	AGE	SEX
1	Florence S. Rogers	32	female

Ancestor: Amanda C. Wyly

Now on this the 20th day of September 1887 comes the above case for a final hearing and having made application pursuant to the provisions of an Act of the National Council approved Dec. 8th 1886, and all evidence having been duly examined and found to be sufficient and satisfactory to the Commission and the name of the ancestor Amanda C. Wyly appearing on the Rolls of 1851 & 52 it is adjudged and determined by the Commission that Florence S. Rogers is a Cherokee by blood and she is hereby re-admitted to all the rights privileges and immunities of Cherokees by blood.

And a certificate of said decision of the Commission and re-admission was made and furnished to said parties accordingly.

Cherokee Citizenship Commission Docket Books
(1880-84, 1887-89) Volume II
Tahlequah, Cherokee Nation

Henry Eiffert	J.T. Adair	Chairman Commission
Clk Commission	D.W. Lipe	Commissioner
		Commissioner

HAIL

Docket #598
Rolls 1851 & 1852

Applicant for Cherokee Citizenship

Post Office: Caney Creek   **Attorney:**

N°	NAMES	AGE	SEX
1	George W. Hail	43	male
2	Martha E. Hail	13	female
3	Wm W. Hail	11	male
4	Hulda E. Hail	10	female
5	Eliza L. Hail	7	"
6	General M. Hail	5	male
7	Alice M. Hail	1	female

Ancestor: Michel[sic] Hail

Now on this the 29th day of September 1887 comes the above case for final hearing and having made application pursuant to the provisions of an Act of the National Council approved December 1886, and all evidence having been duly considered and found to be sufficient and satisfactory to the Commission and the name of the ancestor Michael Hail appearing upon the Rolls of 1851 & 52, it is adjudged and determined by the Commission that Geo W. Hail, Martha E. Hail, Wm W. Hail, Hulda E. Hail, Eliza L. Hail, General M. Hail, and Alice M. Hail are Cherokees by blood and are hereby re-admitted to all the rights privileges and immunities of Cherokees by blood.

And a certificate of said decision and re-admission of the Commission was made and furnished to said parties accordingly.

	J.T. Adair	Chairman Commission
Henry Eiffert	D.W. Lipe	Commissioner
Clk. Com.		Commissioner

Cherokee Citizenship Commission Docket Books
(1880-84, 1887-89) Volume II
Tahlequah, Cherokee Nation

HAMPTON

Docket #599
ROLLS 1851 & 2 O.S.

APPLICANT FOR CHEROKEE CITIZENSHIP
POST OFFICE: Echo I.T.   **ATTORNEY:** J.M. Bryant

NO	NAMES	AGE	SEX
1	Andrew W. Hampton	38	male
2	William C. Hampton	16	"
3	Mattie C. Hampton	9	Female
4	Clara Mary Hampton	5	"
5	Abraham Hampton	15	male

ANCESTOR: Elizabeth Hampton

The decision in this case will be found in Docket "A", page 279 in the Polly White case – Re-admitted.

Cornell Rogers
Clk. Com. on Citizenship

WHITE

Docket #600
ROLLS 1851 & 2 OS

APPLICANT FOR CHEROKEE CITIZENSHIP
POST OFFICE: Prairie City CN.   **ATTORNEY:** J.M. Bryant

NO	NAMES	AGE	SEX
1	James E. White	35	male
2	William H. White	9	"
3	J.S. White	6	

ANCESTOR: Polly White

The decision in this case will be found in Docket "A", page 279 in the Polly White case – Re-admitted.

Cornell Rogers
Clk. Com. on Citizenship

Cherokee Citizenship Commission Docket Books (1880-84, 1887-89) Volume II
Tahlequah, Cherokee Nation

JONES

Docket #601
ROLLS

APPLICANT FOR CHEROKEE CITIZENSHIP
POST OFFICE: Prairie City CN. **ATTORNEY:** J.M. Bryant

NO	NAMES	AGE	SEX
1	~~Francis A. Jones~~	~~40~~	~~Female~~
2	Theodore Jones	21	Male
3	Elizabeth Jones	19	Female
4	Caldona Jones	16	"
5	Margaret A. Jones	10	"

ANCESTOR: James Jones

The decision in this case will be found in Docket "A", page 279 in the Polly White case – Re-admitted.

Cornell Rogers
Clk. Com. on Citizenship

JONES

Docket #602
ROLLS 1851 & 2 OS

APPLICANT FOR CHEROKEE CITIZENSHIP
POST OFFICE: Prairie City CN **ATTORNEY:** J.M. Bryant

NO	NAMES	AGE	SEX
1	Thomas Jones	40	Male
2	William H. Jones	21	"
3	Artilla Jones	19	Female
4	Leroy A Jones	18	Male
5	John S. Jones	16	"
6	Hattie H.C. Jones	8	Female
7	Betsey E. Jones	6	"
8	Joel J.H. Jones	4	Male
9	J.H. Jones	2	"
10	Arvilla Jones	1	"

ANCESTOR: James Jones

Cherokee Citizenship Commission Docket Books
(1880-84, 1887-89) Volume II
Tahlequah, Cherokee Nation

The decision ~~will~~ in this case will be found in Docket "A", page 279 in the Polly White case. Re-admitted.

                    Cornell Rogers
                    Clk. Com. on Citizenship

HEROD

Docket #603
ROLLS 1851 & 52 OS

APPLICANT FOR CHEROKEE CITIZENSHIP

POST OFFICE: Prairie City CN   **ATTORNEY:** J.M. Bryant

NO	NAMES	AGE	SEX
1	Joseph S Herod	21	Male
2	Elzena Herod	19	Female
3	William W. Herod	17	Male
4	Luizo Bell Herod	14	Female

ANCESTOR: James Jones

The decision in this case, will be found on Docket "A", page 279 – in the Polly White case – Admitted.

                    Cornell Rogers
                    Clk. Com. on Citizenship

JONES

Docket #604
ROLLS 1851 & 2 OS

APPLICANT FOR CHEROKEE CITIZENSHIP

POST OFFICE: Prairie City C.N.   **ATTORNEY:** J M Bryant

NO	NAMES	AGE	SEX
1	Dead ~~Meagan Jones~~ Died since enrollment	~~28~~	~~Female~~
2	James Joel Jones	9	Male

ANCESTOR:

The decision in this case will be found on Docket "A", page 279 – Re-admitted – in the Polly White case.

                    Cornell Rogers
                    Clerk Com. on Citizenship

Cherokee Citizenship Commission Docket Books
(1880-84, 1887-89) Volume II
Tahlequah, Cherokee Nation

BLAYLOCK

Docket #605
ROLLS 1851 & 2 O.S.

APPLICANT FOR CHEROKEE CITIZENSHIP

POST OFFICE: Prairie City CN **ATTORNEY:** J M Bryant

NO	NAMES	AGE	SEX
1	Sarah A. Blaylock	26	Female
2	Mary Elizabeth Blaylock	7	"
3	Milly Jane Blaylock	5	"
4	Artela Blaylock	3	"
5	Satu Ann Blaylock	1	"

ANCESTOR: James Jones

The decision in this case will be found in Docket "A", page 279 in the Polly White case. Re-admitted.

Cornell Rogers
Clk. Com. on Citizenship

HURLEY

Docket #606
ROLLS 1851 & 2 OF

APPLICANT FOR CHEROKEE CITIZENSHIP

POST OFFICE: Prairie City I.T. **ATTORNEY:** J M Bryant

NO	NAMES	AGE	SEX
1	Catharine Hurley	37	Female
2	Jane Hurley	16	"

ANCESTOR: James Jones

The decision in this case will be found in Docket "A", page 279 in the Polly White case – Re-admitted.

Cornell Rogers
Clk. Com. on Citizenship

Cherokee Citizenship Commission Docket Books
(1880-84, 1887-89) Volume II
Tahlequah, Cherokee Nation

WHITE

Docket #607
ROLLS 1851 & 2 OS

APPLICANT FOR CHEROKEE CITIZENSHIP
POST OFFICE: Prairie City CN   ATTORNEY: J M Bryant

NO	NAMES	AGE	SEX
1	Mary Jane White	40	Female
2	Ele Herod	20	Male
3	Pally[sic] Brown	16	Female
4	Mont Smith	9	Male
5	John Smith	6	"
6	Eliza Smith	2	Female

ANCESTOR: James Jones

The decision in this case will be found on Docket "A", page 279 in the Polly White case – Re-admitted.

Cornell Rogers
Clk. Com. on Citizenship

WHITE

Docket #608
ROLLS 1851 & 2 OS

APPLICANT FOR CHEROKEE CITIZENSHIP
POST OFFICE: Prairie City CN   ATTORNEY: J M Bryant

NO	NAMES	AGE	SEX
1	Josiah White	25	Male

ANCESTOR: James Jones

The decision in this case will be found in Docket "A", page 279 in the Polly White case – Re-admitted.

Cornell Rogers
Clk. Com. on Citizenship

Cherokee Citizenship Commission Docket Books
(1880-84, 1887-89) Volume II
Tahlequah, Cherokee Nation

JONES

Docket #609
ROLLS 1851 & 52

APPLICANT FOR CHEROKEE CITIZENSHIP
POST OFFICE: Prairie City CN   **ATTORNEY:** J M Bryant

NO	NAMES	AGE	SEX
1	Emily Jones	38	Female

ANCESTOR: James Jones

The decision in this case will be found in Docket "A", page 279 in the Polly White case – Re-admitted.

Cornell Rogers
Clk. Com. on Citizenship

ATCHISON

Docket #610
ROLLS 1851 & 52 OS.

APPLICANT FOR CHEROKEE CITIZENSHIP
POST OFFICE: Prairie City CN   **ATTORNEY:** J M Bryant

NO	NAMES	AGE	SEX
1	Ruth Ann Atchison	14	Female

ANCESTOR: James Jones

The decision in this case will be found on Docket "A", page 279 in the Polly White case – Re-admitted.

Cornell Rogers
Clk. Com. on Citizenship

EBLEN

Docket #611
ROLLS 1835

APPLICANT FOR CHEROKEE CITIZENSHIP
POST OFFICE: Dalton Ga   **ATTORNEY:** Gideon Morgan

NO	NAMES	AGE	SEX
1	Elizabeth L Eblin	66	Female
2	Hugh Mc Hays	18	Male

Cherokee Citizenship Commission Docket Books
(1880-84, 1887-89) Volume II
Tahlequah, Cherokee Nation

3	James Edgar Hays	9	"

ANCESTOR: Elizabeth Lowery

Now on this the 28 day of September 1887 comes the above case for a final hearing and the parties having made application pursuant to the provisions of an Act of the National Council approved Dec. 8th 1886, and all evidence being duly examined and found to be sufficient and satisfactory to the Commission and the name of the ancestor Elizabeth Lowery appearing on the Rolls of 1835. It is adjudged and determined by the Commission that Elizabeth L. Eblen, Hugh Mc Hays, James Edgar Hays are Cherokees by blood. And are hereby re-admitted to all the rights privileges and immunities of Cherokees by blood. And a certificate of said decision of the Commission and re-admission was made and furnished to said parties accordingly.

Henry Eiffert
Clk. Com.

J.T. Adair   Chairman Commission
D.W. Lipe   Commissioner
               Commissioner

HENRY

Docket #612
ROLLS 1835 to 1852

APPLICANT FOR CHEROKEE CITIZENSHIP
POST OFFICE: Guntersville Ala   **ATTORNEY:** Boudinot & R

NO	NAMES	AGE	SEX
1	Patrick Henry	52	Male
2	Gibbs Henry	15	"
3	Albert P. Henry	13	"
4	Maria Henry	5	Female
5	Patrick Henry	2	Male

ANCESTOR: Annie Henry

Now on this the 30th day of Sept. 1887 comes the above case for a final hearing. And the parties having made application pursuant to the provisions of an Act of the National Council approved Dec 8 1886, and all the evidence being duly examined and found to be sufficient & satisfactory to the Commission and the name of the ancestor Annie Henry appearing upon the rolls of 1835 to 1852. It is adjudged and determined by the Commission that Patrick Henry, Gibbs Henry, Albert P. Henry, Maria Henry, Patrick Henry are Cherokees by blood &

Cherokee Citizenship Commission Docket Books
(1880-84, 1887-89) Volume II
Tahlequah, Cherokee Nation

are hereby re-admitted to all the rights privileges and immunities of Cherokees by blood. And a certificate of said decision by the Commission and re-admission was made and furnished to said parties accordingly.

                          J.T. Adair   Chairman Com.
                          John E. Gunter Commissioner

C.C. Lipe
Clerk Commission

HENRY

Docket #613
ROLLS 1835 to 52

APPLICANT FOR CHEROKEE CITIZENSHIP
POST OFFICE: Guntersville, Ala   **ATTORNEY:**

NO	NAMES	AGE	SEX
1	Thomas Benton Henry	21	Male

ANCESTOR: Annie Henry

Now on this the 30th day of Sept. 1887 comes the above case for a final hearing. And the parties having made application pursuant to the provisions of an Act of the National Council approved Dec. 8th 1886, and all the evidence being duly examined and found to be sufficient & satisfactory to the Commission and the name of the ancestor Annie Henry appearing on the rolls of 1835 to 52. It is adjudged and determined by the Commission that Thomas Benton Henry is a Cherokee by blood and are[sic] re-admitted to all the rights privileges and immunities of Cherokees by blood. And a certificate of said decision by the Commission and re-admission was made and furnished to said parties accordingly.

                          J.T. Adair   Chairman Com.
                          John E. Gunter Commissioner

C.C. Lipe
Clerk Commission

Cherokee Citizenship Commission Docket Books (1880-84, 1887-89) Volume II
Tahlequah, Cherokee Nation

SAMUELS

Docket #614
ROLLS 1835 to 52

APPLICANT FOR CHEROKEE CITIZENSHIP
POST OFFICE: Guntersville Ala   **ATTORNEY:** Boudinot & R

NO	NAMES	AGE	SEX
1	Myra Samuels		

ANCESTOR: Annie Henry (nee) Church

Now on this the 30 day of Sept. 1887 comes the above case for a final hearing. And the parties having made application pursuant to the provisions of an Act of the National Council approved Dec 8th 1886, and all the evidence being duly examined and found to be sufficient & satisfactory to the Commission and the name of the ancestor Annie Church appearing on the rolls of 1835 to 52. It is adjudged and determined by the Commission that Myra Samuels is a Cherokee by blood and is hereby re-admitted to all the rights privileges and immunities of Cherokees by blood. And a certificate of said decision of the Commission and re-admission was made and furnished accordingly.

                    J.T. Adair   Chairman Com.
                    John E. Gunter   Commissioner
C.C. Lipe   Commissioner
Clerk Commission

MORRIS

Docket #615
ROLLS 1835 to 52

APPLICANT FOR CHEROKEE CITIZENSHIP
POST OFFICE: **ATTORNEY:** Gideon Morgan

NO	NAMES	AGE	SEX
1	Ellen F. Morris	40	Female
2	Sallie G. Morris	18	"
3	Clyde E. Morris	16	"[sic]
4	Hugh Mc Morris	13	Male
5	Susie Mc Morris	9	Female
6	Mary T. Morris	6	"
7	Thomas F. Morris	2	Male

ANCESTOR: Elizabeth Lowery

Cherokee Citizenship Commission Docket Books
(1880-84, 1887-89) Volume II
Tahlequah, Cherokee Nation

Now on this the 30 day of Sept. 1887 comes the above case for a final hearing and the parties having made application pursuant to the provisions of an Act of the National Council approved Dec. 8th 1886, and all the evidence being duly examined and found to be sufficient & satisfactory to the Commission and the name of the ancestor Elizabeth Lowery appearing on the rolls of 1835 & 52. It is adjudged and determined by the Commission that Ellen F. Morris, Sallie G. Morris, Clyde E. Morris, Hugh Mc Morris, Susie C. Morris, Mary T. Morris, Thomas F. Morris are Cherokees by blood and are hereby re-admitted to all the rights privileges and immunities of Cherokees by blood. And a certificate of said decision of the Commission was made and furnished by[sic] said parties accordingly.

Henry Eiffert
Clk. Com.

J.T. Adair
D.W. Lipe

Chairman Com.
Commissioner
Commissioner

McSPADDEN

Docket #616
ROLLS 1835 to 52

APPLICANT FOR CHEROKEE CITIZENSHIP

POST OFFICE: Madisonville Tenn   **ATTORNEY:** Gideon Morgan

NO	NAMES	AGE	SEX
1	Walter McSpadden	15	Male

ANCESTOR: Gideon & Mary Morgan

Now on this the 28 day of September 1887 comes the above case for a final hearing and the parties having made application pursuant to the provisions of an Act of the National Council approved December 8th 1886, and all the evidence being duly examined and found to be sufficient and satisfactory to the Commission and the name of the ancestor Gideon and Mary Morgan appearing on the rolls of 1835 to 52. It is adjudged and determined by the Commission that Walter McSpadden is a Cherokee by blood. And are[sic] hereby re-admitted to all the rights privileges and immunities of Cherokees by blood. And a certificate of said decision of the Commission and re-admission was made and furnished to said parties accordingly.

Henry Eiffert
Clk. Com.

J.T. Adair
D.W. Lipe

Chairman Commission
Commissioner

Cherokee Citizenship Commission Docket Books
(1880-84, 1887-89) Volume II
Tahlequah, Cherokee Nation

PALMOUR

Docket #617
CENSUS ROLLS 1851 & 2

APPLICANT FOR CHEROKEE CITIZENSHIP

POST OFFICE: Weir Ga. ATTORNEY: A.E. Ivey

NO	NAMES	AGE	SEX
1	Benjamin F. Palmour	38	Male
2	Evaline Palmour	16	Female
3	Amy Palmour	13	"
4	Henry Palmour	11	Male
5	Virginia S. Palmour	9	Female
6	John D. Palmour, Jr.	5	Male
7	Bessie Palmour	3	Female
8	Robert Palmour	2	Male

ANCESTOR: John D. Palmour

Now on this the 22 day of Sept. comes the above case for a final hearing and the parties having made application pursuant to the provisions of an Act of the National Council approved Dec. 8, 1886, and all evidence being duly examined and found to be sufficient & satisfactory to the Commission and the name of the ancestor appearing John D. Palmour appearing on the rolls of 1851 & 2. It is adjudged and determined by the Commission that Benjamin F. Palmour, Evaline Palmour, Amy Palmour, Henry Palmour, Virginia S. Palmour, John D. Palmour, Jr. Bessie Palmour, Robert Palmour are Cherokees by blood. And a hearing[sic] re-admitted to all the rights privileges and immunities of Cherokees by blood. And a certificate of said decision of the Commission and re-admission was made and furnished to said parties accordingly.

       J.T. Adair Chairman Com
       John E. Gunter Commissioner

C.C. Lipe
Clerk Commission

Cherokee Citizenship Commission Docket Books (1880-84, 1887-89) Volume II
Tahlequah, Cherokee Nation

ABERCROMBIE

Docket #618
CENSUS ROLLS 1835

APPLICANT FOR CHEROKEE CITIZENSHIP
POST OFFICE: Sulphur Springs (Tex) Ark. **ATTORNEY:** C.H. Taylor

NO	NAMES	AGE	SEX
1	George Abercombie[sic]	31	Male
2	Clara Abercombie[sic]	5	Female
3	Bertha Abercombie[sic]	3	"
4	Hugh E. Abercombie[sic]	1	"[sic]

ANCESTOR: Angeline Chambers

Rejected April 4th 1889

Adverse
Embraced in decision on page 333
Book "B" in case of Young William
Abercrombie rendered April 4th 1889
    Will P. Ross   Chairman
    John E. Gunter   Commis.

Office Commission on Citizenship
Tahlequah April 4th 1889
    E.G. Ross
        Clk Com on Citizenship

ABERCROMBIE

Docket #619
CENSUS ROLLS 1835

APPLICANT FOR CHEROKEE CITIZENSHIP
POST OFFICE: Sulphur Springs (Tex) Arkansas **ATTORNEY:** C.H. Taylor

NO	NAMES	AGE	SEX
1	Young William Abercombia[sic]	33	Male
2	Riley A. Abercombia[sic]	8	"
3	Edith A. Abercombia[sic]	6	Female
4	Earnest Abercombia[sic]	4	Male
5	Nellia[sic] Dee Abercombia[sic]	2	Female

ANCESTOR: Angelina Chambers

Rejected April 4th 1889

Cherokee Citizenship Commission Docket Books
(1880-84, 1887-89) Volume II
Tahlequah, Cherokee Nation

Now on this the 4th day of April A.D. 1889 comes the above case to wit: Young William Abercrombie VS. the Cherokee Nation for final hearing the same having been submitted by C.H. Taylor, Attorney for the applicant who alleges as the ground of his application for readmission to Citizenship in the Cherokee Nation his descent from Angelina Chambers whose name would be found on the census rolls of the Cherokees for 1835. There being no evidence presented in support of the application and the name of Angeline Chambers not being found on the roll of 1835, it is adjudged by the Commission that Young William Abercrombie is not of Cherokee blood and is not entitled to Citizenship in the Cherokee Nation and it is so decreed. This decision of the Commission embraces the children of said Young William Abercrombie viz Riley A Abercrombie aged eight years, Edith A. Abercrombie aged six years, Earnest Abercrombie aged four years, Nellie Dee Abercrombie aged two years; George Abercrombie and family, Clara aged five years, Bertha aged three years, and Hugh E. Aged one year; Benjamin F. Abercrombie aged twenty six years, John R. Abercrombie aged nineteen years, James C. Abercrombie aged twenty seven years and his family Mollie A, Claud and Callie E. These whose applications were filed before the Commission on the 3rd day of October 1887. Post Office address Sulphur Springs, Ark.

                              Will P. Ross   Chairman
E.G. Ross   John E. Gunter Commissioner
   Clk. Commission

ABERCROMBIE

Docket #620
CENSUS ROLLS 1835

APPLICANT FOR CHEROKEE CITIZENSHIP

POST OFFICE: Sulphur Spgs (Tex) Ark   **ATTORNEY:** C.H. Taylor

NO	NAMES	AGE	SEX
1	James C. Abercombia[sic]	27	Male
2	Mollie A Ambercombia[sic]	6	Female
3	Claud Ambercombia[sic]	4	Male
4	Callie E. Abercombia[sic]	1	Female

ANCESTOR: Angelina Chambers

Rejected April 4th 1889

Cherokee Citizenship Commission Docket Books
(1880-84, 1887-89) Volume II
Tahlequah, Cherokee Nation

Office Commission on Citizenship
Tahlequah I.T. April 4th 1889

Adverse
Embraced in decision on page 333
Book "B" in case of Young William
Abercrombie rendered April 4th 1889
Will P. Ross   Chairman
John E. Gunter   Commis.

E.G. Ross
Clk Com on Citizenship

ABERCROMBIE

Docket #621
CENSUS ROLLS 1835

APPLICANT FOR CHEROKEE CITIZENSHIP

POST OFFICE: Sulphur Spgs (Tex) Ark   **ATTORNEY:** C.H. Taylor

NO	NAMES	AGE	SEX
1	Benj. F. Abercombia[sic]	26	Male

ANCESTOR: Angelina Chambers

Office Commission on Citizenship
Tahlequah I.T. April 4th 1889

Adverse
Embraced in decision on page 333
Book "B" in case of Young William
Abercrombie rendered April 4th 1889
Will P. Ross   Chairman
John E. Gunter   Commis.

E.G. Ross
Clk Com on Citizenship

Cherokee Citizenship Commission Docket Books
(1880-84, 1887-89) Volume II
Tahlequah, Cherokee Nation

ABERCROMBIE

Docket #622
CENSUS ROLLS 1835

APPLICANT FOR CHEROKEE CITIZENSHIP

POST OFFICE: Sulphur Spgs (Tex) Ark   ATTORNEY: C H Taylor

NO	NAMES	AGE	SEX
1	John R Abercombia[sic]	19	Male

ANCESTOR: Angelina Chambers

Rejected April 4th 1889

Adverse

Embraced in decision on page 333 Book "B" in case of Young William Abercrombie rendered April 4th 1889

ABEL

Docket #623
CENSUS ROLLS 1835 to 52

APPLICANT FOR CHEROKEE CITIZENSHIP

POST OFFICE: Alma, Ark   ATTORNEY: A.E. Ivey

NO	NAMES	AGE	SEX
1	John D. Abel	52	Male
2	J.F. Abel	20	"
3	William A. Abel	14	"
4	Harrison E. Abel	12	"
5	Allie B. Abel	9	"[sic]

ANCESTOR: Betsey Pritchet

Rejected July 2nd 1889

Office Commission on Citizenship
Cherokee Nation Ind. Ter.
Tahlequah July 2nd 1889

There being no evidence in support of the above named case the Commission decide that John D. Abel 52 yrs and the following children Jno F. male age 20 yrs, Wm A. male age 14 yrs, Harrison E. male age 12 yrs and Allie B. Abel female age 9 yrs are not Cherokees by blood. Post office Alma Ark.

Cherokee Citizenship Commission Docket Books
(1880-84, 1887-89) Volume II
Tahlequah, Cherokee Nation

Attest
  D.S. Williams
  Asst. Clerk Commission

Will P. Ross   Chairman
John E. Gunter   Com

ABEL

Docket #624
CENSUS ROLLS 1835 to 52

APPLICANT FOR CHEROKEE CITIZENSHIP
POST OFFICE: Mulberry Ark   ATTORNEY: A E Ivey

NO	NAMES	AGE	SEX
1	Samuel Abel	31	Male
2	Emma Abel	6	Female
3	Catharine Abel	4	"
4	L M Abel	2	"
5	J M Abel	Infant	Male

ANCESTOR: John Abel

Rejected June 5th 1889

Office Commission on Citizenship
Tahlequah Cherokee Nation
June 5th 1889

Samuel Abel V.S. C.N. Applicant for Cherokee Citizenship

    The above application was filed on the 5th day of Oct 1887 and on this day the case coming on for final hearing. The Commission fails to find any evidence filed in support of Applicants' claim of Cherokee blood and in view of this fact we decide and so declare that applicant Samuel Abel age 31, & his children Emma Abel Age 6 yrs, Catharine age 4 yrs, L M age 2 yrs & J.M. Abel are not Cherokees by blood & are not entitled to any rights & privileges of citizenship in the Cherokee Nation. Post office Mulberry Ark.

Attest
  D.S. Williams
  Asst Clk Com.

Will P. Ross   Chairman
R. Bunch   Com
J.E. Gunter   Com

Cherokee Citizenship Commission Docket Books
(1880-84, 1887-89) Volume II
Tahlequah, Cherokee Nation

ABEL

Docket #625
CENSUS ROLLS 1835 to 52

APPLICANT FOR CHEROKEE CITIZENSHIP

POST OFFICE: Mulberry Station Ark **ATTORNEY:** A E Ivey

NO	NAMES	AGE	SEX
1	Lucinda E. Abel	32	Female
2	Walter L. Abel	11	Male
3	E B Abel	9	"
4	Mary M. Abel	6	Female
5	Lenard I Abel	4	Male
6	Charles F Abel	2	"

ANCESTOR: John Rogers

Now on this the 17th day of March 1888 comes the above case for a final hearing, and the parties having made application pursuant to the provisions of an Act of the National Council approved December 8th 1886, and all the evidence being duly considered and found to be sufficient and satisfactory, it is adjudged and declared by the Commission, that

Lucinda E. Abel, Walt. L. Abel, E.B. Abel, Mary M. Abel, Lenard I. Abel and Charles F. Abel are not Cherokees and are not entitled to the rights privileges and immunities of Cherokee citizens by blood.

J.T. Adair	Chairman Commission
John E. Gunter	Commissioner
D.W. Lipe	Commissioner

Attest
    C.C. Lipe
    Clerk. Com.

The decision in the James C.C. Rogers case found in Book C, page 627 and testimony on Journal page 325 to 333, governs this case.

Cherokee Citizenship Commission Docket Books
(1880-84, 1887-89) Volume II
Tahlequah, Cherokee Nation

ABEL

Docket #626
CENSUS ROLLS 1835 to 52

APPLICANT FOR CHEROKEE CITIZENSHIP

POST OFFICE: Mulberry Ark   **ATTORNEY:** AE Ivey

NO	NAMES	AGE	SEX
1	James W. Abel	48	Male
2	J F Abel	19	"
3	L C Abel	17	"
4	L A Abel	15	"
5	J H Abel	13	"
6	R A Abel	11	Female
7	S B Abel	9	"
8	S C Abel	7	"
9	R M Abel	5	Male

ANCESTOR: Pritchett

Rejected June 5th 1889

Office Commission on Citizenship
Tahlequah Cherokee Nation
June 5th 1889

James W. Abel VS C.N. Application for Cherokee Citizenship

Now on this day the above case coming on for final hearing & after examing[sic] the application we fail to find any evidence filed in support of applicants claims of Cherokee blood & in view of this fact we decide & so declare that applicant James W. Abel age 48 & his children J F Abel age 19, L C Abel age 17, L A Abel age 15, J H Abel age 13, R A Abel age 11, S B Abel age 9, S C Abel age 7, R M Abel age 5 are not Cherokees by blood & are not entitled to any rights or privileges of Cherokee citizenship in the Cherokee Nation. Post Office Mulberry Ark.

Attest   Will P. Ross
   D.S. Williams   Chairman
   Asst Clk Com   J E Gunter Com

Cherokee Citizenship Commission Docket Books
(1880-84, 1887-89) Volume II
Tahlequah, Cherokee Nation

ARMOUR

Docket #627
CENSUS ROLLS 1835 to 52

APPLICANT FOR CHEROKEE CITIZENSHIP
POST OFFICE: Fort Smith Ark   ATTORNEY: A E Ivey

NO	NAMES	AGE	SEX
1	Armour	22	Male

ANCESTOR: Stephen Moton

Rejected June 5th 1889

Office Commission on Citizenship
Tahlequah Cherokee Nation
June 5th 1889

Mrs. Armour vs C.N. Applicant for Cherokee Citizenship

On this day the above case coming on for final hearing & after examing[sic] the application we fail to find any evidence filed in support of application of Cherokee blood. This alone will justify the Commission in deciding that Applicant Mrs. Armour age 22 yrs is not a Cherokee by blood & not entitled to Citizenship in the Cherokee Nation. Post office Fort Smith Ark.

Attest   Will P. Ross
  D.S. Williams   Chairman
  Asst Clk Com.   J E Gunter   Com

ARMOUR

Docket #628
CENSUS ROLLS 1835 to 52

APPLICANT FOR CHEROKEE CITIZENSHIP
POST OFFICE: Ft Smith Ark   ATTORNEY: A E Ivey

NO	NAMES	AGE	SEX
1	Sarah J Armour	22	Female

ANCESTOR: Pal*(illegible)*

Rejected June 5th 1889

Cherokee Citizenship Commission Docket Books
(1880-84, 1887-89) Volume II
Tahlequah, Cherokee Nation

Office Commission on Citizenship
Tahlequah Cherokee Nation
June 5th 1889

The above application was filed on the 4th day of Oct 1887 and on this day the case coming on for final hearing. The Commission fails to find any evidence in support of applicant's claim of Cherokee blood. This alone will justify the Commission in deciding that Sarah J Armour age 22 years is not of Cherokee by blood & not entitled to any rights & privileges of citizenship in the Cherokee Nation.

Post office Fort Smith Ark.

Attest
   D.S. Williams
   Asst Clk Com

Will P. Ross
        Chairman
J E Gunter Com

AYERS

Docket #629
CENSUS ROLLS OS

APPLICANT FOR CHEROKEE CITIZENSHIP

POST OFFICE: Fort Smith Ark **ATTORNEY:** C H Taylor

NO	NAMES	AGE	SEX
1	Symantha Ayers	35	Female
	Grant "	10	Male
	Sherman "	6	"
	Symantha "	4	Female
	Carry "	6 months	"

ANCESTOR: William Allington

Rejected June 5th 1889

Office Commission on Citizenship
Cherokee Nation Ind. Ter.
Tahlequah June 5th 1889

The above application was filed on this 5th day of Oct. 1887 and on this day the case coming up for final hearing we find after examing[sic] the papers submitted by applicant that she claims to derive her Cherokee blood through one William Alligton[sic] whose name she alleges ought to be found on the Old Settlers rolls

Cherokee Citizenship Commission Docket Books
(1880-84, 1887-89) Volume II
Tahlequah, Cherokee Nation

of Cherokees – The applicant filed as evidence a statement of her Father William Stephens which only states that Symantha Ayers is his daughter. This statement does not state whether the affiant was sworn at the time of making the statement and fails to have a seal of office or an official signature attached to it. In view of the fact that William Allington's name can not be found on the Old Settler Census roll and as this statement of William Stephens can not be taken as evidence we decide and so declare that applicant Symantha Ayers age 35 yrs and her children, Grant age 10 yrs, Sherman age 6 yrs, Symantha age 4 yrs, and Carry Ayers age 6 months are not Cherokees by blood and are not entitled to any rights privileges of Citizenship in the Cherokee Nation. Post office Fort Smith Ark.

	Will P. Ross	Chairman
Attest	R. Bunch	Com
D.S. Williams	John E. Gunter	Com
Asst Clk Com		

AGG

Docket #630
CENSUS ROLLS

APPLICANT FOR CHEROKEE CITIZENSHIP

POST OFFICE: Afton I.T.   **ATTORNEY:** L B Bell

NO	NAMES	AGE	SEX
1	Sarah J Agg		Female

ANCESTOR: Mary Crews

The Commission decide against claimant. See decision in case Andrew Merideth Docket 2180 Book E Page 26 and case John Hanly Docket 1250 Book E Page 386.

Will P. Ross	Chairman
R. Bunch	Com
J E. Gunter	Com

Cherokee Citizenship Commission Docket Books
(1880-84, 1887-89) Volume II
Tahlequah, Cherokee Nation

ARMSTRONG

Docket #631
CENSUS ROLLS 1835 to 52

APPLICANT FOR CHEROKEE CITIZENSHIP
POST OFFICE: Blue Jacket I.T. **ATTORNEY:**

NO	NAMES	AGE	SEX
1	*(Blank on microfilm)*		

ANCESTOR: Charlott Vaughn

Look on Book "C" Docket 957 for this case – Docketed twice –

Cornell Rogers
Clk Com.

ALFRED

Docket #632
CENSUS ROLLS 1835/52

APPLICANT FOR CHEROKEE CITIZENSHIP
POST OFFICE: Childers Station I.T. **ATTORNEY:** L S Sanders

NO	NAMES	AGE	SEX
1	James M Alfred	27	Male
2	Manassa Alfred	4	"

ANCESTOR: William Alfred

Rejected May 9th 1889

Office Commission on Citizenship
Cherokee Nation Ind. Ter.
Tahlequah May 9th 1889

The application in the above case was filed the 4th day of October 1887. It is sustained by no evidence and the parties having been called three several times at intervals of not less than one hour and no answer made. The Commission decide that James M. Alfred aged twenty seven years and his son Manassa Alfred are not of Cherokee blood and therefore not entitled to Citizenship in the Cherokee Nation.

                Will P. Ross   Chairman
Attest   John E Gunter Com
    D.S. Williams
    Clk. Com.

Cherokee Citizenship Commission Docket Books
(1880-84, 1887-89) Volume II
Tahlequah, Cherokee Nation

ALFRED

Docket #633
CENSUS ROLLS 1835/52

APPLICANT FOR CHEROKEE CITIZENSHIP
POST OFFICE: Van Buren Ark   **ATTORNEY:** L S Sanders

NO	NAMES	AGE	SEX
1	William Alfred	59	Male
2	John A Alfred	22	"
3	Andrew J Alfred	19	"
4	Malinda Alfred	16	Female
5	Robert Alfred	14	Male
6	Sarah B Alfred	11	Female
7	Nancy A Alfred	7	"

ANCESTOR: James Alfred

Rejected June 13th 1889

Office Commission on Citizenship
Cherokee Nation Ind. Ter.
Tahlequah June 13th 1889

There being no evidence submitted in the above named case the Commission are of the opinion and so decide that Wm Alfred age 57 years and his children whose names are as follows   John A male age 22 years, Andy J male male[sic] 19 years, Malinda Female age 16 years, Robert male age 14 years, Sarah B. Female age 11 years, and Nancy A Alfred Female age 7 years are not of Cherokee blood and are not entitled to Citizenship in the Cherokee Nation. Post Office address Van Buren Ark.

Will P. Ross
Chairman
Attest   J E Gunter   Com
    D.S. Williams
    Asst Clk Com

Cherokee Citizenship Commission Docket Books
(1880-84, 1887-89) Volume II
Tahlequah, Cherokee Nation

ALFRED

Docket #634
CENSUS ROLLS 1835/52

APPLICANT FOR CHEROKEE CITIZENSHIP
POST OFFICE: Fort Smith Ark.   **ATTORNEY:** L.S. Sanders

NO	NAMES	AGE	SEX
1	Hugh C Alfred	32	Male
2	Callie G Alfred		

ANCESTOR: William Alfred

Rejected June 13th 1889

Office Commission on Citizenship
Cherokee Nation Ind. Ter.
Tahlequah June 13th 1889

There being no evidence in support of the above named applicant we the Commission decide that Hugh C. Alfred age 32 years and his child whose name is Callie G. Alfred is[sic] not of Cherokee blood. Post Office Fort Smith Ark.

Attest   Will P. Ross
   D S Williams   Chairman
   Asst Clk Com   R Bunch   Com
                  JE Gunter   "

ALLEN

Docket #635
CENSUS ROLLS 1835 to 52

APPLICANT FOR CHEROKEE CITIZENSHIP
POST OFFICE: Tahlequah CN   **ATTORNEY:** L.S. Sanders

NO	NAMES	AGE	SEX
1	Nancy Allen	40	Female
2	John McCraw	20	Male
3	Junnetta McCraw	18	Female

ANCESTOR: Strother Burgess

Cherokee Citizenship Commission Docket Books
(1880-84, 1887-89) Volume II
Tahlequah, Cherokee Nation

Office Commission on Citizenship
Tahlequah CN June 13th 1889

There being no evidence in support of the above application we are of the opinion and so decide that applicant Nancy Allen aged 40 years and John McCraw and Junnetta McCraw are not Cherokees by blood. Post Office Tahlequah I.T.

Will P. Ross
Chairman
R. Bunch   Com
J E Gunter   "

ALLEN

Docket #636
CENSUS ROLLS 1835/52

APPLICANT FOR CHEROKEE CITIZENSHIP
POST OFFICE: Van Buren Ark   ATTORNEY:

NO	NAMES	AGE	SEX
1	Jane Allen	33	Female
2	Alice Allen	16	"
3	Julia Allen	14	"
4	Ollie Allen	9	"
5	Wade Allen	7	Male
6	May Allen	4	Female
7	John Allen	1	Male

ANCESTOR: Calew Carlile

Rejected June 6th 1889

Office of Commission on Citizenahip
Cherokee Nation Ind. Ter.
Tahlequah June 6th 1889

The case of Jane Allen was filed the 4th day of October 1887 and was called the 6 of June 1889 3 several times not less than one hour apart and no response from applicant Jane Allen or by Attorney and now the Commission after examing[sic] the papers in said case fail to find any evidence in support of application from the above facts. The Commission decide that Jane Allen age 33 years and her children Alice Allen, Female age 16 years, Julia, Female age 14 year, Ollie Female age 9 years, Wade Male age 7 years, Mary, Female age 4 years and John

Cherokee Citizenship Commission Docket Books
(1880-84, 1887-89) Volume II
Tahlequah, Cherokee Nation

Allen Male age 1 year, are not of Cherokee blood and are not entitled to citizenship in the Cherokee Nation.
Post Office address Van Buren Ark.

                        Will P. Ross
Attest   Chairman
   D S Williams   R Bunch   Com
   Asst Clk Com   J. E. Gunter   "

ALLEN

Docket #637
CENSUS ROLLS

                        APPLICANT FOR CHEROKEE CITIZENSHIP
          POST OFFICE: ATTORNEY: L.B. Bell

NO	NAMES	AGE	SEX
1	Thomas C. Allen		

              ANCESTOR: Sarah Morgan
Rejected June 6th 1889

                 Office Commission on Citizenship
                    Cherokee Nation Ind. Ter.
                     Tahlequah June 6th 1889

The case of Thomas C Allen was filed on the 5th day of October 1887 and was called on 3 several times not less than one hour apart for final action and no response from applicant or Attorney on this 6th day of June 1889. The Commission therefore after investigating the case of Thomas C Allen fail to find any evidence in support of application from that fact decide that Thomas C Allen age not given, is not of Cherokee blood and is not entitled to citizenship in the Cherokee Nation. Post office address is not given.

Attest   Will P. Ross   Chairman
   D S Williams   R Bunch   Com
   Asst Clk Com   J.E. Gunter   "

Cherokee Citizenship Commission Docket Books
(1880-84, 1887-89) Volume II
Tahlequah, Cherokee Nation

ALLEN

Docket #638
CENSUS ROLLS

APPLICANT FOR CHEROKEE CITIZENSHIP
POST OFFICE: **ATTORNEY:** L.B. Bell

NO	NAMES	AGE	SEX
1	Samuel C Allen		Male

ANCESTOR: Sarah Morgan

Rejected June 6th 1889

Office Commission on Citizenship
Cherokee Nation Ind. Ter.
Tahlequah June 6th 1889

The case of Samuel C Allen was filed on the 5th day of Oct. 1887 and was called on 3 several times not less than one hour apart for final action June 6th 1889 and no response from applicant Samuel C. Allen or by Attorney. Therefore the Commission after examing[sic] the papers in said case fail to find any evidence in support of application and from these facts the Commission decide that Samuel C Allen age not given, neither is his Post Office are[sic] not of Cherokee blood and is not entitled to citizenship in the Cherokee Nation.

Attest   Will P. Ross   Chairman
   D S Williams   R Bunch   Com
   Asst Clk Com   J.E. Gunter   Com

ALLEN

Docket #639
CENSUS ROLLS

APPLICANT FOR CHEROKEE CITIZENSHIP
POST OFFICE: Eagletown Ind.   **ATTORNEY:** L B Bell

NO	NAMES	AGE	SEX
1	Samuel C. Allen		Male

ANCESTOR: Martha Elmore

The Commission decide against claimant. See decision in case Lible J. Bogue Docket 2183 Book E Page 29.

                      Will P. Ross   Chairman
                      R. Bunch   Com
                      JE Gunter   Com

Cherokee Citizenship Commission Docket Books
(1880-84, 1887-89) Volume II
Tahlequah, Cherokee Nation

ALLEN

Docket #640
CENSUS ROLLS

APPLICANT FOR CHEROKEE CITIZENSHIP

POST OFFICE: Franklinville NC **ATTORNEY:** L.B. Bell

NO	NAMES	AGE	SEX
1	Hezakiah Allen		Male

ANCESTOR: Martha Elmore

The Commission decide against claimant. See decision in case Lible J. Bogue Docket 2183 Book E Page 29.

                         Will P. Ross   Chairman
                         R. Bunch   Com
                         J.E. Gunter   Com

ALLEN

Docket #641
CENSUS ROLLS

APPLICANT FOR CHEROKEE CITIZENSHIP

POST OFFICE: Emporia, Kan **ATTORNEY:** L.B. Bell

NO	NAMES	AGE	SEX
1	John Allen		Male

ANCESTOR: Sarah Morgan

Rejected June 6th 1889

                         Office Commission on Citizenship
                               Cherokee Nation Ind. Ter.
                                   Tahlequah June 6th 1889

The case of John Allen was filed on the 5th day of Oct. 1887 and was called on 3 several times not less than one hour apart and no response from applicant or by Attorney. The Commission after examing[sic] the case of John Allen find no evidence in support of application and from these facts the Commission decide that John Allen age not given, is not of Cherokee blood and is not entitled to citizenship in the Cherokee Nation. Post Office address Emporia Kansas.

Cherokee Citizenship Commission Docket Books
(1880-84, 1887-89) Volume II
Tahlequah, Cherokee Nation

Attest	Will P. Ross	Chairman
D S Williams	R Bunch	Com
Asst Clk Com	J.E. Gunter	"

ALLEN

Docket #642
CENSUS ROLLS

APPLICANT FOR CHEROKEE CITIZENSHIP

POST OFFICE: Indianapolis Ind **ATTORNEY:** L B Bell

NO	NAMES	AGE	SEX
1	Oliver W. Allen	27	Male

ANCESTOR: Martha Elmore

The Commission decide against claimant. See decision in case Lible J. Bogue Docket 2183 Book E Page 29.

	Will P. Ross	Chairman
	R. Bunch	Com
	J.E. Gunter	Com

ALLEN

Docket #643
CENSUS ROLLS

APPLICANT FOR CHEROKEE CITIZENSHIP

POST OFFICE: Indianapolis Ind **ATTORNEY:** L.B. Bell

NO	NAMES	AGE	SEX
1	Minnie F Allen		Female

ANCESTOR: Martha Elmore

The Commission decide against claimant. See decision in case Lible J. Bogue Docket 2183 Book E Page 29.

	Will P. Ross	Chairman
	R. Bunch	Com
	J.E. Gunter	Com

Cherokee Citizenship Commission Docket Books
(1880-84, 1887-89) Volume II
Tahlequah, Cherokee Nation

ALEXANDER

Docket #644
CENSUS ROLLS 1835 to 52

APPLICANT FOR CHEROKEE CITIZENSHIP

POST OFFICE: Chetopa Kansas **ATTORNEY:** Boudinot & R

NO	NAMES	AGE	SEX
1	William Alexander	45	Male
2	T.G. Alexander	20	"
3	G.W. Alexander	18	"
4	Nellie Alexander	17	Female

ANCESTOR: Chas Hawks

Office Commission on Citizenship Tahlequah I.T. Aug. 10th '88

The above case being set for final hearing by plaintiff's Attorney, Mess. Boudinot & Rasmus for a certain day, and it being called to the notice of the Commission on the 6th inst. by Mr. Alexander's Attys. in the matter of wishing to with-draw the same on the grounds that they were satisfied that they could find no ancestor on the rolls laid down in the 7th Sec. of Act of Dec. 8th 1886, and that they had no proof in support of the allegations set forth in the (his) application for citizenship.   Hon. R.F. Wyly Nation's Attorney moves the Commission to render judgment adversely to claimants whereupon the Commission on Citizenship declares that William Alexander and his three children, viz: T.G. Alexander, G.W. Alexander and Nellie Alexander, are not entitled to any of the rights and privileges or immunities of a Cherokees by blood. See Sec. 7 – Act of Dec. 8th 1886, and are intruders upon the public domain of the Cherokee Nation.

J.T. Adair   Chairman Commission
H.C. Barnes   Commissioner

ALLISON

Docket #645
CENSUS ROLLS 1835/52

APPLICANT FOR CHEROKEE CITIZENSHIP

POST OFFICE: Timson[sic] Texas   **ATTORNEY:** W.A. Thompson

NO	NAMES	AGE	SEX
1	John R. Allison	36	Male
2	Willie Allison	6	"

Cherokee Citizenship Commission Docket Books (1880-84, 1887-89) Volume II
Tahlequah, Cherokee Nation

3	Elma R Allison	3	Female
4	Jennie Allison	2	"

ANCESTOR: J A & Patsey Thompson

Now on this the 12th day of October 1887, comes the above case for a final hearing, and the parties having made application pursuant to the provisions of an Act of the National Council approved December 8th 1886, and all evidence having been duly considered and found to be sufficient and satisfactory to the Commission and the names of the ancestors J.A. & Patsey Thompson appearing upon the Rolls of 1835 to 1852. It is adjudged and determined by the Commission that John R. Allison, Willie Allison, Elma R. Allison, Jennie Allison are Cherokees by blood and are hereby re-admitted to all the rights privileges of Cherokees by blood.

And a certificate of said decision and re-admission was made and furnished to said parties accordingly.

	J.T. Adair	Chairman Commission
Henry Eiffert	D.W. Lipe	Commissioner
Clk. Com.		Commissioner

ALLISON

Docket #646
CENSUS ROLLS 1835 to 52

APPLICANT FOR CHEROKEE CITIZENSHIP
POST OFFICE: Fair Play Texas   **ATTORNEY:** W A Thompson

NO	NAMES	AGE	SEX
1	James T. Allison	40	Male

ANCESTOR: J.A. & Patsey Thompson

Now on this the 12 day of October 1887, comes the above case for a final hearing and the parties having made application pursuant to an Act of the National Council approved December 8th 1886. And all the evidence being duly considered and found to be sufficient and satisfactory to the Commission, and the names of the ancestors J A & Patsey Thompson appearing upon the Rolls of 1835. It is adjudged and decided by the Commission that James T. Allison is a Cherokee by blood and is hereby re-admitted to all the rights privileges and immunities of a Cherokee by blood.

Cherokee Citizenship Commission Docket Books
(1880-84, 1887-89) Volume II
Tahlequah, Cherokee Nation

And a certificate of said decision of the Commission and re-admission was made and furnished to said parties accordingly.

	J.T. Adair	Chairman Commission
Henry Eiffert	D.W. Lipe	Commissioner
Clk. Com.		Commissioner

ALLISON

Docket #647
CENSUS ROLLS 1835/52

APPLICANT FOR CHEROKEE CITIZENSHIP

POST OFFICE: Fair Play Tex   **ATTORNEY:** W A Thompson

NO	NAMES	AGE	SEX
1	Martha A Allison	30	Female

ANCESTOR: J A & Patsey Thompson

Now on this the 12th day of October 1887 comes the above case for a final hearing, and the parties having made application pursuant to the provisions of an Act of the National Council approved Dec 8th 1886 and all the evidence being duly examined and found to be sufficient and satisfactory to the Commission, and the names of the ancestors J A & Patsey Thompson appearing upon the Roll of 1835. It is adjudged and determined by the Commission that Martha A Allison is a Cherokee by blood; and is hereby re-admitted to all the rights privileges and immunities of a Cherokee by blood.

And a certificate of said decision of the Commission and re-admission was made and furnished to said parties accordingly.

	J.T. Adair	Chairman Commission
Henry Eiffert	D.W. Lipe	Commissioner
Clk. Com.		Commissioner

Cherokee Citizenship Commission Docket Books
(1880-84, 1887-89) Volume II
Tahlequah, Cherokee Nation

ARCHER

Docket #648
CENSUS ROLLS 1835 to 52

APPLICANT FOR CHEROKEE CITIZENSHIP

POST OFFICE: Baxter Springs Kan~~sas~~   **ATTORNEY:** Boudinot

NO	NAMES	AGE	SEX
1	John R Archer	23	Male

ANCESTOR: Lucy A Archer

We the Commission on Citizenship after duly considering the testimony in the above case as well as the rolls mentioned in the 7th Sec Sec.[sic] of the Act of Dec. 8th 1886, in relation to citizenship, find that the said rolls contain the name of David M. Harlin, who was the grand father of the applicant John R. Archer, and that said Harlin was, or is, a Cherokee, and hence his grandson must be. We therefore re-admit John R. Archer to all the rights and privileges of a Cherokee citizen by blood, he being entitled to the same under the law creating this Commission.

J.T. Adair   Chairman Commission
D.W. Lipe   Commissioner
H.C. Barnes   Commissioner

ARCHER

Docket #649
CENSUS ROLLS 1835/52

APPLICANT FOR CHEROKEE CITIZENSHIP

POST OFFICE: Baxter Springs   **ATTORNEY:** Boudinot & R

NO	NAMES	AGE	SEX
1	Mary E Archer	20	Female

ANCESTOR: Lucenda A Archer

We the Commission on Citizenship after carefully examining the testimony in the above case, as well as the census and pay rolls laid down in Section 7 of the Act of Dec. 8th 1886, find that Mary E. Propp nee Archer, is the grand daughter of David M. Harlin, whose name is contained on said rolls as a Cherokee, and we do hereby that Mary E. Propp, nee Archer, is a Cherokee by blood, and entitled to all the rights and privileges of a citizen of the Cherokee Nation on account of her blood, and she is hereby re-admitted to the same –

Cherokee Citizenship Commission Docket Books
(1880-84, 1887-89) Volume II
Tahlequah, Cherokee Nation

The applicant married a man by the name of Propp since the filing of this, her application for Citizenship. (See Act of Dec. 8th 1886)

                J.T. Adair   Chairman Commission
                D.W. Lipe   Commissioner
                H.C. Barnes Commissioner

ATKINS

Docket #650
CENSUS ROLLS 1835/52

APPLICANT FOR CHEROKEE CITIZENSHIP

POST OFFICE: Camp Creek CN   **ATTORNEY:** A E Ivey

NO	NAMES	AGE	SEX
1	Sarah A Atkins	23	Female
2	Geo W. Atkins	3	
3	Anna M Atkins	1	

ANCESTOR: Mack Hopper

Rejected June 6th 1889

        Office Commission on Citizenship
           Cherokee Nation Ind. Ter.
            Tahlequah June 6th 1889

The case of Sarah A Atkins was filed on the 3rd day of October 1887 and was called on the 6th day of June 1889 for final action and no response from applicant Sarah A Atkins or by Attorney there being no evidence in support of application the Commission decide that Sarah A Atkins age 23 years and her children Geo. W. male 3 years and Anna M Atkins Female age 1 year, are not of Cherokee blood and are not entitled to citizenship in the Cherokee Nation. Post Office address Camp Creek I.T.

                Will P. Ross   Chairman
                R Bunch   Com
Attest   J.E. Gunter   "
  D S Williams
  Asst Clk Com.

Cherokee Citizenship Commission Docket Books
(1880-84, 1887-89) Volume II
Tahlequah, Cherokee Nation

ARWOOD

Docket #651
CENSUS ROLLS 1835 to 1852

APPLICANT FOR CHEROKEE CITIZENSHIP

POST OFFICE: Mineral Spgs Ga   **ATTORNEY:** A E Ivey

NO	NAMES	AGE	SEX
1	Mary Arwood	53	Female
2	John M McClatchey	26	
3	Thomas W Arwood	18	
4	Rosa Arwood	16	

ANCESTOR: Horatio Talley

Rejected June 6th 1889

Office Commission on Citizenship
Cherokee Nation Ind. Ter.
Tahlequah June 6th 1889

The case of Mary Arwood was filed on the 3rd day of October 1887 and was called on the 6th day of June 1889 3 several times not less than one hour apart for final action and no response from applicant Mary Arwood or by Attorney there being no evidence in support of application the Commission therefore are of the opinion and so decide that Mary Arwood whose age is 53 years and her children names as follows John M McClatchey male age 26 years, Thomas W male age 18 years, and Rosa Arwood Female age 16 years are not of Cherokee blood and are not entitled to citizenship in the Cherokee Nation. Post Office address Mineral Spgs. Ga.

	Will P. Ross	Chairman
	R Bunch	Com
Attest	J.E. Gunter	"
	D S Williams	
	Asst Clk Com.	

Cherokee Citizenship Commission Docket Books (1880-84, 1887-89) Volume II
Tahlequah, Cherokee Nation

ARWOOD

Docket #652
CENSUS ROLLS 1851

APPLICANT FOR CHEROKEE CITIZENSHIP

POST OFFICE: Mineral Spgs Ga.   **ATTORNEY:** A E Ivey

NO	NAMES	AGE	SEX
1	William P Arwood	21	Male

ANCESTOR: Mary Arwood

Rejected June 6th 1889

Office Commission on Citizenship
Cherokee Nation Ind. Ter.
Tahlequah June 6th 1889

The case of Wm P. Arwood was filed on the 3rd day of October 1887 and was called 3 several times not less than one hour apart no response from applicant Wm P. Arwood or by Attorney and there being no evidence in support of application therefore the Commission are of the opinion and so decide that Wm P. Arwood age 21 years is not of Cherokee blood and is not entitled to citizenship in the Cherokee Nation.

                Will P. Ross   Chairman
                R Bunch   Com
Attest   J.E. Gunter   "
   D S Williams
   Asst Clk Com.

AUSTIN

Docket #653
CENSUS ROLLS 1835

APPLICANT FOR CHEROKEE CITIZENSHIP

POST OFFICE: Kansas City Mo.   **ATTORNEY:** A E Ivey

NO	NAMES	AGE	SEX
1	Martha E Austin	36	Female

ANCESTOR: Jessie Hutchins

Rejected June 6th 1889

Cherokee Citizenship Commission Docket Books
(1880-84, 1887-89) Volume II
Tahlequah, Cherokee Nation

Office Commission on Citizenship
Cherokee Nation Ind. Ter.
Tahlequah June 6th 1889

The case of Martha E. Austin was filed on the 3rd day of October 1887 and was called on the 6th day of June 1889 for final action and no response from applicant Martha E Austin or by Attorney and there being no evidence in support of application the Commission are of the opinion and so decide that Martha E Austin age 36 years is not of Cherokee blood and is not entitled to citizenship in the Cherokee Nation. Post Office address Kansas City Mo.

	Will P. Ross	Chairman
	R Bunch	Com
Attest	J.E. Gunter	"
D S Williams		
Asst Clk Com.		

AUSTIN

Docket #654
CENSUS ROLLS 1835/52

APPLICANT FOR CHEROKEE CITIZENSHIP

POST OFFICE: Chalk valley Ark   **ATTORNEY:** A E Ivey

NO	NAMES	AGE	SEX
1	Martha Austin	30	Female

ANCESTOR: Mary S Bell

Rejected June 6th 1889

Office Commission on Citizenship
Cherokee Nation Ind. Ter.
Tahlequah June 6th 1889

The case of Martha Austin was filed on the 3rd day of Oct 1887 and was called on the 6 of June 1889 3 several times not less than one hour apart for final action and no response from applicant Martha Austin or by Attorney. Therefore the Commission after examing[sic] papers in said case fail to find any evidence in support of application and from these facts the Commission decide that Martha Austin is not of Cherokee blood and is not entitled to citizenship in the Cherokee Nation.
Post Office address Chalk valley Ark.

Cherokee Citizenship Commission Docket Books
(1880-84, 1887-89) Volume II
Tahlequah, Cherokee Nation

	Will P. Ross	Chairman
Attest	R Bunch	Com
	J.E. Gunter	"

D S Williams
Asst Clk Com.

ARNOLD

Docket #655
CENSUS ROLLS 1835/52

APPLICANT FOR CHEROKEE CITIZENSHIP
POST OFFICE: Viola Mo.   ATTORNEY: A.E. Ivey

NO	NAMES	AGE	SEX
1	William Arnold	42	Male
2	James B Arnold	14	"
3	William S Arnold	12	"
4	Ralph D Arnold	7	"
5	Elender C Arnold	5	Female

ANCESTOR: James Arnold

Rejected June 6th 1889

Office Commission on Citizenship
Cherokee Nation Ind. Ter.
Tahlequah June 6th 1889

The above named case of William Arnold was filed on the 5th day of October 1887 and was called 3 several times not less than one hour apart on the 6th day of June 1889 for final action and no response from applicant William Arnold or by Attorney there being no evidence in support of application the Commission therefore proceeding with said case fail to find any evidence in support of application from the above facts the Commission decide that William Arnold whose age is 42 years and his children named as follows James B age 14 years, William S. male age 12 years, Ralph D. male age 7 years and Elender C. Arnold Female age 5 years, are not of Cherokee blood and are not entitled to citizenship in the Cherokee Nation. Post Office address Viola Mo.

	Will P. Ross	Chairman
Attest	R Bunch	Com
	J.E. Gunter	"

D S Williams
Asst Clk Com

Cherokee Citizenship Commission Docket Books
(1880-84, 1887-89) Volume II
Tahlequah, Cherokee Nation

ARNOLD

Docket #656
CENSUS ROLLS

APPLICANT FOR CHEROKEE CITIZENSHIP

POST OFFICE: Viola Mo　　ATTORNEY: A E Ivey

NO	NAMES	AGE	SEX
1	James Arnold	40	Male
2	Nicey A Arnold	14	Female
3	John R Arnold	11	Male
4	William E Arnold	9	"
5	Lina M Arnold	6	Female
6	Lonzo J Arnold	3	Male
7	James M Arnold	1	"

ANCESTOR: James Arnold

Rejected June 6th 1889

Office Commission on Citizenship
Cherokee Nation Ind. Ter.
Tahlequah June 6th 1889

The above case James Arnold was filed on the 5th day of October 1887 and was called the 6th day of June 1889 3 several times not less than one hour apart on for final action and no response from applicant James Arnold or by Attorney. The Commission after proceeding with said case fail to find any evidence in support of application from the above facts the Commission are of the opinion and so decide that James Arnold and his children whose names are as follows Nicey A Female age 14 years, John B. male age 11 years, William E. male age 9 years, Lina M Female age 6, Lonzo J. male age 3 years and James M. Arnold male age 1 year, are not of Cherokee blood and are not entitled to citizenship in the Cherokee Nation. Post Office address Viola Mo.

　　　　　　　　　　　　　　Will P. Ross　　Chairman
Attest　　　　　　　　　　　R Bunch　　　Com
　　D S Williams　　　　　 J.E. Gunter　　"
　　Asst Clk Com

Cherokee Citizenship Commission Docket Books
(1880-84, 1887-89) Volume II
Tahlequah, Cherokee Nation

ADAMSON

Docket #656[sic]
CENSUS ROLLS 1835/52

APPLICANT FOR CHEROKEE CITIZENSHIP

POST OFFICE: Van Buren Ark **ATTORNEY:** A E Ivey

NO	NAMES	AGE	SEX
1	G.W. Adamson	35	Male
2	Alva Adamson	9	Female
3	Ina Adamson	7	"
4	Ruby Adamson	6	"
5	Verbal Adamson	2 mo	"

ANCESTOR: Lucy Adams

Rejected June 7th 1889

Office Commission on Citizenship
Cherokee Nation Ind. Ter.
Tahlequah June 7th 1889

The case of Geo. W. Adamson was filed on the 4th day of October 1887 and was submitted for final hearing June 7th 1889 without evidence, the Commission therefore decide that G.W. Adamson whose age 35 years and his children whose names are as follows, Alva Adamson male 9 years, Ina Female age 7 years, Ruby Adamson Female age 6 years and Verbal Adamson male 2 months, are not of Cherokee blood and are not entitled to citizenship in the Cherokee Nation. Post Office address Van Buren Ark.

	Will P. Ross	Chairman
Attest	R Bunch	Com
D S Williams	John E. Gunter	Com
Asst Clk Com		

ANDERSON

Docket #657
CENSUS ROLLS 1835/52

APPLICANT FOR CHEROKEE CITIZENSHIP

POST OFFICE: Aberline Texas **ATTORNEY:** A E Ivey

NO	NAMES	AGE	SEX
1	K G Anderson	34	Male

ANCESTOR: Judith Lewis

Cherokee Citizenship Commission Docket Books
(1880-84, 1887-89) Volume II
Tahlequah, Cherokee Nation

Rejected June 7th 1889

          Office Commission on Citizenship
          Cherokee Nation Ind. Ter.
          Tahlequah June 7th 1889

The case of K.G. Anderson was filed the 4th day of October 1887 and was submitted without evidence in support of application for a final hearing June 7th 1889. Therefore the Commission decide that K.G. Anderson age 34 years is not of Cherokee blood and not entitled to citizenship in the Cherokee Nation. Post Office address Aberline Tex.

	Will P. Ross	Chairman
Attest	R Bunch	Com
D S Williams	J.E. Gunter	"
Asst Clk Com		

ADAMS

Docket #658
CENSUS ROLLS 1835/52

APPLICANT FOR CHEROKEE CITIZENSHIP

POST OFFICE: Mt Carmel Ill   **ATTORNEY:** A E Ivey

NO	NAMES	AGE	SEX
1	Willis J Adams	36	Male

ANCESTOR: Emaline P Denham

Rejected June 7th 1889

          Office Commission on Citizenship
          Cherokee Nation Ind. Ter.
          Tahlequah June 7th 1889

The case of Willis J Adams was filed on the 5th day of Oct. 1887 and was submitted without evidence in support of application for final hearing June 7th 1889. Now therefore we the Commission decide that Willis J Adams is not of Cherokee by blood and is not entitled to citizenship in the Cherokee Nation. Post Office address Mt. Carmel Ill.

	Will P. Ross	Chairman
Attest	R Bunch	Com
D S Williams	John E. Gunter	"
Asst Clk Com		

Cherokee Citizenship Commission Docket Books
(1880-84, 1887-89) Volume II
Tahlequah, Cherokee Nation

ADAMS

Docket #659
CENSUS ROLLS 1835/52

APPLICANT FOR CHEROKEE CITIZENSHIP

POST OFFICE: Mt Carmel Ill   **ATTORNEY:** A E Ivey

NO	NAMES	AGE	SEX
1	Wiley B Adams	35	Male

ANCESTOR: Emaline P Denham

Rejected June 7th 1889

Office Commission on Citizenship
Cherokee Nation Ind. Ter.
Tahlequah June 7th 1889

The case of Wiley B Adams was called the 7th day of June 1889 and now comes A.E. Ivey Attorney and submits the above case without evidence in support of application for final action. Now we the Commission from the above facts decide that Wiley B. Adams age 35 years is not of Cherokee blood and is not entitled to citizenship in the Cherokee Nation.
Post Office address Mt. Carmel Ill.

	Will P. Ross	Chairman
Attest	R Bunch	Com
D S Williams	John E. Gunter	Com
Asst Clk Com		

ADAMS

Docket #660
CENSUS ROLLS 1835/52

APPLICANT FOR CHEROKEE CITIZENSHIP

POST OFFICE: Sumner Ill   **ATTORNEY:** A E Ivey

NO	NAMES	AGE	SEX
1	Mark H Adams	33	Male
2	Fred H Adams	3	"

ANCESTOR: John H Denham

Rejected June 7th 1889

Cherokee Citizenship Commission Docket Books
(1880-84, 1887-89) Volume II
Tahlequah, Cherokee Nation

Office Commission on Citizenship
Cherokee Nation Ind. Ter.
Tahlequah June 7th 1889

The case of Mark H Adams was filed on the 5th day of October 1887 and was submitted for final action June 7th 1889 without evidence in support of application. Therefore we the Commission are of the opinion and so decide that Mark H Adams & Fred H Adams a son age 3 yrs is[sic] not of Cherokee blood and is not entitled to citizenship in the Cherokee Nation.

	Will P. Ross	Chairman
Attest	R Bunch	Com
D S Williams	John E. Gunter	Com
Asst Clk Com		

ADAMS

Docket #661
CENSUS ROLLS 1835/52

APPLICANT FOR CHEROKEE CITIZENSHIP

POST OFFICE: Silom[sic] Spgs Ark   **ATTORNEY:** L.S. Sanders

NO	NAMES	AGE	SEX
1	Anna E Adams	46	Female
2	Elizabeth J Adams	27	"
3	Susan R Gault	17	"

ANCESTOR: Joseph L Mosley

Rejected June 7th 1889

Office Commission on Citizenship
Cherokee Nation Ind. Ter.
Tahlequah June 7th 1889

The case of Anna E Adams was filed on the 3rd day of October 1887 and was submitted for final action June 7th 1889 without evidence in support of application. Therefore we the Commission are of the opinion and so decide that Anna E Adams age 46 years and her children whose names are as follows, Elizabeth J Female age 27 years and Susan R. Gault age 17 years are not of Cherokee blood and are not entitled to citizenship in the Cherokee Nation. Post Office address Siloam Springs Ark.

Cherokee Citizenship Commission Docket Books
(1880-84, 1887-89) Volume II
Tahlequah, Cherokee Nation

	Will P. Ross	Chairman
Attest	R Bunch	Com
D S Williams	John E. Gunter	Com
Asst Clk Com		

ADAMS

Docket #662
CENSUS ROLLS 1835

APPLICANT FOR CHEROKEE CITIZENSHIP
POST OFFICE: Lawrenceville Ill   **ATTORNEY:** A E Ivey

NO	NAMES	AGE	SEX
1	John C Adams	33	Male
2	Martha E Adams	8	Female
3	Emma J Adams	7	"
4	Harley E Adams	5	Male
5	Ollie Flora Adams	1 mo	Female

ANCESTOR: John C Denham

Rejected Sept 9th 1889

Office Commission on Citizenship
Cherokee Nation Ind. Ter.
Tahlequah June 7th 1889

Application for Cherokee Citizenship.

The above case was called and submitted by Att'y A.E. Ivey without evidence the Commission now decide that John E. Adams age 33 yrs, Marthey E Adams Female 8 yrs, child Emma J Adams Female 7 yrs. child, Harley E Adams male 5 yrs, Ollie Flora Adams Female 3 week old child are not Cherokees by blood.

	Will P. Ross	Chairman
Attest	R Bunch	Com
D S Williams	J. E. Gunter	Com
Asst Clk Com		

Cherokee Citizenship Commission Docket Books
(1880-84, 1887-89) Volume II
Tahlequah, Cherokee Nation

BROOKS

Docket #663
CENSUS ROLLS 1835/52

APPLICANT FOR CHEROKEE CITIZENSHIP
POST OFFICE: Lawson Mo.   ATTORNEY: L S Sanders

NO	NAMES	AGE	SEX
1	Geo W Brooks	60	Male
2	John T Brooks	30	"
3	Mary T Brooks	28	Female
4	Fedora J Brooks	23	"
5	William M Brooks		

ANCESTOR: Anna Jourdon

Rejected [sic] 7th 1889

Office Commission on Citizenship
Cherokee Nation Ind. Ter.
Tahlequah June 7th 1889

The case of Geo W. Brooks was filed on the 3rd day of Oct. 1887 and was submitted June 7th 1889 without evidence in support of application. The Commission therefore are of the opinion and so decide that Geo W. Brooks age 60 years and his children whose names are as follows, John T. male age 30 years, Mary Female 28 years, Fedora J Female 23 years, and William M Brooks male age 19 years are not of Cherokee blood and are not entitled to citizenship in the Cherokee Nation.

Attest
    D S Williams
    Asst Clk Com

Will P. Ross   Chairman
R Bunch   Com
John E. Gunter   Com

BAXTER

Docket #664
CENSUS ROLLS 1835/52

APPLICANT FOR CHEROKEE CITIZENSHIP
POST OFFICE: ATTORNEY: L S Sanders

NO	NAMES	AGE	SEX
1	Eliza J Baxter	56	Female
2	Taylor Baxter	33	Male
3	John Baxter	31	"

Cherokee Citizenship Commission Docket Books
(1880-84, 1887-89) Volume II
Tahlequah, Cherokee Nation

4	Florence Jackson	27	Female
5	Bell Stevens	24	"
6	William Baxter		

ANCESTOR:

Rejected June 7th 1889

Office Commission on Citizenship
Cherokee Nation Ind. Ter.
Tahlequah June 7th 1889

The case of Eliza J Baxter was filed on the 3rd day of October 1887 and was called 3 several times not less than one hour apart and no response from Applicant Eliza J. Baxter or by Attorney June 7th 1889 for a final hearing. The Commission after examining the papers fail to find any evidence in support of application. Therefore we the Commission decide that Eliza J Baxter age 56 years, Taylor male age 33 years, John male age 31 years, Flornence[sic] J. Female age 27 years, Bell Stevens Female age 24 years, and William Baxter male age 20 years, are not of Cherokee blood & are [sic] entitled to citizenship in the Cherokee Nation.
Post Office address Lawson Mo.

                        Will P. Ross   Chairman
Attest   R Bunch   Com
    D S Williams   John E. Gunter Com
    Asst Clk Com

BROOKS

Docket #665
CENSUS ROLLS 1835

APPLICANT FOR CHEROKEE CITIZENSHIP
POST OFFICE: Lawson Mo   **ATTORNEY:** L S Sanders

NO	NAMES	AGE	SEX
1	Isaac J Brooks	58	Male
2	Joseph Brooks	19	"
3	Louisa Brooks	17	Female
4	James Brooks	15	Male
5	William Brooks	13	"
6	Lucinda Brooks	9	Female
7	Mack Brooks	7	Male

Cherokee Citizenship Commission Docket Books
(1880-84, 1887-89) Volume II
Tahlequah, Cherokee Nation

8	Charles Brooks	1	"

ANCESTOR:

Rejected June 7th 1889

                      Office Commission on Citizenship
                            Cherokee Nation Ind. Ter.
                                Tahlequah June 7th 1889

The case of Isaac J Brooks was filed on the 3rd day of Oct. 1887 and was called 3 several times not less than one hour apart for final action the 7th of June 1889 and no response from Applicant Isaac J Brooks or by Attorney. The Commission after examining the papers fail to find any evidence in support of application. Therefore the Commission are of the opinion and so decide that Isaac J Brooks age 58 years and his children whose names are as follows, Joseph male 19 years, Louisa Female 17 years, James male 15 years, William male age 13 years, Lucinda Female age 9 years, Mack male age 7 years, and Charles Brooks, age 1 year, are not of Cherokee blood and not entitled to citizenship in the Cherokee Nation. Post Office address Lawson Mo.

	Will P. Ross	Chairman
Attest	R Bunch	Com
D S Williams	John E. Gunter	Com
Asst Clk Com		

BRACKETT

Docket #666
CENSUS ROLLS 1835

APPLICANT FOR CHEROKEE CITIZENSHIP

POST OFFICE: Wah hil lau IT.   **ATTORNEY:** A E Ivey

NO		NAMES	AGE	SEX
1	Rejected	Benj J Brackett Sr	76	Male
2		Sarah Brackett	39	
3	Admitted	Arminda L Brackett	10	

ANCESTOR: Benjamin Brackett

Re-Admitted Aug 16th 1889

                      Office Commission on Citizenship
                              Cherokee Nation Ind. Ter.
                              Tahlequah August 16th 1889

Cherokee Citizenship Commission Docket Books
(1880-84, 1887-89) Volume II
Tahlequah, Cherokee Nation

The evidence in the above named case shows that Benjamin J Brackett is a shite man. The Commission therefore reject his application. The evidence futher[sic] shows that Sarah Brackett is the daughter of said Benjamin J Brackett and Susie Brackett nee Susie Hubbard a grand daughter of Nellie Williamson from whom she derives her Cherokee blood. It also shows that Arminda Brackett is the daughter of the before named Sarah Brackett. The Commission, therefore deide that Sarah Brackett aged 39 yrs and Arminda Brackett aged 10 years are of Cherokee blood and are entitled to re-admission to Citizenship in the Cherokee Nation. See Census Roll of 1852 (Siler)
P.O. Wah-hil-lau Ind. Ter.

                  Will P. Ross
Attest   Chairman
   D S Williams   John E. Gunter Com
   Asst Clk Com

BRACKETT

Docket #667
CENSUS ROLLS 1835

APPLICANT FOR CHEROKEE CITIZENSHIP
POST OFFICE: Wah hil lau IT   **ATTORNEY:** A E Ivey

NO	NAMES	AGE	SEX
1	Adam Brackett	41	Male
2	Asalline Brackett	12	Female
3	Mary Brackett	10	"
4	Dora Brackett	8	"
5	Ethel Brackett	6	"
6	Benj Brackett	4	Male

ANCESTOR: Benj Brackett

Rejected Aug 16th 1889

                Office Commission on Citizenship
                    Cherokee Nation Ind. Ter.
                    Tahlequah Aug 16th 1889

The applicant is the son of Benj. J. Brackett and Susan Brackett nee Susie Hubbard and grand son of Nellie Wilkerson from whom he derives his Cherokee blood. His name also appears on the Siler roll of Cherokees taken and made in the year 1852. The Commission therefore adjudge that he is entitled to re-admission to Citizenship in the Cherokee Nation as a Cherokee by blood, as are

Cherokee Citizenship Commission Docket Books (1880-84, 1887-89) Volume II
Tahlequah, Cherokee Nation

also his daughters Rosaline or (Asalline) age 12, Mary age 10 yrs, Dora age 8 yrs, Ethel age 6 yrs and son Benjamin Brackett, Jr. age 4 yrs. See case of Benj. J. Brackett, Docket 666 Book B, Page 381. P.O. Wah-hil-lau I.T.

	Will P. Ross	
Attest		Chairman
D S Williams	John E. Gunter	Com
Asst. Clerk Commission		

BEAVER

Docket #668
CENSUS ROLLS 1835

APPLICANT FOR CHEROKEE CITIZENSHIP
POST OFFICE: Huntsville Ark   **ATTORNEY:** C.H. Taylor

NO	NAMES	AGE	SEX
1	Addie Beaver	33	
2	Annie Beaver	15	
3	Cora Beaver	12	
4	Albert Beaver	10	
5	Addie Beaver	8	

ANCESTOR: Temby Vaughn

Rejected June 10th 1889

Office Commission on Citizenship
Cherokee Nation Ind. Ter.
Tahlequah June 7th 1889

The above case was filed on the 1st day of October 1887 and was submitted the 10th day of June 1889, without evidence in support of application. The Commission therefore decide that Adda Beaver age 33 years and her children whose names are as follows Adda[sic] Beaver Female age 15 years, Cora Female age 12 years, Albert Male age 10 years & Addie Beaver Female age 8 years are not of Cherokee blood and are not entitled to citizenship in the Cherokee Nation. Post Office address Huntsville Ark.

	Will P. Ross	Chairman
Attest	R Bunch	Com
D S Williams	J.E. Gunter	"
Asst Clk Com		

Cherokee Citizenship Commission Docket Books
(1880-84, 1887-89) Volume II
Tahlequah, Cherokee Nation

BELLEW

Docket #669
CENSUS ROLLS

APPLICANT FOR CHEROKEE CITIZENSHIP

POST OFFICE: Chelsea CN   ATTORNEY: J M Bryan[sic]

NO	NAMES	AGE	SEX
1	Levi J Bellew	24	Male
2	Raymond Bellew	7	"
3	Joseph B Bellew	5	"

ANCESTOR: Governor Bellew

Rejected March 18th 1889

Adverse
Embraced in decission[sic] on page 431
Book B. in the Aaron Bellew case.
Rendered 18th day of March 1889

Office Commission on Citizenship   Will P. Ross
Tahlequah I.T. March 18-1889   Chairman Com
            DS Williams   John E. Gunter   Com
            Clk Com

BELLEW

Docket #670
CENSUS ROLLS

APPLICANT FOR CHEROKEE CITIZENSHIP

POST OFFICE: Chelsea I.T.   ATTORNEY: J M Bryant

NO	NAMES	AGE	SEX
1	M E Bellew	25	Male

ANCESTOR: Governor Bellew

Rejected March 18th 1889

Adverse
Embraced in decission[sic] on page 431
Book. B.   in the Aaron Bellew case.
Rendered 18th day of March 1889.

Cherokee Citizenship Commission Docket Books
(1880-84, 1887-89) Volume II
Tahlequah, Cherokee Nation

Office Commission on Citizenship
Tahlequah I.T   March 18 – 1889
  D S Williams
    Clk Com

  Will P. Ross
    Chairman Com
  John E Gunter   Com

BAYLESS

Docket #671
CENSUS ROLLS 1835/52

APPLICANT FOR CHEROKEE CITIZENSHIP
POST OFFICE: Dover Ark   **ATTORNEY:** Boudinot & R

NO	NAMES	AGE	SEX
1	Ella *(or Etta)* Bayless	21	Female
2	Allie Bayless	18	"
3	John Bayless	13	Male
4	Jennie Bayless	11	Female
5	Sarah Bayless	7	"
6	Benj Bayless	10 mo	Male

ANCESTOR: Bashaba Goodrich

Rejected June 13th 1889

Office Commission on Citizenship
Cherokee Nation Ind. Ter.
Tahlequah June 13th 1889

There being no evidence in support of the above named case, We the Commission decide that Etta Bayless age 21 yrs, and the following named children Alice Female age 18 yrs, John male age 13 yrs, Jennie Female age 11 yrs, Sarah Female age 7 yrs and Benj Bayless, male age 10 months, are not of Cherokee blood and are not entitled to Citizenship in the Cherokee Nation.

	Will P. Ross	Chairman
Attest	R. Bunch	Com
D S Williams	J.E. Gunter	"
Asst Clk Com.		

Cherokee Citizenship Commission Docket Books
(1880-84, 1887-89) Volume II
Tahlequah, Cherokee Nation

BONDS

Docket #672
CENSUS ROLLS 1835

APPLICANT FOR CHEROKEE CITIZENSHIP
POST OFFICE: Dover Ark   **ATTORNEY:** Boudinot & R

NO	NAMES	AGE	SEX
1	George G Bonds		Male

ANCESTOR: Bashaba Goodrich

Rejected June 13th 1889

Office Commission on Citizenship
Cherokee Nation Ind. Ter.
Tahlequah June 13th 1889

There being no evidence in support of the above named case, The Commission decide that Geo G Bonds age not given is not of Cherokee blood. Post Office address Dover, Ark.

	Will P. Ross	Chairman
Attest	R. Bunch	Com
D S Williams	J.E. Gunter	"
Asst Clk Com.		

BROWN

Docket #673
CENSUS ROLLS 1835/52

APPLICANT FOR CHEROKEE CITIZENSHIP
POST OFFICE: Clarksville Ark   **ATTORNEY:** Boudinot & R

NO	NAMES	AGE	SEX
1	Susan Brown	40	Female
2	Lou Brown	18	"
3	Lillian Maud Brown	12	"
4	Jessie Brown	8	"
5	Benton Brown	4	Male
6	Susan Brown	2	Female

ANCESTOR: Bashaba Goodrich

Rejected June 13th 1889

Office Commission on Citizenship
Cherokee Nation Ind. Ter.
Tahlequah June 13th 1889

Cherokee Citizenship Commission Docket Books
(1880-84, 1887-89) Volume II
Tahlequah, Cherokee Nation

There being no evidence in support of the above named application, We the Commission are of the opinion and so decide that Susan Brown age 40 yrs, and her children whose names are as follows Lou Brown Female age 18 yrs, Lillian Brown Female 12 yrs, Jessie Female age 8 yrs, Benton J. male age 4 yrs, and Susan Brown, Female age 2 years, are not of Cherokee blood. Post Office Clarksville Ark.

	Will P. Ross	Chairman
Attest	R. Bunch	Com
D S Williams	J.E. Gunter	"
Asst Clk Com.		

BONDS

Docket #674
CENSUS ROLLS 1835/52

APPLICANT FOR CHEROKEE CITIZENSHIP
POST OFFICE: Russellville, Ark   **ATTORNEY:** Boudinot & R

NO	NAMES	AGE	SEX
1	T K Bonds	28	Male
2	William J Bonds	4	"
3	Jessie Knights Bonds	2	Female

ANCESTOR: Barsheba Bonds

Rejected June 13th 1889

Office Commission on Citizenship
Cherokee Nation Ind. Ter.
Tahlequah June 13th 1889

There being no evidence in support of the above application, We are of the opinion and so decide that applicant T K Bonds age 28 yrs and his children William J Bonds age 4 yrs and Jessie Knights Bonds age 2 years, are not Cherokees by blood and are not entitled to Cherokee Citizenship in the Cherokee Nation.

	Will P. Ross	Chairman
Attest	R. Bunch	Com
D S Williams	J.E. Gunter	"
Asst Clk Com.		

Cherokee Citizenship Commission Docket Books
(1880-84, 1887-89) Volume II
Tahlequah, Cherokee Nation

BOATRIGHT

Docket #675
CENSUS ROLLS 1835/52

APPLICANT FOR CHEROKEE CITIZENSHIP

POST OFFICE: Van Buren Ark   ATTORNEY: L S Sanders

NO	NAMES	AGE	SEX
1	Francis A Boatright	49	Female
2	John J Boatright	20	Male
3	Franklin Boatright	13	"
4	Albert B Boatright	10	"
5	Joseph B Boatright	7	"
6	Elizabeth Edna Boatright	3	Female
7	James B Boatright	1	Male

ANCESTOR: Elizabeth Blackburn

Rejected June 13th 1889

Office Commission on Citizenship
Cherokee Nation Ind. Ter.
Tahlequah June 13th 1889

There being no evidence in support of the above named case The Commission decide that Francis A Boatright age 49 years and the following named children John J male age 20 yrs, Franklin male age 13 yrs, Albert B. male age 10 yrs, Joseph B. male age 7 yrs. Elizabeth E. Female age 3 yrs, James B Boatright age 1 year, are not of Cherokee blood. Post Office address, Van Buren Ark.

Attest
D S Williams
Asst Clk Com

Will P. Ross   Chairman
R. Bunch   Com
J.E. Gunter   "

BAIN

Docket #676
CENSUS ROLLS 1835/52

APPLICANT FOR CHEROKEE CITIZENSHIP

POST OFFICE: Prairie City IT.   ATTORNEY: C H Taylor

NO	NAMES	AGE	SEX
1	Andrew J Bain	62	Male

ANCESTOR: Agnes J Bain

Cherokee Citizenship Commission Docket Books
(1880-84, 1887-89) Volume II
Tahlequah, Cherokee Nation

Rejected June 10th 1889

Office Commission on Citizenship
Cherokee Nation Ind. Ter.
Tahlequah June 10th 1889

The above case was filed on the 1st day of Oct. 1887 and on this day the [sic] coming up for final hearing, we find after examining the papers submitted by applicant that he fails to name any of the rolls of Cherokees that might contain the name of his ancestor. As Sect 7 of the law governing this Commission expressly provides that all applicants for Cherokee Citizenship must names their ancestor on some of the Cherokee Census rolls. This alone will justify the Commission in deciding that applicant Andrew J. Bain age 62 yrs, Post office Prairie City is not of Cherokee blood & not entitled to any rights or privileges of Cherokee citizenship.

                    Will P. Ross   Chairman
Attest   R Bunch   Com
    D S Williams   J.E. Gunter   "
    Asst Clk Com

BAIN

Docket #677
CENSUS ROLLS 1835/52

APPLICANT FOR CHEROKEE CITIZENSHIP
POST OFFICE: Ottawa Kansas   **ATTORNEY:** C H Taylor

NO	NAMES	AGE	SEX
1	Lughton S Bain	28	Male

ANCESTOR: Agnes Bain

Rejected June 10th 1889

Office Commission on Citizenship
Cherokee Nation Ind. Ter.
Tahlequah June 7th 1889

The above application was filed on the 1st day of Oct. 1887 and on this day the case coming ing[sic] for final hearing, we find that applicant fails to submit any evidence to sustain his claim of Cherokee blood. And further he fails to names the census rolls of Cherokees that may contain the name of his ancestor. Sec. 7 of the law governing this Commission expressly says, that all applicants for Cherokee Citizenship must be a descendant of a person whose name must

Cherokee Citizenship Commission Docket Books
(1880-84, 1887-89) Volume II
Tahlequah, Cherokee Nation

appear upon some of the Census rolls of Cherokees. This fact & the fact that applicant produces no evidence in support of his application will justify as in deciding that applicant Lughton S Bain age 28 yrs is not a Cherokee by blood & is not entitled to any rights & Privileges of Cherokee Citizenship.
Post Office Ottawa Kansas

                        Will P. Ross   Chairman
Attest   J.E. Gunter   Com
    D S Williams
    Asst Clk Com

BLACK

Docket #678
CENSUS ROLLS 1835/52

APPLICANT FOR CHEROKEE CITIZENSHIP
POST OFFICE: Forth Worth Texas   **ATTORNEY:** Boudinot & R

NO	NAMES	AGE	SEX
1	Eliza M Black	44	Female
2	Dora C Black	16	"
3	Forrest C Black	10	Male
4	J Elliott Black	9	"
5	Kennie D Black	7	Female
6	Della May Black	5	"

ANCESTOR: D. Caldwell

Rejected June 10th 1889

Commission on Citizenship.

CHEROKEE NATION, IND. TER.

Tahlequah, June 14th 1889

Eliza M. Black   The above application for Citizenship came
    vs   up this day for the final hearing. The appli-
The Cherokee Nation   cant alleges that at the time of filing her
                              application (the 5th day of October 1887)
forty four years old and is the grand daughter of one D Caldwell <u>nee</u> Sevier & her name should be found on the rolls of Cherokees by blood taken in the years

Cherokee Citizenship Commission Docket Books
(1880-84, 1887-89) Volume II
Tahlequah, Cherokee Nation

1835, 48, 51-52 or "Old Settler" and that her residence is Fort Worth, Texas. The most important witness in this case on the part of the claimant, is one Thomas G. Smith, who represents in his affidavit taken before the Clerk of Tarrant County, Texas, on the 27th day of December 1887, ~~His represents states~~ that he was born in 1834, 15 miles above Gunthersville[sic], in Alabama, and was well acquainted with the Bushyhead and Sevier families, knew them to be Cherokees by blood; knew Serena Sevier, niece of David Bushyhead to be Cherokee by blood a half breed, ~~knew~~ who married Andrew Caldwell a white man in the Old Nation that their daughter Elizabeth D. Caldwell married John C. Jackson, white and that their daughter Elizabeth Jackson, the applicant, married Wm. P. Black in Hunt County Texas, and that his permanent Post Office in Fort Gibson, Ind. Ter. Witnesses who are well acquainted with the families referred to and who have resided for many years at Fort Gibson, (know nothing of the persons named as ancestors of applicant and fail to recall to mind any such persona, Thomas G. Smith. In addition to the insufficient character of the evidence as showing the Cherokee blood of the applicant a careful examination of all the rolls referred to fails to reveal the names of Serena Caldwell nee Sevier, of David Bushyhead and of Elizabeth D. Jackson nee Caldwell, The Commission have therefore come to the convulsion that the application has no foundation in fact and decide that Eliza M. Black and her daughters, Dora L. Black, aged 16 years, Kennie D. Black aged 7 years and Della May Black aged 5 years, and her sons, Forrest C. Black aged 11 years and J. Elliott Black aged 9 years are not of Cherokee blood and not entitled to readmission to Citizenship in the Cherokee Nation.

P.O. address, Fort Worth, Texas.

Will P. Ross
Chairman

(Illegible)
John E. Gunter   Commissioner

O'BRYANT

Docket #679
CENSUS ROLLS 1835/52

APPLICANT FOR CHEROKEE CITIZENSHIP
POST OFFICE: Lancaster, Ark   **ATTORNEY:** Boudinot & R

NO	NAMES	AGE	SEX
1	Mary L O'Bryant	33	Female
2	Minnie O'Bryant	7	"

Cherokee Citizenship Commission Docket Books
(1880-84, 1887-89) Volume II
Tahlequah, Cherokee Nation

3	Eula O'Bryant	6	"
4	James A O'Bryant	4	Male
5	Sarah J O'Bryant	2	Female
6	Cora O'Bryant	1	"

ANCESTOR: Eliza J Brooks

Rejected June 13th 1889

Office Commission on Citizenship
Cherokee Nation Ind. Ter.
Tahlequah June 13th 1889

There being no evidence in support of the above named case The Commission decide that Mary L. O.Bryant age 33 years and the following named children, Minnie L. O. female age 7 years, Eula O. Female age 6 years. James A. male age 4 years, Sarah J. Female age 2 years, and Cora O.Bryant, Female age 1 year, are not of Cherokee by blood. Post Office address, Lancaster Ark.

                    Will P. Ross   Chairman
Attest   J.E. Gunter   Com
    D S Williams
    Asst Clk Com

BONDS

Docket #680
CENSUS ROLLS 1835/52

APPLICANT FOR CHEROKEE CITIZENSHIP
POST OFFICE: Dover Ark.   **ATTORNEY:** Boudinot & R.

NO	NAMES	AGE	SEX
1	J Clark Bonds	51	Male
2	Jessie V. Bonds	20	
3	Maggie A Bonds	18	
4	Mary E Bonds	15	

ANCESTOR: Barsheba Bonds

Rejected June 13th 1889

Cherokee Citizenship Commission Docket Books
(1880-84, 1887-89) Volume II
Tahlequah, Cherokee Nation

Office Commission on Citizenship
Cherokee Nation Ind. Ter.
Tahlequah June 13th 1889

There being no evidence in support of the above named case The Commission therefore decide that J. Clark Bonds age 51 yrs and the following named children Julia[sic] V. Female age 20 yrs, Maggie A Female age 18 yrs, and Mary E. Bonds age 15 years, Post Office address Dover Ark. are not of Cherokee blood.

Attest
   D S Williams
   Asst Clk Com

Will P. Ross
          Chairman
R. Bunch   Com

BRACKET

Docket #681
CENSUS ROLLS 1851

APPLICANT FOR CHEROKEE CITIZENSHIP
POST OFFICE: Carlise[sic] Ga.   **ATTORNEY:** A E Ivey

NO	NAMES	AGE	SEX
1	Francis J Bracket	44	Male[sic]

ANCESTOR: Migi Bracket

Admitted Aug 16th 1889

Office Commission on Citizenship
Cherokee Nation Ind. Ter
Tahlequah Aug 16th 1889

The applicant is the Daughter of Midge and Cynthia Brackett nee Cynthia Hubbard who was the Daughter of Nellie Wilkerson and from where she derives her Cherokee blood. Her name is found on the census rolls of Cherokees by blood taken and made in 1852, by the United States. The Commission therefore decide that Francis J. Brackett age 44 yrs is entitled to readmission to Citizenship in the Cherokee Nation as a Cherokee by blood. PO Carlisle Georgia. See case Ben J. Brackett D. 666 B.B. P38

Attest
   D S Williams
   Asst Clk Com

Will P. Ross
          Chairman
J.E. Gunter   Com

Cherokee Citizenship Commission Docket Books
(1880-84, 1887-89) Volume II
Tahlequah, Cherokee Nation

BACON

Docket #682
CENSUS ROLLS 1835/52

APPLICANT FOR CHEROKEE CITIZENSHIP
POST OFFICE: Evansville Ark   **ATTORNEY:**

NO	NAMES	AGE	SEX
1	Catherine Bacon	63	Female

ANCESTOR: William Lee

Rejected June 12th 1889

Office Commission on Citizenship
Cherokee Nation Ind. Ter.
Tahlequah June 12th 1889

There being no evidence in support of the application in the above case The Commission decide that Catherine Bacon aged Sixty three years, P.O. address Evansville Ark. is not of Cherokee blood.

                Will P. Ross
Attest   Chairman
  D.S. Williams   J.E. Gunter   Com
  Asst Clk Com

BACON

Docket #683
CENSUS ROLLS 1835/52

APPLICANT FOR CHEROKEE CITIZENSHIP
POST OFFICE: Evansville Ark   **ATTORNEY:**

NO	NAMES	AGE	SEX
1	Mark S Bacon	19	Male

ANCESTOR: William Lee

Rejected June 12th 1889

Office Commission on Citizenship
Cherokee Nation Ind. Ter.
Tahlequah June 12th 1889

The case of Mark S Bacon was filed on the 4th day of October 1887 and was called 3 several times not less than one hour apart and no response from

Cherokee Citizenship Commission Docket Books
(1880-84, 1887-89) Volume II
Tahlequah, Cherokee Nation

applicant Mark S. Bacon. Therefore we the Commission find no evidence in support of application and are of the opinion and so decide that Mark S Bacon age 19 years is not of Cherokee by blood and are[sic] not entitled to citizenship in the Cherokee Nation Post Office address Evansville Ark.

Attest
    D S Williams
    Asst Clk Com

          Will P. Ross
          Chairman
    J.E. Gunter   Com

BACON

Docket #684
CENSUS ROLLS 1835/52

APPLICANT FOR CHEROKEE CITIZENSHIP

POST OFFICE: Evansville Ark

ATTORNEY:

NO	NAMES	AGE	SEX
1	A.H. Bacon	38	Male
2	James H Bacon	12	"
3	John W Bacon	11	"
4	Maggie Bacon	9	Female
5	Benj H Bacon	6	Male
6	May Bacon	4	Female
7	Estella Bacon	1	"

ANCESTOR: William Lee

Rejected June 12th 1889

    Office Commission on Citizenship
    Cherokee Nation Ind. Ter.
    Tahlequah June 12th 1889

There being no evidence in support of the application in the above named case, The Commission decide that A.H. Bacon aged 38 yrs and his sons James H Bacon aged 12 yrs, John W. Bacon 11 yrs, Benjamin H. Bacon 6 yrs and daughters Maggy Bacon 9 yrs, May Bacon 4 yrs and Estella Bacon one year are not of Cherokee blood. P.O. Evansville Ark

          Will P. Ross
Attest   Chairman
    D S Williams   J.E. Gunter   Com
    Asst Clk Com

Cherokee Citizenship Commission Docket Books
(1880-84, 1887-89) Volume II
Tahlequah, Cherokee Nation

BATEMAN

Docket #685
CENSUS ROLLS 1835/52

POST OFFICE: Evansville Ark

APPLICANT FOR CHEROKEE CITIZENSHIP
ATTORNEY:

NO	NAMES	AGE	SEX
1	Benjamin F Bateman	34	Male
2	Frank Bateman	11	"
3	John Bateman	9	"
4	Mark Bateman	7	"
5	Walter Bateman	6 mo	"

ANCESTOR: William Lee

Rejected June 12th 1889

Office Commission on Citizenship
Cherokee Nation Ind. Ter.
Tahlequah June 12th 1889

There being no evidence in the above named case found, The Commission decide that Benjamin F. Bateman aged 34 yrs and his children, Frank Bateman aged 11 yrs, John Bateman aged 9 yrs, Mark Bateman aged 7 yrs and Walter Bateman aged 6 months are not of Cherokee blood and are not entitled to Citizenship in the Cherokee Nation. P.O. address Evansville Ark

Attest
   D.S. Williams
   Asst Clk Com

Will P. Ross
           Chairman
J.E. Gunter Com

BACON

Docket #686
CENSUS ROLLS 1835/52

POST OFFICE: Evansville Ark

APPLICANT FOR CHEROKEE CITIZENSHIP
ATTORNEY:

NO	NAMES	AGE	SEX
1	John A Bacon	31	Male
2	Amos Lee Bacon	2	"

Cherokee Citizenship Commission Docket Books
(1880-84, 1887-89) Volume II
Tahlequah, Cherokee Nation

3	Mark J Bacon		

ANCESTOR: William Lee

Rejected June 12th 1889

Office Commission on Citizenship
Cherokee Nation Ind. Ter.
Tahlequah June 12th 1889

There being no evidence in support of the application in the above named case, The Commission decide that John A Bacon aged 31 yrs, Amos Lee Bacon 3 yrs and Mark J Bacon aged three months at the filing of this application on 4th day of October 1887, are not of Cherokee blood. P.O. Evansville Ark

Will P. Ross
Attest   Chairman
   D S Williams   J.E. Gunter Com
   Asst Clk Com

BACON

Docket #687
CENSUS ROLLS 1835/52

APPLICANT FOR CHEROKEE CITIZENSHIP
POST OFFICE: Evansville Ark   **ATTORNEY:**

NO	NAMES	AGE	SEX
1	Nancy B Bacon	22	Female

ANCESTOR: William Lee

Rejected June 12th 1889

Office Commission on Citizenship
Cherokee Nation Ind. Ter.
Tahlequah June 12th 1889

There being no evidence in support of the application in the above case, The Commission decide that Nancy B. Bacon aged twenty two years is not of Cherokee blood. P.O. address Evansville Ark

Will P. Ross
Attest   Chairman
   D S Williams   J.E. Gunter Com
   Asst Clk Com

Cherokee Citizenship Commission Docket Books
(1880-84, 1887-89) Volume II
Tahlequah, Cherokee Nation

BURGESS

Docket #688
CENSUS ROLLS 1835/52

APPLICANT FOR CHEROKEE CITIZENSHIP

POST OFFICE: Morehead IT **ATTORNEY:** L S Sanders

NO	NAMES	AGE	SEX
1	Reuben E Burgess	34	Male
2	Arthur L Burgess	7	"
3	David L Burgess	5	"
4	Hettie Delilah Burgess	3 mo	Female

ANCESTOR: William Burgess

See Decision in this case in that of
William Burgess Docket 695 Book B Page 408

Adverse June 17th 1889

Attest Will P. Ross
  D S Williams   Chairman
  Asst Clk. Com. J.E. Gunter   Com

BURGESS

Docket #689
CENSUS ROLLS

APPLICANT FOR CHEROKEE CITIZENSHIP

POST OFFICE: Sherman Texas **ATTORNEY:** Boudinot & R

NO	NAMES	AGE	SEX
1	Strother Burgess	38	Male

ANCESTOR: William Burgess

See Decision in this case in that
of William Burgess Docket 693 Book B Page 408

Attest Will P. Ross
  DS Williams   Chairman
  Asst Clk. Com J.E. Gunter   Com

Cherokee Citizenship Commission Docket Books
(1880-84, 1887-89) Volume II
Tahlequah, Cherokee Nation

BURGESS

Docket #690
CENSUS ROLLS

APPLICANT FOR CHEROKEE CITIZENSHIP

POST OFFICE: Tahlequah CN   **ATTORNEY:** Boudinot & R

NO	NAMES	AGE	SEX
1	Mary P. Burgess	34	Female

ANCESTOR: William Burgess

See Decision in this case in that of
William Burgess Docket 693 Book B Page 408

Attest   Will P. Ross
   DS Williams   Chairman
   Asst Clk. Com   J.E. Gunter   Com

BURGESS

Docket #691
CENSUS ROLLS

APPLICANT FOR CHEROKEE CITIZENSHIP

POST OFFICE: Rome Ga   **ATTORNEY:** Boudinot & R

NO	NAMES	AGE	SEX
1	John T Burgess	42	Male

ANCESTOR: William Burgess

See Decision in this case in that of
William Burgess Docket 693 Book B Page 408

Attest   Will P. Ross
   DS Williams   Chairman
   Asst Clk. Com   J.E. Gunter   Com

Cherokee Citizenship Commission Docket Books
(1880-84, 1887-89) Volume II
Tahlequah, Cherokee Nation

BURGESS

Docket #692
CENSUS ROLLS

APPLICANT FOR CHEROKEE CITIZENSHIP
POST OFFICE: Morehead IT. **ATTORNEY:** Boudinot & R

NO	NAMES	AGE	SEX
1	William P Burgess	40	Male

ANCESTOR: William Burgess

See Decision in this case in that of William Burgess Docket 693 Book B Page 408

Attest
  DS Williams
  Asst Clk. Com

Will P. Ross
        Chairman
J.E. Gunter Com

BURGESS

Docket #693
CENSUS ROLLS

APPLICANT FOR CHEROKEE CITIZENSHIP
POST OFFICE: Tahlequah CN **ATTORNEY:** Boudinot & R
                                              LS Sanders

NO	NAMES	AGE	SEX
1	William Burgess	65	Male

ANCESTOR: William Burgess

We the Commission on Citizenship after duly examining the testimony in the above cases for there are eight of them all claiming a *(illegible)* descent from one William Burgess, Sen. Who the testimony shows lived in Cherokee Co. North Carolina about the years 1835 to 1842 or 3 and there is no evidence before the Commission that he was not there in 1851 and 1852. The name of William Burgess, Sen, does not appear in the census & pay rolls of Cherokees taken & made in the Old Nation in the years of 1835, 1848, 1851 & 1852, neither do these records of Cherokees contain the names of any of the applicants. There is no use in accounting the testimony in this case in the absence of the fact that the mentioned rolls of Cherokees fail to contain the names of their Cherokee ancestor, or themselves, *(illegible)* under the law of Dec. 8th 1886 in relation to citizenship. William Burgess, Elizabeth F Smith,

Cherokee Citizenship Commission Docket Books
(1880-84, 1887-89) Volume II
Tahlequah, Cherokee Nation

John T. Burgess, William G. Burgess, Strother S. Burgess, Mary P. Burgess, Reubin E. Burgess, Arthur L. Burgess, David L Burgess, Hettie Delilah Burgess and James H Burgess are ~~not~~ declared not to be Cherokees by blood and not entitled to any of the rights of such on account of their blood, an are intruders upon the public domain of the Cherokee Nation.

                        J.T. Adair   Chairman Commission
                        D.W. Lipe   Commissioner
                        H.C. Barnes   Commissioner

Office Com. on Citizenship
Tahlequah I.T. Oct. 24th 1888

BURGESS

Docket #694
CENSUS ROLLS

APPLICANT FOR CHEROKEE CITIZENSHIP
POST OFFICE: Tahlequah CN   **ATTORNEY:** Boudinot & R

NO	NAMES	AGE	SEX
1	James H Burgess	29	Male

ANCESTOR: William Burgess

See Decision in this case in that of William Burgess Docket 693 Book B Page 408

Attest   Will P. Ross
  DS Williams   Chairman
  Asst Clk. Com   J.E. Gunter   Com

BURGESS

Docket #695
CENSUS ROLLS 1835/52

APPLICANT FOR CHEROKEE CITIZENSHIP
POST OFFICE: Morphisville Mo   **ATTORNEY:** L S Sanders

NO	NAMES	AGE	SEX
1	Dudley Burgess	40	Male

ANCESTOR: Reuben Burgess

Rejected June 13th 1889

Cherokee Citizenship Commission Docket Books
(1880-84, 1887-89) Volume II
Tahlequah, Cherokee Nation

Office Commission on Citizenship
Cherokee Nation Ind. Ter.
Tahlequah June 13th 1889

There being no evidence in support of the above named case, The Commission decide that Dudley Burgess age 40 years is not of Cherokee blood. Post Office address Morphisville Mo.

                  Will P. Ross
Attest   Chairman
    D S Williams   J.E. Gunter Com
    Asst Clk Com

BUTLER

Docket #696
CENSUS ROLLS 1835/52

APPLICANT FOR CHEROKEE CITIZENSHIP
POST OFFICE: Hico Ark   ATTORNEY: Geo O Butler

NO	NAMES	AGE	SEX
1	Pleasant A Butler	41	Male
2	Arva L Butler	19	Female
3	James T Butler	17	Male
4	Byrnie M Butler	15	Female
5	John N Butler	13	Male
6	Georgia Ann Butler	12	Female
7	Alice V Butler	10	Female

ANCESTOR: Joe Watt

Office Commission on Citizenship
Tahlequah CN June 13th 1889

The above application was filed on the 5th day of October 1887 and on this day the case coming on for final hearing, the Commission fails to find any evidence in support of applicant's claim of Cherokee blood and in view of this fact we decide that applicant Pleasant A Butler age 41 years and his children, Arva L Butler age 19 years, James T Butler age 17 years, Byrnie M Butler age 15 years, John N Butler age 13 years, Georgia Ann Butler age 12 years, Alice V Butler age 10 years are not Cherokees by blood and not entitled to any rights in the Cherokee Nation. Post Office Hico Ark.

Cherokee Citizenship Commission Docket Books
(1880-84, 1887-89) Volume II
Tahlequah, Cherokee Nation

Will P. Ross Chairman
Attest   J.E. Gunter   Com
   E.G. Ross
   Clk Com

BUTLER

Docket #696[sic]
CENSUS ROLLS 1835/52

APPLICANT FOR CHEROKEE CITIZENSHIP
POST OFFICE: Hico Ark   ATTORNEY: Geo O Butler

NO	NAMES	AGE	SEX
1	James C Butler	33	Male
2	David L Butler	14	"
3	Andrew M Butler	9	"
4	Columbus Lee Butler	4	"
5	Ocei T Butler	2	Female
6	Julia M Butler	6 mo	"

ANCESTOR: Joe Watts

Rejected June 13th 1889

Office Commission on Citizenship
Cherokee Nation Ind. Ter.
Tahlequah   June 13th 1889

There being no evidence in support of the application in the above case, the Commission decide that James C. Butler age 33 yrs, Ella L Butler age 38 yrs, David L Butler age 14 yrs, Andrew M Butler age 9 yrs, Columbus Lee Butler age 4 yrs, Ocei T. Butler age 2 yrs and Julia M Butler age 6 months, are not Cherokees by blood and not entitled to citizenship in the Cherokee Nation. Post Office Hico Ark.

Will P. Ross
Attest   Chairman
   D S Williams   J.E. Gunter   Com
   Asst Clk Com

Cherokee Citizenship Commission Docket Books
(1880-84, 1887-89) Volume II
Tahlequah, Cherokee Nation

BUTLER

Docket #697
CENSUS ROLLS 1835/52

APPLICANT FOR CHEROKEE CITIZENSHIP

POST OFFICE: Siloam Springs **ATTORNEY:** Geo P Butler

NO	NAMES	AGE	SEX
1	J Vann Butler	21	Male

ANCESTOR: Joe Watts

Office Commission on Citizenship
Tahlequah CN June 13th 1889

The above application coming up for a final hearing and after examining the papers submitted by applicant, we fail to find any evidence submitted with the application in support of applicant's claim of Cherokee blood, and in view of this fact we decide that applicant J Vann Butler age 21 years is not a Cherokee by blood and is not entitled to Cherokee Citizenship in the Cherokee Nation. Post Office Siloam Springs Ark.

Will P. Ross
Attest   Chairman
E.G. Ross   J.E. Gunter   Com
Clk. Com.

BUTLER

Docket #698
CENSUS ROLLS 1835/52

APPLICANT FOR CHEROKEE CITIZENSHIP

POST OFFICE: Prairie Grove Ark **ATTORNEY:** Geo O Butler

NO	NAMES	AGE	SEX
1	H Milton Butler	28	Male
2	Sue Butler	27	Female
3	Erastus Butler	7	Male
4	Joe S Butler	6	"
5	Ethel Butler	5	Female
6	Arrilla Butler	4	"
7	Milton Butler	2	Male

ANCESTOR: Joe Watts

Cherokee Citizenship Commission Docket Books
(1880-84, 1887-89) Volume II
Tahlequah, Cherokee Nation

Office Commission on Citizenship
Tahlequah CN June 13th 1889

  The above application was filed on the 5th day of Oct. 1887 and on this day the case coming up for final hearing, and after examining the application we fail to find any evidence submitted by applicant and in view of this fact we decide and so declare that applicant H Milton Butler age 28 years, Sue Butler age 27 years, Erastus Butler age 7 years, Joe S Butler age 6 years, Ethel Butler age 5 years, Arrilla Butler age 4 years, Milton Butler age 2 years are not Cherokees by blood, and are not entitled to Citizenship in the Cherokee Nation. Post Office Prairie Grove Ark.

         Will P. Ross Chairman
Attest   J.E. Gunter Com
 E G Ross
    Clerk Commission

BUTLER

Docket #699
CENSUS ROLLS 1835/52

APPLICANT FOR CHEROKEE CITIZENSHIP
POST OFFICE: Hico Ark ATTORNEY: Geo O Butler

NO	NAMES	AGE	SEX
1	William C Butler	38	Male
2	Cherry L Butler	38	Female
3	John L Butler	17	Male
4	Lenora Butler	15	Female
5	Lou Ellen Butler	13	"
6	Earnest Watts Butler	11	Male
7	Jessie Butler	8	Female
8	Margaretta Butler	6	"
9	Alice Butler	2	"

ANCESTOR: Joe Watts

Tahlequah IT
June 13th 1889

  There being no evidence filed in support of the above application, the Commission decide that applicant William C Butler aged 38 years and Cherry L

Cherokee Citizenship Commission Docket Books
(1880-84, 1887-89) Volume II
Tahlequah, Cherokee Nation

Butler aged 38 years, John L Butler aged 17 years, Lenora Butler aged 15 years, Lou Ellen aged 13 years, Earnest Watts age 11 years, Jessie age 8 years, Margaretta age 6 years, Alice Butler age 2 years are not Cherokees by blood and are not entitled to citizenship in the Cherokee Nation. Post Office Hico Ark.

                          Will P. Ross
E G Ross   Chairman
    Clerk Commission   John E. Gunter Com

BOGUE

Docket #700
CENSUS ROLLS

APPLICANT FOR CHEROKEE CITIZENSHIP
POST OFFICE: Spiceland Ind   **ATTORNEY:** L B Bell

NO	NAMES	AGE	SEX
1	Martha E Allen Bogue	45	Female
2	Josephine S Bogue	18	"

ANCESTOR: Martha Elenore

The Commission decide against claimants in case. See decision in case Lible J Bogue Docket 2183 Book E Page29

                          Will P. Ross   Chairman
                                    J.E. Gunter   Com

Attest
    D.S. Williams
    Asst Clk. Com.

BURNSIDES

Docket #701
CENSUS ROLLS

APPLICANT FOR CHEROKEE CITIZENSHIP
POST OFFICE: Iowa   **ATTORNEY:** L B Bell

NO	NAMES	AGE	SEX
1	Sibbley Burnsides		Female

ANCESTOR: Martha Elenore

Cherokee Citizenship Commission Docket Books
(1880-84, 1887-89) Volume II
Tahlequah, Cherokee Nation

The Commission decide against claimants. See decision in case Lible J Bogue Docket 2183 Book E Page29

                Will P. Ross   Chairman
                         J.E. Gunter   Com

Attest
    D.S. Williams
    Asst Clk. Com

BALLENGER

Docket #702
CENSUS ROLLS

APPLICANT FOR CHEROKEE CITIZENSHIP
POST OFFICE: ATTORNEY:

NO	NAMES	AGE	SEX
1	Albert Ballenger	33	Female[sic]
2	Roda Ballenger	18	"
3	Walter Ballenger	16	Male
4	Edward Ballenger	11	"

ANCESTOR: Anna Crews

The Commission decide against claimants in decision in case of Andrew Meredith Docket 2180 Book E Page 26 and John Henley Docket 1250, Book C Page 376.

                Will P. Ross   Chairman
                John E. Gunter   Com

Attest
    D.S. Williams
    Asst Clk. Com

Cherokee Citizenship Commission Docket Books (1880-84, 1887-89) Volume II
Tahlequah, Cherokee Nation

BARRETT

Docket #703
CENSUS ROLLS

APPLICANT FOR CHEROKEE CITIZENSHIP

POST OFFICE: Afton IT   **ATTORNEY:** L B Bell

NO	NAMES	AGE	SEX
1	Mary Jane Barrett	62	Female

ANCESTOR: Anna Crews

The Commission decide against claimant in decision in case of Andrew Meredith Docket 2180 Book E Page 26 and John Henley Docket 1250, Book C Page 376.

        Will P. Ross   Chairman
        John E. Gunter   Com

Attest
    D.S. Williams
    Asst Clk. Com

BALLENGER

Docket #704
CENSUS ROLLS

APPLICANT FOR CHEROKEE CITIZENSHIP

POST OFFICE: Afton Ind Terry   **ATTORNEY:** L.B. Bell

NO	NAMES	AGE	SEX
1	Chas W Ballenger	28	Male

ANCESTOR: Anna Crews

The Commission decide against claimant. See decision in case Andrew Meredith Docket 2180 Book E Page 26 and case John Henly Docket 1250, Book C Page 376.

        Will P. Ross   Chairman
        J. E. Gunter   Com

Attest
    D.S. Williams
    Asst Clk. Com

Cherokee Citizenship Commission Docket Books
(1880-84, 1887-89) Volume II
Tahlequah, Cherokee Nation

BROWN

Docket #705
CENSUS ROLLS

APPLICANT FOR CHEROKEE CITIZENSHIP

POST OFFICE: Afton IT. **ATTORNEY:** L B Bell

NO	NAMES	AGE	SEX
1	Margarett E Brown	41	Female

ANCESTOR: Anna Crews

The Commission decide against claimant. See decision in case Andrew Meredith Docket 2180 Book E Page 26 and case John Henly Docket 1250, Book C Page 376.

         Will P. Ross Chairman
         J. E. Gunter Com

Attest
  D.S. Williams
  Asst Clk. Com

BEEBEE

Docket #706
CENSUS ROLLS

APPLICANT FOR CHEROKEE CITIZENSHIP

POST OFFICE: Wilmington Del **ATTORNEY:** L.B. Bell

NO	NAMES	AGE	SEX
1	Mary Beebee		Female

ANCESTOR: Anna Crews

The Commission decide against claimant. See decision in case Andrew Meridith Docket 2180 Book E Page 26 and case John Henly Docket 1250, Book C Page 376.

         Will P. Ross Chairman
         J. E. Gunter Com

Attest
  D.S. Williams
  Asst Clk. Com

Cherokee Citizenship Commission Docket Books
(1880-84, 1887-89) Volume II
Tahlequah, Cherokee Nation

BUTLER

Docket #707
CENSUS ROLLS

APPLICANT FOR CHEROKEE CITIZENSHIP
POST OFFICE: Kingstown[sic] Ind   **ATTORNEY:** L.B. Bell

NO	NAMES	AGE	SEX
1	Luzetta Ellen Butler		Female

ANCESTOR: Anna Crews

The Commission decide against claimant. See decision in case of Andrew Meredith Docket 2180 Book E Page 26 and case John Henly Docket 1250, Book C Page 376.

        Will P. Ross Chairman
        John E. Gunter Com

Attest
 D.S. Williams
 Asst Clk. Com

BUTLER

Docket #708
CENSUS ROLLS

APPLICANT FOR CHEROKEE CITIZENSHIP
POST OFFICE: Kingston Ind.   **ATTORNEY:** L.B. Bell

NO	NAMES	AGE	SEX
1	Francis F Butler		Female

ANCESTOR: Anna Crews

The Commission decide against claimant. See decision in case of Andrew Meredith, Dock 2180 Book E Page 26 and John Henly Docket 1250, Book C Page 376.

        Will P. Ross Chairman
        John E. Gunter Com

Attest
 D.S. Williams
 Asst Clk. Com

Cherokee Citizenship Commission Docket Books
(1880-84, 1887-89) Volume II
Tahlequah, Cherokee Nation

BUTLER

Docket #709
CENSUS ROLLS

APPLICANT FOR CHEROKEE CITIZENSHIP

POST OFFICE: Sterling Kansas **ATTORNEY:** L.B. Bell

NO	NAMES	AGE	SEX
1	Eva Butler	24	Female

ANCESTOR: Anna Crews

The Commission decide against claimant. See decision in case of Andrew Meredith Dock 2180 Book E Page 26 and case John Henly Docket 1250, Book C Page 376.

Will P. Ross   Chairman
John E. Gunter   Com

Attest
D.S. Williams
Asst Clk. Com

BUTLER

Docket #710
CENSUS ROLLS

APPLICANT FOR CHEROKEE CITIZENSHIP

POST OFFICE: Sterling Kans **ATTORNEY:** L.B. Bell

NO	NAMES	AGE	SEX
1	William H Butler	50	Male
2	Fannie H Butler	12	Female
3	Flora Butler	9	female
4	Howard Butler	4	Male

ANCESTOR: Anna Crews

The Commission decide against claimant. See decision in the case of Andrew Meredith Docket 2180 Book E Page 26 and case John Henly Docket 1250, Book C Page 376.

Will P. Ross   Chairman
John E. Gunter   Com

Attest
D.S. Williams
Asst Clk. Com

Cherokee Citizenship Commission Docket Books
(1880-84, 1887-89) Volume II
Tahlequah, Cherokee Nation

BUTLER

Docket #711
CENSUS ROLLS

APPLICANT FOR CHEROKEE CITIZENSHIP
POST OFFICE: Afton IT   ATTORNEY: L.B. Bell

NO	NAMES	AGE	SEX
1	Hardy H Butler	48	Male
2	Alva R Butler	18	female
3	Joseph H Butler	16	Male
4	Hanlin J Butler	14	"
5	Ollie B Butler	5	female

ANCESTOR: Anna Crews

The Commission decide against claimant. See decision in case Andrew Meredith Docket 2180 Book E Page 26 and case John Henly Docket 1250, Book C Page 376.

Will P. Ross   Chairman
J. E. Gunter   Com

Attest
D.S. Williams
Asst Clk. Com

BUTLER

Docket #712
CENSUS ROLLS

Applicant for Cherokee Citizenship
Post Office: *(Illegible)* Ind.   Attorney: L.B. Bell

NO	NAMES	AGE	SEX
1	James H Butler	46	Male
2	Lizzie Butler	17	Female
3	Albert Butler	15	Male

ANCESTOR: Anna Crews

The Commission decide against claimant. See decision in case of Andrew Meredith Docket 2180 Book E Page 26 and case John Henly 1250, Book C Page 376.

Cherokee Citizenship Commission Docket Books
(1880-84, 1887-89) Volume II
Tahlequah, Cherokee Nation

                Will P. Ross   Chairman
                John E. Gunter Com

Attest
    D.S. Williams
    Asst Clk. Com

BUTLER

Docket #713
CENSUS ROLLS

Applicant for Cherokee Citizenship
Post Office: **Attorney:** L.B. Bell

NO	NAMES	AGE	SEX
1	H.H. Butler	47	

ANCESTOR: Anna Crews

The Commission decide against claimant. See decision in case of Andrew Meredith Docket 2180 Book E Page 26 and John Henly Docket 1250, Book C Page 376.

                Will P. Ross   Chairman
                John E. Gunter Com

Attest
    D.S. Williams
    Asst Clk. Com

BELEW

Docket #714
CENSUS ROLLS 1835

APPLICANT FOR CHEROKEE CITIZENSHIP
POST OFFICE: *(Illegible)*   ATTORNEY: CH Taylor

NO	NAMES	AGE	SEX
1	Giles D Belew	62	Male
2	Francis B Blew	28	Female
3	Giles D Blew Jr	7	Male

ANCESTOR: John Bryant

Rejected March 18th 1889

Cherokee Citizenship Commission Docket Books
(1880-84, 1887-89) Volume II
Tahlequah, Cherokee Nation

Ad<u>ve</u>rse
Embraced in decission[sic] on page 431
Book B in the Aaron Bellew case.

Office Commission on Citizenship
    Tahlequah I.T   March 18th 1889

D.S. Williams   Will P. Ross
    Asst Clk Com   Chairman Com
                           John E Gunter   Com

BELEW

Docket #715
CENSUS ROLLS

APPLICANT FOR CHEROKEE CITIZENSHIP
POST OFFICE: Vinita Ind Ter   **ATTORNEY:** L.B. Bell

NO	NAMES	AGE	SEX
1	Aaron Belew	67	Male
2	Samuel Belew	43	female[sic]
3	Elizabeth Belew	47	"
4	John Belew	40	Male
5	Polly Ann Belew	37	female
6	Novascotia Belew	34	"
7	Levi Belew	31	Male
8	Tennessee Belew	28	female

ANCESTOR: John Bryant

Rejected March 18th 1889

Now on this the 18th day of march 1889, comes the above case to wit; Aaron Bellew for himself and children to wit: Samuel Bellew age 43 years, Elizabeth Bellew age 47 years, John Bellew aged 40 years, Polly Ann Bellew aged 37 years, Novascotia Bellew aged 34 years, Levi Bellew aged 31 years, Tennessee Bellew aged 28 years for a final hearing, he having made application for re-admission to Citizenship in the Cherokee Nation pursuant to the provisions of an Act of the National Council approved December 8th 1886. After careful examination of all the testimony submitted in this case on behalf of the Plaintiff and of the defendant, The Commission have reached the conclusion that it has not been established that John Bryant the grand father of the applicant and

Cherokee Citizenship Commission Docket Books
(1880-84, 1887-89) Volume II
Tahlequah, Cherokee Nation

descent from whom he claims Cherokee blood and a right to admision[sic] to Citizenship as a native Cherokee, was of Cherokee blood. The testimony shows that he was not at any time known to the witnesses to have resided within the limits of the Cherokee Nation and that his percentage and relationship were unknown. This alleged Cherokee descent is based upon common report except in the case of one or two witnesses who give no reason for the statement that John Bryant was a Cherokee Indian except that they knew him to be part Cherokee as they knew him to be part white, there is no identification of John Bryant as a Cherokee and none of Lucy Bryant or that she was either his mother or sister. It is also worthy of note that although John Bryant is shown to have resided within the state of South Carolina when he first became known as a stragling[sic] young man, and afterwards in Alabama and finally for many years in Gibson County Tennessee near the Cherokee Country that he does not appear to have sought residing at any time within the Cherokee Nation or to have availed himself of any of the privileges and benefits to which if a Cherokee he was entitled before and at the time of the removal of the Cherokees under the Treaties of 1817, 1819 and 1835 and such is the fact *(illegible)* to his descendants also until of recent date. Neither the names of John Bryant, Zachariah Bryant nor of the claimant Aaron Bellew, nor of any of their relatives or descendants so far as shown are found on the census or pay rolls of 1835 or 1851 or 1852 nor of other date. In accordance therefore with these facts and with the provisions of the Act in force defining the authority of this Commission they decide that Aaron Belew, et. al. named above, are not of Cherokee blood and are not entitled to the rights and privileges of Citizenship in the Cherokee Nation which belong to native Cherokees, but not intruders and will be reported as such to the Principal Chief. This decision includes the following named applicants for Citizenship who claim Cherokee blood by descent from the before named John Bryant and whose applications were submitted by the consent of parties for final hearing and determination by the Commission on Citizenship along with the case of Aaron Bellew, et. al. herein described to wit.

                    Will P. Ross
                    Chairman
          JE Gunter   Com

Attest
   D.S. Williams
   Asst Clk. Com.

Cherokee Citizenship Commission Docket Books
(1880-84, 1887-89) Volume II
Tahlequah, Cherokee Nation

Commission on Citizenship.

CHEROKEE NATION, IND. TER.

Tahlequah, March 18th 1889

Familys	Giles D. Bellew	aged	62	years	
"	Francis B. Bellew	"	28	"	daughter
"	Giles D. Bellew	"	17	"	male
"	Governor Bellew	"	54	"	
"	M.E. Bellew	"	12	"	male
"	Levi J Bellew	"	24	"	
"	Ramond Bellew	"	7	"	male
"	Joseph B. Bellew	"	5	"	"
"	M.E. Bellew	"	25	"	"
"	Zack Bryant	"	69	"	
"	George W. Bryant	"	52	"	
"	John Bryant	"	20	"	male
"	Jim Bryant	"	18	"	"
"	Only Bryant	"	14	"	Female
"	Willie Bryant	"	10	"	"
"	Daniel Boyd Bryant	"	32	"	male
"	Audery Bryant	"	12	"	Female
"	Julian Bryant	"	10	"	male
"	Giles H. Bryant	"	61	"	"
"	Mose Z Bryant	"	19	"	"
"	Mary A Bryant	"	17	"	Female
"	James H Bryant	"	15	"	male
"	Gersham C. Bryant	"	12	"	"
"	David F. Bryant	"	10	"	"

Cherokee Citizenship Commission Docket Books
(1880-84, 1887-89) Volume II
Tahlequah, Cherokee Nation

BRYANT

Docket #715
CENSUS ROLLS

APPLICANT FOR CHEROKEE CITIZENSHIP

POST OFFICE: Miland[sic] Tenn   ATTORNEY: C H Taylor

NO	NAMES	AGE	SEX
1	Brinkley Bryant	23	Male

ANCESTOR: John Bryant

Rejected March 18th 1889

Adverse

Embraced in decission[sic] on page 431
Book B in the Aaron Bellew case
Rendered March 18th 1889.

Will P. Ross
    Chairman Com.
John E. Gunter   Com

Office Commission on Citizenship
Tahlequah I.T   March 18th 1889

D.S. Williams
Clk Com

BRYANT

Docket #717
CENSUS ROLLS 1835

APPLICANT FOR CHEROKEE CITIZENSHIP

POST OFFICE: Choatea IT.   ATTORNEY: C.H. Taylor

NO	NAMES	AGE	SEX
1	William C Bryant	24	Male

ANCESTOR: John Bryant

Rejected March 18th 1889

Adverse

Embraced in decission[sic] on page 431
Book B in the Aaron Bellew case
Rendered March 18th 1889.

Cherokee Citizenship Commission Docket Books
(1880-84, 1887-89) Volume II
Tahlequah, Cherokee Nation

Will P. Ross
Chairman Com.
John E. Gunter   Com

Office Commission
on Citizenship
Tahlequah I.T.
March 18th 1889

D.S. Williams
Clk Com

BRYANT

Docket #716[sic]
CENSUS ROLLS

APPLICANT FOR CHEROKEE CITIZENSHIP
POST OFFICE: Miland[sic], Tenn   **ATTORNEY:**

NO	NAMES	AGE	SEX
1	Brinkley Bryant	23	Male

 Commission on Citizenship.

CHEROKEE NATION, IND. TER.

Tahlequah,   March 18th 1889

Familys	Scotea Ann Beaty	aged	37	years	
"	Giles Earl Beaty	"	3	"	male
"	Z.B. Newhouse	"	27	"	male
"	A.E. Newhouse	"	24	"	Female
"	A.M. Newhouse	"	6	"	male
"	Thomas Newhouse	"	3	"	"

Office Commission   Will P. Ross
on Citizenship   Chairman of Commission
Tahlequah I.T.   John E. Gunter   Commis.
March 18th 1889

D.S. Williams
Clk Com

Cherokee Citizenship Commission Docket Books
(1880-84, 1887-89) Volume II
Tahlequah, Cherokee Nation

BRYANT

Docket #718
CENSUS ROLLS 1835

APPLICANT FOR CHEROKEE CITIZENSHIP

POST OFFICE: Miland[sic] Tenn   **ATTORNEY:** C H Taylor

NO	NAMES	AGE	SEX
1	Giles H. Bryant	61	Male
2	Moses C Bryant	19	Male
3	Mary A Bryant	17	female
4	James H Bryant	15	Male
5	Gersham C. Bryant	12	Male
6	David F. Bryant	10	"

ANCESTOR: John Bryant

Rejected March 18th 1889

Adverse

Embraced in decission[sic] on page 431
Book B. in the Aaron Bellew case.
Rendered March 18th 1889.

Will P. Ross
Chairman Com.
John E. Gunter   Com

Office Commission on Citizenship
Tahlequah I.T. March 18th 1889
D.S. Williams
Clk Com

ABEL
- Allie B 256
- Catharine 257
- Charles F 258
- E B 258
- Emma 257
- Harrison E 256
- J F 256, 259
- J H 259
- J M 257
- James W 259
- Jno F 256
- John 257
- John D 256
- L A 259
- L C 259
- L M 257
- Lenard I 258
- Lucinda E 258
- Mary M 258
- R A 259
- R M 259
- S B 259
- S C 259
- Samuel 257
- Walt L 258
- Walter L 258
- William A 256
- Wm A 256

ABERCOMBIA
- Benj F 255
- Callie E 254
- James C 254
- John R 256

ABERCOMBIE
- Bertha 253
- Clara 253
- George 253
- Hugh E 253

ABERCROMBIA
- Earnest 253
- Edith A 253
- Nellia Dee 253
- Riley A 253
- Young William 253, 255

ABERCROMBIE
- Benjamin F 254
- Bertha 254
- Callie E 254
- Clara 254
- Claud 254
- Earnest 254
- Edith A 254
- George 254
- Hugh E 254
- James C 254
- John R 254
- Mollie A 254
- Nellie Dee 254
- Riley A 254
- Young William 253, 254, 255, 256

ADAIR
- J R 105
- J T   2, 5, 7, 13, 21, 22, 24, 25, 26, 27, 28, 29, 34, 41, 44, 46, 47, 48, 56, 57, 58, 64, 69, 72, 75, 77, 78, 84, 91, 102, 103, 104, 106, 110, 111, 112, 116, 120, 126, 129, 132, 133, 135, 136, 137, 140, 148, 149, 150, 151, 152, 159, 160, 161, 162, 164, 173, 185, 189, 190, 191, 192, 193, 198, 199, 209, 211, 212, 213, 214, 215, 216, 218, 219, 222, 223, 224, 233, 235, 236, 237, 238, 239, 240, 241, 248, 249, 250, 251, 252, 258, 271, 272, 273, 274, 275, 308
- Judge 131

ADAMS
- Anna E 284
- Elizabeth J 284

Emma J 285
Fred H 283, 284
Harley E 285
John C 87, 88, 285
Lucy 281
Mark H 283, 284
Martha E 285
Marthey E 285
Nancy 87
Nancy A 88
Ollie Flora 285
Powhattan 87, 88
Wiley B 283
Willis J 282
ADAMSON
  Alva 281
  G W 281
  Ina 281
  Ruby 281
  Verbal 281
ADDINGTON
  Adaline 5
  Altha 5
  China J 5
  Cynthia 5
  Lucinda 5
  Mollie 5
  R N 5
  Texas 5
ADINGTON
  Lucinda 5
AGG
  Sarah J 262
ALBERTY
  Bluford W 227
ALEXANDER
  G W 271
  Nellie 271
  T G 271
  William 271
ALFRED
  Andrew J 264
  Andy J 264

Callie G 265
Hugh C 265
James 264
James M 263
John A 264
Malinda 264
Manassa 263
Nancy A 264
Robert 264
Sarah B 264
William 263, 264, 265
Wm 264
ALLEN
  Alice 266
  Hezekiah 269
  Jane 266
  John 266, 269
  Julia 266
  Mary 266
  May 266
  Minnie F 270
  Nancy 265, 266
  Oliver W 270
  Ollie 266
  Samuel C 268
  Thomas C 267
  Wade 266
ALLIGTON
  William 261
ALLINGTON
  William 261, 262
ALLISON
  Elma R 272
  James T 272
  Jennie 272
  John R 271, 272
  Martha A 273
  Willie 271, 272
ALSUP
  Martha 136
AMBERCOMBIA
  Claud 254
  Mollie A 254

Index

ANDERSON
  K G 281, 282
ARCHER
  John R 274
  Lucenda A 274
  Lucy A.......................................274
  Mary E.......................................274
ARMOUR...260
  Mrs 260
  Sarah J 260, 261
ARMSTRONG 263
ARNOLD
  Elender C...................................279
  James 279, 280
  James B 279
  James M 280
  John R 280
  Lina M.......................................280
  Lonzo J......................................280
  Nicey A 280
  Ralph D 279
  William......................................279
  William E 280
  William S 279
ARWOOD
  Mary 276, 277
  Rosa 276
  Thomas W 276
  William P 277
  Wm P 277
ASBELL 117
  M 117
ATCHISON
  Ruth Ann 247
ATKINS
  Anna M 275
  Geo W 275
  Sarah A......................................275
AUSTILL
  Iven 165, 166, 171
  Ivin 165
  Sarah 165, 166, 171
AUSTIN
  Martha..278
  Martha E.............................277, 278
AYERS
  Carry 261, 262
  Grant 261, 262
  Sherman 261, 262
  Symantha............................261, 262
AZBILL
  Elizabeth 65
  Indian Bill 65
  John 65
  Neomas 65
BACON
  A H 302
  Amos Lee 303, 304
  Benj H 302
  Benjamin H 302
  Catherine....................................301
  Estella 302
  James H.....................................302
  John A 303, 304
  John W 302
  Maggie 302
  Maggy 302
  Mark J 304
  Mark S................................301, 302
  May 302
  Nancy B 304
BAILY
  Alice 215
BAIN
  Agnes 296
  Agnes J......................................295
  Andrew J 295, 296
  Lughton S..........................296, 297
BAKER
  Eliza J 95
  Geo S 98
  George S......................................98
  Henry 167
  Melissa Jane 42
  Samuel B 95
  William A....................................95

BALES
  David 131
BALLARD
  Eliza 139
BALLENGER
  Albert 314
  Chas W 315
  Edward 314
  Roda 314
  Walter 314
BARBER
  Ailcy J 23
  Atta 23
  Caliway 23
  Edgar 23
  Emma 23
  Irena 23
  Joel 23
  Jounnah 17, 23
  Mary 23
  Ouice 23
  Riley 23
  Toliven 23
BARNES
  H C 7, 25, 41, 46, 77, 84, 91,
         126, 133, 136, 150, 173,
         175, 198, 216, 233, 271,
         274, 275, 308
BARNETT
  John 150
BARNHILL
  Mary 78, 217, 220, 225
BARRETT
  Mary Jane 315
BARTHEL
  Florence 232, 234
  Josephine 231, 232, 234
BATEMAN
  Benjamin F 303
  Frank 303
  John 303
  Mark 303
  Walter 303

BATES
  F M 131
BAXTER
  Eliza J 286, 287
  Flornence J 287
  John 286, 287
  Taylor 286, 287
  William 287
BAYLESS
  Alice 292
  Allie 292
  Benj 292
  Ella 292
  Etta 292
  Jennie 292
  John 292
  Sarah 292
BEATY
  Giles Earl 325
  Scotea 325
BEAVER
  Adda 290
  Addie 290
  Albert 290
  Annie 290
  Cora 27, 28, 290
  Frank 28
  Jane 27, 28
  Lucinda 27, 28
  Lucy 27, 28
BEEBEE
  Mary 316
BELEW
  Aaron 321, 322
  Elizabeth 321
  Francis B 320
  Giles D 320
  Giles D, Jr 320
  John 321
  Levi 321
  Novascotia............................321
  Polly Ann 321
  Samuel 321

Index

Tennessee 321
BELL
   James 107
   L B   19, 21, 23, 49, 50, 225, 228,
         229, 230, 235, 236, 237,
         238, 239, 262, 268, 269,
         270, 313, 315, 316, 317,
         318, 319, 320, 321
   Mary 107, 108
   Mary S 278
   W M 108
BELL & AKIN 48
BELL & AKIN 47
BELL & BRYANT 16
BELLEW
   Aaron 291, 321, 322, 324, 326
   Elizabeth 321
   Francis B 323
   Giles D 323
   Governor 291, 323
   John 321
   Joseph B 291, 323
   Levi 321
   Levi J 291, 323
   M E 291, 323
   Novascotia 321
   Polly Ann 321
   Ramond 323
   Raymond 291
   Samuel 321
   Tennessee 321
BELLU
   Adah H 104
   George G 104
   Job C 104
   John A 104
   Peter A 104
   W H 104
   William C 104
   Wm C 104
BENUM
   Nancy 173, 175
BERRYHILL

Louisa 60
BIBLE
   Eliza 89
   Geo 89
   Rebecca 89
BISWELL
   Artimiss 64, 65
   Dillie M 65
   Elizabeth A 64, 65
   Emily T 65
   Emily T B 65
   Martha D 64, 65
BLACK
   Della May 297, 298
   Dora C 297
   Dora L 298
   Eliza M 297, 298
   Elliott 298
   Forrest C 297, 298
   J Elliott 297
   Kennie D 297, 298
   Wm P 298
BLACKBURN
   Elizabeth 295
   Polly 20, 29, 48
BLACKSTONE
   R C 3
BLANCETT
   Akie 139
   Desdemonia 138, 139
   Harden 139
   Hardin 138
   Laur A 139
   Laura A 138
   Myrtie F 138, 139
   Sarah E 138, 139
BLAYLOCK
   Artela 245
   Mary Elizabeth 245
   Milly Jane 245
   Sarah A 245
   Satu Ann 245
BOATRIGHT

Albert B 295
Catharine E 194
Catherine E 194
Elizabeth E 295
Elizabeth Edna 295
Eveline 194
Francis A 295
Franklin 295
Geo M 194
George M 194
James B 295
James R 194
Jas R 194
Jesse 194
John J 295
Joseph B 295
Julia M 194
Medora P 194
Mr 196
Myrtle 194
BOATS
    Bell 47
    Cora 47
    Lula 47
    Stealla 47
BOBO
    Alabama 86, 87
    Charles 87
    Charlie 86, 87
    George 87
    Nellie 86, 87
BOGUE
    Josephine S 313
    Lible J 268, 269, 270, 313, 314
    Martha E Allen 313
BOLIN
    Annie 2
    Stephen 2
BOND
    Abel J 179
    Almeeda 187
    Anna P 179
    Annie 189

    Bertha 179
    Christina 179
    Earl 187
    Ethel 187
    Ida 187
    Isom H 187
    Isom R 187
    J A 179
    J S 189
    Laura 179
    Mabel 188
    Sarah A .. 134, 175, 176, 177, 178, 179, 187, 188, 189
    Wm 179
BONDS
    Barsheba 294, 299
    Geo G 293
    George G 293
    J Clark 299, 300
    Jessie Knights 294
    Jessie V 299
    Julia V 300
    Maggie A 299, 300
    Mary E 299, 300
    T K 294
    William J 294
BOUDINOT 274
    E C 6
    E C, Jr 40
    Mr 271
BOUDINOT 13
BOUDINOT & R 248, 250, 271, 274, 292, 293, 294, 297, 298, 299, 305, 306, 307, 308
BOUDINOT & RASMUS 7, 8, 9, 10, 11, 12, 15, 22, 29, 39, 51, 52, 54, 85, 90, 94, 95, 96, 117, 118, 119, 133, 135, 141, 195
BOUDINOT and RASMUS 50, 53, 135, 142

BOWLIN
- Annie 2
- Stephen 2

BOYD
- Albert 15
- Janna 15
- John 15
- Luther 15

BRACKET
- Francis J 300
- Migi 300

BRACKETT
- Adam 289
- Arminda 289
- Arminda L 288
- Asalline 289, 290
- Benj 289
- Benj J 289, 290
- Benj J, Sr 288
- Benjamin 288
- Benjamin J 289
- Benjamin, Jr 290
- Cynthia 300
- Dora 289, 290
- Ethel 289, 290
- Francis J 300
- Mary 289
- Midge 300
- Rosaline 290
- Sarah 288, 289
- Susan 289
- Susie 289

BRADY
- Ida 231, 233, 234
- John G 233, 235

BREMER
- Eliza 49
- George 49, 60, 61, 76
- Wm 49

BREWER
- Rebecca M 205

BRINK
- G F 238

- Lidia 238
- Lydia 238
- Mary 238
- Mary A 238

BROOKS
- Adell 102
- Charles 288
- Eliza J 299
- Elizabeth 95
- Fedora J 286
- Geo W 286
- Isaac J 287, 288
- James 287, 288
- John T 286
- Joseph 287, 288
- Louisa 287, 288
- Lucinda 287, 288
- Mack 287, 288
- Mary 286
- Mary Manervia 102
- Mary T 286
- Rosa Maybell 102
- William 287, 288
- William M 286

BROWN
- Alex 123, 124, 201, 202, 203
- Baby 202
- Benton 293
- Benton J 294
- Charles F 123, 124
- Jessie 293, 294
- John 123, 124
- John Thomas 123, 124
- Lillian 294
- Lillian Maud 293
- Lou 293, 294
- Margarett E 316
- Pally 246
- Sarah A 200
- Sarah T 202
- Susan 293, 294
- Susan Lona 123, 124

BROWNING

Index

Jennie 158
Jessie 153
Lillie 158
BRUNER
   David 76
   Edward 76
   Geo S 13
   George S 13
   Isaac A 13
   Isaac N 13
   John R 13
   Katy 76
   Lethia 13
   Mary 13
   Nancy 76
   Polly 76
   Theodore S 13
   Thomas 76
   Walter 76
BRYAN
   J M 291
BRYANT
   Audery 323
   Brinkley 324, 325
   Daniel Boyd 323
   David F 323, 326
   George W 323
   Gersham C 323, 326
   Giles H 323, 326
   Hiram 140, 141
   J M 242, 243, 244, 245, 246, 247, 291
   James H 323, 326
   Jim 323
   John 320, 321, 322, 323, 324, 326
   Julian 323
   Lucy 139, 322
   Mary A 323, 326
   Mose Z 323
   Moses C 326
   Only 323
   William C 324

Willie 323
Zachariah 322
Zack 323
BULLOCK
   Alvo C 73, 74
   Cynthia E 73, 74
   Dennis 73, 74
   Henry 73, 74
   Joseph W 73, 74
   Walter 73, 74
   William H 73, 74
BUNCH
   R   6, 16, 17, 18, 32, 47, 51, 52, 53, 54, 55, 60, 61, 62, 65, 66, 67, 68, 70, 71, 73, 76, 79, 85, 86, 88, 91, 93, 94, 95, 96, 97, 99, 101, 108, 109, 111, 113, 114, 116, 119, 122, 123, 138, 139, 140, 141, 142, 143, 147, 149, 153, 154, 155, 156, 157, 158, 163, 164, 165, 166, 167, 168, 169, 170, 171, 172, 185, 186, 188, 194, 200, 201, 202, 203, 204, 206, 208, 228, 229, 230, 231, 257, 262, 265, 266, 267, 268, 269, 270, 275, 276, 277, 278, 279, 280, 281, 282, 283, 284, 285, 286, 287, 288, 290, 292, 293, 294, 295, 296, 300
BUNCH
   R 124, 145
BURGESS
   Arthur L 305, 308
   Cornell 107
   David L 305, 308
   Dudley 308, 309
   Hames H 308
   Hettie Delilah 305, 308
   James H 308

John T	306, 308
Mary P	306, 308
Reuben	308
Reuben E	305
Reubin E	308
Strother	265, 305
Strother S	308
William	305, 306, 307, 308
William G	308
William P	307
William, Sr	307

BURK
Mary 68

BURNSIDES
Sibbley 313

BUSHYHEAD
David 298

BUTLER
Albert	319
Alice	312, 313
Alice V	309
Alva R	319
Andrew M	310
Arrilla	311, 312
Arva L	309
Byrnie M	309
Cherry L	312
Columbus Lee	310
David L	310
Earnest Watts	312, 313
Ella L	310
Erastus	311, 312
Ethel	311, 312
Eva	318
Fannie H	318
Flora	318
Francis F	317
Geo O	309, 310, 311, 312
George O	68, 91, 154, 204
Georgia Ann	309
H H	320
H Milton	311, 312
Hanlin J	319
Hardy H	319
Howard	318
J Vann	311
James C	310
James H	319
James T	309
Jessie	312, 313
Joe S	311, 312
John L	312, 313
John N	309
Joseph H	319
Julia M	310
Lenora	312, 313
Lizzie	319
Lou Ellen	312, 313
Luzetta Ellan	317
Margaretta	312, 313
Milton	311, 312
Ocei T	310
Ollie B	319
Pleasant A	309
Sue	311, 312
William C	312
William H	318

CAH LAH TO LI TU 227

CALDWELL
Andrew	298
D	297
Elizabeth D	298
J T	90
Serena	298

CAMPBELL
Annie D	42
Annie Duncan	41
Daniel A	42
Dan'l Alford	41
Jesse K	42
Jesse Kenneth	42
Oscar D	42
Oscar Dunreath	41

CAMPE
James M	47
Missouri	47

Index

Ora M 47
CANADA
   Absalome 172
   Alonzo 173
   Biddie 172
   G L 172, 173
   James 173
   James L 172, 173
   Mansfield 173
   Viney J 173
CANNADA
   Absalome 172
   Alonzo 172
   G L 172
   James 172
   Mansfield 172
CAPP
   Pricey 127
   Richard 127
   Samuel 127
CAPPS
   Pricy 127
   Samuel 127
CARLILE
   Calew 266
CARMICLE
   Allen F 237
   Annie J 237, 238
   Clarence 237
   Mary 237
   Ora 237
   Wm C 237
CAULK
   Arthur 227, 228
   Bessie 227, 229
   Edward H 227, 228
   Edward L 225, 228
   Fannie E 227
   Jesse 227
   Jessie 229
   Laura 227, 229
   Laura E 225, 228
   Lena M 227, 228
   Mary A 227, 229
   Milton M 227, 228
   Nellie L 227, 228
   Pleasant H 225, 228
   Rhoda 225, 226, 227, 228, 229, 230, 231
   Rosa M 227, 228
CHAMBERS
   Angelina 253, 254, 255, 256
   Angeline 253, 254
   Emily J 99
   Josephine Bell 99
   Milly A 99
   Sarah C 99
   Thomas S 99
CHASTIAN
   Edward D 116
   James R 116
   John B 116
   John E B 56
   John S 116
   Joseh E 56
   Leona C 116
   Lucinda E 56
   Milton B 116
   William 55
   William A J 56
CHASTINE
   John E B 55
   Joseph E 55
   Lucinda E 55
   William A J 55
   William M 55
CHES-QUAY-AH 88
CHILDERS
   Catherine 225, 228, 229, 230
   Lem 227
   Lemuel 226, 227
   Nancy 226, 235, 236, 237, 238, 239
CHILDRESS
   Agnes 134

Index

CHISHOLM
    Frank 26
    Jessie 26, 27, 28
    Mary 26
    William................................27
CHOATE
    Elizabeth...........................185
    John B................................137
    John B, Jr...........................111
    John B, Sr...................111, 112
    Laura E..............................111
    Mary C...............................112
    Rufus M.............................111
    Silas 112
    William S 111
CHOTE
    John Brown 112
    Laura Etta.........................112
    Mary Carolina 112
    Rufus Marc.......................112
    William Silas....................112
CHRISTEY
    Ellen L...............................186
    John H...............................186
    John L................................186
CHRISTIAN
    Walt 18
CHURCH
    Annie 250
CLARK
    Austin 169
    Bettie A 86
    Dalis 86
    Donie 169
    Elizabeth...........................169
    Ennia 169
    Mary 86
    Nellie 86
    Ollie L...............................169
    Ora 169
CLARKES
    (Illegible)...........................195
CLEMMONS
    Jodie 134
    Jodie R 134
    M P 134
    Ottis D...............................134
CLINE
    D F 167
    David 167
    G W 167
    R D 167
CLUBB
    Billetty..............................202
    Isiah 201, 202
    James 201, 202
    Lovenia.....................201, 202
    Villetty..............................201
COATS
    Bell 46
    Cora 46
    Lola 46
    Stella 46
CODY
    Cloris C 54, 55
    Elmer B 54, 55
    Sarah A 54, 55
COLEMAN
    James F 119
    Margaret G.........................119
    Nancy A 119
COLLINS
    Aurora............................10, 11
    Bessie 11
    Roscoe S 11
COMBS
    Cora 199, 200
    Cornelia.....................199, 200
    Jennie J......................199, 200
    Lillie 199, 200
    Sallie A 199, 200
    Wm A 199, 200
COMINGDEER...........................186
COMPTON
    Nancy 47
COOPER

Index

Lou Eva 115
Lou Eve 114
T C 114, 115
Thomas C 115
Willie May 114, 115
COPE
   David 188
   Martha A 188
   William 188
CORK
   Laban 226
CORN
   Archie 192
   Arden 192
   Earl 192
   Hannah 192
   Ola 192
   Ola S 192
   William H 192
   Wm H 192
CORTNER
   Pauline 138
COTNER
   Allie 138
   Babe 138
   Melt in 138
   Pauline 138
   Robert J H 138
   William 138
COUCH
   M A 164
   Mary A 159, 160, 164
COVINGTON
   George A 30
   Mordicia J 30
COX
   Edward 200
   Frances 19
   Francis 19
   Isaac 200
   Isabell 200
   Serena 19, 20
COZBY

Andrew L 164, 165
Eva J 165
Frank 165
James R 164, 165
John H 164, 165
Virginia J 164, 165
Wm A 165
CRAIG
   Braister M 132
   Brassiter 129
   Caleb 128, 129, 131
   Dartha J 128, 129, 131
   David B 132
   David M 129
   G W 130, 131, 132
   George W 131
   J E 129, 132
   James W 131
   Jim 131
   John 128, 131, 132
   John W 128, 129, 131
   Josiah 131
   L M 128, 129, 132
   Lee N 128, 129, 132
   Maggie J 129, 132
   Martha C 131
   Mary E 128, 129, 131
   Saah A 131
   Sam 131
   Samuel 128, 129, 132
   Tom 131
   William A 128, 129
   Wm A 132
CRAWFORD
   Elmyra J 228, 229
   Ollie 228, 229
CREWS
   Anna 314, 315, 316, 317, 318, 319, 320
   Mary 262
CROW
   Alla A 69, 70
   Allie M 69

Index

Annie 70
Flora 70
Florence 69, 70
Hellen 70
John M 69, 70
L H 69
Levi M 69, 70
M E F 69
Margaret 70
Margarett 69
Robt W 70
William M 67
CRUCHFIELD
   Claud 133
   Claude 133
   John 133
   Mary 133
   S W 133
   W W 133
CRUTCHFIELD 133
   Annie 58
   John H 58
   Josephine 58
   Leroy L 58
DALE
   James 174
DARNELL
   Eliza E 219
   Enla 219
   Eva 219
DAUGHERTY
   Lear 19
DAVIDSON
   (Illegible) 203
   (Illegible) B 204
DAVIS
   Addie 199
   Alfred 43, 44
   Amanda 193
   Andy 43, 44
   Berrella E 193
   Berrilla 199
   Biddie 199

Charles 43, 44
Daniel 190
Daniel B 193
Danl 191
Dan'l 198
Danl B 193
Dock 193
Earl 184
Elizabeth 44, 175
Emma J 125
Eva 43, 44
Florence 193
Georgia 43, 44
J W 193
James 43, 44
Johny 43, 44
Joseph C 198
Joseph J 193
Lorenzo D 184, 190, 192, 193, 198, 199
Lorenzo D, Jr 199
Manda 125
Mary E 193
Maude 175
Miller 184
Nancy 43, 44
Newton L 190
Rachel 191
Susan 184
Susan M 193
William E 190
DAWSON
   America J 16
   Andrew J 17
   Claud 16
   Cleveland 16
   Elias F 16
   Emma 16
   Fanny 16
   G R 21
   J G 16
   James K P 17
   Jane 17

Index

Jaunnah 17
John Riley 16
Katharine J 16
L R 23, 29
Mrs 66
Parlee 16
Robt E 16
S R 16
Samuel 16
Samuel R 16, 17
Toliver 16
DENHAM
   Emaline P 283
   John C 285
   John H 283
   John S 161
   William 161
   Wm 161
DESHAZO
   Eddie 92
   Hellen 92
   Tennessee 92
   Tilda 92
   Willie 92
DICKERSON
   Clarence 195, 197
   Ernest 195, 197
   Everet 197
   Everet Male 196
   Harry 195, 197
   James L 196
   John M 196, 197
   Mary P 195, 196, 197
DILLON
   Kesiah 207
   Kusiah 208
   Richard 208
DINSMORE
   Lizzie 120, 121
   Louisa J 122
   Malisa 122
   William L 120, 121
   Wm L 121, 122

DOBINS
   George C 176
DORN
   Bernard 90
   Joseph B 90
DORNS
   Bernard 90
   Joseph B 90
DOUGHERTY
   Benjamin 216, 223, 224
   Callie D 218
   Charles E 217, 218
   Elizabeth 224
   Elsie M 218
   Essie M 218
   Homer 218
   James 220, 224
   John H 224
   Maud 218
   Sarah M 223, 224
   Susan J 216, 218
DRAKE
   Charles S 107
   D W 107
DRINEN
   Rosetta 131, 132
DUNCAN
   Allen T 2
   Charles 38
   Charles M 1, 2
   George W 1, 2
   Georgia Ann 2
   Hiram 1, 2
   Mary Ellen 2
   Sarah C 1, 2
DUNHAM
   John S 161
DUNSON
   Mrs 70, 71, 78
DUNSTON
   Mrs 67, 69
DURBIN
   Amanda 206, 207

Sarah 206, 207
Willis 206, 207
DYE
   Isaac 197
EARLE
   Albert 154
   Benjamin 154
   Cora 154
   George..............................154
   Grantburn 154
   John 154
   Sarah 154
   William.............................154
EAVES
   Etta 203
   Pete 203
   Viletta 203
   Villetty 202
EBLEN
   Elizabeth..........................189
   Elizabeth L 248
   Elizabeth Morgan 189
EBLIN
   Elizabeth L 247
EDWARDS
   Anna L..............................162
   Anna Lee 103
   Elizabeth..........................103
   G W 162
   George W 103
   Henry 162
   James Daniel 103
   James W 162
   Lucy A..............................162
   Mary M 162
   Mima 64, 101, 102, 103, 104, 105, 106, 109, 159, 160, 162, 164
   Perry W 162
   Sarah E 167, 168
   Silas 103
   Silas P 101, 102
   W H 168

W J 167
William C P......................103
Wm C P............................103
EIFFERT
   Henry .. 13, 21, 24, 34, 44, 57, 75, 137, 152, 211, 212, 213, 235, 236, 237, 238, 239, 240, 241, 248, 251, 272, 273
ELENORE
   Martha..............................313
ELLIS
   Martha J 205
ELMORE
   Martha...............268, 269, 270
   Sarah 205, 206, 207, 208
ELROD
   Columbia..........................155
   Mertle 155
ELRODE
   Columbia..........................156
   Myrtle 156
ENHAMD
   Emaline P 282
EWART
   Alford P....................165, 166
   Amrilla N 165, 166
   Dora 165, 166
   Lethea A 165, 166
   Myrtle 165, 166
FERGUSON
   John H 59
   Joseph 59
   Oceola 59
   Ophelia...............................59
   Pearl 59
FIELDS
   Rebecca....................169, 170
FISHER
   Carrie 10
   Geo G 33, 34
   Leoda T 33, 34
   Lucy B................................10

Olley	10
Ollie	10
Oslah Hailey	10
Viva C	34

FLOTHO
- Francis G 96, 97
- James 96
- Oscar 96, 97

FORBES
- Agnes E 223
- Cora 209
- Francis E 209
- Nancy 209
- Nancy E 223
- Nancy L 223
- Robert F 223
- Susan L 223
- William M 223

FOREMAN
- Joe 75
- Stephen 75
- Susie 75
- Thomas 75

FRANKLYN 41, 42, 43, 44

FURGUSON
- John H 59
- Joseph 59
- Oceola 59
- Ophelia 59
- Pearl 59

GABBOR
- Thos 45

GAULT
- Susan R 284

GAY
- Amand 166
- Amanda 166
- R B 166

GAYLOR
- America O 179
- Bertha R 179
- Garland G 179
- Mary A 179

GENTRY
- Eleza 138, 139
- Shade 138, 139

GEORGE
- Calvin M 85
- Ellennora 85
- Ellenora 85
- Ester J 85
- Isaac C 52
- James T 85
- John W 50, 51
- Maggie J 85
- Margaret I 85
- Robert 85
- Robert H 85
- Willie 50, 51

GERMANY
- Florida 66
- Mary C 66
- Wm E 66

GIDEON
- Rhoda 145, 146, 147, 148

GIDEONS
- Rhoda 145, 146, 147

GLASS
- Iks 150

GOBBERT
- Thomas 83

GOBBEST
- Thomas 25

GOODRICH
- Bashaba 292, 293

GORDON
- Author T 205
- Daniel E 205
- David E 205
- Isham F 205
- Margaret 205
- Margaret L 205
- Nathan F 205
- Rachel L 205
- Rachel S 205

GOURD

Index

John R 108
GRANT
  Eddie 7
  Edith 7, 136
GRAVITT
  Alfred 72
  Artemissa 72
  Columbus F 72
  Ella 72
  Frances M 72
  Infant 73
  James M 72, 73
  Jefferson M 72
  Luther O 72, 73
  Minta A 72
  Ora B 72, 73
  Pearl 72, 73
GRAY
  Aurilla P 171
  Fannie E 227, 230
  Ora 227, 230
  S H 171, 172
  William N 171, 172
GRAYSON
  Claud 120
  Claud R 120
  Della 120
  Della E 120
  Kate R 120
  Late 120
GREEN
  Drewsiller 39
  Eliza 89
GRIST
  Emma 170, 171
  Sadie 170, 171
GUNTER
  J E   4, 6, 16, 18, 21, 23, 29, 47,
      49, 50, 51, 52, 53, 55, 60,
      61, 62, 65, 66, 70, 71, 73,
      76, 79, 83, 86, 88, 90, 93,
      94, 95, 96, 97, 99, 100, 109,
      111, 113, 114, 116, 119,
      122, 123, 124, 125, 127,
      134, 139, 140, 141, 142,
      143, 144, 145, 146, 147,
      149, 153, 157, 163, 164,
      165, 166, 167, 168, 170,
      171, 172, 180, 181, 182,
      183, 184, 185, 186, 188,
      194, 200, 201, 202, 203,
      204, 205, 208, 210, 228,
      229, 230, 231, 257, 259,
      260, 261, 262, 264, 265,
      266, 267, 268, 269, 270,
      275, 276, 277, 278, 279,
      280, 282, 283, 292, 293,
      294, 295, 296, 297, 298,
      299, 300, 301, 302, 303,
      304, 305, 306, 307, 308,
      309, 310, 311, 312, 313,
      314, 315, 316, 319, 322
  Jno E 67
  John E 1, 5, 7, 8, 9, 10, 11, 12,
      13, 15, 17, 19, 20, 24, 30,
      31, 32, 33, 35, 36, 37, 38,
      39, 41, 42, 43, 44, 45, 47,
      48, 54, 56, 58, 59, 62, 63,
      64, 67, 68, 72, 74, 75, 78,
      81, 82, 83, 87, 92, 97, 101,
      102, 103, 104, 105, 106,
      108, 110, 111, 115, 116,
      117, 118, 120, 121, 128,
      129, 132, 135, 137, 148,
      149, 151, 161, 162, 169,
      185, 189, 190, 191, 192,
      193, 195, 198, 199, 208,
      209, 214, 215, 217, 218,
      220, 221, 225, 249, 250,
      252, 254, 255, 257, 258,
      262, 263, 281, 282, 284,
      285, 286, 287, 288, 289,
      290, 291, 292, 313, 314,
      315, 317, 318, 320, 321,
      324, 325, 326
HAGER

Horato Leroy	43
Mary Adaline	43
Mary Adeline	43
Nevada L	43
Nevada Lillian	43

HAGGINS
Berdie K E	144, 145
Charles	144
James A	144, 145
Lulu May	144, 145

HAIL
Alice M	241
Eliza L	241
General M	241
Geo W	241
George W	241
Hulda E	241
Joseph	84
Joseph L	24, 25, 84
Martha E	241
Michael	24, 241
Micheal	24, 84
Michel	241
Wm W	241

HAILEY
Sallie M	8, 9

HALL
Amanda	100, 101
Annie L	100, 101
Archie C	186
Catharine	238
Catherine	235
D H	239
D M	100, 101
Daisy M	186
David A	100, 101
Dora	228, 230
Effie M	186
Frank	235, 238
Fredrick	235
Henry	228, 230
Ibie	235, 238
J W	239
John	100, 101
Lee Ann	100, 101
Martha	235, 238
Mary K	186
Minnie J	186
Newton	228, 230
Paty L	186
Rebecca	235, 238
Rhoda	235
Robert	101, 228, 230
Thrusetta	100
Thursetta	101
William	239
William O	239
Wm A	186

HAMMACK
Samuel M	145

HAMPTON
Abraham	242
Andrew W	242
Clara Mary	242
Elizabeth	242
Mattie C	242
William C	242

HANLY
John	262

HARDCASTLE
John F	85

HARLIN
David M	274

HARRELL
Bettie	153
Rosie	153

HARRIS | 68
C J	13

HASLAW
Eliza	131
Nancy	131

HAUKS
R T	47, 185, 190, 192, 193, 198, 199

HAWKINS
Celia	157

Dora 157
Golden..............................157
Money 157
Nancy 157
Rebecca 157
Samuel..............................157
HAWKS
   Chas 271
HAYES
   Bertha 96
   Elizabeth Morgan 189
   James L 96
   John H 94
   Kia 96
   Rachel M 94
   Walter 94, 95
   William M 94, 95
HAYS
   Hugh Mc 247, 248
   James Edgar 248
HENDRIX
   Daisy C N 23, 24
   Henrietta 23, 24
   Milo ....,24
   Theodosha 24
HENLEY
   Alphena 206
   Glenn 206
   John 314, 315
   John R 206
   Louisa 206
   Richard 206
   Sarah 206
HENLY
   Alphena 207
   John 207, 315, 316, 317, 318, 319, 320
   John R 205, 206, 207, 208
   Phineas 207
   Sarah 207
HENRY
   Ada A 56
   Albert P 248

   Amelia D 56
   Annie 248, 249, 250
   Archie B 56
   Elsie A 56
   Elzie A 56
   Eva M 56
   Gibbs 248
   Maria 248
   Mary B 56
   Patrick 248
   Rchie B 56
   Thomas Benton 249
HERNDON
   Elwood 168
   Grover C 168, 169
   J M 168
   Wallace 168
HEROD
   Ele 246
   Elzena 244
   Joseph S 244
   Luizo Bell 244
   William W 244
HESELRODE
   George Alice 143, 144
HESLERODE
   Bertha A 143
   Bertha Ann 144
   Charles O 144
   Charles Otto 144
   Eli Walter 144
   Elie W 143
   Katie E 143
   Katie Elmyra 144
   Robert E 144
   Robert Edward 144
HIBBS
   David Andrew 77
   John Alexander 77
   Mary Elizabeth 77
   Nancy Malissa Jane 77
HILL
   Caroline 28

Index

Mary 28
HITCHCOCK
   Isaac 232
   M 172
   Mr 114
HOOD
   Raleigh 101
   Thursetta 101
HOOKER
   Ellie 91
   Ellis 73, 115
HOPPER
   Mack 275
HOUSE
   Charles 157
   Charlie 156
   Elizabeth .. 153, 154, 155, 156, 158
   George 153, 155, 156, 157, 158
   Ida 156, 157
   James 156
   Thomas 156, 157
   Virginia 156, 157
HOWARD
   Charles P 212, 213
   Ellen 212, 213
   Hellen 212, 213
   Mary E 212, 213
   Russell 212, 213
HOWELL
   Charles C 151, 152
   Eaton E 151, 152
   Emily C 151, 152
   Evan C 152
   Frank R 152
   Mary D 151, 152
   Robert E Lee 152
   Robert Edie 151
   Thomas C 151, 152
HUBBARD
   Alvilda 170
   Cynthia 300
   Susie 289
HUDSON

Barnet 20
Edney E 20
Harrison 20
L B 20
Leuan 20
Mandy 20
Samuel 20
Sarah Francis 20
HUGHES
   Charles B 7
   Martha E 221
HULSEY
   Ada 61
   Alonzo 219, 220
   Catherine 60
   Charles 219, 220
   Earl 219, 220
   Eliza 60, 61
   Ella V 219, 220
   Emma 60, 61
   Geo W 60
   George W 61
   Ida 60
   Katharine 61
   Loucinda 219, 220
   Louisa 60, 61
   McAfee 61
   Rosalee 219, 220
   Roscoe 219, 220
   Ross 60, 61
   Sarah M 219, 220
HUNNICUT
   John Thomas 4
   Mary Ann 4
   Mrs 4
   Robert Lee 4
HURLEY
   Catharine 245
   Jane 245
HUTCHINS
   Jessie 277
   Mr 2
HUTCHISON

Thomas J 150
IRVING
  Hester L 44
  Hester Luvina 44
  Lowell 44
IVEY
  A D 78, 103
  A E ..1, 5, 6, 55, 64, 66, 67, 68,
    69, 71, 72, 75, 77, 78, 79,
    80, 97, 98, 99, 100, 101,
    102, 104, 105, 106, 109,
    110, 111, 112, 113, 114,
    115, 116, 123, 128, 129,
    130, 132, 133, 138, 139,
    140, 149, 151, 158, 159,
    160, 161, 162, 163, 164,
    165, 166, 167, 171, 172,
    175, 176, 177, 178, 179,
    186, 187, 188, 189, 199,
    200, 201, 202, 203, 209,
    210, 212, 213, 214, 215,
    216, 217, 218, 219, 220,
    221, 222, 223, 224, 225,
    231, 233, 234, 239, 240,
    252, 256, 257, 258, 259,
    260, 275, 276, 277, 278,
    279, 280, 281, 282, 283,
    285, 288, 289, 300
  G W 130
  George W 130
  James G 130
  John 130
  Josiah 130
  Martha C 130
  Mr 2
  Sarah A 130
IVEY & SANDERS 17, 18
JACKSON
  Arka J 117, 118
  Arthur E 117, 118
  Chester E 117, 118
  Elizabeth 298
  Elizabeth D 298

Florence 287
Frank A 117, 118
George P 117, 118
Hugh 118
Hugh J 117
John C 298
Martha 117
Martha A 118
Maud E 117, 118
JAMISON
  Elija 107
  Harriet 107
  Henry 107
  Herschal 107
  James 107
  James W 107, 108
  Maggie E 107
  Nancy 107
  Sidney R 107
  William 107
JOHNSON
  Amanda 175
  Dicey 175
  George 181
  Hubbard 174
  John H 113, 114
  Lillie 181
  Mary 175
  Mitchell 175
  Rebecca 173, 175
  Rena .6, 180, 181, 182, 183, 184
  Robert 175
  Sarah E 164
JONES
  Anna 183, 184
  Artilla 243
  Arvilla 243
  Betsey E 243
  Caldona 243
  Elizabeth 243
  Emily 247
  Emma E 71
  Ester 183, 184

Francis A 243
Hattie H C 243
Homer C 71
J H 243
James 128, 243, 244, 245, 246, 247
James Joel 244
Jane L 71
Jesse 128
Joel J H 243
John S 243
Leroy A 243
Margaret A 243
Margaret L 71
Mary 183
Mary Jane 184
Mary O 71
Meagan 244
Samuel 183, 184
Theodore 243
Thomas 243
William H 243
William J 71
Wm J 71
JORDAN
   Alva D 35
   Ettie 35
   River 35
   William 35
JOURDAIN
   Laura 32
JOURDAN
   Annice 38
   Annis 37
   Charles 36, 37
   Chisterfer 14
   Christopher 15
   Emma 32
   Ettie 35
   Frank 36, 37
   Fred 36, 37
   Jackson 37, 38
   James 37, 38

Jefferson 15
Jefferson D 14
Jesse 15, 34, 35
Jesse P 32
Jessie 14, 36, 37, 38
Jessie P 32
John A 34
Josie 37
Laura 32
Martin 37, 38
Mary 32, 36, 37
Mary S 14, 15
Nora 36, 37
River 14, 15, 32, 34, 36
Ruver 37
Sam 32
Samuel 32
Sarah 32
Susan 37, 38
Taylor 32
William A 32
William S 36, 37
Willie 35
JOURDON
   Anna 286
JULIAN
   Edwin C 222
   Ella P 222, 223
   Eva M 222
   Robert W 222
   Susan J 222
   Wm B 222
KANSAS
   Chetopa 90
KEITH
   Elmer 177
   James M 177
   Jefferson 177
   Minnie 177
   Sarah 177
   Stella 177
KEY
   Thomas Tikonees 77

KILL-ER-NE-TER 232
KILL-ER-NEE-TER
   Peter 232
KILL-ER-NIGGER 232
LANDRETH
   Geo R 45
   George R 45
LANDREW
   H T 88
LANGLEY
   Charles O 110
   Joannie 195
   John F 195
   John W D 110
   Joseph M 195
   Lock 110
   Loncella 195
   Louisa H M C 110
   Marion J 110
   Martha E 110
   Nellie C 195
   Robert R 110
   Sarah J 195
   Susan 110
   Zachary T 110
LARKIN
   Columbia 61
   Columbus 61
   Henry A 61
   Nora 61
   Olla 61
LAWRENCE
   Daniel B 141
   James F 139
   T R 140, 141
LAYTON
   Emma B 93
   Ida J 93
   Martha C 93
   Sarah F 93
LEE
   Dick 109
   Ellen 108, 109
   Frank 109
   James 109
   Margaret 109
   Mary B 108, 109
   Oliver 108, 109
   Richard 108, 109
   S 109
   Susan A 108, 109
   William ... 109, 301, 302, 303, 304
   Z B 108, 109
LEWELLEN
   Dica 173
LEWIS
   Annie 7
   Annie C 14
   Dilsy 108
   E B 6, 7
   Judith 281
   Martha 6, 7
   Mary 108
LIPE
   C C   5, 22, 48, 56, 58, 64, 69, 77,
         78, 102, 103, 104, 105, 106,
         110, 116, 120, 133, 148,
         159, 160, 162, 189, 191,
         209, 214, 215, 249, 250,
         252, 258
   D W 2, 5, 8, 9, 10, 11, 12, 21, 22,
         25, 26, 27, 28, 29, 34, 38,
         41, 46, 56, 57, 69, 72, 84,
         102, 103, 104, 105, 106,
         110, 112, 115, 116, 129,
         132, 137, 140, 148, 150,
         152, 159, 160, 161, 162,
         164, 175, 191, 209, 211,
         212, 213, 216, 217, 218,
         219, 220, 221, 222, 223,
         224, 225, 233, 235, 236,
         237, 238, 239, 240, 241,
         248, 251, 258, 272, 273,
         274, 275, 308
   E G 5, 7
LLEWELLYN

(Illegible) J 191	Fernecy Jane 150
(Illegible) M 191	George F 150
Alfred B 175	George T 150
Alonzo 175	Rebecca E 150
Bertie A 175	Serena C 150
Cordora 175	LOWERY
Dicey 173, 174, 175, 192	Elizabeth 248, 250, 251
Dora 175	Geo 24
Florence 175	Jane 79, 80
Henry J 173, 175	LYON
Hugh 175	Lenora 117
James 175	MCALLISTER
James L 173, 175	John M 38
John 175	MCCLATCHEY
Laura 175	John M 276
Lawson 175	MCCLURE
Nettie M 175	Alice L 151
Oscar 175	MCCOY
Robert 175	Alexander 197
Sarah F 175	J L 66, 196
Stephen 175	J S 197
Steve 173, 175	Jack 197
Vincent B 175	Maria 196
William C 173, 175	Oliver 196, 197, 198
LLOYD	Richard 196, 197
Dr 231	MCCRAW
Dr George 231	John 265, 266
G C 231, 232, 233, 234, 235	Junnetta 265, 266
Ida 233	MCGUIRE
James P 231, 233	Hettie Bell 185
James R 232	James T 185
John G 232, 233	James Taylor 185
Mary 231	Rosa Lee 185
Minnie M 232, 234	Rosey Lee 185
Mr 231	William A 185
Mrs 231	MCINTOSH
Virgil M 231, 232, 233	Susanah 8
William W 232, 233	Susannah 8, 9, 10, 11, 12
Wm W 234	Susannah M 9
LONG	MCLEMORE
Daniel E 150	Elizabeth 155, 156, 157
Fernecy 150	MCNAIR
Fernecy J 150	C V 34

Index

Clem V 34, 56
Clement V 56
MCSPADDEN
   Walter 251
MARSHAL
   E F 163
   Wm B 211
MARSHALL
   Mrs M J R 211
MARSHFIELD
   M J R 211
   Wm B 211
MARTIN
   Jack 196
   Joseph L 227
   Mary 38
MATEA
   James 152
   Phillip 152
MEARS
   Oliver 196, 197
MENDENHALL
   Evan 204
   Francis V 204
   Lawrence E 204
   Walter H 204
MEREDITH
   Andrew...314, 315, 316, 317, 318, 319, 320
MERIDETH
   Andrew 262
MERRIL
   Elizabeth 67
MIDDLETON
   Mary Jane 144
MIDLETON
   Mary Jane 144
MILES
   Rosalee Ross 208, 209
MILLER
   Ada M 66
   Addie M 67
   Andrew 50, 51, 52, 53, 54, 55, 85, 118, 119, 194
   Caladonia 3
   Clara 17, 18
   Clelan J 66
   Cleland J 67
   Esbella J 66
   Ethel 67
   Francis 3
   G W 3
   George 18
   George E 47
   George Washington 3
   Henry 3
   Isaac 194
   Jack 3, 4
   James Dick 17, 18
   James J 3, 4
   James Jackson 3
   Jessie Bell 17, 18
   John 3, 4
   Louisa 3
   Lucy 3
   Mabel 17, 18
   Mary Catherine 3
   Ola D 66, 67
   Othelan 18
   Othelia 17
   Pearlie J 66, 67
   Pleasant Henry 3
   Polly 121
   Richard 18
   Richard J 17
   Samuel A 18
   Thomas 3
   Walter D 67
   William 17, 18
   William Franklin 3
   Wm F 3
MILLS
   James E 122
   Malisa 122
   Otto 122
MITCHEL

Alta	181
Stella	181
MITCHELL	
Alta	182
Stella	182
MOLDEN	
Aleis	180
Alice	180
Arthur	180
Mattie	180
Sissie	180
MONTGOMERY	
Alfred	46
Alverd	45
James H	25
James N	25
James W	46
Janus H	83
Jno S	45
John S	46
Jos W	45
N B	25
Nora B	25, 83
Thomas	25, 46, 83
Thos W	45
William A	25
William H	25, 83
MORGAN	
Gideon	189, 247, 250, 251
Mary	251
Sarah	267, 268, 269
MORRIS	
Clyde E	250, 251
Ellen F	250, 251
Hugh Mc	250, 251
Mary T	250, 251
Sallie G	250, 251
Susie C	251
Susie Mc	250
Thomas F	250, 251
MORTON	
Annie R	215, 216
Henry H	215, 216
J ?	210
James M	215, 216
Quinn	215, 216
Samantha	215, 216
Sherard	215, 216
William	210, 215, 216
MOSLEY	
Joseph L	284
MOSS	
Della	183
Elbert	183
Elizabeth	201
Hugh	183
Mary M	218
Roxey	183
Sissie	183
MOTON	
Stephen	260
MURRELL	
Amanda R	136
Fanney E	136
Fannie E	136
Geo Ross	136
George Ross	136
Lewis Edward	136
Rosanna E	136
NEAL	
Mary R	22
Mary Rebecca	22
NEWHOUSE	
A E	325
A M	325
Thomas	325
Z B	325
NICHOLS	
Oceola T	29
Oceola Taylor	29
NULL	
Nancy J	131, 132
O.BRYANT	
Cora	299
Eula O	299
James A	299

Mary L.................................299
Minnie L O...........................299
Sarah J.................................299
O'BRYANT
   Cora 299
   Eula 299
   James A...............................299
   Mary L..................................298
   Minnie..................................298
   Sarah J.................................299
OSSR
   E G 92
OUMILLER
   Lizzie 114
   Mary E.........................113, 114
PALMOUR
   Alaska 213
   Amy 252
   Asa 214
   Benjamin F............................252
   Bessie 252
   Charles F...............................214
   Evaline 252
   Iva 214
   Jemru 252
   John D 213, 214, 215, 252
   John D, Jr 252
   Keziah 213
   Keziah M..............................213
   Mollie O...............................213
   Robert 252
   Sarah 213
   Virginia S 252
PARKER
   Clauda 88
   E A 88
   Earnest....................................88
   George W...............................88
PARKS 61
   George E...............................123
   George W.............................123
   Samuel...........................46, 123
   Samuel R..............................123

PARRIS
   Frank 236
   George..................................174
   George, Jr..............................174
   James 173, 191
   Jim 174
   Lemuel.........................226, 227
   Levi 236
   Nancy 173
   Polly 174
   Robert 174
   Sally 73
   W F 236, 237
PARSON 232
   Peter 232
   Susan 232
PARSONS
   Susan 231
PASSON 232
PAULEY
   Sarah A 51
PERIMAN
   Ada 135, 136
   Agnes 135, 136
   Glenard........................135, 136
   Mary E 135, 136
   Mattie 136
   Minnie..........................135, 136
   Oscar 135, 136
   William 135, 136
PETERS
   Dora S................................78, 79
   Eudora...............................78, 79
   Ivin L 78, 79
   Jennie E..................................78
   Jinnie E...................................79
   John W..............................78, 79
   Mattie L............................78, 79
   Sarah M..................................79
   Sarah W............................78, 79
PETTIT 200
PETTITT 201
PREWITT

Alcey 21
Alcy 23
Anna 21
PRITCHET
   Betsey 256
PRITCHETT 259
PROPP 275
   Mary E 274
PRUITT
   Epilsy 16
QUEEN
   E G 21
   E M 21
   E O 21
   H A 21
   Jane 17, 21
   O J 21
   S D 21
   S P 21
RAGSDALE
   Obediah 156
   Thomas 156
RAPER
   Charles, Jr. 135
   Charles, Sr. 135
   Cora 135
   Infant 135
   Young 135
RASMUS 13
   Mr 271
REASONER
   Elizabeth 113
   J W 113
REDMON
   Richard 112
REED
   Infant 53
   Julia A 53
   Lula 53
   Nannie A 53
RICH
   Bennett 91
   F 91

Ferhia 91
Fred 79
James P 67
Jane 80
Jessie 144
John H 80
John R 68
Lucetta 91
Nancy 91
Nancy J 91
Reil 91
Thomas T 79
RICHARDSON
   James U 119
RICHERSON
   James W 142
   John 142
   Mattie Ann 142
   Wm Brice 142
   Wm Rice 142
RIDGE
   A J 41, 42, 43, 44, 128, 152
RIGGSLEE
   Sarah H 205
RISS
   Will P 45, 54
ROBERTS
   Alexander C 13
   Henry G 13
   Rozella 14
ROBISON
   Elizabeth J 50
   George G 50
   Jane 50
   Mr 49
   William 49
   Wm 50
ROBNSON
   Wm 68
ROGERS
   Anna 114
   Captain John 16
   Chas W 100

Cornell 88, 129, 130, 132, 134, 161, 175, 176, 177, 178, 179, 180, 187, 188, 189, 192, 217, 220, 221, 225, 233, 234, 235, 242, 243, 244, 245, 246, 247, 263
Daisie B 100
F C 147
Florence S 240
H L 100
Henry C 151
J C 147, 148
James C C ..56, 100, 116, 148, 258
James M 147, 148
James O 147, 148
John 16, 21, 23, 55, 100, 116, 147, 258
John C 100
Lillie May 100
Mary M 100
P C 148
Pink 100
Polly 16
R B 147, 148
Robert 150
Robt 150
Rose 100
S C 147, 148
Sarah 150
William C 100

ROSE
America 131

ROSS
Andrew 208
E G 1, 16, 33, 37, 39, 51, 52, 53, 55, 59, 60, 61, 65, 66, 70, 73, 79, 81, 82, 83, 85, 87, 88, 90, 94, 95, 96, 97, 108, 117, 119, 122, 123, 125, 127, 138, 142, 144, 145, 146, 147, 149, 153, 154, 155, 156, 158, 169, 171, 172, 185, 188, 194, 195, 200, 201, 202, 203, 204, 205, 253, 254, 255, 310, 311, 312, 313
Elizabeth 65
Jennie P 208, 209
John 22
John Yagu 208
John Yargu 209
Joshua 208, 209
Joshua Ewing 208, 209
Lewis 136
Martha 199
Richard 120
Richard Lewis 208, 209
Susan Lowery 208, 209
W P 120
Will P 1, 4, 5, 6, 7, 15, 16, 17, 18, 19, 20, 21, 23, 29, 30, 31, 32, 33, 35, 36, 37, 39, 41, 42, 43, 45, 47, 49, 50, 51, 52, 53, 55, 59, 60, 61, 62, 63, 65, 66, 67, 70, 71, 73, 74, 75, 76, 79, 81, 82, 83, 85, 86, 87, 88, 90, 91, 92, 93, 94, 95, 96, 97, 99, 100, 101, 108, 109, 111, 113, 114, 116, 117, 118, 119, 121, 122, 123, 124, 125, 127, 128, 134, 138, 139, 140, 141, 142, 143, 144, 145, 146, 147, 149, 153, 154, 155, 156, 157, 158, 163, 164, 165, 166, 167, 168, 169, 170, 171, 172, 180, 181, 182, 183, 184, 185, 186, 188, 194, 195, 200, 201, 202, 203, 204, 205, 206, 208, 210, 228, 229, 230, 231, 254, 255, 257, 259, 260, 261, 262, 263, 264, 265, 266, 267, 268, 269, 270, 276, 277, 278, 279, 280, 281, 282,

283, 284, 285, 286, 287, 288, 289, 290, 291, 292, 293, 294, 295, 296, 297, 298, 299, 300, 301, 302, 303, 304, 305, 306, 307, 308, 309, 310, 311, 312, 313, 314, 315, 316, 317, 318, 319, 320, 321, 322, 324, 325, 326
    Wm P 136
RUSH
    Z F 207
RUSK
    Ada E 175
    America E 173
    America Ellen 175
    Eliza E 175
    John M.......................................175
    Lula 175
    Mary 175
    William D................................175
RUSSELL
    Ed W 212
    Edward W 212
    Fannie L 210
    Robert L 210
    Susan 210, 211, 212, 225
    W H 217, 220, 221
    W R 210
    William H................................212
SAMUELS
    Myra 250
SANDERS 191
    L S 185, 186, 194, 195, 263, 264, 265, 284, 286, 287, 295, 305, 307, 308
    Walt 76, 77
    Walter 49
    Wat 60, 61
    Water Walter.............................49
SATERSFIELD
    Lucy 218
SCALES

    J A 3
    S A 4
SCHELL
    Rebeccah 59
SCHRIMSER
    John 226
SCHRIMSHER
    Edith 226, 227
    John 226
    Mrs 227
    Rhoda 226
SCOTT
    Daniel 9
    Kiah 9
SCUDDER
    Addie E 48
    Gordon H 48
    Ida J 48
    Laura ? 48
    Maggie L 48
    Mary E 48
    Nellie V 48
    Newton G 48
    Wm H H 48
SEITZ
    Amanda E................................191
    Eliza M....................................191
    George A.................................191
    Jennie L............................190, 191
    Jetta A 191
    John C 191
    Mary D 190, 191
SEVIER
    D 297
    Serena 298
SEWELL
    Benjamin 76
    George..77
    Sophia 76
    Sophie 68
SHANNON
    Daisy 12
    Floyd 12

Floyd D 12
Lucy 12
Mary B 12
Pauline 12
Sallie H 12
SHAW
  G W C 143
  George W C 142
  Hardy Rodman 143
  James G W 142
  Jas G W 143
  Mathew Benj F 143
  Samuel B 142, 143
SHIPMAN
  Gustina 150
SHOEMAKE
  Altha J 30, 31
  Amy E 40
  Annie 40, 39
  Annie E 39
  Bettie Ann 40
  Bulah 30
  Bulah B 31
  Cyrus D 39, 40
  Eli 30
  Eli B 30, 31, 33
  Elis B 29
  Frances J 31
  Francis J 31
  Ida B 33
  James D 40, 39
  Jas D 39
  Jesse B 31
  Jessie B 31
  John H 39, 40
  Lena 31
  Marion F 40, 39
  Ric'd E 39
  Richard E 40
  Rosetta 33
  Tammie 31
  W H 40
  William L 31

Wm L 31, 33
Zidda W 33
SILER
  Mr 24, 38, 84
SIMMONS
  Malinda 94, 96
SIZEMORE
  Adolph A 177
  Allen G 177
  America A 176
  Andrew J 178
  Charles A 178
  Della V 178
  Gertrude 177
  Gracie M 187
  Hattie G 178
  Henry 134
  Ida 176
  Isom 179, 186, 188, 189
  James A 178
  James C 176
  James K 187
  Jessie 178
  Leander 134
  Lissa A 178
  Richard ... 175, 176, 177, 178, 179, 187
  Richard G 178
  Tennessee 134
  Willis D 133
  Wm F 176
SKYLOCK
  Burton 7
SLATON
  Chas 38
  Elner 39
  Jas V 38
  Jesse 39
  Jessie 39
  Martha E 38
SLATTON
  Charles 39
  James V 39

Martha E 39
SLAUGHTER
　　Lawrence S 163
SLOOP
　　Harvey 182
　　Jane 182
　　Josie 182
SMITH
　　Alice M 6
　　Andrew J 6
　　Cynthia 5, 6
　　Eli T 115
　　Eliza 246
　　Elizabeth 74
　　Elizabeth F 307
　　Emma V 6
　　Fred 115
　　J L 6
　　J R 6
　　James M 115
　　James S 175
　　John 246
　　John B 74
　　John C 115
　　John W 175
　　Louisa 74
　　Lula A 6
　　Mary 6
　　Mary Ann 109, 110
　　Mary M 109, 110
　　Mont 246
　　Nancy J 74
　　Phillip 90
　　Polly 120, 121, 122
　　Robert 5
　　Robt 5, 6
　　Sallie A 215
　　Samuel 109, 110
　　Thomas G 298
　　William L 175
SNYDER
　　Aleson 203
　　Martesen E 203

　　Mary C 203
　　Oscar L 203
SOMMERS
　　Martha 60
SPRAGGINS
　　C C 111
　　John 111
STEPHENS
　　William 262
STEVENS
　　Bell 287
STEWARD
　　Dr Thomas 62
STEWART
　　Agnes 63
　　Claud 63
　　Daisy Bell 64
　　Delilah May 64
　　Della M 63
　　Dennis 63
　　Dr Thomas 62
　　Earnest 62, 63
　　Florence 62
　　John 62
　　Leandrew 63
　　Mariah 62, 63
　　Ralf 63
　　Ralph 63
　　T C 64
　　William 63
　　Windfield 63
STONE
　　B H 24, 43, 45, 83, 84, 91,
　　　　　　　107, 108
　　Bean 159
　　H B 25, 59
　　J A 158, 159
　　James C 159
　　Lelia M 158, 159
　　Robert A 158, 159
　　Samuel H 160
　　W R 158, 159
STORY

Geo Henry 41
George Henry 41
Sarah Nevada 41
SWEET
  C S 148, 149
  Carrie J 146, 147
  Cleveland 147
  Emma C 147
  Guardie 146, 147
  Hester L 148, 149
  Isam T 148, 149
  J Y 147
  John F 146
  John M 146
  John P 148, 149
  Manda B 147
  R A 146, 147
  Walter R 146, 147
  William E 147
  Wm E 146
SWEETEN
  Carrie 89
  Clem 89
  Emaline 89
  Emeline 89
  Eng 89
  Phillip 89
  Phillip G 89
  Rebecca 89
  Sam M 89
SWEETON
  Phillip 68
SYLEOX
  Burton 7
TALLEY
  Horatio 276
TAYLOR
  Alma R 137
  Arazona 125, 126
  Billy 22
  C H ..14, 29, 30, 31, 32, 33, 34,
      35, 36, 37, 38, 45, 46, 61,
      62, 63, 80, 81, 82, 86, 87,
      92, 120, 121, 122, 123, 124,
      125, 126, 127, 134, 142,
      153, 154, 155, 156, 157,
      158, 169, 170, 173, 180,
      181, 182, 183, 253, 254,
      255, 256, 261, 290, 295,
      296, 320, 324, 326
  Davenport 22
  David 22
  Delilah 87
  Emerson 126
  Emily A 124, 126
  Emmerson 124
  Geo 125, 126
  George 124, 125, 126
  Idia 125, 126
  J M 121
  James E 122
  John A 124, 125, 126
  John H 124, 126
  John M 108
  Levada 125, 126
  Louisa J 121, 122
  Louiza 121
  Port 22
  Sarah 124, 126
  Susan 15
  Susan C 137
  Susie C 137
  Tennessee C 124, 126
  William 22, 124, 126
  William E 124, 126
  William S 107
TERRY
  A M 140
  Dora Bell 140
  Elizabeth 140
  Isaac 140
  John 140
  Joseph R 140
  Manda 140
  Robert 140
  Wiley C 140

Index

William 140
THOMPSON
  Isom 174
  J A 272, 273
  John 97, 98, 99
  Patsey 272, 273
  W A 56, 93, 271, 272, 273
  William A 168
  Wm A 20, 33, 143, 144, 145, 146,
      147, 148, 149, 150, 195
THRIFT
  Charles F B 205
  Chas F B 205
  David A 205
  Davis M 205
  Mary 204, 205
  Samuel ? 205
  Samuel L 205
  Thomas H 205
  William L 205
  Wm T 205
TIMMS
  Ethan Comonodon 112
  Mary Jane 112
  Mathias 112
  Osceola 112
  V G 112
TUCKER
  Calvin 149
  E A J 149
  E J 149
  J W E 57
  James 57
  Lennie 57
  Mary M 57
  Polly 149
  Sally M 149
  Sally May 149
  Thomas T 149
  Thomas Taylor 149
  Wesley 149
TURNHAM
  Edgar M 118, 119

  Ellen M 118, 119
  Irvan W 119
  Irvin W 118
  Joseph M 118
  Miney L 118, 119
  Pinkney B 118, 119
  Sarah A 118, 119
  Sarah J 118, 119
  William A 118, 119
TWIST
  Rachel 232
VANN
  Edith 226
  Jane 50
  John 225, 226, 227, 228, 229,
      230
  Miss 70, 78
  Nancy 226
  Reuben 50
VAUGHN
  Charlott 263
  Temby 290
WAGONER
  Disia L 105
  James W 105
  Julia A 105
  Lavina N 105
  Mary E 105
  Peter G 105
  Soloman E 105
WALDON
  Berry 1
  John 98
  Nannie 1
  Nona 1
  Robbie 1
WALDROOP
  Betsey 143
  Martha J 144
WALKER
  Joseph 93
  Sallie Nunoly 93
WARD

360

(Illegible) C 54
(Illegible) K 54
(Illegible) V 54
Bergess 54
Bergess C 54
Burgess 53
Daniel 54
David 54
George W 54
John 54
Martin 151
Nathan 54
Rhoda 54
Richard 54
Sallie 151
Samuel C 53, 54
Samuel F 54
WARREN
   Jacob E 29
   James L 29
   Mary E 29
WATER
   Nancy 113, 114
WATER HUNTER 231, 232, 233, 234
WATERS
   Elmina 152
   George 3
   Mary Catharine 3
WATKINS
   Charles 81
   Charles W 82, 83
   Dora 81
   G D 82
   Garland 81
   Gordon 80, 81
   Grover 81
   Helen 82
   Hellen 82
   Ida 82
   Jack ...80, 81, 82, 83, 86, 87, 92
   Joe 82
   John 82, 197
   Johnie 82
   Larkin 81
   Mack 80, 81
   Mary 80, 81
   Nellie 82
   Nettie 82
   Paschal 81, 82
   Paschall 82
   Thomas 80, 81
WATSON
   Josephine 98
WATT
   Joe 309
WATTS
   Fits 126
   Fitts 127
   Francis M 126, 127
   Joe 310, 311, 312
   Minnie 126, 127
   Sarah L 126, 127
WELDON
   Rebecca D 8
WEST
   Bell 8
   Elizabeth 35, 36
   Nettie 8
   Robt Lee 8
   Viola 8
   William A 36
WHEELER
   Lucrecy 114, 115
WHITE
   J S 242
   James E 242
   Josiah 246
   Mary Jane 246
   Polly 242, 243, 244, 245, 246, 247
   Sally 4
   William H 242
WHITSON
   Collumbus 106
   Emma 106

Etta	106	Ester J	217
James	106	Esther J	217
John	106	George E	222
Ollie	106	John P	217
Tempie	106	Mary E	222
William	106	Nathaniel D	217

WILDER
   Rachel 140

WILKERSON
   Geo 131
   George................................. 130
   Nellie 289, 300

WILLIAMS
   D S 4, 6, 14, 17, 18, 19, 20,
      21, 23, 29, 30, 31, 32, 35,
      36, 41, 42, 43, 45, 50, 52,
      62, 63, 67, 68, 71, 74, 75,
      76, 77, 79, 80, 83, 86, 89,
      93, 97, 99, 100, 101, 109,
      111, 113, 114, 116, 118,
      121, 122, 124, 128, 134,
      139, 140, 141, 143, 163,
      164, 165, 166, 167, 168,
      169, 170, 180, 181, 182,
      183, 184, 186, 206, 208,
      210, 257, 259, 260, 261,
      262, 263, 264, 265, 267,
      268, 270, 275, 276, 277,
      278, 279, 280, 281, 282,
      283, 284, 285, 286, 287,
      288, 289, 290, 291, 292,
      293, 294, 295, 296, 297,
      299, 300, 302, 303, 304,
      305, 306, 307, 308, 309,
      310, 313, 314, 315, 316,
      317, 318, 319, 320, 321,
      322, 324, 325
   D W 15, 301
   Lucinda Jane 163

WILLIAMSON
   Nellie 289

WILLIS
   Andrew E 217

   Pickens E........................ 217, 222
   Priestly 217, 220, 221
   Priestly E 78, 219, 221
   William P 222

WILLISON
   Howard D 11
   Irene B..................................... 11
   James D 11
   Jim M 11
   May C 11

WILSON
   Oda 170

WING
   Malissa 59
   Mallissa 59

WOMACK
   Daisey Dell.......................... 141
   Daisy Dell 141
   Elizabeth 141
   John Everts........................... 141
   John W 141

WOODARD
   Guie 155
   James 155
   Mollie 155

WOODWARD
   Guie 155
   Guy 155
   James 155

WORCESTER
   Mr 232

WYLEY
   R F 2

WYLY
   Amanda C 239, 240
   Oliver L 239, 240
   R F 271

    Robert N 239
    Robt M 240
YOUNG
    Gus   97
    J D   97
    James 98
    Mollie 97
    Oscar 97
ZARTMAN
    Catharine B 90
    Eliaz R 90
    Erdie W 90
    Lizzie R 90
    Oscar B 90, 91
    Owen L 90, 91
    Perlie E 90

www.ingramcontent.com/pod-product-compliance
Lightning Source LLC
Chambersburg PA
CBHW020239030426
42336CB00010B/546